POLARIZING JAVANESE SOCIETY

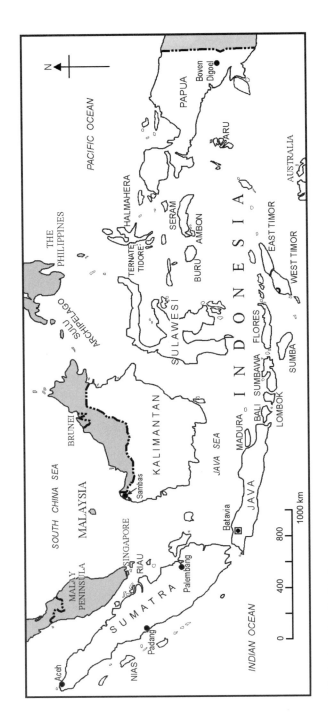

The Indonesian Archipelago

POLARIZING JAVANESE SOCIETY

Islamic and Other Visions

c. 1830–1930

M.C. Ricklefs

UNIVERSITY OF HAWAI'I PRESS
HONOLULU

Published in North America by:

University of Hawai'i Press
2840 Kolowalu Street
Honolulu, HI 96822
www.uhpress.hawaii.edu

Published in Asia by:

NUS Press
National University of Singapore
AS3-01-02, 3 Arts Link
Singapore 117569

Library of Congress Cataloging-in-Publication Data

Ricklefs, M. C. (Merle Calvin)
  Polarizing Javanese society: Islamic, and other visions, 1830–1930 / M. C. Ricklefs.
     p. cm.
  Includes bibliographical references and index.
  ISBN 978-0-8248-3152-3 (pbk. : alk. paper)
  1. Java (Indonesia)—Social conditions. 2. Islam—Indonesia—Java. 3. Java
(Indonesia)—Religious life and customs. I. Title.
  HN710.J3R53 2007
  305.6'972809598209034—dc22
                              2007007633

Cover photo: Students at a Javanese *Qur'an* school in the front gallery of a small
prayer-house, c. 1910 (Collection of KITLV, Leiden)

Cover design: Winnifred Wong

Printed in Singapore

For
Margaret

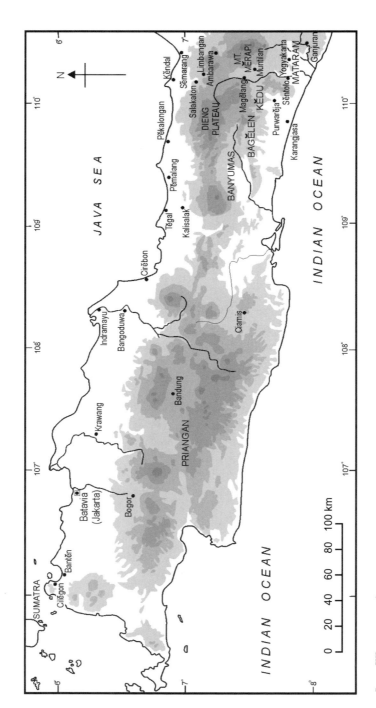

Java: Western portion

Contents

Illustrations

Maps

Tables

Abbreviations

A.	Ajĕng (female aristocratic title)
Ad.	Adipati (aristocratic title)
AD	*Anno Domini*, the Christian Era
AH	*Anno Hijrae*, the Islamic era
AJ	*Anno Javanico,* the Javanese era
Ar.	Arya (aristocratic title)
ARZ	Archief Raad voor de Zending, held in the Utrecht city archives (het Utrechts Archief)
BKI	*Bijdragen tot de Taal-, Land- en Volkenkunde*
BM	*Bramartani* (in the period 1864–11 Aug. 1870 entitled *Jurumartani*)
c.	circa
dd.	dated
f., ff.	folio, folios
fl.	florin, Dutch guilder
GG	Governor-General of the Netherlands East Indies, Batavia
H.	Haji

IPO   *Overzigt van de Inlandsche en Maleisch-Chineesche Pers.*
             Weltevreden: Kantoor voor de Volkslectuur, 1918–38

ISDV   Indische Sociaal-Democratische Vereeniging (Indies
             social-democratic union)

km, kms   kilometre, kilometres

Ky.   Kyai

LOr   Leiden University Oriental manuscript

M.   Mas (middle-ranking aristocratic title)

MNZG   *Mededeelingen van wege het Nederlandsche
             Zendelinggenootschap*

MR   Mail report, Netherlands National Archives, The Hague

MS, MSS   manuscript, manuscripts

n.d.   no date, undated

Ng.   Ngabei (aristocratic title)

n.s.   new series

NZG   Nederlandsche Zendelinggenootschap (Netherlands
             mission society)

OSVIA   Opleidingscholen voor inlandsche ambtenaren
             (training schools for native officials)

PKI   Partai Komunis Indonesia (Indonesian Communist Party)

Png.   Pangeran (title for a prince)

PNRI   Perpustakaan Nasional Republik Indonesia, the
             Indonesian National Library, Jakarta

r.   reigned; if with a MS reference: recto

R.	Raden (aristocratic title of the middle rank)
SH	*Sinar Hindia* (Light of the Indies)
SI	*Studia Islamika*
SI	Sarekat Islam (Islamic Union)
SOAS	School of Oriental and African Studies, London, MS
SR	*Soeara ra'jat* (peoples' voice)
STOVIA	School tot opleiding van inlandsche artsen (school for training native doctors)
TBG	*Tijdschrift van het Bataviaasch Genootschap van Kunsten en Wetenschappen*
Tg.	Tuměnggung (aristocratic title)
TNI	*Tijdschrift voor Nederlandsch Indië*
VKI	*Verhandelingen van het Koninklijk Instituut voor Taal-, Land en Volkenkunde*
VOC	Vereenigde Oost-Indische Compagnie, (Dutch) East India Company
v.	verso

Transcription and Orthography

The transcription system employed here for Javanese is that normally used in Indonesia, with the addition of ě for /ə/ (like the e in "fallen") to distinguish it from e for the character *taling* which is pronounced as either /é/ or /è/ (like either the a in "fate" or the e in "set"). For the rest, vowels are pronounced as in English except for a which is pronounced rather like English o when it is found in penultimate and final syllables without final consonants. Consonants have generally the same value as in English except for c which is pronounced like ch in "chair". Dh and th are retroflexes. Stress in Javanese words is generally on the penultimate syllable.

In Javanese place names, retroflexes have been ignored so as to avoid confusion with contemporary Indonesian usage, e.g. Kědiri is found here rather than Kědhiri.

Consistency in transliterating Javanese personal names becomes impossible after they came to be written in the western alphabet. Javanese individuals often varied in their choice of transcription. I have attempted to follow those personal preferences where they are known. In the colonial period, these transcriptions normally followed the Dutch-based system. Thus, one finds here Tjokroaminoto rather than the "correct" transcription Cakraaminata.

Old Javanese, Sanskrit and Arabic words follow currently accepted systems of transliteration.

Preface

This book aims to answer questions that have been bothering me for many years. I learned when I began studying Indonesia in the 1960s, and observed personally when I first arrived there in 1969, that Javanese society was deeply conflicted by differing degrees of commitment to Islam. Very many people — several hundred thousand — were killed in the mid-1960s in political violence in which those differing degrees of religiosity played a major role in defining loyalties. If that was so, I wondered over the following years, why in my research in the pre-nineteenth century history of Java did I not see the deeper historical roots of these categories? And why, as the decades passed in the later twentieth century, did the categories themselves seem to subside? There was a mystery here, but I knew that I could only confidently attempt to unravel it after I had done significant research on Javanese history before the nineteenth century, for I needed that background. Now, having written five books on that earlier history and having committed several years to researching the nineteenth and early twentieth centuries, I feel that I can attempt to provide some answers to those bothersome questions. Moreover, I feel that if we can understand this history in Java, we might understand something valuable about human societies more generally. For we are dealing with the question of what circumstances can make religion into a source of social conflict.

Readers will need to decide for themselves whether this book sheds light on questions of such import. I hope that they will think that it does. In particular, I hope that they will agree with me that an understanding of the Javanese case leads us to think about the risks involved when religious differences — and here we are talking about differences *within* a religious tradition, not differences *between* religions — become replicated in educational systems, political organisations and political action. That is an issue not just for the period 1830–1930 covered in this book, or just for Indonesia, but for all places and all times.

In researching the materials for this book I have been fortunate to receive vital help from others. I thank three people in particular.

Dr. Michael Laffan plowed through the Dutch archives, seeking anything relevant in the voluminous *Mailrapporten.* I had expected to find little of value there, for the Dutch colonial bureaucracy was not very qualified or inclined to assess the social developments of interest in this book. But the search had to be undertaken, so I was grateful that Michael Laffan was prepared to do it. In the course of this, he found more material of value to his own research than to mine — a happy outcome all around. He also compiled a voluminous bibliography of Dutch periodical publications that might prove relevant.

Having worked through that bibliography, I turned to Dr Paule Maas, who then sought out those publications — sometimes quite obscure as they were — in the Netherlands, photocopied them and sent them to me. She employed her own academic judgment to omit those that, on examination, proved to be irrelevant. She thus saved me much time, while also providing me with a mountain of material to study.

Mr Nindya Noegraha of the Indonesian National Library played a crucial role. That library holds the most complete set of the Javanese newspaper *Bramartani,* which is of central importance to this book. I read Javanese script comfortably, but because it is one of those scripts in which words are not divided from one another, and because *Bramartani* did not use headlines like a modern newspaper, it is very difficult to skim it — an essential tactic if one is to get through multiple years of a weekly newspaper. So we decided to transcribe the paper into the roman alphabet. This not only made it eminently skimmable but also raised the possibility that, when the series was all done, we could publish the transcriptions, probably in a searchable CD-ROM format, so that the newspaper would be available to other scholars. It was Nindya Noegraha who organised people to do these transcriptions, maintained control of their quality and kept the documents flowing to me, right through one of the most troubled times of recent Indonesian history. In the interest of accuracy, however, when I discovered items of interest in the transcriptions, I always checked those passages in the original copies of *Bramartani* in the National Library. The CD-ROM has not yet materialised, but I hope that it will one day do so.

Financial support for all of this activity has been essential. I particularly thank the Australian Research Council and the Asia Research Institute of the National University of Singapore, especially its Director and my old friend Professor Tony Reid, for their support. The latter gave me a

year of uninterrupted research and writing time and an office so remote
that I was almost never bothered by anyone. That was crucial to getting
through a backlog of piled-up research material and starting the writing.

Several libraries and archives have made their resources available to
me. I have already mentioned the central importance of the Indonesian
National Library, Perpustakaan Nasional Republik Indonesia (Jakarta).
I am grateful also to the Netherlands National Archives (Het Nationaal
Archief, The Hague) and to the librarians of the School of Oriental and
African Studies (London), the Koninklijk Instituut voor Taal-, Land- en
Volkenkunde (Leiden) and Leiden University. Vital missionary sources
were made accessible through the advice of Dr Chris de Jong, archivist
of the mission records at the Samen op Weg Kerken (Utrecht), and the
assistance of the archivists of the Archief Raad voor de Zending collection
itself, held in the Utrecht city archives (het Utrechts Archief).

Several colleagues have been willing to read parts of the book and
to give me their suggestions. I am grateful to Professor Martin van
Bruinessen, Professor Robert Elson, Professor Nancy Florida, Professor
Vincent Houben, Dr Werner Kraus, Dr Ruth McVey and Professor
Karel Steenbrink for their help. None of them, of course, bears any
responsibility for the final outcome.

The sources for this period are voluminous, and not without their
own particular difficulties of interpretation. The topic considered here
is complex and, I think, important not only in its own right, but also
in a context broader than Java or Indonesia. I hope that readers will feel
that this book has done justice to both the sources and the topic.

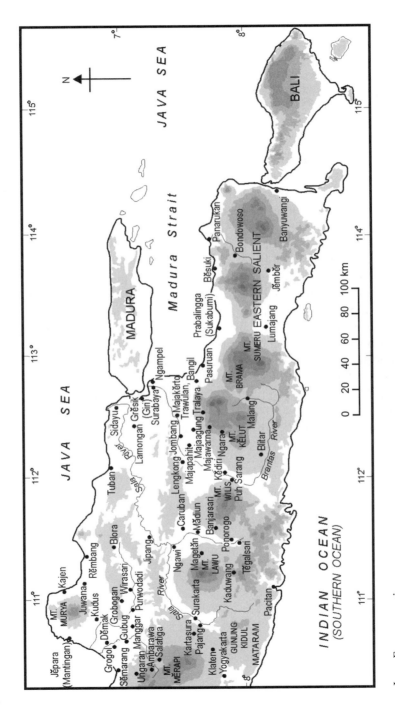

Java: Eastern portion

1

The Javanese Islamic Legacy to c. 1830: The Mystic Synthesis*

The Javanese have long had opportunities to sample new, foreign ways of doing and believing and the imagination to embrace whatever seemed to be of value. As world trade passed through their waters, stopped at their ports and sought their trade items, new technologies and new faiths were displayed to the people of Java. From early in the first millennium AD they adopted Hinduism and Buddhism, and then combined them into Javanese Hindu-Buddhism. When the Prophet Muhammad revealed Islam to the Arabs, he thereby also introduced the new faith to the wide network throughout which Arabs traded, a network that encompassed the waters of Indonesia. The merchants and mystics who sailed these routes — many of them non-Arab Muslims — brought Islam to Java, but it seems that for several centuries there was no significant local response. So far as can be discerned from surviving evidence, it was only in the fourteenth century that Javanese began to embrace this new faith.

The first evidence suggesting that Javanese were converting to Islam is found in gravestones which evidently mark the burial of elite figures from the Hindu-Buddhist court of Majapahit. The earliest is found at

---

* This chapter is a brief summary of M.C. Ricklefs, *Mystic synthesis in Java: A history of Islamization from the fourteenth to the early nineteenth centuries* (Norwalk: EastBridge, 2006). More detailed discussion should be sought there. Only direct quotations from primary sources will be referenced here.

1

the graveyard of Trawulan and is dated Ś 1290 (AD 1368–69). While logic might suggest that Islam would first have gained adherents along the northern littoral (called *pasisir* in Javanese), in fact this first evidence comes from the interior, near the site of the court. Half a century later, the Chinese observer Ma Huan still recognised no Javanese Muslims on the north coast. Not until much later is there unequivocal evidence — this time from the early Portuguese observer Tomé Pires — that Javanese Muslims were also found on the coast. By his time, in the second decade of the sixteenth century, Islamic states had been established on the *pasisir*. Most of these were led by Muslims of foreign origin, who were accommodating themselves to the cultural style of the Hindu-Buddhist Javanese aristocracy and were thereby becoming Javanese. So there were processes of both Islamisation of Javanese and Javanisation of foreign Muslims going on. The king in the interior, however, had not converted. In the end, Majapahit fell to a coalition of Islamic states c. 1527.

The evidence from these early centuries of the spread of Islam suggests both conflict and accommodation of identities. Some people believed that being Javanese and being Muslim were two irreconcilable identities. Others believed that one could be both. For some Javanese, the new faith may have been a means of gaining yet another source of supernatural power. For some, it was the key to salvation. For others, it was anathema. Adherence to Islam meant changing significant social customs, notably abandoning pork (but probably not alcohol, to judge from later evidence), burying rather than cremating the dead and circumcising the young. But it was evidently the case that in the minds of those who adopted the new faith, older ideas about the supernatural survived formal conversion. From the sixteenth century we have Javanese manuscripts which confirm that orthodox Islamic mysticism was taught in Java, but their use of Javanese rather than Arabic terms for crucial concepts tells us also of Islam's accommodation within Javanese society, and of Javanese concepts being assimilated within local Islam. As is true in the spread of any great world religion, a cross-cultural process of mutual fertilisation was under way.

Sometimes religious and cultural boundaries were clear: you were either Muslim or Javanese. Sometimes they were not: Pires said that there were still thousands of pre-Islamic ascetics in Java and that the *pasisir* Muslims greatly honoured them. Nevertheless, it seems reasonably clear that by the end of the sixteenth century, at the elite level of Javanese society there were people who were both Javanese and Muslim. In that age of ethnic and cultural fluidity, the ancestry of these Javanese Muslims lay in two directions. They were descendants of Javanese who had embraced Islam on the one hand and of non-Javanese Muslims (Indians, Chinese and others) who had become Javanese on the other.

It is important to note that such evidence as we have from the early centuries of Islam in Java supports the view that mysticism — Sufism — was the dominant style of Islam there. The two sixteenth-century manuscripts that survive are both mystical. Later Javanese legends about Islamisation tell of people with mystical insights and magical powers. The transition from mystical Hindu-Buddhism to mystical Islam was thus presumably eased by conceptual continuities.

In the later years of the sixteenth century, political hegemony shifted from the *pasisir* states to the interior of Java, where the court of Mataram became at least *primus inter pares* by the end of the century and the dominant court by c. 1625. But the Mataram court was still very imperfectly Islamised. Its literary traditions, its rituals, its very calendar, were still substantially Hindu-Buddhist in character.

In the reign of Sultan Agung (1613–46) the first major reconciliation of Javanese royal and Islamic traditions took place that we know of. In large part responding to military reverses and rebellions that were led by Islamic religious figures, which undermined his claims to invincibility and divine support, Agung turned to Islamic supernatural forces. These he sought to domesticate and to bend to his purposes rather than allowing them to challenge him. He undertook a royal pilgrimage to the holy site of Těmbayat in 1633. In the same period, he reconciled with the defeated princely line of Surabaya who claimed descent from one of Java's original Islamic saints (the legendary nine *walis*), converted the Javanese Hindu Śaka calendar into a Javano-Islamic hybrid lunar calendar using the Islamic months, and imported into court culture major works of literature that were of Islamic inspiration and evidently regarded as supernaturally potent. Legends also say that he met with the spirit of the local saint, Sunan Bayat, who taught Agung the secret essence of mystical sciences. It may be these lessons that are captured in a text called *Suluk Garwa Kancana,* which depicted the art of Javanese kingship as an exercise in Sufi devotion and which was evidently Sultan Agung's own political philosophy. Here the martial traditions of Javanese kingship were reconciled with the Sufi tradition of the "greater *jihad*" (*al-jihad al-akbar*), the struggle against one's own carnal self. The Islamising thrust of the Mataram court under Sultan Agung coincided with major expressions of courtly piety elsewhere in the archipelago as well, notably in Bantěn in West Java and in Aceh.

But this reconciliation of Islamic and royal identities seems to have been fragile, for in subsequent reigns Islam became the rallying standard of those who opposed the kings of Mataram. Agung's son and successor Amangkurat I (r. 1646–77) presided over the largest slaughter of Islamic leaders in Java's history, when 5–6,000 Muslim clerics and their families were murdered on the great square before the court. His murderous reign collapsed in rebellion in the 1670s. Thereafter, for a period of about 50 years until the mid-1720s, Java suffered wars and rebellions. In these conflicts, the dynasty turned to the Dutch East India Company (VOC) for support. The Company had established a foothold in West Java in 1619 by its conquest of Batavia. It intervened into the interior of Java in 1677 in support of the Mataram dynasty against the rebellion of Trunajaya, who denounced the ruler for his alliance with Christians. Trunajaya was in the end defeated and killed. So was his supporter the *Panĕmbahan* (lord) of Giri, one of the holiest of Java's Islamic leaders, who was slaughtered along with many of his family and followers in 1680.

The alliance between the VOC and the Mataram dynasty was vexed, with complaints, misunderstandings and conflicts occurring frequently. In 1686 the VOC's ambassador François Tack was ambushed and killed at the court of Amangkurat II (r. 1677–1703) along with 74 of his men. This caused an 18-year breach between Company and king, but it did not bring about reconciliation between the court and its Islamically inspired critics. As his kingdom began to disintegrate towards the end of his life, Amangkurat II made tentative gestures towards reconciliation with the VOC, to no avail. His immediate successor was regarded as the Company's enemy, but his throne was then usurped by his uncle, who successfully won the support of the VOC and became Pakubuwana I (r. 1704–19). The VOC-Mataram alliance was now stronger than ever, and so was the hatred felt by enemies of the monarchy for its alliance with *kafirs*.

There followed a series of bloody wars, mainly fought in East Java. Opponents of the monarchy and its VOC allies repeatedly justified their actions in Islamic terms. They believed that they were fighting Holy Wars. Within the court of Pakubuwana I, however, his queen Ratu Pakubuwana (d. 1732) began to emerge as a major political force. She was also a *litterateur* of significance, a master of the occult and a pious Sufi mystic. Within court circles it was she who would engineer the second major reconciliation of the *kraton* (court) and Islam in Java. But she had no opportunity to do this until the accession of her malleable, 16-year-old grandson Pakubuwana II (r. 1726–29).

Java was at peace in Pakubuwana II's early years, giving Ratu Pakubuwana and her followers an opportunity to make the *kraton* again a centre of Islamic mystic piety, as it had been in the time of Sultan Agung. Agung indeed seems to have been a direct inspiration for the Ratu. She sponsored the rewriting of the supernaturally potent books from his time: *Carita Sultan Iskandar, Carita Yusuf* and *Kitab Usulbiyah*. The last of these claimed to contain the very words of God. It was the aim of Ratu Pakubuwana and her circle of Islamisers to turn Pakubuwana II into the model Sufi monarch. After the old Ratu's death in 1732, others continued her Islamising influence in court circles, but they were not without opponents.

Royal piety culminated in the midst of the Chinese-VOC war of 1741–43 when, in July 1741, Pakubuwana II attacked and besieged the VOC fortress at his court. The VOC garrison surrendered after three weeks: some were executed, the rest were circumcised and obliged to convert to Islam. So Pakubuwana II was now the triumphant Sufi warrior, the victor over Company infidels. But when he saw that the VOC was turning the tide of battle elsewhere in Java, he sought reconciliation with his erstwhile Christian enemies. This turned the rebel forces against the king. In June 1742 they conquered the court, putting the monarch to flight. In his abject defeat, Pakubuwana II abandoned his demonstrations of Islamic piety and became again the ally of the VOC, like his predecessors. With Company support, after five months the king eventually reentered his *kraton*. The last prominent members of the circle of Islamisers at the restored court were surrendered to the VOC and exiled from Java. In 1745 the old, battered *kraton* at Kartasura was abandoned and a new one occupied at Surakarta, which still stands today.

Sultan Agung was the greatest of Javanese kings and Pakubuwana II probably the least, but it was their two reigns that defined a dominant mode of religiosity in Java, a mode for which the term "mystic synthesis" seems appropriate. In the case of the latter reign, of course, it was not the king but his pious grandmother Ratu Pakubuwana and her followers who contributed to shaping this mode. The mystic synthesis was the fruit of many years of conflicts and accommodations, and never constituted a formal or established orthodoxy that the courts were able, or concerned, to enforce. It was no established church, but its lineaments are nevertheless reasonably clear.

We may see this mystic synthesis as the Javanese understanding of Sufism, resting on three prominent distinguishing features. The first of these was a strong sense of Islamic identity. Javanese society was a society of Muslims. While there were small pockets of population where pre-Islamic faiths were still adhered to, for the vast majority of Javanese, Islam was the only conceivable religious element of identity. We know most about this at the level of the elite, of course, for most of our evidence concerns that level of society. Here we find devout aristocratic men and women, some of whom engaged in major acts of asceticism and piety. The first Sultan of Yogyakarta, Sultan Mangkubumi (Haměng-kubuwana I, r. 1749–92) was reputed in his youth to have engaged in extreme forms of asceticism and to have defeated attacking spirits by reciting memorised passages of the *Qur'an*. Prince Mangkunagara I (r. 1757–95) led a life of exemplary piety. He frequently attended Friday prayers at the mosque, taught his people how to perform ritual prayer, personally copied out the *Qur'an* several times and patronised Qur'anic recitations by large numbers of religious students (*santri*). Other leading figures, too, revealed a sense that Islam was central to their identity as Javanese.

The second prominent feature of the mystic synthesis was fulfill-ment of the five pillars of Islamic ritual life — reciting the confession of faith, ritual prayer five times a day, the giving of alms, fasting in the month of Ramadan and the pilgrimage to Mecca for those who were able to undertake it. Late in his life, Sultan Mangkubumi was reported by the Dutch Resident at the court to carry out "his religious service" as part of his daily routine. As noted above, Mangkunagara I was also exemplary in his religious devotions. Several works of religious literature are ascribed to Pakubuwana IV (r. 1788–1820). The most famous, *Sěrat Wulangreh*, admonishes mystics not to neglect their five daily prayers or any other of the five pillars of the faith.

The third characteristic — perhaps surprisingly for some readers, given the two previous ones — was acceptance of an array of local spiritual forces. When Pakubuwana II was driven from his court by rebels in 1742, he turned to the indigenous spirit-king Sunan Lawu for supernatural support. When Mangkubumi's son Haměngkubuwana II (r. 1792–1810, 1811, 1826–28), while still crown prince, wrote out the most supernaturally powerful book of the later eighteenth century, entitled *Surya Raja*, he placed it in a context of Islamic piety but included the Goddess of the Southern Ocean (Ratu Kidul) in its story. Mangku-nagara I — a model of princely piety in so many ways — also had a particular link with Sunan Lawu and seems to have believed equally in the Goddess of the Southern Ocean. In this respect, the dominant mystic synthesis may have departed from what Ratu Pakubuwana would have wished, for it is notable that the works of literature ascribed to her — works whose origins go back to the time of Sultan Agung — do not mention local forces such as Sunan Lawu or Ratu Kidul. But by the later eighteenth century these figures — and of course very many other local spirits — were accepted as a part of Javanese Islam.

We would do well not to idealise these pious aristocrats, to imagine that eighteenth-century Java was a place of saintly princes and rulers. It was a tough place, with less bloody violence after the peace settlements that ended the Third Javanese War of Succession in 1755–57, but nevertheless always full of intrigues, plots, poisonings and other forms of oppression, brutality and homicide. There were certainly figures whom we may rightly admire. But without doing too much injustice to Javanese historical reality, we might bear in mind Mark Twain's comments on the English aristocracy in his satirical *A Connecticut Yankee in King Arthur's Court*: "I will say this much for the nobility: that, tyrannical, murderous, rapacious, and morally rotten as they were, they were deeply and enthusiastically religious."

Java's mystic synthesis may be seen in its full flowering in the early nineteenth century. The monumental Javanese poem *Sěrat Cěnthini* provides one view of this. *Cěnthini* was composed in 1815 in the court of Surakarta but is attended by multiple problems of interpretation, for its content mainly concerns the time of Sultan Agung. So one may wonder whether it tells us about the seventeenth century or the nineteenth, or whether it is fiction or a sort of sociology. We may reasonably accept, however, that its depiction would at least have seemed believable to early nineteenth-century Javanese aristocrats and that it thus helps us to grasp where Javanese Islam stood in their time. For all of its problems, *Cěnthini* therefore remains a work of interest, particularly for shedding light on the place of Islam in the countryside of Java.

Sěrat Cěnthini treats mystical teachers — called *kyais* in Javanese — with respect and makes light of Islamic legal and ritual functionaries. But in the earlier parts of the book Sufi adepts are expected to adhere to the *shari'a* (religious law). The mystical doctrines taught in the text are of various kinds, including radical monism that teaches the unity of God with humankind, and therefore at least borders on — perhaps transgresses — the boundaries of orthodox Sufism. Whatever the case, Islamic sensibility permeates the text. Days are divided by prayer-times, actors frequently engage in *dhikr* (the recitation of pious formulae as a mystic exercise), attend the mosque and discuss mystical teachings.

The doctrines conveyed in *Cĕnthini* reflect the writer's (or writers') knowledge of Sufi works from the Middle Eastern heartlands of Islam. The main hero Amongraga follows the *dhikr* of the Shattariyya and Naqshabandiyya mystical brotherhoods (*tarekat*). One of the characters says that "every blade of grass in the land of Java" embraced Islam. The superiority of Islam over other faiths is stressed. But the text also introduces the Goddess of the Southern Ocean. It accommodates local culture, attributing the continued use in Islamised Java of the *wayang* theatre and its Hindu-derived stories to the conversion of the pre-Islamic hero Yudisthira to Islam. In its later sections, *Cĕnthini* also describes licentious mystic sects in the countryside, the *wong birai* or *santri birai*, who will be seen in Chapter 3 below to have been reported in various places in the later nineteenth century.

 Cĕnthini thus reflects the characteristics of Java's mystic synthesis. It is mystical in nature. It conveys a strong sense of Islamic identity. It reflects observance of the ritual obligations of Islam. And it admits the reality of local spiritual forces.

 Similar qualities are evident in the life of Java's most heroic figure of the earlier nineteenth century, prince Dipanagara (1785–1855) of Yogyakarta. Here was a devout Muslim mystic who travelled the countryside in search of new learning and mystical experiences. He was alienated by the debauched irreligiosity and corruption of the Yogyakarta court and spent much of his youth at the countryside residence of his pious great-grandmother, the widow of Sultan Mangkubumi. There he studied Islamic literature along with Javanese legends and history. He was familiar with the Hindu-Buddhist-derived literary classics of Java and admired the figure of Sultan Agung. He was aware of being part of a world-wide fellowship of Muslims. As a result of visions that helped to propel him into rebellion, he adopted a name taken from that of the Ottoman Sultan. Those visions also brought him into contact both with the spirit of Sunan Kalijaga, one of Java's *walis*, and with Ratu Kidul, the Goddess of the Southern Ocean. He was charged with the awesome task of purifying Java of its corruption through bloody war. In July 1825 Dipanagara went into rebellion. Thus began the devastating five-year Java War. When it finally ended in the defeat of Dipanagara, the stage was set for the period of interest in the following chapters of this book.

 Dipanagara personified the mystic synthesis. He was a devout Muslim mystic who believed himself to be part of the international community of Muslims. Yet he was also visited by the Goddess of the Southern

Ocean, who promised him the supernatural help in war that she promised
only to kings.

Most of what has been discussed above concerns elites. We have few
sources about Javanese commoners, but insofar as they exist they support
the depiction of the mystic synthesis as described here. An account of
Grĕsik in East Java in 1822 by A.D. Cornets de Groot, who was Dutch
Resident there, reported widespread observation of the five pillars of
Islam:

> In domestic life, the Javanese observes just a few of the practices
> prescribed for him by the *Qur'an*. The main points of the Islamic faith,
> which are carried out by many, are the *Shahada* [Confession of faith],
> the *sĕmbayang* [daily prayer], the *puasa* (fast), the *zakat* [alms], *fitrah*
> [contribution at the end of the fast] and *hajj* [pilgrimage].... The
> *puasa* (fast) is carried out by most Javanese of all classes.[1]

Another report came from Surakarta in 1824, on the eve of the
outbreak of the Java War. This was by J.W. Winter, who had worked as
a translator there since the late eighteenth century. In Chapter 6 below,
the Winter family will be seen to play a significant role in the intellectual
changes of the nineteenth century. J.W. Winter's report on Surakarta is
a combination of insights and ignorance. His observations of Javanese
Islam reflected both self-defining distance and years of observation,
much of it evidently unsympathetic. At the start of a section entitled
"superstitions", Winter wrote,

> I'm not saying that the Javanese don't practice well their religion of the
> faith of Muhammad, which is professed by them across the whole of
> Java. Its adherents are devoted to it as strongly as possible. But the
> exorbitant superstition which seems native to them makes them wholly
> incapable of paying attention ... to the fact that anything which is not
> part of nature also cannot be brought into being [through magic] by
> any mortal.[2]

---

[1] A.D. Cornets de Groot, "Bijdrage tot de kennis van de zeden en gewoonten der
Javanen", *TNI* 14, pt. 2 (1852): 271–2. Cornets de Groot's report is summarised in
Ann Kumar, *Java and modern Europe: Ambiguous encounters* (Richmond, Surrey:
Curzon, 1997), p. 111 *et seq.*, but her summary of this passage on p. 161 renders
it as "Observance of Islam is slight". The quotation given here shows this to be
inaccurate.

[2] J.W. Winter, "Beknopte beschrijving van het hof Soerakarta in 1824", *BKI* 54
(1902): 82.

Winter's report confirms from a contemporary but culturally distanced observer the outlines of the dominant mode of religion in Java at this time: self-consciously, indeed tenaciously Muslim in identity, but admitting indigenous supernatural ideas.

During the British interim administration of Java (1811–16), Sir Thomas Stamford Raffles (1781–1826) and John Crawfurd (1783–1868) both wrote about the Javanese. Of the two, Crawfurd had greater direct knowledge of Javanese society and the Javanese language. Their reports are valuable, if their judgments tell us at least as much about the self-conscious modernity of early nineteenth-century Britain as they do about Java. Raffles noted the perseverance of pre-Islamic ideas. He wrote,

> Their profession of Mohamedanism has not relieved them from the superstitious prejudices and observances of an anterior worship; they are thus open to the accumulated delusions of two religious systems.

"Pilgrimages to Mecca are common", he noted, and "every village has its priest, and ... in every village of importance there is a mosque or building set apart adapted to religious worship". He reported the practice of circumcision of both boys and girls, the latter said to "suffer a slight operation, intended to be analogous".[3]

All Javanese supported and respected Islam's doctrines:

> Some there are who are enthusiastic, and all consider it a point of honour to support and respect its doctrines: but as a nation, the Javans by no means feel hatred towards Europeans as *infidels*; and this perhaps may be given as the best proof that they are very imperfect Mahomedans.[4]

John Crawfurd, a fiercely judgmental Scottish Protestant, described the Javanese as "semibarbarians".[5] He provides us with a rather different picture of the Javanese from that in the other sources we have encountered here. He wrote,

---

[3] Thomas Stamford Raffles, *The history of Java* (2 vols.; 2nd ed.; London: John Murray, 1830), vol. II, pp. 3–4.

[4] Ibid., vol. II, p. 5.

[5] John Crawfurd, *History of the Indian Archipelago, containing an account of the manners, arts, languages, religions, institutions, and commerce of its inhabitants* (3 vols.; Edinburgh: Archibald Constable and Co., 1820), vol. I, p. 47 and elsewhere.

Of all Mahomedans the Javanese are the most lax in their principles and practice.... In most of the Mahomedan institutions of the Javanese, we discover marks of Hinduism. The institutions of the latter have in reality been rather modified and built upon than destroyed.... Neither the prayers nor the fastings of the Indian islanders, commonly speaking, are very rigid. The lower orders know little, and care less, about these matters.... Some of the higher classes, *now and then*, pay a more sober and decent regard to the exterior observances of religion, but it is not very general, and it is never severe.... The pilgrimage to Mecca is frequently undertaken by the Javanese, and all the other Mahomedan tribes, less on account of piety, than on account of the distinctions and immunities which the reputation of the pilgrimage confers among a simple and untaught people.... The only negative precept of the Koran by which the Javanese can be said strictly to abide, is the prohibition against eating the flesh of hogs.[6]

Crawfurd's judgments prefigured those of later colonial rulers, of anthropologists and indeed of Islamic reformers. He evidently measured Javanese religious practices by the strictness he expected in any faith, and found wanting in a version of Islam so open to local influences. His judgments are not, however, inconsistent with the argument here, supported in the other sources we have cited, that Islam was the core religious element in Javanese senses of identity, while also accommodating older spiritual forces.

These European observations are important for showing that in the opening decades of the nineteenth century Java's mystic synthesis seems to have been embraced by commoners as well as the elite. We must not forget that our picture of Javanese society c. 1800–30 remains patchy. There is much that we would like to know that the sources do not tell us. But, insofar as the evidence allows us to draw conclusions, it is reasonable to believe that Javanese society was relatively unified in terms of its religious identity. For this religious identity we are using the term mystic synthesis which, as noted above, had three characteristic features within the mystical variant of Islam that it represented: a strong commitment to Islamic identity, widespread observation of the five pillars of the faith, and acceptance of local spiritual forces.

The shattering of this unifying religious identity by the dramatic forces of the nineteenth century is the subject of the remaining chapters of this book.

---

[6] Ibid., vol. II, pp. 260–71.

2

Javanese Society's Nineteenth-century Colonial Context

In Java, 1830 was one of those remarkable years that truly mark a historical watershed. Most years that we take as turning-points are just useful short-hand indicators of longer periods of transition, some particular event being taken to stand for a larger train of events. But 1830 really mattered in Java, for in that year began unprecedented and profound changes in Javanese life.

In 1830 the Java War ended in victory for the colonial forces. With the surrender of Prince Dipanagara and his supporters, for the first time Javanese faced a situation in which there was no serious competitor to the power being exercised by the Dutch colonial regime. In January of that year, a new Governor-General arrived in Batavia, bringing with him ideas about a more profitable way to run Java for the benefit of the Netherlands. This was Johannes van den Bosch (1780–1844), the architect of the *cultuurstelsel* (cultivation system). His contribution to the Netherlands was so great that in 1835 he was ennobled as a Baron and in 1839 was made a Count.[1] Millions of Javanese, however, would have found little to be grateful for his ideas.

Van den Bosch's *cultuurstelsel* was an attempt to solve a persistent problem in the Dutch administration of Java: it lost money. After nearly

---

[1] Biographical information is available at <http://www.iisg.nl/bwsa/bios/bosch.html>.

two centuries in the Indonesian archipelago, the Dutch East India Company (VOC) went bankrupt at the end of the eighteenth century, at which point the Netherlands government took over its role in Java. But still Java remained a financial loss. In the wake of the costs of the Napoleonic wars in Europe and then the secession of the southern provinces of the Netherlands to become the state of Belgium in 1830 — followed by a fruitless war to regain those provinces — the embattled Netherlands treasury was still less able to carry a loss-making colony. Van den Bosch proposed to King Willem I (1813–40), however, that it would be possible to extract agricultural products from Java in a volume and at a price that would enable the Netherlands to become one of the world's greatest suppliers of tropical products, particularly indigo, sugar and above all coffee. And this could be done, he proposed, in a way that would benefit the Javanese themselves. This no doubt attracted the monarch with that particular ring made by coins being piled up.

These ideas for what was called the *cultuurstelsel* rested upon the fact that, since the days of the British interregnum administration of Java (1811–16), Javanese were in principle obliged to pay a land tax to the sovereign government in Batavia. This was theoretically set at 40 per cent of the main crop of a village and was to be paid in cash, but numerous problems of administration and limited circulation of money meant that it had never worked well in practice. There was great variety in application across Java.[2] The land tax as a source of income was unreliable and unsatisfactory to Batavia, and at the same time a nuisance at best and a burden at worst to the Javanese who actually paid it — or in most cases paid a part of it.

Van den Bosch proposed to continue with the land tax, but believed that it could only work if it was backed up by greater compulsion, which was to be the core administrative mechanism of his system. Javanese peasants would be compelled to grow valuable tropical produce and deliver that to the government at a fixed price. Van den Bosch's estimations suggested that, to cover their land-tax obligations with the payments they would receive for the government-assigned crops, villages would need only to set aside about 20 per cent of their land — a more beneficial

---

[2] W.R. Hugenholtz, "Taxes and society: Regional differences in Central Java around 1830", *Papers of the fourth Indonesian-Dutch history conference, Yogyakarta, 24–29 July 1983*, vol. I: *Agrarian history*, ed. Sartono Kartodirdjo (Yogyakarta: Gadjah Mada University Press, 1986), pp. 145–56.

arrangement for them than paying 40 per cent of the value of their main crop as the tax. Thus, both the government and the farmers of Java should benefit.

But this *stelsel*, this "system", was in fact barely a system at all. It amounted to a wide variety of arrangements across Java. The link between land tax and crop payments was never entirely clear and became less so as time went on, except in the perverse sense that if village incomes from crop payments rose, then administrators tended to raise the land tax as well, thus recouping the surplus "profit" of the village. The main investment by the Javanese was, in fact, not land but labour, as will be seen below. There was a great deal of corruption and multiple scandals emerged, particularly in the sugar industry. But the Netherlands home government did indeed make a great deal of money. The prosperity, development and industrialisation of the Netherlands in the course of the nineteenth century rested in significant measure on the agricultural products squeezed out of the Javanese.

Our concern here, however, is not with the impact of the *cultuurstelsel* in the Netherlands, but with the changes it brought to Javanese society. This is a complex and difficult topic for several reasons. The very variety of developments across different places and different groups and social classes of the population makes generalisation difficult. The statistical evidence from the nineteenth century is voluminous but often of dubious reliability. And there is a legacy of heated political controversy about the *cultuurstelsel* from earlier generations of Dutch authors that makes much of the discussion of it in earlier works tendentious. Fortunately, several modern scholars have dedicated themselves to making sense of the evidence, so that we know much more than we did only a few decades ago. In this chapter, we will attempt to capture both the general aspects of the Javanese experience and something of the immense variety that lurked within general patterns.

As noted above, the key factor underlying *cultuurstelsel* output was the investment of Javanese labour into agricultural production for the government: the key to this labour investment was rising population. The rate of population growth in Java during the nineteenth century was indisputably high, but just how high has been vigorously disputed. The problem is that no one knows what the population was at the start of the century. It might have been anything between about 3 and 5 million. By 1890 it was approaching 24 million. So the increase was of the order of five- to eight-fold over a century. At the time, people were aware that something remarkable was happening. The missionary Carel Poensen remarked in 1886 from Kědiri about "the alarming increase in population".[3] Both increasing fertility and declining mortality seem to have played a role. Boomgaard applied sophisticated statistical analysis to the very unsatisfactory data to attempt to measure and explain Java's population increase, but asserted at the end that "Of course this model leaves many questions unanswered."[4]

This book concentrates on the ethnic Javanese, who occupied the heartland of Central and East Java. The island was also occupied also by the Sundanese of West Java and many Madurese who migrated to East Java. Bantěn in West Java was a Javanese-speaking pocket. What were the proportions of each of these ethnic groups in Java's population is not clear, except that the ethnic Javanese were by far the greatest number. Veth, writing in 1875, estimated that of a total indigenous population in Java at the end of 1872 which he thought to be 17.1 million, 23.4 per cent were Sundanese, 9.4 per cent were Madurese, and 67.3 per cent, or 11.5 million, were ethnic Javanese.[5]

For the purposes of this book, readers should keep in mind that everything discussed here took place in a context in which population was growing at a significant rate in Java, unused land was being progressively more opened up for agriculture and settlement, and population density was increasing. The colonial context was changing rapidly, the demographic context at the same time and, as will be seen in subsequent chapters, so were the intellectual and religious contexts. This was a society in flux, not some so-called "traditional" society tied to a "traditional" way of life.

Javanese involvement in the *cultuurstelsel* was significant at all levels. The elite of the society — collectively known as the *priyayi*[6] — were essential to the large-scale organisation of labour that made the system

---

[3] C. Poensen, "Iets over het Javaansche gezin", Kědiri, Dec. 1886, in ARZ 161; also in *MNZG* 31 (1887): 225.

[4] Peter Boomgaard, *Children of the colonial state: Population growth and economic development in Java, 1795–1880* (Amsterdam: Free University Press, 1989), pp. 166–98. The debates on this subject were commenced by Bram Peper, *Grootte en groei van Java's inheemse bevolking in de negentiende eeuw* ([Amsterdam]: Afdeling Zuid en Zuidoost-Azië, Antropologisch-sociologisch Centrum Universiteit van Amsterdam, publicatie nr. 11, 1967).

[5] P.J. Veth, *Java: Geographisch, ethnologisch, historisch* (3 vols.; Haarlem: Erven F. Bohn, 1875–82), vol. I, pp. 265–6.

[6] This is an old term for the Javanese aristocratic elite, deriving from *para yayi*, younger brothers; i.e. the younger brothers of the king.

work. From the regional heads known as *regenten* in Dutch and *bupati* in Javanese down to lower-level village leaders, Javanese involvement was *sine qua non*. The Europeans, or their Indonesian subjects from outside Java, did not have enough local knowledge, authority or even numbers of personnel to do the job on their own. To encourage their enthusiastic participation, Javanese officials were paid percentages of the agricultural deliveries, which proved to be a rich source of corrupt dealings. Some of Java's higher *priyayi* elite became very wealthy. There was a difference, however, between the experience of *priyayi* in the districts directly ruled by the Dutch and those in the principalities of Yogyakarta and Surakarta, where in theory Dutch control was indirect (but in fact no less dominant). These states had been greatly reduced in size and resources by the colonial government's confiscation of their outer districts at the end of the Java War. As a result, these were lean times for many of the principalities' *priyayi*.

Javanese peasant families were obliged to cultivate government crops. The statistics for this are as bewildering and doubtful as any others from this period, but several scholars have made enough sense of the data to give a remarkable picture of what the *cultuurstelsel* meant for millions of Javanese peasants. Van Niel calculated that over 70 per cent of all agricultural families were committed to raising crops for the government, over half of them in coffee.[7] Fasseur's figures for all of Java give 57 per cent of agricultural families involved in 1840, falling to 46 per cent (of an increasing total population) in 1850.[8] Elson's all-Java data reports 67 per cent of agricultural families engaged in compulsory agricultural activities in 1836, with the figure not declining below 60 per cent until 1858 and only below 50 per cent in 1866, as the *cultuurstelsel* was being wound up.[9]

There were great variations. In some regions the percentages of peasant households compulsorily committed to growing and processing government crops was much higher than the mean figures suggest. A few examples from various parts of Java will illustrate this point. In 1840, 69 per cent of agricultural families in Cirĕbon were compulsorily producing government crops, 72 per cent in Pacitan, 79 per cent in

---

[7] Robert Van Niel, "Measurement of change under the cultivations system in Java, 1837–1851", *Indonesia* no. 14 (Oct. 1972): 98.

[8] C. Fasseur, *Kultuurstelsel and koloniale baten: De Nederlandse exploitatie van Java, 1840–1860* (Leiden: Universitaire Pers, 1975), p. 16.

[9] Elson, *Village Java*, p. 185.

Kědu, 81 per cent in Bagělen and 68 per cent in Banyumas.[10] In the same year, other figures for Bantěn, Banyumas, and Kědu reported that over 100 per cent of agricultural families were involved, an outcome produced either by requiring even non-agricultural families to work on the crops, or by obliging families to work on more than one crop, and thus counting them twice. The same sorts of figures appear for Kědu and Pacitan in 1850.[11] In Jěpara, in 1858, 41 per cent of families were committed to government cultivations and another 50 per cent to forestry work; in Kudus 38 per cent of the families were obliged to grow crops for sale to the government and a further 18 per cent were obliged to work in the forestry industry.[12] In the sugar-growing area of Pasuruan, 80 per cent of the families in the "circles" of the sugar factories were obliged to grow cane or to perform other services for the industry c. 1855, a situation described by Elson as "coerced drudgery on a massive and relentless scale".[13] In Madiun, the main crops were coffee and indigo. There were over 3 million coffee trees planted there by 1835, 6.5 million by 1856 and over 5.7 million in 1859. Nearly 17,000 families were compulsorily growing coffee trees in 1859, each with an average of 340 trees to tend. Another 10,200 families were forced to work in the indigo industry, which involved both growing the indigo plants and working in the factories — indigo being one of the most hated crops in Java because the work was so relentless and dirty. In all, about 64 per cent of Madiun's peasant households were committed to compulsory government agricultural work.[14]

[10] Fasseur, *Kultuurstelsel*, p. 16. See also Djoko Suryo, *Sejarah sosial pedesaan karesidenan Semarang 1830–1900* (Yogyakarta: Pusat Antar Universitas Studi Sosial, Universitas Gadjah Mada, 1989), p. 23. Readers who do not command Dutch should note that Fasseur's book is also available in English translation as *The politics of colonial exploitation: Java, the Dutch and the cultivation system*, transl. R.E. Elson and Ary Kraal (Ithaca: Cornell University Southeast Asia Program, 1992).

[11] R.E. Elson, *Village Java under the cultivation system 1830–1870* (Sydney: Asian Studies Association of Australia in association with Allen & Unwin, 1994), pp. 90, 111.

[12] Frans Hüsken, *Een dorp op Java: Sociale differentatie in een boerengemeenschap, 1850–1980* (Overveen: ACASEA, 1988), p. 60.

[13] R.E. Elson, *Javanese peasants and the colonial sugar industry: Impact and change in an East Java residency, 1830–1940* (Singapore, New York: Oxford University Press, 1984), p. 77.

[14] Onghokham, "The residency of Madiun: Priyayi and peasant in the nineteenth century", PhD dissertation, Yale University, 1975, pp. 179–80.

Figures gathered at the level of residencies, however, often conceal
dramatic variations at lower levels of Javanese society. When information
about the average number of coffee trees being tended by agricultural
families in Sěmarang — information like that reported for Madiun
above — is tested at district level, the mean residency data can be seen
to be quite misleading about the actual experience of peasant families.
For all of Sěmarang residency, the figure shows 123.3 coffee trees grown
compulsorily per agricultural family in 1837. But this ranged from a low
of just one tree per family in Purwadadi and 6.0 in Wirasari to 279.7
in Selakaton and 272.6 in Limbangan. By 1845, the all-residency figure
had increased dramatically to 536.6 trees per family. But again this
concealed wide variations at district level, where the figure ranged from
58.0 trees in Purwadadi to 1014.5 in Ambarawa.[15] No doubt, if we
could penetrate to the level of the village or household, we would see
similarly wide variations.

The peasant population was highly mobile. People moved for
many reasons: to escape the burdens of compulsory labour, to take up
wage labour, to escape harvest failures (in many cases caused by
competition between export crops and food crops for access to land,
labour and water), to open up new agricultural lands, to flee oppression
by local officials, or to seek opportunities in the growing towns and
cities. In Sěmarang and Cirěbon the number of agricultural families
fell over 1837–51, but the total population of those residencies was
stable, suggesting significant inward migration to towns and cities as
people escaped indigo cultivation in Cirěbon and unprofitable sugar
cane production in Sěmarang.[16] In Madiun, emigration in the 1880s
from Pacitan to the Mangkunagaran principality in Surakarta prompted
government enquiries into the causes, which reported that an oppres-
sive local official, the belief that corvée was less burdensome in the
Mangkunagaran and that it was easier to open new agricultural lands
there had all played roles.[17] In the last quarter of the nineteenth century,
the growth of population was continuing to require people to move to
new areas to open up agricultural land. In his report on the declining
welfare of Javanese — a sweeping denunciation of the colonial system
— C. Th. van Deventer pointed particularly to large-scale migrations
from Central Java to Banyuwangi in the Eastern Salient of Java, of

[15] Djoko Suryo, *Sejarah sosial*, p. 27
[16] Van Niel, "Measurement", p. 103.
[17] Onghokham, "Madiun", pp. 219–23.

Madurese and Javanese to Jĕmbĕr, and of people from the Central Javanese principalities (the *Vorstenlanden*) and Madiun to the highlands of Malang.[18]

Detailed analysis down to district level in the residency of Sĕmarang has revealed dramatic population movements. Again, a few examples across the residency will illustrate this. In 1837 the district of Grogol was reported as having a population of 7,474; in 1845 it had 27,824, giving a mean rate of annual population growth of 17.9 per cent, which can only be explained by large-scale immigration. In Manggar district the population went from 17,807 to 50,503, for an annual rate of growth of 13.9 per cent. In Dĕmak the figures were 30,541 and 55,067 respectively, for a mean annual rate of population growth of 7.6 per cent. But in Ambarawa, population fell between these two years from 44,598 to 42,998. In the midst of such massive social flux, any idea that Javanese villages were of a roughly similar size became irrelevant — if indeed, it had ever been relevant. Reported mean population in Sĕmarang as a whole was 180 per village, but at district level in 1837 this ranged from a low of 81 to a high of 539. The rate at which those numbers multiplied between then and 1845 ranged from 0.98 times (i.e. a slight decrease in the mean population of villages in Ambarawa district) to 2.25 times (as mean village population in Manggar district grew from 213 to 272 over these eight years).[19]

Mobility was enhanced by improving transportation infrastructure, required by the expansion of commercial agriculture and the attendant need to move crops to railheads and ports, and thence overseas. Roads, lesser paths and very many bridges were needed to link together the ever-expanding networks of settlements in Java's undulating land. Where previously porters had carried much of the goods traffic, in many places wheeled vehicles — drawn by horses, cattle or men — replaced them. Railways were being proposed for Java from the 1850s. The first section of railway to be constructed was from Sĕmarang to Tanggung, begun in 1864 and completed in 1867, a segment of 24.6 kms. In 1870 the rail line reached Surakarta. Building the line and the many bridges that it required was a significant source of employment to wage labourers. Over a period of 14 months in 1867–68, this work required nearly two

---

[18] C. Th. Van Deventer, *Overzicht van den economischen toestand der inlandse bevolking van Java en Madoera* (Koloniaal-economische bijdragen I; 's-Gravenhage: Martinus Nijhoff, 1904), p. 8.

[19] Djoko Suryo, *Sejarah sosial*, pp. 11–7.

million man-days of labour. But this was hard, dangerous work. Many
workers suffered from cholera, typhoid and malaria; many died. After
the line was completed, it represented a revolution in land transport for
Javanese.[20] Javanese were well aware of how important such developments
were. The introduction of a horse-drawn tramway in Batavia in 1869
even inspired a poem in classical Javanese verse.[21] In subsequent years
the rail network was expanded across other parts of Java. By 1903 there
were 1,788 kms of government-owned railways in Java and Madura, 261
kms of privately-owned railways, and 1,838 kms of steam tramways, for
a total of 3,887 kms.[22]

Did the Javanese peasantry benefit as Johannes van den Bosch had
proposed? Van Niel attempted to answer this question for Cirĕbon,
Bagĕlen, Sĕmarang and Surabaya over 1837–51. His conclusion is of
interest:

> Van den Bosch had assumed that his plan would bring increased
> welfare and prosperity to the Javanese. In the main, despite shortfalls
> in some areas, the System did that. By all material bases of calculation
> such as area of land under cultivation per family, amount of livestock
> per family, and availability and price of basic food commodities it
> would appear that material well-being was growing more rapidly than
> population during the period under consideration here. But this is a
> very generalised observation and says nothing about the manner in
> which these material gains were distributed among the population....
> In actuality, many families received no benefits unless they were included
> among the village landholders.[23]

One test of the welfare thesis is to look at the balance between crop
payments to agricultural villages and the tax imposed upon them. Some
observers have argued that if crop payments were sufficient, or more than
enough, to pay the land rent tax, then villages were prospering because
they had surplus income. The results of such analysis are of interest,

---

[20] Ibid., ch. 4.
[21] *Tramweg (Kareta Gĕrbong)* in 4 cantos and 46 pp., published in Batavia in 1869;
Poersoewignja and Wirawangsa, *Javaansche bibliographie gegrond op de boekwerken in
die taal, aanwezig in de boekerij van het Bataviaasch Genootschap van Kunsten en
Wetenschappen/Pratélan kawontenaning boekoe-boekoe Basa Djawi (tjitakan) ingkang
kasimpen wonten ing gĕdong boekoe (Museum) ing pasimpenan (bibliothek) XXXIII*
(Batavia: Bataviaasch Genootschap, 1920), vol. I, p. 425.
[22] Van Deventer, *Overzicht*, p. 214.
[23] Van Niel, "Measurement", pp. 104–5.

although it will be seen in the following paragraph that there are reasons to doubt that the relationship between crop payments and land tax can tell us much about the prosperity or otherwise of peasants.

Djoko Suryo examined Sĕmarang, also one of Van Niel's cases, at district level, and there some of the patterns visible at higher administrative levels become more complicated in the varieties of local experiences. Looking at the balances between land rent taxes paid and crop payments received, Djoko Suryo showed that for some districts there was surplus cash, for some not. In Selakaton over 1836–45, there was surplus cash of the order of fl. 0.82–1.62 per agricultural household. But in Grobogan the situation was reversed: land rent exceeded crop payments each year from fl. 0.91 to 1.67 per agricultural household. In Grogol, land tax exceeded crop payments by fl. 1.98 to fl. 3.45 per agricultural family in 1837–39. As noted above, however, it is doubtful whether such calculations by themselves tell us much about peasant experiences of welfare or otherwise. Consider this example: in the district Ambarawa, crop payments consistently exceeded land rent assessments over 1836–45, by fl. 1.31 to fl. 2.17 per agricultural household.[24] Yet this did not attract Java's highly mobile peasantry to move to Ambarawa in search of "profit". Instead, as noted above, Ambarawa's population actually fell between 1837 and 1845 and its mean village population size decreased. Peasants were leaving. Meanwhile in Grogol, where land tax exceeded crop payments by some of the highest figures in the whole residency of Sĕmarang, so that in principle the *cultuurstelsel* there was "unprofitable" to the peasantry, the greatest influx of population took place, as noted above.

Peasants reacted to their new challenges in many ways, including resistance. The burning of cane fields occurred fairly commonly but was not necessarily a major problem for the sugar producers, for if the burned cane was milled quickly sugar could still be extracted. But at times it became serious. In Prabalingga in 1846 there were 144 incidents. Thereafter cane-burning declined in Pasuruan residency for a time, but again became a major problem from the 1880s onward.[25] In early twentieth-century Madiun, cane-burning became serious enough that the factory owners agreed to pay for a special police force to guard the fields.[26] In Klaten in Central Java, where also the sugar industry had a

---

[24] Djoko Suryo, *Sejarah sosial*, pp. 33–5.
[25] Elson, *Javanese peasants*, pp. 79, 148–55
[26] Onghokham, "Madiun", p. 230.

major impact, there was widespread vagabondage, highway robbery, cattle robbery and cane-burning.[27]

As Elson observes, however,

> by around 1840 the disturbing pace of the System's establishment had given way to a measured tread, a smooth organisational routine, as peasants and their masters accustomed themselves to annually recurring patterns of labour for the cause of the Dutch treasury.... By far the most common response of peasants ... was simply to make the best of their circumstances.... Most ... had become immersed in a system of exploitation that forced them to work regularly and onerously, from which they drew only moderate and often scanty recompense in relation to the work they performed, and which taxed them with increasing severity.[28]

The 1840s were a time of crisis for the *cultuurstelsel* and for the peasants who bore its burdens. There were several devastating famines, outbreaks of epidemics — notably typhoid in 1846–50 — and other general problems arising from corruption and abuse by officials. As already noted above, food shortages were commonly caused by competition for land, labour and water between food crops and export crops. For example, in the Grobogan and Děmak areas of Sěmarang residency, some 80,000 people died of famine and related causes in 1849–50.[29] Yet the arrangements carried on, bolstering the reserves of the Netherlands treasury and expanding the Netherlands home economy, until its oppression, abuses and scandals made it politically untenable in Dutch domestic politics in the course of the 1850s and 1860s. This was among the reasons why the *cultuurstelsel* began to be abandoned piecemeal on the ground in Java from the 1860s.[30]

For many members of the administrative elite of Java, the *priyayi*, however, the nineteenth century brought some new and profitable experiences. As noted above, the *priyayi* were essential to the entire system. It was they, in the end, who had to organise the labour without which the *cultuurstelsel* could not succeed. This was not because the

---

[27] Suhartono, "The Impact of the sugar industry on rural life, Klaten, 1850–1900", in Sartono Kartodirdjo (ed.), *Papers of the Fourth Indonesian-Dutch history conference, Yogyakarta, 24–29 July 1983*, vol. I: *Agrarian history* (Yogyakarta: Gadjah Mada University Press, 1986), pp. 187–92.

[28] Elson, *Village Java*, pp. 88–9, 96, 97–8.

[29] Ibid., pp. 99–127.

[30] See Fasseur, *Kultuurstelsel*, chs. 6–12.

pre-colonial Javanese kingdoms had efficient administrative systems that the *priyayi* controlled. In fact, the old kingdoms were utterly ramshackle administrative entities. Limited means of communication, difficult mountainous topography, scattered pockets of population and traditions of local autonomy meant that pre-colonial monarchs hardly had an administrative structure at all outside of the core territories around the court. Taxes and corvée were mostly *ad hoc*, labour mobilisation was short-term and much depended on the willingness of local elites to cooperate with higher levels of authority. That cooperation could be ensured by royal threats, military action, murder, efficient spying, delivery of rewards (in money, control over manpower, wives, etc.) and, perhaps above all, by monarchs mobilising their presumed supernatural powers to become cultural axioms. If in modern democratic and supposedly egalitarian societies, people still rise when the head of state enters the room, in profoundly undemocratic and inegalitarian Java, people dropped to the floor in the presence of the monarch. They believed that he communicated with the Goddess of the Southern Ocean, was the shadow of God upon the earth, possessed supernaturally powerful weapons and was the heir to sacred and secret powers. At every level below the king, elites sought to emulate his grandeur without so obviously competing with it that it meant rebellion — unless, of course, it was their intention to rebel. *Bupatis* built residences that looked and functioned like lesser *kratons*. At the bottom of the hierarchy, village heads had *krisses* that were thought to be "alive" with spiritual powers This was what "traditional" authority meant in Java.

The early nineteenth-century Franco-Dutch and British administrations of Java, inspired by the ideals of the French Revolution, had been hostile to this *ancien régime* in Java, but in the age of the *cultuurstelsel* the Dutch needed this "traditional" authority. There was no other way that several million peasants could be organised to grow coffee, sugar, indigo, tea, pepper, cinnamon, tobacco and so on, or to undertake the labour needed to prepare these crops for export. So the *cultuurstelsel* period was marked by a social conservatism. The Javanese elite became more secure in their positions than they had ever been in the days of the tumultuous, violent and murderous pre-colonial kingdoms. The *pax neerlandica* of post-1830 Java brought them greater physical security, their positions became normally inheritable by their sons, and they had opportunities to become wealthy. It will be seen in Chapter 6 that for the *priyayi* the nineteenth century was also time of rapidly widening intellectual horizons.

As noted above, a key decision by the colonial regime was to pay percentages of crop values to the elite who organised their growing, in order to inspire them to press as much as possible from the peasantry. From *Bupatis* at the top to village heads at the bottom, percentages were paid. In 1858–60, for example, *Bupatis* received from fl. 1,301 to fl. 25,064 per annum in crop percentages, on top of a *Bupati's* regular salary that was normally about fl. 15,000.[31] The significance of these sums would be clearer if we had a contemporary figure for the cash, or cash-equivalent, income of villagers. We do not have that, but we do have an estimate from the beginning of the twentieth century that the total cash-equivalent income of Javanese village land-owners was on average (readers by now, I hope, being distrustful of the idea of an average in Java) of the order of fl. 80 per annum.[32] If one accepts that estimate, then the *Bupati* of Pasuruan would have had a total cash income some 500 times that of a village land-owner, in addition to which he could call upon villagers for various forms of compulsory labour. These crop percentages and the general opportunities for black market trading provided multiple opportunities for corruption. Yet only rarely was a *Bupati* dismissed from office. Anyone who thinks large-scale corruption to be an invention of twentieth-century independent Indonesian governments might do well to look at nineteenth-century colonial Java.

These percentages and the various abuses associated with the role of the local aristocratic elite were addressed by the colonial government reluctantly and piecemeal. Over time various measures were taken to restrict oppression and dishonesty. And there were *priyayi* who conducted themselves honourably and with the welfare of their subjects in mind, at least as they saw it. But the fundamental facts of the colonial power structure were not greatly altered. A foreign-run colonial state depending on the indigenous elite to organise labour and taxes successfully exploited an ever-increasing Javanese peasantry.

Yet Java was the home not only to Dutch colonial officials and sugar-concessionaires, to Javanese elite and to peasants. Nor was all of the work done during the nineteenth century compulsorily organised. In association with the *cultuurstelsel* and with the "liberal" period that succeeded it from c. 1870 — when Java was opened to private capitalism — there were also opportunities for "free labour" and entrepreneurship. Many of

---

[31] Fasseur, *Kultuurstelsel,* p. 29; see also Elson, *Village Java,* p. 182.
[32] Van Deventer, *Overzicht,* p. 34.

the people who grasped such opportunities and prospered from them were locally domiciled Chinese, but there were also Arabs (who played an important role in the Islamic developments discussed in the following chapter) and indigenous Javanese. There arose village-level entrepreneurs and, particularly in the towns, a nascent middle class that will be seen to play a major role in this book.

While much of the growing of crops and associated factory work was done by compulsory labour, there were many ancillary tasks that were done with wage labour. In textiles, agricultural processing, land transport, entertainment, smithing, bricklaying, shipbuilding, pottery- and gunny sack-making and similar tasks, even in some cane harvesting, there were opportunities for small- (and sometimes larger-)scale entre- preneurs and wage labourers. When the Dutch abolished the market tax in 1851, Javanese markets flourished as items not previously worth selling because of the tax became commercially viable. Improving transportation networks that linked together the ever-expanding areas under habitation and cultivation also stimulated indigenous commerce. There was substantial Javanese shipping trade along the north coast. Some Javanese sailed across the Java Sea to Kalimantan and to Singapore — the latter being attractive as a source of opium for smuggling.[33] Along the coast of Central and East Java, Javanese were engaged in deep-sea fishing and fish-farming.[34]

The Javanese textile industry was seriously challenged by cheap imported textiles, but the nineteenth century provided opportunities for growth for most branches of industry and trade. Elson's conclusion is that, except for textiles, "There came about an intensification, elaboration, broader diffusion and greater penetration of commerce and industrial activity throughout Java.... Javanese peasant society was now profoundly commercial."[35] The increasing money supply was an important element of this commercialisation. This became particularly significant in the last quarter of the nineteenth century, during the "liberal" period of colonial rule, when private enterprise and free wage labour were encouraged. In Jĕpara, for example, in the early 1890s the annual inflow of cash from the sugar, coffee and timber industries was around fl.2 million.[36]

---

[33] Ibid., pp. 108–9.
[34] Ibid., pp. 116–9.
[35] Elson, *Village Java*, pp. 222–5, 264–77; quotation from p. 277.
[36] Hüsken, *Dorp*, p. 66.

Most Javanese who engaged in wage labour or entrepreneurship did so on a part-time basis in addition to agricultural work, but by the end of the century those fully engaged in non-agricultural work were becoming a significant minority. In the census of Java and Madura in 1900, 5.5 million working adult males were reported. Of these, some 900,000 (i.e. about 16 per cent) were exclusively employed in non-agricultural work as government officials, school teachers, religious leaders, traders, fishermen, factory workers, craftsmen, carters and shippers. Another 850,000 (15 per cent) were agriculturalists but had outside income as well. That leaves about two-thirds of those adult males finding their sole income from agriculture.[37] Women have long been involved in trade in Java, but unfortunately the source just cited, while commenting that women dominated small-scale trading,[38] does not have statistics on the matter.

In 1904, C. Th. van Deventer compiled a report for the Netherlands Minister of Colonies on the economic circumstances of the indigenous population of Java and Madura.. Van Deventer was a lawyer who had spent nearly 20 years in Indonesia and was one of the principal architects of the "ethical" colonial policy of the early twentieth century.[39] This policy was inspired by the widespread conviction that under Dutch rule Javanese welfare had declined during the nineteenth century. Van Deventer's report provides a useful overview of what life was like for Javanese at the turn of the twentieth century.

According to Van Deventer, welfare was declining throughout Java, regardless of whether people lived in heavily or lightly populated areas, or in areas with particular forms of land tenure.[40] Evidently concentration of land ownership was underway. Village officers — who received land as part of their office — and higher officials were becoming major landowners. As were indigenous money lenders.

Shortages of cash led farmers into indebtedness and thus into the hands of usurers.[41] Cash was needed for taxes as well as for ordinary daily needs, but the burdens on ordinary Javanese took not only the form of cash. Throughout most of the nineteenth century, they also owed the

---

[37] Van Deventer, *Overzicht*, p. 8.
[38] Ibid., p. 98.
[39] See M.C. Ricklefs, *A History of Modern Indonesia Since c. 1200* (3rd ed.; Basingstoke: Palgrave; Stanford: Stanford University Press, 2001), pp. 193–4.
[40] Van Deventer, *Overzicht*, pp. 7, 16.
[41] Ibid., p. 17.

government various forms of compulsory labour. While many compulsory services were abolished in principle in 1867, that abolition did not take effect until 1882. At that stage, there still remained compulsory services such as construction of jails, resthouses, roads, bridges, dams, irrigation canals and other public works; guarding of warehouses; services of various sorts for the postal service, and so on. These obligations were abolished over subsequent years and were replaced by the requirement to pay a head tax, which may have been an even more difficult burden to bear because of the shortage of currency. As of 1904, villagers in Java were still obliged to render labour service for the maintenance of roads, dams, waterworks, dikes and water channels.[42]

A good deal of the trade of Java was in the hands of Chinese, Indians, Arabs and — of particular importance here — Javanese who had made the pilgrimage to Mecca, the *hajis*. It was mainly these Javanese *hajis* who initiated the Islamic reform and revival movement that is of interest in this volume. Van Deventer says of them that,

> by undertaking the pilgrimage to Mecca, [they] have already shown that they have more energy and also rather more capital than their fellow village-dwellers and, upon their return, moreover regard themselves as a good deal more elevated in esteem than ordinary natives. With greater success, to their peddling trade they can add the role of money-lender, i.e. usurer; their status as *hajis* elevates their social significance.[43]

Interest rates were very high. Usurers in Java demanded 100 to 200 per cent annual interest at the beginning of the twentieth century. When rice was loaned for consumption or as seed, a return of 2 : 1 after six months was normal, which van Deventer calculated (given the reasonable expectation of production from seed rice) to be the equivalent of a rate of 50 per cent. Accumulation of debts led land owners to lose their land. Because Indians and Chinese were legally "foreign Orientals" under Dutch colonial law, they and European money lenders could not own land, and thus could only foreclose on mortgaged land by using indigenous Indonesians as middle-men. This was not a problem for money lenders who were Javanese *hajis* and consequently some among them were becoming major land owners. But the Arabs were,

---

[42] Ibid., pp. 138–42.
[43] Ibid., p. 99.

said van Deventer, "in general ... the most dreadful usurers".[44] To diminish peasant indebtedness to money lenders, agricultural credit banks were established from 1897, but they were short both of working capital and competent personnel. In a few places the agricultural credit banks worked well, but for the most part they brought few benefits to common villagers. In fact, most of the credit went to Javanese officials.[45] Van Deventer's picture of Javanese society in 1904 is a dreary one. But the experience of Javanese in the nineteenth century, however dreary it was for ordinary peasants, was not so for everyone.

The information assembled in this chapter illustrates that the experience of Javanese in the middle and later nineteenth century varied greatly. For many members of the upper *priyayi* elite, these were good times. Subsequent chapters will explore the new horizons, the cultural initiatives and the progress that were pioneered by leaders from this group. For lower officials, often there were opportunities for increasing land holdings and incomes and for sharing in the more cosmopolitan culture being developed in *priyayi* circles. For many Javanese there were opportunities in small-scale trade and industry. Out of this there emerged a nascent middle class, people with money to build better houses, to develop their trade and money-lending businesses, to educate their children better, to go on the *hajj* to Mecca and to embrace Islamic reform movements. They often had business and religious links with the Arab communities found especially in the coastal towns and cities of Java. Among the peasants at the bottom of the heap, however, it is doubtful if any significant number found the nineteenth-century colonial age to be of benefit. Population pressure on resources was increasing, the burdens of the colonial state were relentless, and there was little that might offer a way out of the confinements of village poverty.

From the point of view of the colonial experience alone, it therefore seems that Javanese society was polarising. The three main poles of this social division were (1) the *priyayi* elite, (2) a nascent bourgeoisie of Islamic bent and (3) a peasantry being ground down by colonialism and by their social superiors. This not to suggest that pre-colonial Javanese society had in any sense been egalitarian. It was always hierarchical in the way of aristocratic societies. But the divisions that emerged in the nineteenth century were rather new in style, for they were only partly

---

[44] Ibid., pp. 228–30.
[45] Ibid., pp. 232–8.

differences of class in a hierarchical society. They were also differences of cultural orientation and aspirations and of relationship to the dominant colonial power. To the Dutch colonial regime, the *priyayi*, the increasingly devout Islamic traders and the peasantry were not just different sorts of people, not just an upper, middle and lower class. They were also fundamentally different in how they related to the regime: the *priyayi* being essential to its administration and indeed very existence, the Islamic middle class essential economically but deeply suspect politically, and the peasantry needed to generate the wealth that drove the entire structure.

In subsequent chapters it will be seen that this apparent polarisation in relation to the colonial experience was paralleled in cultural and religious spheres. This was a society progressively being pulled, and pulling itself, into multiple categories. In the course of the nineteenth century these categories became visible, then progressively more distinct and in some cases antagonistic. Subsequent chapters of this book are dedicated to exploring this phenomenon. While colonialism may be thought of as a major initiator of social changes and population growth may be thought to have made them more pressing, it is to the realm of religion and culture that we turn to understand how these divisions became sharper and sometimes hostile.

3

The Diverging Worlds of Pious Islam

As noted in Chapter 1, Javanese Islamic traditions around 1830 brought together a sense of Islamic identity, fulfillment of the five pillars of Islamic ritual life and acceptance of an array of local spiritual forces — all within the Javanese understanding of Sufism — marking what I have called the "mystic synthesis" of Javanese Islam. In the course of the nineteenth century, contending versions of Islam would appear in Java to challenge the consensus represented by this mystic synthesis.

Readers should be warned that the evolution of Javanese Islam during the nineteenth century is a complex matter, with transitional stages and hybrid states that are unclear in the evidence and difficult to untangle. But with the help of other scholars who have worked on materials from that period, and with the riches of Javanese literature and Dutch archival sources before us, we may hope at least to understand more than the hapless Dutch missionary who said, in 1884, "The native Mohammedan world is like a sphinx. One observes it, sees its movements, and yet one does not penetrate it."[1] Ironically, as will be seen later in this book, among the most valuable evidence about religious changes in the nineteenth century is that of Dutch missionaries, but the cultural distance between them and Javanese society must always be kept in mind.

---

[1] B., "De godsdienstig beweging op Java", *Indische Gids* 1884, vol. 2: 742, citing C. Albers, who was working in the Sundanese-speaking area of Cianjur.

THE MYSTIC SYNTHESIS

The mystic synthesis style of Islam, while it came under challenge in nineteenth-century Java, did not disappear. Nor has it disappeared today. Rather than remaining the dominant consensus, however, it became one of several variants of the Islamic faith adhered to by Javanese. In some of the literature on this subject, one can find this variant of the faith labeled "Javanism", a term reportedly invented by the missionary S.E. Harthoorn (1831–83).[2] This seems misleading, however, for at a later stage there came into being a genuine distinction and conflict between Islam and a "Javanist" rejection of Islam. That is not what the mystic synthesis was. Its adherents certainly thought of themselves as Muslims; those who composed the Javanese works that reflect ideas of the mystic synthesis no doubt thought of themselves as particularly pious Muslims.

Javanese literature of the nineteenth century is full of examples of the mystic synthesis still being written about, debated and believed. Within this vast literature there are of course differences of emphasis and doctrine. One finds both of the theoretical types of mystical unity set out by Martin Buber:[3] both the dynamic mysticism of becoming, in which the godhead becomes one with the being of the mystic or the mystic becomes one with the godhead, thus a mysticism resting on the concept of unification; and on the other hand the static mysticism of being, in which the being of the mystic discovers the godhead within by realising the unreality of distinctions between self and godhead, thus a mysticism resting on the idea that there is no unification because in reality there is no prior duality. Similarly, Javanese mystic synthesis texts vary in their view of the *shari'a*, Islamic religious law. For some, the practices of a mystic should stay within the law: she or he should still recite the confession of faith, pray five times a day, fast in Ramadan, pay the alms and undertake the *hajj* to Mecca if able to do so.[4] Others assert that, at the higher levels of insight, a mystic is freed of the

---

[2] According to B.M. Schuurman, *Mystik und Glaube in Zusammenhang met der Mission auf Java* (Haag: Martinus Nijhoff, 1933), p. 4.

[3] M. Buber, *Ich und Du* (Leipzig, 1923), pp. 98–9, as cited in Schuurman, *Mystik und Glaube*, p. 11.

[4] This was not a new idea after 1830, of course. Yasadipura II's *Sĕrat Sana Sunu* of AD 1819 also takes this position, for example. See Yasadipura II, *Serat Sana Sunu* (transl. Jumeiri Siti Rumidjah; Yogyakarta: Kepel Press, 2001), text p. 119, transl. p. 9.

obligations of the law. But all of this occurs within the general boundaries of the mystic synthesis, defined by that sense of Islamic identity, commitment to the five pillars of Islamic ritual life — except where it is asserted that those who had achieved the highest levels of mystic experience were freed of the law — and recognition of local spiritual forces. Most of this literature is notable for its prolixity, multiple layers of meaning, paradoxical propositions, deliberate obscurity, technical Arabic terms, similes, metaphors and word-play. The mystical path was not meant to be easy for adepts. Its study is no more so for historians.

P.J. Zoetmulder studied a particularly valuable set of Javanese mystical poems (*suluk*) found in a two-volume work written in AJ 1763 (AD 1835–36).[5] The place where the MS was written is not clear, but its style suggests one of the Central Javanese court cities. Here are found dozens of *suluks* illustrating the range of doctrines within the world of mystic synthesis in the 1830s. Zoetmulder brought to the study of these works a philosophical rigor that has yet to be surpassed. A few examples of these texts will give readers a taste of the mystical doctrines contained in such works.

One of the *suluks* published by Zoetmulder says this of the mode of mystic worship:

> When you worship, seek to see Him who is worshipped. Let it be as it is with a mirror: one must see the reflection, then the true form becomes visible. What is visible in the mirror, that is the form,
>
> (or, better) it is the form, yet it is not. Be sure to note carefully correspondence and difference. Ask for a true explanation that you might find guidance.
>
> Turn your face towards the visible world. All that is indeed His face. The countenance of existing things, of all that is visible, conceals His face....
>
> Now I see clearly and because of the illumination which I receive, it seems to me as if my being is become the being of the Lord....

---

[5] The MSS referred to here are LOr 1795 and 1796. P.J. Zoetmulder, *Pantheisme en monisme in de Javaansche soeloek-litteratuur* (Nijmegen: J.J. Berkhout, 1935); in English as P.J. Zoetmulder, *Pantheism and monism in Javanese suluk literature: Islamic and Indian mysticism in an Indonesian setting*, ed. and transl. M.C. Ricklefs (KITLV translation series 24; Leiden: KITLV Press, 1995). Zoetmulder also uses other Javanese sources in this invaluable work. References here are to the English edition for the convenience of readers who are presumed to be more likely to read English than Dutch (or all of the 11 other languages Zoetmulder deploys in the original version).

We are one and not one, and certainly two and yet not two. It looks like (the connection between) soul and body. Thus my Being seems one with the Lord and yet two.[6]

Another text tells of the moment of mystical union in a way that at first seems contradictory, speaking of unity with the godhead and then denying its possibility. Zoetmulder observes that this reflects the concept of human Being as relative in relation to the absolute Being of the divine, "an image as against reality, an attribute as against essence. And although it cannot be said that attribute becomes essence and essence becomes attribute, yet they constitute a unity and cannot be separated." We see here also an example of the antinomian tendencies of mysticism, where ultimate insight may free the mystic of the obligations of the law:

For the chosen person who has already achieved the highest Truth, vision becomes completely clear at the same moment when he meets Him. For disappeared and melted away is the screen which this world forms. He is overwhelmed (by God); seeing in his heart only the true form of the Immaterial. Unceasingly he keeps Him before him; he thinks only of the Lord.

All his doings are dominated by the (only) Real. He hears not and speaks not and sees not, but the Most High is his ear, his tongue and his eye. He is really "nothing", without soul or body. He is entirely permeated by the Creator; he is destroyed and is no more to be seen, as stars struck by the rays of the sun disappear and become invisible because they are overwhelmed by the sun's light. For it is not possible that the servant becomes the Lord and the Lord becomes the servant. For the Holy, the being of the Immaterial, is eternal, without cause.

All his actions become worship of God; his is the "everlasting *salat*" [prayer], which is without time limits and for which no hours are set. This is not (ordinary) *salat* with ablutions.[7]

Javanese mystics often turned to the *wayang* shadow theatre for inspiration and metaphors, linking the abstruse doctrines of their mysticism to the Javanese cultural world, with its attendant spirit forces. When the *wayang* is performed, there are spiritual forces at play, and the *dhalang* (puppeteer) must be qualified to control them. In Javanese

---

[6] Zoetmulder, *Pantheism and monism*, pp. 93–4, with minor departures from Zoetmulder's translation.

[7] Ibid., pp. 145–7, with minor departures from Zoetmulder's translation.

suluks, the *dhalang* is often taken as a metaphor for God and the screen on which the *wayang* is performed as a metaphor for the phenomenal world, with its characters that move only by the will of the *dhalang*. It is therefore interesting in the following text to find *wayang* metaphors that present both that relationship and its reverse. In Javanese paradoxical fashion, this passage seems to make the Being of God contingent upon the existence of His creation, encloses its mysticism within the orthodox duality between creator and creation, presents an orthodox view of divine grace, and then denies the duality it asserted a moment before. It finally resolves its paradoxes in a fine example of elitist Javanese monism:

> There is a surpassing mystic union (which can be described) like the *wayang*, which calls up (*or* controls) the *dhalang* with all his movements. The movements of the *dhalang* are caused by the puppets; the speaking of the *dhalang* comes from the puppets; all that the *dhalang* does comes from the *wayang*. But all that the puppets do comes from the *dhalang*.
>
> There is another surpassing mystic union: like the *dhalang* who calls up (controls) the puppets with all their movements....
>
> *Dhalang* and puppets are like the shadow image and the Creator. There is an interaction between them. Neither of them is real if there is no interaction between the Creator and the shadow image. Thus is it also with Lord and servant: they do not manifest themselves without interaction, any more than Allah and Muhammad....
>
> But understand this well: it is immutably reserved to every servant to receive signs of grace as one who is distinct (from the Lord). This being distinct in receiving signs of grace means: the creation may not become one (with the Creator). To be both Lord and servant, slave and Master, is in truth not allowed. This receiving of grace means that one is subject to separation.
>
> But you must know also this: it immutably belongs to every servant to be from God, with God, through God and for God. This means that every servant is a shadow image which (in everything) is united with the Immaterial. Firmly orient yourself towards the Immaterial. Take care that you heed this well....
>
> But this is merely *wayang* from the sphere of relativity, a false *wayang* which can be called Non-Being. It is not true *wayang* but merely something which resembles it.
>
> If that is called *wayang*, then that which is Real is called *dhalang*. This is an idea which is spread among the common people. This is true, yet one can go a higher stage regarding the true meaning of

wayang and *dhalang*. The true meaning of puppet and *dhalang* is the meeting of servant and Lord. Pay attention to this....

It is the ultimate mystery.... In truth *dhalang* and *wayang*, Lord and servant, even your own Being are relative things which count for nothing; Muhammad, too, retreats to the background.... All is overwhelmed and concealed by the One. That is the ocean of blessedness....

That is the true being of the servant. To praise not nor venerate, and to recognise no one as Lord.... There is no twofold Being. Like pure Non-Being is this emptiness. Understand well the disappearance of the servant without becoming the Lord. That is the ultimate vision.[8]

Such works would have confused the neophyte, demanded the guidance of a teacher and led the advanced adept to that mystical realm where mere worldly logic had little role.

And when one reached the ultimate understanding, in some texts the very foundations on which the orthodox Islamic view of God rested would be called into question:

All the meaning of ... allusions is to be found in just a single word. For it is to be found in: you. Allah, that are you; the Prophet of God, that also are you; *bismi'llah* [the invocation "in the name of God"] are you, *fatiha* [the opening *sura* of the *Qur'an*] are you.[9]

Antinomianism lurks in mysticism at any time, a situation that Islam (and other faiths) sought to contain by insisting on the observance of religious law even by the most advanced mystic. In Zoetmulder's two-volume source of 1835–36 are found examples of doctrines that overthrow the law and embrace antinomianism:

He (who understands not) is confused in spirit because he lacks true insight; he is absorbed in words and practices, in the question of whether something is recommended or obligatory. Unceasingly he carries out *salat* [prayer], but all of this hinders his vision. Fasting and alms-giving, *jakat* and *pitrah* [paying of tax at the end of the fasting month] are regarded as idols. He who is absorbed in them shows that he lacks true insight; his concepts are still those of a novice.

In confusion he sits absorbed in the books and continually engages in discourse. His knowledge becomes ever broader. He speaks of

---

[8] Ibid., pp. 258–60, with some variations from Zoetmulder's translation.
[9] Ibid., p. 222.

practices which one must maintain, about what is permitted and what
is not permitted. This is all a sign that he still has no insight. He loses
himself in (fixed prayer-)times....

Endlessly he prattles abut the law and the prophets, of *walis* and
believers, but ever more does he depart from the rightful path. All of
this is wrong.... It would be better to get some sleep.

For those who have true insight, there is nothing that they pretend
to practice. Recommended or prescribed works, *iman* [faith], *tokid*
[oneness], and *makripat* [gnosis], exist no longer for them. That is all
just idle prattle (?), still polytheism, knowledge fumbling about in the
dark. Failed and come to naught, if one persists in such worship, one
is rewarded with nothing but a bump on the head (from the prostrations
in prayer).

Such is not the doing of a superior person.... Rather *his* knowledge
is heresy.... One is not yet a Muslim if one is not yet an infidel....

In the true exercise of unity, there is nothing to which one turns
one's sight, one thinks no more of oneself, nor of a single other thing,
not even heaven or hell. They who have a pure insight speak no more
of servant and Lord. In truth they are perfectly *one*.[10]

There were indeed Javanese who engaged in extreme antinomian
conduct in the nineteenth century in the name of religious ecstasy. These
were the so-called *santri birai* or *wong birai* (the religious students or
people of ecstasy), also called followers of *ngelmu dul* (the mystical
science of *dul*, evidently from the name of the founder, an Arab named
Abdul Malik, as will be seen below). They are described in the early
nineteenth-century monumental work *Sĕrat Cĕnthini*, where they are
said to have abandoned themselves to sexual indulgence:

> Men and women mixed together,
> whoever on top of anyone else,
> just so they were naked.
> There was no law,
> that was the way of the *wong dul-birai*.[11]

The Dutch missionary-scholar Carel Poensen (1836–1919), who
spent the years 1862–91 in Kĕdiri, was told by a Javanese Christian
informant of *santri birai* existing in the countryside.[12] A Dutch source

---

[10] Ibid., pp. 225–6, with departures from Zoetmulder's translation.
[11] Ricklefs, *Mystic synthesis*, pp. 203–4.
[12] LOr 5762, pp. 42–4. The MS also comments on Javanese belief in the Goddess
of the Southern Ocean, on the perseverance of Buddhist ideas, etc.

from 1855 describes the followers of *dul* as a deviant sect of men and women who gathered where they thought they would not be bothered by the local authorities, then they would sing and shout the confession of faith that there is no God but God (*La ilaha illa 'llah*) until entering a trance and achieving a vision of the Almighty. They were hated by Javanese heads and orthodox Islamic leaders, this source reported.[13] The Mennonite missionary Pieter Jansz also recorded information he received in 1855 about the *dul* sect, which gathered in Mantingan on the north coast, used a secret language among themselves and achieved a state of ecstasy by repeating certain phrases while moving their heads in a prescribed fashion[14] — a description of *dhikr*.

Poensen's informants provided him with a Javanese text — there is no indication when this was written — describing *santri dul* who engaged in extravagant forms of *dhikr* leading to mystic ecstasy and sexual excess at Mantingan.[15] This text is written in the form of a prose dialogue between the *santris'* leader, Kyai Běstari, and a sceptical aristocrat named Raden Atma, who later also talks with a bitter enemy of these people named Mas Danuwikrama. Because this is framed as a pair of contrived dialogues, it is hard to know how literally to take the content, but it may at least reflect the grounds on which some Javanese objected to this sect. Kyai Běstari is aggressive: he criticises the "*abangan* dogs" (*abangan* nominal Muslims are discussed in the following chapter) for loving this world, ridiculing Allah and lying when they claimed that those who engaged in *dhikr* were entered by the spirit of the Prophet, whereas it was instead a case of God appearing to another. He tells Atma that he, Atma, probably enjoyed dance parties (*tayuban*), dancing like a madman, and watched *wayang* but did not know the mosque. Atma responds that in Java each was allowed to exercise his religion in his own way, but now this was being opposed by religious leaders who were lacking in judgment. Atma then sings a verse in which people were warned not to believe in *santri brahi* for they were like eggs that are white on the outside but rotten on the inside. Ky. Běstari tells him not

---

[13] J.L.V. "Bijdrage tot de kennis der residentie Madioen", *TNI* 17, pt. 2 (1855): 14–5.

[14] Pieter Jansz, *"Tot heil van Java's arme bevolking": een keuze uit het dagboek (1851–1860) van Pieter Jansz, doopsgezind zendeling in Jepara, Midden–Java*, ed. A.G. Hoekema (Hilversum: Verloren, 1997), pp. 102–3.

[15] Dialogues on *santri Dul* by Ky. Běstari, R. Atma and M. Danuwikrama. 19 pp., 20.5 × 32.5 cm. Poensen collection, LOr 5787.

to make fun. So R. Atma and his companions depart from these "*santris of deviant character (budi)*".

In Poensen's text, the *santri dul* return to their ever-louder *dhikr* until reaching a state like drunkenness, to the amazement of watching *abangan*. The *guru* even cries out (as if he were a Hindu invoking the descent of a god), "O Lord, descend! Descend! And do a miracle, a miracle — a divine miracle!", a cry echoed by the ecstatic. Eventually the *guru* cries out that the ecstatic is possessed and all shout, "Thanks be to God!". Ky. Běstari then says that in five moments the Prophet will appear in their gathering. When R. Atma discusses all of this with Mas Danuwikrama, the latter denounces these people. Their *gurus*, he says, were in one case a former duck- and chicken-seller who had twice been jailed, and in the other a former carpenter; "They are both commoners." He says that they often set sibling against sibling, elders against children, husband against wife and servant against master. They offended the words of the *Qur'an* and the prohibitions of the *walis*. Women were led astray from their affections to their husbands and subject to sexual exploitation. In other words, they destroyed the social order and Javanese Islam as created by the *walis* — that is, they assaulted Java's mystic synthesis. There were many such, said Danuwikrama, at Mantingan near Jěpara, for there was found the grave of their Arab founder, Seh (*sheikh*) Dul (i.e. Abdul) Malik, after whom they were called "Dul". Danuwikrama then sings two verses composed by an earlier poet of Surakarta poking fun at the *santri dul*.

A similar account was provided by Harthoorn regarding groups called *pasek dul* (*dul* unbelievers) who were still found in some places, notably in the area of Majakěrta, in the late 1850s.[16] The famous poem *Wedhatama* — discussed below — also says that there were thousands of *santri dul* and *santri brai* along Java's south coast,[17] in this case evidently referring to the 1870s. In 1876 in Jěmběr (East Java) the leaders of a sect teaching a "new religion" in which devotees came together naked were arrested.[18] Presumably these were also *santri dul*.

There were certainly Javanese for whom mystical piety and the magical manipulation of supernatural forces were part of a single

---

[16] S.E. Harthoorn, "De zending op Java en meer bepaald die van Malang", *MNZG* 4 (1860): 240–1.
[17] Stuart Robson (ed. and transl.), *The Wedhatama: An English translation* (KITLV working papers 4; Leiden: KITLV Press, 1990), pp. 40–1.
[18] MR 1876 no. 452/14 June.

continuum called Islam. The general Indonesian and Malay claim to understand and to command such spirit forces lay behind their renown as "possessors of articles of magic and of preservatives [*jimat*] against evil spirits" in nineteenth-century Mecca.[19] Another volume of nineteenth-century *suluks* held in Leiden University illustrates this.[20] Here are 41 *suluks*, some of them the same as in Zoetmulder's collection, but others different. They all, however, fit within the mystic synthesis style of Javanese Islam. One of these works, *Suluk Raden Putra*, for example, denies the possibility of gaining ultimate insight through ritual piety or consulting conventional Islamic clerics. Only a teacher can guide one to the mist-shrouded ultimate:

> If you know not yet that which is true,
> from beginning to end,
> then your being is not yet perfected;
> you should ask for knowledge
> from a teacher who is learned.
> You must really have a teacher.
> Don't borrow insights,
> Don't go to just any teacher,
> to someone who brings innovations (*bidngah*, i.e. *bid'a*), who
> > transgresses, a polytheist and infidel,
> for this is yet more sinful.

> They worship the sounds of words,
> praised and taken for God,
> taken as something holy...
> They go still farther astray
> because they know not.
> The unity of servant
> and lord is not yet true,
> for their knowledge is very deficient....

---

[19] C. Snouck Hurgronje, *Mecca in the latter part of the 19th century: Daily life, customs and learning; The Moslems of the East-Indian-archipelago,* transl. J.H. Monahan (Leiden: E.J. Brill; London: Luzac & Co., 1931; reprinted Leiden: E.J. Brill, 1970), p. 96.
[20] LOr 7375, originally from Cirĕbon, presented to Snouck Hurgronje in 1896, consulted for this book via Simuh *et al.* (eds. and transl.), *Suluk: The mystical poetry of Javanese Muslims (41 suluks/LOr 7375)* (Yogyakarta: IAIN Sunan Kalijaga, 1987). Readers wishing to turn to this should be advised that, despite the English title, the contents are entirely in Javanese and Indonesian.

> Manifestly Raden Putra [taken here as the ultimate Being]
> is in a place hidden in the mist
> called *a'yan sabita*.[21]....
>
> If any teacher is asked,
> a *pangulu* [mosque head] and his subordinates,
> a *modin* [lesser mosque official],
> *lĕbes* [village religious officials] and *santris* [students of religion],
> none can answer
> because they know not truly....
>
> There are those that say they have the ability,
> ... or who are like ones intoxicated,
> who claim that they are Lord,
> or claim to be the servant;
> both are wrong....[22]

In a world so shrouded in mystery, it is not surprising that another text in this collection, called *Kidung Nabi* (song of the Prophet) is a series of spells for warding off sickness, black magic, fire, theft, poisons, agricultural pests and other dangers and evils, and for winning the love of others, the protection of angels, and so on.[23]

Yet while some texts were intent on overthrowing the *shari'a* and conventional modes of conduct, others argued against this:

> Even though your mystical science (*ngelmu*) is already perfected,
> if you should alter the *shari'a*
> you have been improperly taught,
> such a person has been carried away by the *ngelmu*,
> joining in disguise in the company
> of Satan entirely.
> You absolutely must not
> destroy the *shari'a* of the Prophet
> the Messenger of God, for that will mean sin everywhere.[24]

---

[21] *A'yan thabita*, the fixed essences in the scheme of seven-fold emanation. See Zoetmulder, *Pantheism and monism*, ch. 7.

[22] Simuh, *Suluk*, pp. 66–70.

[23] Ibid., pp. 316–21. The text calls itself at the start, *Kidung rumaksa ing wĕngi* (song for guarding in the night), of which there are multiple versions known in other MSS.

[24] SOAS 231925, dated AJ 1803 [AD 1874–75], f. 61.

Bust of Mangkunagara IV (r. 1853–81)
(from A.K. Pringgodigdo, *Geschiedenis
der ondernemingen van het
Mangkoenagorosche rijk*, 's-Gravenhage:
Martinus Nijhoff, 1950)

Prince Mangkunagara IV (b. 1811; r. 1853–81) was a major figure
in nineteenth-century Java, including being a major *litterateur*.[25] Among
the many writings ascribed to him,[26] probably the most famous — and
the one still most frequently cited by devotees of Javanese literature —
is *Wedhatama* (superior wisdom).[27] As its most recent editor Stuart
Robson comments, this work represents "an ideal of literary beauty, to
be sought in the use of noble language appropriate to its subject,

---

[25] See Soebardi, "Prince Mangku Nagara IV: A ruler and a poet of 19th century Java",
Journal of the Oriental Society of Australia (Dec. 1971): 28–58, for an overview.
In my view, however, Soebardi overemphasises the direct influence of al-Ghazali
in this discussion. On Mangkunagara IV's modernising of his domains, see
A.K. Pringgodigdo, *Geschiedenis der ondernemingen van het Mangkoenagorosche rijk*
('s-Gravenhage: Martinus Nijhoff, 1950), ch. 2.

[26] A four-volume collection of his works is in Mangkunagara IV, *Sĕrat-Sĕrat anggitan-
dalĕm Kangjĕng Gusti Pangeran Adipati Ariya Mangkunagara IV* (Jakarta: Kolĕp
[Kolff], 1953). There is also a 3-volume collection, also entitled *Sĕrat-Sĕrat anggitan-
dalĕm Kangjĕng Gusti Pangeran Adipati Ariya Mangkunagara IV*, edited by Th.G.Th.
Pigeaud and published in Soerakarta by the Java Instituut in 1928.

[27] Mangkunagara IV's authorship of *Wedhatama* has been disputed. As early as 1885,
contributors to *Bramartani* doubted that he had written the work (see *BM* 2 April
and 9 April 1885), which had been serialised in the paper earlier in the year (*BM*
8 Jan. and 17 Jan. 1885). Robson, *Wedhatama*, pp. 5–6, discusses the authorship
issue. Here I accept the convention that the work was by Mangkunagara IV.

expression echoing with elegant vocabulary and laden with alliteration and assonance. And ... heavy with the authority of teaching on sublime subjects such as philosophy and mysticism."[28]

Wedhatama is presented as Mangkunagara IV's advice and admonitions to his sons, "in the hope that they may prosper in their practice of the noble sciences (*ngelmu*) that are found in the land of Java".[29] Its approach to Islam is consistent with that of Mangkunagara IV's pious and combative ancestor, the founder of his principality, Mangkunagara I (r. 1757–95), whose exemplary piety in the mystic synthesis style is noted in Chapter 1 above. It is not known when the poem was composed, but Robson believes it to have been done in the late 1870s, which is a reasonable suggestion. By that time, as will be seen below, developments in Java were challenging the mystic synthesis that was dominant in Javanese aristocratic circles, and which *Wedhatama* espoused.

The poem assures its audience, the prince's sons and untold numbers of readers since,

> Whoever gains Gods' inspiration
> soon shines at the practice of the *ngelmu* of insight.
> He is skilled at grasping the ways of gathering up
> the scattered pieces of himself.
> In that case he may be called an "old" man —
> "old" in the sense of free from desires,
> with clear insight into the two-in-one....
>
> Truly such a man
> has been granted the grace of God.
> He has returned to the realm of the void....[30]

Wedhatama then admonishes the prince's sons to take as a model in life the founder of the Mataram dynasty, Panĕmbahan Senapati Ingalaga (r. c. 1584–1601). It tells of his legendary asceticism and his meeting with the Goddess of the Southern Ocean — whose reality is not questioned in *Wedhatama*.[31]

---

[28] Robson, *Wedhatama*, p. 3.

[29] Ibid., pp. 20–1.

[30] Ibid., pp. 24–5.

[31] Ibid., pp. 26–9.

However, at the present time
what the youth are obsessed with
is taking as their model and example the Prophet,
Guide of the World, the Messenger of God.
They constantly make this grounds for boasting
and whenever they attend court they call first at the mosque,
in the hope of a miracle and carrying off an official position.

Constantly they appeal to the *shari'a*
but the essence they do not grasp....

If you insist on imitating
the example of the Prophet,
O, my boys, you overreach yourself.
As a rule you will not hold out long:
seeing that you are Javanese,
just a little is enough.[32]

Thus, for Javanese — at least for Javanese princes — if they were attracted to the Prophet Muhammad as a model, "just a little is enough". Mangkunagara IV described himself in his youth, leading an ascetic life and "taking lessons from any *haji*". But the *Wedhatama* made it clear that such an approach could lead the youth of Java astray. It bemoaned "the present time":

Many are the young people who boast of their theological knowledge.
Though not yet qualified,
they are in a hurry to show off.
The way they interpret Arabic texts
is like a Sayid from Egypt.
Every time they belittle the abilities of others.

Such persons
can be reckoned as frauds:
where is their common sense?
Oddly enough they deny their Javaneseness
and at all costs bend their steps to Mecca in search of knowledge....

Now in days gone by
things were orderly and correct from one generation to the next.

---

[32] Ibid., pp. 28–31, with a few minor departures from Robson's translation.

Matters of *shari'a* were not mingled with spiritual practice.
So unconfused
were those who worshipped the All-Seeing.

As for the *shari'a*,
it can be called a discipline.
First, it calls for regularity and in the second place for diligence.
Its use, my sons,
is to keep refreshing the body in order to improve it.

For when the body is refreshed, ...
the peace of mind becomes focused
and banishes inner confusion.[33]

Another well-known poem by Mangkunagara IV is the brief seven-stanza *Tripama* (three exemplars).[34] These were his ethical teachings to soldiers, who in the case of the Mangkunagaran principality were not toy-soldier fantasies of a demilitarised monarchy, for the Dutch supported the Mangkunagaran Legion, set up in 1808 with 1,150 men to provide supplementary military backing for the colonial government. By Mangkunagara IV's time the Legion was a serious military force of infantry, cavalry and artillery which served the Dutch colonial regime in several combat theatres. *Tripama* is of interest here particularly because the three examples that it placed before Mangkunagara IV's soldiers were all taken from the pre-Islamic legacy of Java as preserved in Javanese literature and *wayang* stories. They were Patih Suwanda, the giant Kumbakarna and Raden Suryaputra — all of them examples of loyalty to their monarchs, even unto death. At the end of *Tripama*, Mangkunagara IV wrote,

These three are exemplars from Java:

it is fitting for all warriors
to emulate with all their capacities
the merits (of these three).
Do not go so far as to reject these examples
even if you should hit rock-bottom
and think yourself not up to it.

---

[33] Ibid., pp. 36–7, 40–1, with minor departures from Robson's translation.
[34] Mangkunagara IV, *Sĕrat-Sĕrat* vol. IV, pp. 3–6.

Although their faith was Buddhist[35]
their character was no different from that of other created beings
who strive for excellence.

Tripama was very much in the style of Java's mystic synthesis:
honouring the pre-Islamic heritage and turning there for models of
soldierly conduct rather than to Islamic tradition. Other works of
admonition by Mangkunagara IV are included in a study by Moh.
Ardani, who observes that these works "emphasise the importance of
maintaining both Javanese and Islamic characteristics.... There is a
distinction here between that which is Islamic and that which is Arab."[36]

Another major literary figure of nineteenth-century Surakarta was
Ronggawarsita (1802–73), who is conventionally regarded as the last
of Java's great poets, although in his own time not all thought that his
work equaled the standard of the great poets of the past.[37] Among
his works is the monumental *Sěrat Pustakaraja Purwa* (the book of kings
of ancient times), discussed in Chapter 6 below, which reflected the
nineteenth-century Javanese elite's fascination with the pre-Islamic past.
Mangkunagara IV, too, produced his own version of *Sěrat Pustakaraja
Purwa*.[38]

Ronggawarsita's prose *Sěrat Maklumat Jati* (the book of true teachings)
is another example of speculative writing in mystic synthesis style. Its
teachings include an exposition of the five "pillars of the true Islam":

> The pillars of Islam are said to be five: (1) the confession of faith
> (*sahadat*) ... (2) fasting (*siyam*) ... (3) paying the tax (*jakat*) ...
> (4) ritual prayer (*salat*) ... (5) the pilgrimage (*kaji*).
> [But:] (1) a silent mouth, (2) a closed nose, (3) unseeing eyes,
> (4) unhearing ears, (5) a dead body: indeed it is these which provide
> what is necessary as pillars of the true Islam, for this means that we

---

[35] The printed text (ibid., p. 6) actually has *buta* (blind) not *buda* ("Buddhist", but
having the more general sense of "pre-Islamic") but I presume that to be an error for
buda. The term *budi* is used in the next line (translated as "character"), suggesting
that a play on the words *buda* and *budi* is to be found here, as in other later
nineteenth-century works. This is explored more fully in Chapter 7 below.

[36] Moh. Ardani, *Al Qur'an dan sufisme Mangkunagara IV: Studi serat-serat piwulang*
(Yogyakarta: Penerbit Dana Bhakti Wakaf, 1995), pp. 38–9.

[37] See the debate about Ranggawarsita's writings conducted in the correspondence
columns of *Bramartani* from late 1866 to early 1867, brought to a close in the
edition of 9 Feb. 1867. This is discussed further in Chapter 6 below.

[38] *Sěrat Pustaka Raja*, written by (*yasan-dalěm*) Mangkunagěgara IV, covering the
years 1–800; undated; KITLV Or. 661.

can die within life. Whosoever can die within life, truly can live within death. Indeed if we are just to accept life as it comes, then we must be able to kill our passions; our body's task is just to pass them by.[39]

As will become clear shortly, this sort of mystic synthesis speculation was coming under challenge in the later years of the nineteenth century. It is therefore interesting to note the existence of a manuscript owned by the *bupati* of Purwarĕja (Kĕdu) in 1907. It asserts a statement of identity in its title *Agami Jawi*: Javanese religion. But it does not imply an opposition between Islam and this "Javanese religion". Rather, here "Javanese religion" is just what we have been calling the mystic synthesis. The entire context of the manuscript, its referents and its teachings, are rooted in an Islamic identity, but one that is committed to mysticism, secret doctrines and hidden truths. "This is a book to note down the Javanese religion", it says at the beginning, "to be taken as an indication for life, in order to achieve deliverance."[40]

This *Agami Jawi* manuscript helps to underline that we should not take the religious controversies of the nineteenth century to mean a general conflict between a sort of pristine Javaneseness on the one hand and a Muslim identity on the other. It was rather a conflict between different sorts of Islam, between different kinds of Muslims, among whom the adherents of the mystic synthesis saw themselves as authentically Javanese as well as authentically Muslim. As will be seen below, by the 1870s there were also Javanese who did indeed turn away from Islam. But that is not what the proponents of the mystic synthesis were doing.

This variant of Islam was not just confined to the *priyayi* elite of Java. At lower levels of society, where literacy was much more limited and life was harsher, there was probably little of the abstruse, paradoxical, obscuring speculations of the kind discussed so far. But there was certainly interest in local spirit forces, magical ploys and ascetic practices. At this level, occasionally Islamic leaders of the mystic synthesis variety mobilised protest movements against the local power structure and the Dutch colonial regime that stood behind it and thereby came to the notice of the government.

---

[39] SOAS 310763(D), ff. 17v.–18r. More extensive analysis of Ronggawarsita's mysticism can be found in Simuh, *Sufisme Jawa: Transformasi tasawuf Islam ke mistik Jawa* (Yogyakarta: Bentang, 1996). Further discussion of the concept of "dying within life" is found in Zoetmulder, *Pantheism and monism*, pp. 170, 172–4, where it is argued that this expresses the mystical concept of "achieving oneness in ecstasy".
[40] LOr 6548, *Agami Jawi*, p. 1.

Messianic protest movements tended to emerge particularly at the turning of the centuries, of which there were two in nineteenth-century Java. Locals cared little about the *Anno Domini* calculations of their Dutch masters. What mattered to them was the turning of the centuries in *Anno Javanico* and *Anno Hijrae*. AJ 1800 began in March 1871 and AH 1300 began in November 1882. Not surprisingly, the early 1870s and early 1880s proved to be times of rising protest in Java. One Akhmad Ngisa, for example, led a messianic movement in Banyumas in 1871, promising the arrival of the Ratu Adil, the "just king" of Javanese messianic traditions, who would expel the foreign rulers from Java.[41] Similar Ratu Adil ideas, mystical doctrines, magical powers and messianic hopes were deployed in teachings called Akmaliyah, spread by three men whose activities spanned the 1840s to the 1880s. These were Kyai Hasan Maulani, Mas Malangyuda and Kyai Nurhakim. They won significant peasant followings and were regarded as sufficiently dangerous that Ky. Hasan Maulani and M. Malangyuda were exiled by the colonial government. Only Ky. Nurhakim escaped this fate. Although by this time a reform movement was under way within Islam in Java, it was not reflected in the ideas of these three.[42] It will be seen below that the increasing number of Javanese *hajis* played a leading role in that reform movement. It is not surprising to discover that, according to a Dutch investigation, "among the 490 followers of Nurhakim whose names are known, there is only one *haji*". That gentleman was arrested for fraud and banished to Batavia.[43]

A peasant uprising in Těgal in 1864 was led by another figure of the pre-reform model of Javanese Islam named Mas Cilik. He was a healer, seller of amulets (*jimats*) and teacher of mystical doctrines (*ngelmu*). He gathered a significant following by promising that a golden age would come under his supernatural leadership, when people would be freed of taxes. A special ritual was conducted to ensure Cilik's invulnerability and to enable him to fly. After praying at a holy tomb, Cilik had a dream that led him to take the title Raden Haji, but he was no *haji*. Cilik's uprising claimed a few lives, including that of one Dutch

---

[41] Sartono Kartodirdjo, *Protest movements in rural Java: A study of agrarian unrest in the nineteenth and early twentieth centuries* (Singapore: Oxford University Press, 1973), p. 77.

[42] G.W.J. Drewes, *Drie Javaansche goeroe's: Hun leven, onderricht en messiasprediking* (Leiden: Drukkerij A. Vros, 1925).

[43] The Assistant Resident of Lědok, cited in ibid., p. 49.

sugar industry overseer, but the rebellion was put down within days.[44] In the wake of the more significant peasant uprising in Bantĕn, West Java, in 1888,[45] Dutch authorities in the Javanese-speaking heartland of Central and East Java cracked down on movements that they thought dangerous there. But whereas the Bantĕn revolt was led by *hajis* and Sufi *tarekat* figures, the leaders who were arrested in Central and East Java appear to have been devotees of the mystic synthesis school. They dealt in amulets and Ratu Adil hopes, but they were evidently not *hajis* and, at least in one case, reportedly did not observe Islamic ritual obligations.[46]

One Mas Rahmat left a diary from the 1880s that records the life of a wandering adept of mystic synthesis. He had links with Malangyuda and with a weak-minded Yogyakarta prince named Suryengalaga, whose mother plotted a quixotic and short-lived rebellion in 1883.[47] Rahmat was summoned to Yogyakarta to join Suryengalaga, but got there only after the arrest of the prince and his mother. So he set off wandering in search of insight. His first destination was the collection of ancient Hindu temples high on the mist-shrouded Dieng plateau. He then went to the *pasisir* (north coast) to visit holy graves of *walis* (early saints of Islam) and thence to Madura, where he stayed at an Islamic boarding school (*pĕsantren*) and meditated in caves.[48] This was the pious, searching Islam of the mystic synthesis, not the *shari'a*-oriented Islam that we will consider below.

By the time Mas Rahmat was wandering from Hindu temples to religious schools to meditation caves, another interpretation was spreading

---

[44] Tine Ruiter, "The Tegal revolt in 1864", in Dick Kooiman *et al.* (eds.), *Conversion, competition and conflict: Essays on the role of religion in Asia* (Amsterdam: Free University Press, 1984), pp. 81–98.

[45] Sartono Kartodirdjo, *The peasants' revolt of Banten in 1888: Its conditions, course and sequel; a case study of social movements in Indonesia* (*VKI* vol. 50; 's-Gravenhage: Martinus Nijhoff, 1966).

[46] Based on the brief description in Kartodirdjo, *Peasants' revolt*, pp. 269–73. See also *BM* 19 Oct. 1888 on a rebel in Mangkunagaran lands who called himself Imam Sampurna. His followers engaged in *dhikr*, so Imam Sampurna may have been from a Sufi background. When attacked by colonial and Mangkunagaran forces, he cried out *Sabilullah* (war in the path of God). Imam Sampurna died in the attack along with several of his followers.

[47] A.L. Kumar, "The "Suryengalagan affair" of 1883 and its successors: Born leaders in changed times", *BKI* 138, nos. 2–3 (1982): 251–84.

[48] Ann Kumar, *The diary of a Javanese Muslim: Religion, politics and the pesantren 1883–1886* (Canberra: Faculty of Asian Studies Monographs, new series no. 7, 1985).

of what it meant to be a Muslim. It is to these newer ideas that we now turn.

Reform and Revival Movements Among the *Putihan*

In the 1840s there existed significant numbers of professionally religious in Javanese society — mosque officials, religious teachers, guardians of holy sites, students at *pěsantrens* — who were known collectively as *kaum* (the religious folk) or *putihan* (the white ones). On the north coast, evidently this group was sometimes also called *santri* (students of religion), foreshadowing a usage that would become common in the mid-twentieth century. The Dutch called them *geestelijken:* clericals, religious. There is no evidence, however, that they yet formed a force for puritanism, fundamentalism or revivalism.[49] In mid-century, large numbers of religious lived around Madiun, for example. There were reported to be 42 *pěsantrens* in the area that attracted students from across Java. Some of these schools had 2–300 *santris* and the total number of students at the area's schools could be up to 1800. Other religious looked after holy graves. Such schools and holy grave sites had *pěrdikan* status, that is, they had been freed of tax obligations by rulers in pre-colonial times and the Dutch colonial government continued to maintain that privileged status.[50]

Education is usually an essential element of Islamic reform movements. In general, provision of education was still very limited and of a low standard in the first half of the nineteenth century in Java. In the 1850s the Madiun-area *pěsantrens* mentioned above taught the *Qur'an* and Arabic prayers by rote but not the Arabic language itself. And this although some of those schools were among the most famous *pěsantrens* in Java — notably Banjarsari and Těgalsari near Panaraga.[51] The colonial government ordered a survey of education in 1819, but not all residencies

---

[49] L.W.C. van den Berg, "De Mohammedaansche geestelijkheid en de geestelijke goederen op Java en Madoera", *TBG* 27 (1882): 8–9. See also P. Bleeker, "Hoofdstuk II: Pasoeroean", *TNI*, pt. 2 (1849): 26–7; Anon, "Algemeen overzigt van den toestand van N.I., gedurende het jaar 1846", *TNI* (n.s.) 10, no. 1 (1848): 371; Martin van Bruinessen, "*Pesantren* and *kitab kuning*: Continuity and change in a tradition of religious learning", *Ethnologica Bernensia* 4/1994: *Texts from the islands* (Bern: Institut für Ethnologie, 1994), pp. 132–3.

[50] J.L.V., "Bijdrage" pp. 10–1, 15.

[51] Ibid., pp. 12–6. Těgalsari had strong connections with the court of Surakarta. Těgalsari tradition has it that Pakubuwana II (r. 1726–49) gave Těgalsari special

Students at a Javanese *Qur'an* school in the front gallery of a small prayer-house, c. 1910 (Collection of KITLV, Leiden)

responded. Enough results are known, however, to suggest that the general picture was poor. For example, in Grěsik no one taught literacy in Javanese, but young people were taught to read and to pray in Arabic by village *kaum*. It was estimated that only 1 per cent of the population had any degree of literacy in Javanese. This included some of the *Bupatis* and other Javanese heads who were literate in their native tongue, of whom some could also write Malay in romanisation. In Těgal, only 3–4 of 850 village heads could write their own names but religious leaders taught Javanese literacy and spoken Malay to the elite. In Surabaya, education for most people was restricted to learning the *Qur'an* by rote, but elite children were taught to read and write Javanese along with arithmetic by their elders, relatives and friends. In Pěkalongan there were eight major *pěsantrens* where pupils were taught to read the *Qur'an* and *kitabs*. For more advanced study of Islam, students went to the *pěsantrens* of Madiun and Panaraga. In the Sundanese-speaking area of Bogor, it

status as the cradle of Islam in his kingdom, but other records raise doubts about the antiquity of this tradition; see M.C. Ricklefs, *The seen and unseen worlds in Java, 1726–49: History, literature and Islam in the court of Pakubuwana II* (Honolulu: Asian Studies Association of Australia in association with Allen & Unwin and University of Hawai'i Press, 1998), pp. 277–87.

was estimated that only one in a thousand was literate. Most indigenous heads there were illiterate.[52]

Another survey of education was ordered by the colonial government in 1831.[53] Responses came in from fourteen residencies and, although they are probably not to be relied upon in detail, they indicated that there had been little or no improvement since 1819. Among Javanese-speaking residencies, in almost all cases Islamic education was simply a matter of elementary instruction in rote recitation of the *Qur'an*, sometimes supplemented with study of other Arabic religious works. In Tĕgal about 1,000 *santri* learned to read the *Qur'an* and to recite prayers; few of the *kyais* there knew Javanese script. The *Bupati* of Tĕgal said that it was difficult to get any other education for his children. In Pĕkalongan there were now nine *pĕsantrens* offering religious education and in Jĕpara ninety, but *santri* numbers were not reported in either case. The *pĕsantrens* of the former were probably significant in size, those of the latter presumably small. In Kĕdu, in the interior, there were only five *pĕsantrens*. There, elite children who persisted longer with their studies could learn to read and write in Javanese as well as Arabic script, but most such learning was done outside the *pĕsantrens*. In Bagĕlen, village *kaum* offered very limited religious education. In Banyumas there were few religious schools but some children of *Bupatis* were taught reading and writing in the western alphabet at the regency office. In the Eastern Salient, Bĕsuki had 5–600 religious schools but *santri* numbers were not reported. Some youths in the *Bupati*'s entourage were taught to write, but there even some *priyayi* were illiterate.

Cirĕbon, Sĕmarang and Surabaya had the largest number of religious educational institutions and *santri* reported in 1831. Cirĕbon was said to have 190 *pĕsantrens* with between 2 and 100 *santri* each, for a total of nearly 2,800 pupils. Those who wanted to learn Malay or Sundanese, however, had to study with friends or relatives. In Sĕmarang residency there were 180 *pĕsantrens* with a total of almost 3,000 *santris*. Adults as well as children attended these *pĕsantrens*, but only few *santri* progressed far enough to understand what they were reciting. A few gurus taught reading of the *Qur'an* in Javanese — the only place where this was

---

[52] Anon., "Het onderwijs op Java, en de invloed daarvan op den toestand der bevolking", *TNI* (1849): 329–35; J.A. van der Chijs, "Geschiedenis van het inlandsch onderwijs in Nederlandsch-Indië, aan officiëele bronnen ontleend", *TBG* 14, nos. 3–4 (1864): 214–9.

[53] Van der Chijs, "Geschiedenis", pp. 227–31.

reported. In Surabaya teaching took place in prayer houses (*langgar*), of which there were reportedly 410 with nearly 4,400 pupils, including 355 girls, while in Grěsik were 238 *langgars* with over 2,600 pupils. *Priyayi* who wished their children to learn reading, writing and arithmetic still used private teachers.

Two things are noteworthy about the educational information reported in 1831. Firstly, although we see that *pěsantrens* were a feature of life in some areas — particularly on the *pasisir* — they were not yet a common phenomenon across Java and the proportion of Java's population educated in them was very small. Secondly, there was evidence of a gap between Islamic education (mainly a matter of rote recitation of the *Qur'an*) and knowledge of Javanese language and culture. According to van der Chijs's analysis of the 1831 reports, this was because devout Muslims believed that "man is not capable of understanding any other education until he is completely familiar with the teachings of his faith. Also, anyone who has completed his studies in Mohammedan teachings and thereupon has gone on the pilgrimage to Mecca is regarded as a scholar, for whom all other knowledge has become unnecessary."[54] Such a gap does not seem to have been a feature of Javanese life in the period before c. 1830. In the coming decades, *pěsantrens* would become a much more common feature of the Javanese countryside, while the gap between Islamic and Javanese knowledges would widen.

In this rather poorly educated society, the early Dutch Christian missionaries in the interior of Java found that there were still many traces of pre-Islamic ideas in local practice and little of what they regarded as fanaticism. These were, of course, conditions they hoped to find in a mission field. In 1855, from the area of Majawarna (near Jombang in the interior of East Java), D.J. ten Zeldam Ganswijk sent one of the most valuable early missionary evaluations. He wrote of a low level of observance of daily prayers or other pillars of Islam by local Javanese. There was, he said, much gambling, drinking of arak, and opium usage in violation of Islamic norms. In the mountains there were still hermits (*tapa*) with anti-Islamic sentiments. "Indifferent ignorance goes so far that not only all sorts of laymen, but even indigenous heads and priests[55] without reflection often agree with things that are said that

---

[54] Ibid., p. 231.
[55] He uses the term *priesters*, commonly used by the Dutch for Islamic religious leaders, even though there are no priests in Islam. The term is kept here as a reminder to readers of the limits of Dutch understanding of Islam at the time.

are in conflict with Islam." Almost no one knew the Arabic language or the contents of the *Qur'an*. Religious schools just taught external formalities. Thus the negative side of Ganswijk's evaluation.

Yet there was much more to the picture, for Ganswijk observed that Islam was not just superficial. He was more impressed with the influence that Islam had than with the remnants of pre-Islamic beliefs. After all, he reminded his readers, the influence of heathen ideas in Christian Europe was still significant. He was, in fact, observing the presence of the mystic synthesis style of Islam:

> Against ignorance there is, especially among the more prominent people, if not knowledge then an unorthodox interest in Islam. Many of its foremost prescriptions are, in general, faithfully observed. The religious foundation of the Javanese is, although also tallying with his character, always genuinely Mohammedan.[56]

Ganswijk wrote that Javanese observed the fast during Ramadan (albeit accompanied by binging in the nighttime); abhorred pork (so much so that even some of the first Javanese Christians could not bring themselves to eat it); practised circumcision, polygamy and divorce; and honoured the pilgrimage to Mecca (although many who claimed to have completed the *hajj* had in fact not done so).[57] Other missionaries like Hoezoo took the view that the Javanese weren't really Muslims and prayed that God would prevent them becoming so,[58] but Ganswijk was already warning them that things were more complicated.

W. Hoezoo took a trip through the interior of Java in 1850, staying mostly with European officials but speaking in Javanese to local people and, in most places, visiting the mosque and speaking to mosque officials. He reported that he encountered little sign of fanaticism and, in general, an attachment to Islam expressed mainly in outward formalities — or, as Hoezoo dubbed them, "meaningless externals". In this, he reflected the common European inability to grasp that correctly observing the requirements of the *shari'a* and Islam's ritual formalities was a significant a part of Islamic identity. In Panaraga he visited the famous local *pĕsantrens*, where he was pleased to see that little "fanaticism" was taught.

---

[56] Another inappropriate term, but preserved here to remind readers of the limits of Dutch understanding of Islam and to preserve the flavour of the original document.
[57] D.J. ten Zeldam Ganswijk, who had arrived in Majawarna only a few months before, 1 Sept. 1855 in ARZ 209 (also as "Iets over de Javanen, in betrekking tot de evangelieprediking in oostelijk Java", *MNZG* 1 [1857]: 105–8).
[58] W. Hoezoo, Beantwoording der vragen, Sĕmarang, 6 Nov. 1855 in ARZ 210.

On Java's *pasisir*, however, Hoezoo saw the first signs of what was to become a significant phenomenon: the emergence of a devout, self-consciously pious group of Javanese. In his first two years in Sĕmarang, he wrote, he saw "only a *few* zealots for Islam", who attended the mosque regularly or prayed five times a day in groups in their houses. But there were also Javanese Muslims in the mystic synthesis style, who felt themselves to be elevated above the *shari'a*, the fulfilling of which they could leave to lesser persons. Among these, some were ready to criticise Islamic leaders ("priests") and to undermine popular trust in them. "Such a liberalism, however," warned Hoezoo, "is as disadvantageous for Christianity as it is for Islam."[59]

The *pasisir* was a place where attitudes were becoming different from those deeper in Java's interior, one major element in this difference being the presence there of Arab and other international Muslim communities. Arabs had particular social standing both because they were commonly members of the commercial elite and were from the heartlands of Islam and, in the case of *sayyids*, because they claimed direct descent from the Prophet. Their family and business connections with the Middle East exposed them to events there more directly than was true of most Javanese. The Wahhabi conquest of Mecca in 1803 was one of many dramatic Middle Eastern events in the first half of the nineteenth century, for it threatened the integrity of the Ottoman Empire and unleashed an iconoclastic puritan movement within the holiest city of Islam. The Wahhabis were expelled from Mecca in 1818 by Ottoman forces. But by this time they may already have contributed to inspiring the violently reformist Padri movement in West Sumatra — the first such movement of the modern era in Indonesia — which itself precipitated Dutch intervention and the subsequent Padri War (1821–38).[60] The impact of Middle Eastern political and intellectual

---

[59] W. Hoezoo, Sĕmarang, to Bestuurders NZG, Rotterdam, 23 Jan. 1852, in ARZ 210.

[60] The extent to which the Wahhabis directly inspired the Padris is disputed. Christine Dobbin sees direct inspiration at work but Werner Kraus is inclined to see the Padris more as part of a wider reformist atmosphere within the Islamic world at that time. See Christine Dobbin, *Islamic revivalism in a changing peasant economy: Central Sumatra, 1784–1847* (London & Malmö: Curzon Press, 1983), p. 128; Werner Kraus, *Zwischen Reform und Rebellion: Über die Entwicklung des Islams in Minangkabau (Westsumatra) zwischen den beiden Reformbewegungen der Padri (1837) und der Modernisten (1908): Ein Beitrag zur Geschichte der Islamisierung Indonesiens* (Wiesbaden: Franz Steiner Verlag, 1984), pp. 15–6.

ferment in the nineteenth century[61] was thus already felt in West Sumatra before the time that this study of the Javanese commences. From about the 1850s, ongoing developments in the Middle East began to have significant impacts in Java as well, and the Arabs seem to have been a major conduit for those impacts amongst Javanese society. In the early 1880s, the Dutch scholar L.W.C. van den Berg wrote that there were particularly large numbers of Arabs in the *pasisir* towns, notably in Cirĕbon, Pĕkalongan, Sĕmarang and Grĕsik, where even Javanese notables were exposed to their "Mohammedan or rather Arabic" influence.[62]

The missionary J.E. Jellesma found Surabaya in the 1850s to be less congenial than some of his colleagues found the interior, in part because of the Arab presence, it seems. "The Mohammedans here are hostile, and still more uninterested, about Christianity," he wrote. "Those who live nearest to me are under the authority of the Pangeran (prince), the landowner, a half Arab."[63] But it was not only Arabs that Jellesma thought hostile. In 1853 he warned the governors of the Netherlands Missionary Society that there were also Javanese who were hostile to Christianity. He spoke of "the fanaticism of the Mohammedan priests" and "the opposition of the heads".[64] A decade later, his colleague H. Smeding similarly regarded the head of Blitar to be a "so-to-say full-blooded Mohammedan, many say indeed a fanatic, a man strict in formalities who in the eyes of the world holds firmly to the prescriptions of Islam". He was, claimed Smeding, a false, low character feared by his subjects and loved by none.[65] Yet it nevertheless seems clear that it was the *pasisir* with its Arab communities that played a leading role in early Islamic reform movements and in opposing the first fitful European efforts at Christian missionising among Javanese.

---

[61] See Albert Hourani, *Arabic thought in the liberal age, 1798–1939* (London: Oxford University Press, 1970).

[62] Van den Berg, "Geestelijkheid", pp. 35–7.

[63] J.E. Jellesma, Dagverhaal Aug. 1849–15 Jan. 1850, dd. Surabaya, 1 Feb. 1850, in ARZ 509.

[64] J.E. Jellesma, Majawarna, to Bestuurders NZG, Rotterdam, 15 Aug. 1853, in ARZ 509.

[65] H. Smeding, Rotterdam, to Bestuurders NZG, Rotterdam, 21 Mar. 1862, in ARZ 206. Note that Smeding had by this time returned to the Netherlands for health reasons; S. Coolsma, *De zendingseeuw voor Nederlandsch Oost-Indië* (Utrecht: C.H.E. Breijer, 1901), p. 266.

One report from 1848 suggests that the number of Arabs and other foreign Muslims in the coastal areas was small in terms of the total population, but large enough to have a significant impact. In that year, Tĕgal reportedly had a total population of 317,446, of whom 98 per cent were Javanese. There were 3025 Chinese and 2,275 Arabs, Bengalis, Malays and other Asian Muslims (Moors). Of Europeans there were only 286.[66] In considering missionary strategies, in 1846 Jellesma wrote that it was better to begin in the interior than on the coast, "where most of the Mohammedan priests and Arabs are found". Yet even in the interior, he said — employing a military metaphor that occurs more than once in missionary sources — the stronghold of Javanese Islam was firm, "for the number of priests is nevertheless great and *hajis* and Arabs continuously arrive".[67] G. Brückner — one of the first, most experienced and most frustrated of missionaries in Java, who had arrived in 1814 — said that in Sĕmarang in 1850 there was strong devotion to Islam among the populace, particularly amongst the more eminent citizens, "because of the great number of priests and Arabs who live or travel from here and who have a remarkable influence on the people".[68] Hoezoo, too, saw Sĕmarang as a hostile place for missionising. This was partly because irreligious Europeans there gave a bad impression of what sorts of people Christians were, he thought. But it was more because of the influence of the many Arabs,

> who avidly profit from the indifference of the [European] Christians to instill in the Javanese an aversion to the "already obsolete" religion of the Prophet Jesus, who openly call us *kafirs* (unbelievers) and teach the pious Muslims to pray for the destruction of our faith, who in all sorts of ways pave the way to superstition and promote a fanaticism that can only nourish hatred for anyone who is not a follower of the honoured Prophet.... Not to mention the known scoundrels and fanatics who are banished to here from the interior and entrusted to the watchful oversight of the police.[69]

---

[66] Anon, "Algemeen overzigt 1846", p. 99.

[67] J.E. Jellesma, Surabaya, to Bestuurders NZG, Rotterdam, 31 Dec. 1846, in ARZ 509.

[68] G. Brückner, Sĕmarang, to Bestuurders NZG, Rotterdam, 12 Jan. 1850, in ARZ 511.

[69] W. Hoezoo, Sĕmarang, to Bestuurders NZG, Rotterdam, 20 Feb. 1854, in ARZ 210.

Kudus on the *pasisir* was a place of piety, too. It is the only city in Java to have acquired permanently the name of a Middle Eastern Islamic holy site, for it is named after al-Quds (Jerusalem). There many Javanese revealed "a certain zeal for Islam".[70] The people of Kudus were known as great traders as well as pious Muslims, for there were many *kaum, hajis* and *santris*. But not all were pious, for there were also 80 dancing-girls (i.e. prostitutes) there for whom the colonial government provided a clinic and a Javanese medical officer.[71]

Technological changes were enhancing communication between the Middle East and Java in the mid-nineteenth century and were supportive of religious reform efforts. The spread of printing was important. A Javanese translation of the *Qur'an* was printed for the first time in Batavia in 1858.[72] Later in the century, the Hadhrami Arab Sayid Uthman bin Aqil bin Yahya al-Alawi (1822–1913)[73] became a major voice for reformist Islam. He remained based in Batavia and his many publications — over 100 titles in all — were all originally published in Arabic or Malay. But some were also published in Javanese translations[74] and undoubtedly his works were influential also among Arabs living among the Javanese.

The advent of steam shipping made the pilgrimage from Java to Mecca easier, a matter of serious concern to the Dutch. The colonial regime in Java was suspicious of the influence of religious, whether Christian or Muslim, and disliked the interference of Christian missionaries almost as much as it feared the influence of Arabs and *hajis*. But there were far more Arabs and *hajis* than there were Dutch Protestant missionaries, so more vigorous efforts were needed with regard to the former. The latter, in any case, always had a potential to call on allies

---

[70] W. Hoezoo, Sĕmarang, to Bestuurders NZG, Rotterdam, 5 Dec. 1855, in ARZ 210.
[71] Purwalĕlana [pseud. for Condranagara V], *Cariyos bab lampah-lampahipun Raden Mas Arya Purwalĕlana* (2 vols.; Batavia: Landsdrukkerij, 1865–66), vol. I, pp. 200–2. See also Marcel Bonneff (transl.), *Pérégrinations javanaises: Les voyages de R.M.A. Purwa Lelana: Une vision de Java au XIXe siècle (c. 1860–1875)* (Paris: Editions de la maison des sciences de l'homme, 1986), pp. 191–2.
[72] Poerwasoewignja and Wirawangsa, *Pratélan*, vol. I, p. 181.
[73] Azyumardi Azra, "Hadrâmî scholars in the Malay-Indonesian diaspora: A preliminary study of Sayyid 'Uthmân", *SI* 2, no. 2 (1995): 1–33; Karel A. Steenbrink, *Beberapa aspek tentang Islam di Indonesia abad ke-19* (Jakarta: Bulan Bintang, 1984), pp. 134–7.
[74] Poerwa Soewignja and Wirawangsa, *Pratélan*, vol. II, p. 121.

in the Netherlands, which the Arabs and *hajis* could hardly do. So while Dutch records reflect irritation with Christian missionaries, they more clearly reflect a *haji*-phobia throughout most of the nineteenth century.

In 1825, Batavia established regulations and procedures for the *hajj* which required that fl. 110 be paid for a special passport to travel to Mecca — that being a large sum at the time — and *Bupatis* were asked to discourage Javanese from undertaking the *hajj* as much as possible. But this attempt to restrict the pilgrimage was of limited success. Pilgrims bypassed the regulation by travelling via Sumatra or Singapore. So in 1852 these rules were abandoned. A *haji* still needed a passport, but the financial burdens were thrown out. Then in 1859 new regulations were introduced. Now it was necessary for *bupatis* to certify that aspirant *hajis* had sufficient means to undertake the pilgrimage and to support families left behind. The pilgrims had to report to the Dutch consul in Jeddah when they arrived in the Middle East. On their return, they must be examined by Javanese officials to verify that they had really gone to Mecca — as opposed to spending time in a place such as Singapore and claiming on their return to have completed the *hajj* — before they could adopt the title and dress of a *haji*. This policy remained in place until the beginning of the twentieth century.[75]

It was not only the reduction of the cost of the *hajj* that encouraged greater numbers of Javanese to go, but also the advent of steam shipping.[76] In 1869 an entrepreneur, an Arab to judge from his name, given as Sayid Muhammad Aidit, announced that he had bought a steam ship specifically for the transport of *hajis* from Batavia to Mecca. Previously, he said, pilgrims who had gone by sail had to endure cramped conditions and many became ill. But now they would travel in comfort in Muhammad Aidit's steamship for only Rp. 150.[77] Over the years this improvement in technology — greatly enhanced by the opening of the Suez Canal in 1869 — contributed to a major increase in *hajj* traffic from Java.

The numbers of *hajis* travelling from Java (or from Java and Madura, which were amalgamated administratively and thus appear together in many Dutch records) vary slightly in different sources. Sometimes they

[75] S. Keijzer, *Onze tijd in Indië, beschreven in bundles* ('s-Gravenhage: H.C. Susan, C. Hzoon, 1860), pp. 9, 56–7; Jacob Vredenbregt, "The haddj: Some of its features and functions in Indonesia", *BKI* 118, no. 1 (1964): 98–100.
[76] G.M. van der Linden, "Wat zijn hadjie's en welke is hun invloed op het volksleven der Javanen", *Indisch Genootschap: Algemeene vergadering op 21 Maart 1859*, pp. 1–3.
[77] *BM* 19 Aug. 1869.

include ethnic Sundanese from West Java as well as the Madurese. So for much of the nineteenth century it is not always possible to isolate ethnic Javanese from Central and East Java within these statistics. Fortunately we can do so for the period 1850–58 with regard to both departures and returns. The two figures often differ significantly because some Javanese stayed in Mecca or elsewhere in the Middle East for a time — a few of them for many years — before returning home, while not a few died before completing their journey, particularly from cholera and smallpox. Ignoring all of these complexities and accepting that the statistics did not capture all of the *hajis* from Java, for there were still those travelling via Sumatra and Singapore, it is nevertheless obvious that a major increase in *hajis* from Java occurred during the 1850s.

TABLE 1: *Hajj* **departures and returns from Javanese-speaking residencies, 1850–58**[78]

Year	Departures	Returns
1850	48	190
1851	23	83
1852[79]	238	403
1853	610	235
1854	995	235
1855	1,137	546
1856	1,739	546
1857	1,715	976
1858	2,283	848

This increase continued. Figures for all of the Netherlands Indies (of which, at this time, Java and Madura represented the core) reported the departure of 2,212 aspirant *hajis* in 1866 and 3,258 in 1870.[80] By 1867, shortly before the opening of the Suez Canal, the total number

[78] Calculated from F.G.P. Jaquet, "Mutiny en hadji-ordonnantie: Ervaringen met 19e eeuwse bronnen", *BKI* 136, nos. 2–3: 310–1. Jaquet also comments on the limited reliability of such figures. Cf. Keijzer, *Onze tijd*, pp. 186, 188–91, giving similar results covering all of Java and Madura, 1849–58.
[79] When payments for the passport ceased.
[80] Johan Eisenberger, *Indië en de bedevaart naar Mekka* (Leiden: Boekhandel M. Dubbeldeman, 1928), p. 204.

of *hajis* recorded as living in Java had grown to 73,658 and by 1868 to 96,670.[81] Thereafter, with much of the Indonesia-Europe steam navigation going via the Suez Canal, and thus past Mecca's doorstep, numbers grew still further. The 1872–73 *hajj* season saw peak figures. This was a year of a so-called *hajj akbar*, when the day of Arafat fell on a Friday. Popular belief had it that a *hajj* performed in such a year carried seven times the merit of another.[82] The Dutch consul in Jeddah reported that some 150,000 pilgrims came to Mecca in that season, about one-third from outside Arabia. From Java came 3,554. That may be compared with the total from all of British India of 5,620, or from nearby Egypt and Turkey of 11,170. The Javanese — who had a greater distance to come than almost any *hajis* — were, in other words, a significant element in the overseas pilgrims in Mecca. In general, pilgrims from the Dutch territories in Indonesia were also regarded there as being among the more prosperous.[83]

In the previous chapter, we already noted the comment of C. Th. van Deventer at the end of the century that,

> by undertaking the pilgrimage to Mecca, [*hajis*] have already shown that they have more energy and also rather more capital than their fellow village-dwellers and, upon their return, moreover regard themselves as a good deal more elevated in esteem than ordinary natives.... Their status as *hajis* elevates their social significance.[84]

The procedure by which the *Bupati*s and other officials examined anyone claiming to be a returned *haji* was meant to prevent the fraudulent use of that title and its attendant advantages. People were asked about their experience in Mecca and must have the stamps of the Netherlands consulate in Jeddah in their passport. Only after successfully passing the examination process were they given authorisation to call themselves a *haji* and to wear the associated Arab-style clothing. This was part of a general responsibility laid upon *Bupatis* to oversee the professional religious and their establishments in their areas. The implementation of

---

[81] [C.E. van Keesteren] v.K., "De Koran en de driekleur", *Stemmen uit Indië*, no. 1 (1870): 34.

[82] This idea was common at the time, and is specifically reported in *BM* 19 Aug. 1880, another *hajj akbar* year, but is often rejected now. E.g. see <http://www.islamicity.com/dialogue/Q431.HTM>

[83] Anon., "De Indische bedevaartgangers", *TNI* (n.s.) 3 (1874): 60–1.

[84] Van Deventer, *Overzicht*, p. 99.

this policy was not, however, always satisfactory. Records were not always kept accurately, so readers must accept that figures given for religious in this book are not to be regarded as entirely reliable.[85]

Some Europeans did not share the prevalent *haji*-phobia, believing that the social influence of *hajis* would diminish as their numbers grew. Others thought this folly:

> When their number in relation to the population is big enough, then [their influence] will plunge to nil, so people hope. Fortunately they've not experimented with this, for the number of *hajis* could have rapidly become so great that the dangers associated with that would have come into being before the desired number was reached.[86]

Yet this view was not necessarily entirely false. While the growth in the number of *hajis* was an important part of the story of Islamic revivalism, it will be seen in the following chapter that reformist Islam also distanced itself progressively from much of Javanese society. The Javanese newspaper *Bramartani* reflected something of that declining social influence when, in 1873, it reported on the implementation of the post-1859 procedures for testing the validity of pilgrimage claims in the Panaraga (Madiun) area, the site of the famous *pĕsantrens* of Banjarsari and Tĕgalsari and other schools. Previously, a *haji* returning from Mecca was met with a carriage by the learned scholars and *priyayi* and was grandly received. But with the changed regulations, now a returning *haji* was tested by an official about his understanding of texts, then examined by the *bupati* and his most senior official about religion, then tested by an assistant for knowledge of the holy places in Mecca and Medina and of the seas crossed during the trip, being required to point these out on a map. As a result of this, in Panaraga many who claimed to be *hajis* failed when they were examined, *Bramartani* reported.[87]

The most extreme fundamentalist movement sparked by a returned *haji* in the mid-nineteenth century was that of Kyai Haji Ahmad Rifa'i (or Rifangi), the founder of a movement known as Rifa'iyah or Budiah. He was born near Sĕmarang in 1786 and spent the years 1833–41 in Mecca. He returned to Java and eventually settled in the *pasisir* village

---

[85] Van den Berg, "Geestelijkheid", p. 2; L.Th. Mayer, *Een blik in het Javaansche volksleven* (2 vols.; Leiden: E.J. Brill, 1897), vol. I, pp. 209–10.
[86] Keijzer, *Onze tijd*, p. 181.
[87] *BM* 10 July 1873.

of Kalisalak, where he set up a *pĕsantren*. His teachings were uncom-
promisingly puritanical, seeking to rid local Islam of the accretions
which, in his view, had obscured the original message of God as delivered
to His Prophet in the *Qur'an*. As was to be expected, education was a
key strategy for Rifa'i. He wrote numerous works in Javanese to spread
what he understood to be the true and reformed meaning of Islam. He
denounced local cultural forms such as the *wayang*. He rejected the
validity of rituals conducted by the established religious elite who were
not only generally ignorant but, by working under the rule of the *kafir*
Dutch, had rendered themselves unfit to lead Muslims, he said. But it
is important to note that — unlike some reformers who would come
after him — he did not reject Sufism. Several of his works deal with
Sufism, but of course as a reformed, orthodox mysticism freed of what
he saw as deviant practices and local accretions. He did not, however,
declare himself to be a member of any particular Sufi order (*tarekat*).

As part of a general withdrawal from the surrounding society, Rifa'i's
followers built their own separate mosques, rigidly adhered to the ritual
requirements of their faith, generally avoided association with their
fellows and rejected the authority of officials who served under the
authority of the colonial regime. They did not, for example, recognise
as valid marriages conducted by a Pangulu (the head of a mosque)
appointed by the colonial regime. Rifa'i's followers grew to significant
numbers, particularly in the Pĕkalongan and Kĕdu residencies. Unlike
the Padri reformers of West Sumatra, however, Rifa'i did not attempt
violent restructuring of society or physical resistance to the Dutch, but
he was regarded as a danger by the local religious and *priyayi* elite. These
elites, after some difficulty in doing so, persuaded the Dutch authorities
to exile Rifa'i to Ambon in 1859, where he died in 1876. A century and
a half after his exile, his movement reportedly still has around seven
million followers today, mainly on Java's *pasisir*, where they have continued
from time to time to find themselves in conflict with local society and
religious officials. Ky. H. Rifa'i's books are still read in some Javanese
pĕsantrens.[88]

---

[88] Kartodirdjo, *Protest movements*, pp. 118–27; Abdul Djamil, *Perlawanan Kiai desa:
Pemikiran dan gerakan Islam KH. Ahmad Rifa'i Kalisalak* (Yogyakarta: LKiS, 2001);
Ahmad Adaby Darban, *Rifa'iyah: Gerakan sosial keagamaan di pedesaan Jawa Tengah
tahun 1850–1982* (Yogyakarta: Tarawang Press, 2004); Jaquet, "Mutiny en hadji-
ordonnanie", pp. 303–6.

The divisions already opening up in pious Javanese Islamic circles by the 1850s are exemplified in the following verse by Ky. H. Ahmad Rifaʻi:

Truly it is cruel of the learned scholars (*alim*) and of the *hajis* it is a great sin,
when they submit to serving the Tumĕnggung [a high Javanese official],
the Tumĕnggung who serves the exalted *kafir* king.[89]

The colonial environment was requiring various sorts of compromises to be made, not all of them acceptable to movements as fundamentalist as the Rifaʻiyah.

The number of *hajis* and consequently of the professionally religious *putihan* as a group continued to grow in Java. It was reported that an increasing number of people whom the Dutch regarded as notables (*aanzienlijken*) were going on the pilgrimage: up to 242 such in 1872, which, as noted above, was the year of a so-called *hajj akbar*.[90] Figures for the number of *hajis* present in Java in 1874 fortunately allow us to distinguish Javanese-speaking residencies (Table 2).[91]

These figures reflect the significant numbers of *hajis* found especially on the *pasisir*, and particularly in the major commercial cities of Sĕmarang and Surabaya. In the interior, only the court city of Surakarta had numbers of *hajis* comparable to those found in the larger towns of the coast. The link between trade and piety that so often arises in the history of Islam was also discernible here. Poensen observed in 1881 that "insofar as the native trade is of significance, it is mainly in the hands of *hajis* and of *santris* who follow their example. Even the peddling trade of the markets is in their hands to a considerable extent."[92]

Such numbers continued to grow. The *hajj akbar* years of 1880, 1885 and 1888 produced particularly large numbers from across the

---

[89] Cited in Abdul Djamil, *Perlawanan Kiai desa*, p. 211; Abdul Djamil gives a slightly different reading of the Javanese text on p. 44, but it makes less sense than that on p. 211.

[90] E. de Waal, *Onze Indische financien: nieuwe reeks aanteekeningen* (9 vols.; 's-Gravenhage: M. Nijhoff, 1876–1907), vol. I, p. 245.

[91] Ibid., pp. 246–7. See also the figures for departing and returning *hajis* broken down by residencies in Java in anon., "De regeering van Nederlandsch Indie tegenover den Islam", *TNI* (n.s.) 7 (1878): 208–9.

[92] C. Poensen, "Naar en op de pasar", Kĕdiri, May 1881, in ARZ 261; also in *MNZG* 26 (1882): 1 *et seq.*

TABLE 2: *Hajis* in Javanese residencies, 1874

Pasisir Residencies	Hajis Present
Cirĕbon	1,463
Tĕgal	1,158
Pĕkalongan	972
Sĕmarang	4,998
Jĕpara	2,059
Rĕmbang	651
Surabaya	3,110
Pasuruan	746
Prabalingga	117
Bĕsuki	149
Banyuwangi	143
Interior Residencies & Principalities	
Kĕdiri	502
Madiun	843
Surakarta	1,312
Yogyakarta	836
Kĕdu	923
Bagĕlen	798
Banyumas	467

Dutch-ruled Indonesian territories, but the figures that are readily available do not enable us to separate out the Javanese-speaking territories. We can, however, give such figures for Central and East Java, Madura, Surakarta and Yogyakarta for some years later in the nineteenth and at the beginning of the twentieth centuries, which show a steady flow of significant numbers on the *hajj* (Table 3).[93]

Fed by the rising numbers of *hajis*, the number of professionally religious and their schools grew significantly in the later years of the century. There are problems with getting comparable definitions so that statistics can tell a meaningful story, but nevertheless the general trend is clear enough, as can be seen in Table 4.[94]

---

[93] Vredenbregt, "Haddj", pp. 140–2.
[94] De Waal, *Indische financien*, vol. 1, pp. 251–2.

TABLE 3: *Hajj* departures from Javanese-speaking areas and Madura, selected years, 1884–1911

Year	hajis
1884	2,568
1885	2,501
1898	5,322
1899	NA
1900	2,274
1901	1,546
1902	1,232
1903	1,172
1904	NA
1905	2,543
1906	2,940
1907	1,128
1908	4,630
1909	3,243
1910	3,602
1911	7,614

TABLE 4: Professional religious (*geestelijken*) and religious students in Java, 1863–74

Year	Religious (geestelijken)	Students
1863	64,980	93,680
1864	65,103	97,384
1865	72,440	103,699
1866	73,832	110,315
1867	73,658	109,242
1868	95,670	121,590
1869	78,816	129,575
1870	NA	142,178
1871	138,775	189,955
1872	90,023	162,474

Thus, the number of professional religious and religious students roughly doubled in the years 1863–71. It is possible also to break these figures down amongst the Javanese-speaking residencies in 1872:

TABLE 5: Religious (*geestelijken*) and religious students in Javanese-speaking residencies, 1872[95]

Pasisir Residencies	Religious (geestelijken)	Students
Cirĕbon	5,983	6,590
Tĕgal	2,478	4,832
Pĕkalongan	2,592	3,202
Sĕmarang	7,978	15,911
Jĕpara	4,151	11,750
Rĕmbang	3,422	6,370
Surabaya	7,409	13,740
Pasuruan	2,782	7,211
Prabalingga	752	4,937
Bĕsuki	3,797	6,382
Banyuwangi	291	3,772
Interior Residencies & Principalities		
Kĕdiri	3,338	4,859
Madiun	2,821	6,526
Surakarta	7,367	3,386
Yogyakarta	2,446	4,361
Kĕdu	4,537	9,636
Bagĕlen	6,766	4,338
Banyumas	2,704	2,010

As was true of the figures about *hajis* given in Table 2, in Table 5 we again see the prominence of the *pasisir*, and particularly of Sĕmarang and Surabaya. Among interior areas, only the court city of Surakarta had numbers of religious like those of the larger towns of the coast, although its total number of *santris* (students) was lower than for the major coastal towns. Nevertheless the numbers of religious in the interior were significant. In 1884, the unhappy missionary H.C. Kruyt wrote to the head of his mission society in Rotterdam,

---

[95] Ibid., p. 253.

The diligence of the Mohammedans appears above all in Sukabumi,[96] because the *patih* [the senior Javanese administrator] is a great zealot. The prayer-times are observed faithfully and punctually. Those who don't know the usual formulae are taught daily in the mosque. That building is chock-full on Fridays. Sukabumi is swarming with *hajis*.[97]

It would not, however, be consistent with the evidence to see these developments as a single religious phenomenon — simply as pious people enhancing the observance of their faith across Javanese society — for this growth in religious life seems to have fed diverging trends. Sharp-eyed readers will already have noted something odd between

TABLE 6: Religious (*geestelijken*) 1872: number of *hajis* 1874, in Javanese-speaking residencies

Pasisir Residencies	*Religious (1872) : hajis (1874)*
Cirĕbon	4.09 : 1
Tĕgal	2.14 : 1
Pĕkalongan	2.67 : 1
Sĕmarang	1.60 : 1
Jĕpara	2.02 : 1
Rĕmbang	5.26 : 1
Surabaya	2.38 : 1
Pasuruan	3.73 : 1
Prabalingga	6.43 : 1
Bĕsuki	25.48 : 1
Banyuwangi	2.03 : 1
Interior Residencies & Principalities	
Kĕdiri	6.65 : 1
Madiun	3.35 : 1
Surakarta	5.62 : 1
Yogyakarta	2.93 : 1
Kĕdu	4.92 : 1
Bagĕlen	8.48 : 1
Banyumas	5.79 : 1

[96] There are several Sukabumis, the best-known being in the Sundanese-speaking area of West Java. I presume, however, that Kruyt, who was writing from East Java (see the following note) probably meant Sukabumi in Prabalingga, East Java.
[97] H.C. Kruyt, Majawarna, 20 Oct. 1884, in ARZ 145.

Tables 2 and 5. One might imagine that, in this context of increasing religiosity, where there were more religious teachers and other professionally religious *putihan*, there would also be more *hajis*. That is, that a generally high level of religious activity and a high level of *hajis* would go together. But it was not so. Consider the comparison in Table 6, setting the number of religious (*geestelijken*) in Javanese-speaking residencies in 1872 (Table 5) against the number of *hajis* in Javanese residencies in 1874 (Table 2).

The statistical variations there tell us that high numbers of religious in a population did not produce comparably high levels of pilgrims or, at least, if it did the returning *hajis* did not always go back to their places of origin. *Hajis* and professionally religious both tended to be found in high numbers on the central *pasisir*, the categories relating to each other in the range of 1.6–2.6 professional religious:*hajis* in most places. Along the coast to the southeast of Surabaya, however, the numbers of religious were not reflected in those of *hajis*. In that region — an area of significant Madurese immigration — except in remote Banyuwangi where numbers in both categories were too small to be significant, the ratio was in the range from 3.7 to a remarkable 25.48 religious per *haji*. In the interior of the island, the ratio of professional religious to *hajis* was in the range 3.4–8.5, except for Yogyakarta, where the ratio was closer but the number of both was low when compared to its peer court city of Surakarta.[98] Sartono Kartodirdjo provides figures for religious teachers and *hajis* in 1887, which show a similar pattern. In Javanese-speaking residencies, where there were higher numbers of religious teachers (called *kyai* in Javanese) there tended to be lower figures of *hajis*, and vice-versa.[99]

This suggests that there were at least two statistically evident categories of religious leaders in Java in this time and they were tending to stay out of each other's way. Not all *hajis* came back from Mecca with revivalist ideas which they tried to spread among their compatriots, of course, but many did, and they were, it seems, concentrating in areas where there were fewer established religious. There were certainly *kyais* who were also *hajis*, but there were many who were not and who, we

---

[98] Given the link between Islam and commerce, this difference between Surakarta and Yogyakarta may reflect in part a higher level of commercial activity in Surakarta. There the presence of the Solo River facilitated trade, while pre-railway Yogyakarta was relatively poorly served by trade routes.

[99] Kartodirdjo, *Peasants' revolt*, p. 332.

may guess, found the new-fangled ideas coming out of the Middle Eastern experience of *hajis* to be inconsistent with their understanding of the true Islam. So where the Islam of the *kyais* was strong — the teachings of pious men whose faith in many cases was close to the mystic synthesis of the aristocratic elite — the new ideas of *hajis* may have found a less cordial reception than elsewhere. That is not to suggest that *kyais* or the aristocratic elite were actually opposed to the pilgrimage. In 1879, for example, Sultan Haměngkubuwana VII of Yogyakarta sent four emissaries on the *hajj* with orders to construct accommodation in Mecca on his behalf so that pilgrims could stay at no cost.[100] But the statistics suggest that there was a contest of ideas developing in Islamic circles, in which *kyais* and *hajis* tended to play separate roles. We have already noted above, for example, that among the nearly 500 followers of Ky. Nurhakim there was known to be only one *haji*.[101] Similar circumstances were noted by the colonial government's advisor for Islamic and indigenous affairs, E. Gobée, in 1928. He drew a distinction between the leaders of Sufi brotherhoods on one hand — who would have been *kyais* — and on the other the teachers of *kitab* — the less mystically inclined, more *shari'a*-oriented figures. "In many areas conflict is prevalent between the *tarekat* gurus and the *kitab* gurus", he said.[102]

Religious schools (*pěsantrens*) were essential to all groups of Islamic leaders — as schools also were to the Christian missionaries — and they were growing rapidly in number, as the figures for religious students seen in Table 4 already have suggested. There are serious problems of definition in assessing this growth, however, for sources disagree as to what constituted a *pěsantren*. There was little agreement on how many students, what sort of syllabus, or what facilities were needed to meet the definition of a school. Oddities in the table below also reflect the simple inadequacy of colonial statistical services at the time, of course. But the pattern is nevertheless clear, as will be seen in Table 7.

---

[100] *BM* 28 Aug. 1879. It is worth noting, however, that no Sultan of Yogyakarta or Susuhunan of Surakarta himself undertook the *hajj* — nor would the Dutch probably have allowed one to do so — until the following century, after Indonesian independence.
[101] Assistant Resident of Lědok, cited in Drewes, *Drie Javaansche goeroe's*, p. 49.
[102] E. Gobée to Resident of Kědiri M.H. Doornik, 8 May 1928, in Arsip Nasional Republik Indonesia, *Laporan-laporan tentang gerakan protes di Jawa pada abad-XX* (Jakarta: Arsip Nasional Republik Indonesia, 1981), p. 217.

**TABLE 7: Islamic religious schools and students
in Java and Madura, 1882–93**[103]

Year	Number of Schools	Number of Pupils
1882	5,009	80,846
1883	12,947	164,953
1887	19,108	291,721
1892	18,202	262,416
1893	10,830	272,427

Other sources provide different figures, but they are generally of a similar magnitude. One set of official statistics, for example, counted 15,000 religious schools in Java in 1885, with 230,000 students. Among those, the *pěsantrens* that taught more than elementary Islam, taking students to the study of law, theology and more advanced topics, may have been no more than about 200.[104] The spread of railways improved communications in general in Java and, the Dutch Resident of Surakarta believed, also made it almost universal for young Javanese males to spend at least some time in a *pěsantren* if they wished to claim any cultivation or knowledge of the world. Even the poorest could attend a *pěsantren*, living on alms. The *pěsantrens* thus became nodes for ongoing social networks among young Javanese men from across Java.[105]

Many of Java's *pěsantrens* were small. In the table above, the mean number of students per school ranges from 12.7 in 1883 to 25.2 in 1893. In the early 1880s Punjul and Wanantara in Cirěbon, Brangkal in Bagělen, Těgalsari and Banjarsari in Madiun and Sidasrěma in Surabaya were the only schools with over 100 students and which attracted *santris* from outside their immediate area. Sidasrěma was the

[103] *Algemeen vijfjarig verslag van het inlandsch onderwijs in Nederlandsch-Indië, loopende over de jaren 1878 t/m 1882* (Batavia: Landsdrukkerij, 1885), p. 260; *Algemeen vijfjarig verslag van het inlandsch onderwijs in Nederlandsch-Indië, loopende over de jaren 1883 t/m 1887* (Batavia: Landsdrukkerij, 1890), p. 282; *Algemeen vijfjarig verslag van het inlandsch onderwijs in Nederlandsch-Indië, loopende over de jaren 1888 t/m 1892* (Batavia: Landsdrukkerij, 1894), p. 218; *Algemeen vijfjarig verslag van het inlandsch onderwijs in Nederlandsch-Indië, loopende over de jaren 1893 t/m 1897* (Batavia: Landsdrukkerij, 1901), p. 191.
[104] L.W.C. van den Berg, "Het Mohammedaansche godsdienstonderwijs op Java en Madoera en de daarbij gebruikte Arabische boeken", *TBG* 31 (1886): 518–9.
[105] A.J. Spaan, Surakarta, to GG, 15 Oct. 1888, in MR 1888 no. 728/26 Oct.

largest and had surpassed the fame of Tĕgalsari, previously the premier *pĕsantren* of Java.[106] The latter had students from across most of Java, except from the Surabaya area whose *santris* went to Sidasrĕma. But whereas Tĕgalsari was said once to have had 2,000 students, now it had only some 250. Most students stayed at Tĕgalsari (or other *pĕsantrens*) for only one or two years, but some stayed for ten or twenty and themselves became professional religious.[107] Even if most schools were small, the cumulative effect of so many was significant. In Kĕdiri, for example, where the population was a bit under a million in the 1880s, there were 650 *pĕsantrens*. All the teaching in them was reportedly based on Arabic books.[108]

Many *pĕsantrens*, especially in the interior, still taught the mystic synthesis tradition of Javanese Islam, with its attendant doctrines of supernatural powers and hidden forces, but not all. L.W.C. van den Berg visited *pĕsantrens* in the 1880s and reported that, while Arabic books were found in them, in many cases the teachers had little or no command of Arabic. Much of what was taught consisted of magic arts, that is, the older *ngelmus* of Javanese Islamic traditions. The Islamic schools on the *pasisir*, however, particularly in the main commercial cities, were generally of a higher standard. Teachers there had mostly spent years in Mecca, were well-educated and fluent in Arabic. In some places an Arab taught, but most of the teachers in the coastal schools were Javanese. In such schools, students learned to recite the *Qur'an* and could study Qur'anic interpretation (*tafsir*), law (*fiqh*), grammar (*nahw*), scholastic theology (*usul* [*al-din*]), and Sufism (*tasawwuf*).[109] We noted above that a distinction between the *pasisir* and the interior is suggested also in statistical sources regarding two categories of religious leaders, the *kyais* with their interior schools and the *hajis* with their greater concentration on the *pasisir*.

While some schools maintained older Javanese traditions, others embraced a reformist, *shari'a*-oriented orthodoxy including, it seems, the most famous *pĕsantren*, that at Sidasrĕma in Surabaya. The Yogyakarta

[106] Van den Berg, "Geestelijkheid", p. 22; idem, "Godsdienstonderwijs", pp. 520–1.
[107] F. Fokkens, Jr., "De priesterschool te Tegalsari", *TBG* 24 (1877): 328–32; Veth, *Java*, vol. I, p. 384.
[108] C. Poensen, "Iets over den Javaan als mensch", Kĕdiri, July 1884, in ARZ 261; also in *MNZG* 29 (1885): 64; population figure from Kartodirdjo, *Peasants' revolt*, p. 332, giving 996,385 in 1887.
[109] Van den Berg, "Godsdienstonderwijs", pp. 521–5.

aristocrat R. Natarata (also known as Sasrawijaya) set out to seek mystical wisdom by travelling from teacher to teacher around 1870–71. At Sidasrěma he found over 3,000 *santris*. But he discovered that the *kyai* there would not teach him Sufism, for he was a defender of *shariʿa*-oriented orthodoxy. The *kyai* reportedly said,

> As for Sufism (*'ilmu tarekat*), I have declared it truly forbidden (*kula haramakěn*). In this life, a person should do no more than carry out the obligations of the five pillars of Islam: ... the confession of faith, the prayer, paying the religious tax, fasting in the month of Ramadan and the fifth, if you are able, to go on the *hajj*.... Oh, my son, do not persist in searching for secret knowledge and then cast off the *shariʿa* of God's Emissary.

In the wake of this rejection, Natarata went to an Arab in Surabaya who eventually — after Natarata had undertaken further travels — was willing to teach him Sufism.[110]

This *shariʿa*-oriented orthodoxy occasionally even crept into the correspondence pages of the Javanese newspaper *Bramartani* (at that stage entitled *Jurumartani*), which was generally an unsympathetic venue for such ideas. One contributor objected to the Javanese practice of having a lavish communal meal (the *sidhěkah malěman*) on certain nights of the fasting month, on the grounds that this had no Islamic origin.[111] Another who called himself "the mendicant" (*tiyang pěkir*) wrote of the increasing number of people who were praying, attending the mosque and reading the *Qurʾan*. But there were still many young people dedicated to pleasures that were improper for one committed to religion, he said: raising dogs, playing cards and watching dancing-girls. All this must be stopped.[112] At the same time, the missionary-scholar Carel Poensen noted how the "orthodox Muslims" rejected the various mystical sciences (*ngelmus*) of Javanese religious tradition.[113] A rather bitter exchange took place in *Jurumartani* in 1868. A contributor who was impressed (as were most) with the scientific advances of the modern world wrote critically of religious folk (*kaum*) who could only read out

[110] Tanaya, *Sang Pinudyasma R. Natarata iya R. Sasrawijaya sarta jasané kang arupa kasusastran 'ilmu luhung* ([Surakarta:] Para kadang mitra tresna budaya, 1977 [mimeo]), pp. 1–8.
[111] *BM* 25 Feb. 1869.
[112] *BM* 7 Oct. 1869.
[113] C. Poensen, "Bijdragen tot de kennis ...", Kědiri, June 1869, in ARZ 261.

the contents of Islamic books and traditions but could not set out all the human discoveries that were being published in newspapers. A *kyai* from Cirĕbon wrote in reply that these *kaum* could not set out the deeper meaning of things in *Jurumartani* because it was not a suitable place for religious teachings.[114]

Bramartani received a reformist contributor's letter in 1879 that represented iconoclastic Islamic orthodoxy. The author, who signed himself only with the initial "D", complained of the many superstitions of village folk — which received condemnation from many of the newspaper's contributors — and of searching for worldly benefits through veneration of spiritually sacred places, holy graves and hidden powers. This diminished the worship of God, "D" wrote, echoing the orthodox rejection of *shirk* (polytheism, the ascribing of partners to God or the worship of other than God). Did "my people the Javanese" think that a *haji* who had died could rise again from the grave and dispense medicines, hand out money or guarantee a long life? Should not humankind instead concentrate on the Lord Allah who is all-powerful and be thankful to Him? But if one prayed to God, one must observe preconditions: if one wanted to be cured of illness, one must take medicine; if to be rich, one must engage in trade. There were no spirits (*setan*): many Europeans had entered caves and other places never before visited by humans and had never seen a spirit, "D" said, curiously acknowledging an implicit epistemological superiority of European observation. *Bramartani*'s Javanese editor reacted to this final touch by adding the comment that in Europe there were still people who believed in superstition, but there were far more in Java. "My people the Javanese", he wrote, were reluctant to free themselves of everything handed down from their ancestors, but nowadays there were many of the elite who were capable of wisdom and they would be an example to the common folk.[115] Between the near-Wahhabism of "D" and the faith in science of *Bramartani*'s editor yawned a chasm of contending visions of reform.

As the *shari'a*-oriented reformers progressed so also, we may presume, did a sense of distance from the European colonisers of Java — a distancing that, as will be seen in later chapters, contributed also to the

---

[114] *BM* 2 Jan. and 16 Jan. 1868.
[115] *BM* 17 Apr. 1879. I am uncertain of the editor's name at this stage. He referred to the Javanese as *bongsa kula tiyang Jawi* so he was clearly Javanese, but he only signed himself on this occasion as *Juru ngarang* (the writer).

gap between reforming Muslims and the *priyayi* elite with its taste for things Western. Amongst the many Islamic legal opinions (*fatwa*) available to Javanese *hajis* in the later nineteenth century were those in an 1892 collection compiled in Mecca specifically for Indonesian pilgrims, among whom of course a large proportion were Javanese. One question dealt with there was whether a Muslim could wear clothes of a kind worn by Christians. On the authority of Ahmad ibn Zaini Dahlan (1817–86), the head of the Shafi'i school of law in Mecca — the school adhered to by Indonesian Muslims — the *fatwa* declared that Muslims must reject clothing worn by *kafirs* (infidels).[116] In societies such as nineteenth-century Java, clothing had long been a way of expressing who you were and who you were not. For pious Muslims under Christian colonial rule, the latter may have been growing even more important than the former. And it was not just that they were not European Christians. It will become clear later in this book that they were also demonstrating that they were not peasants, not *priyayi* and, indeed, in some sense not Javanese. As *Wedhatama* put it, "Oddly enough they deny their Javaneseness, and at all costs bend their steps to Mecca in search of knowledge."[117] Similarly, from the vantage point of Kĕdiri in East Java, Poensen observed that when a returned pilgrim donned his Arab-style dress, "He feels himself to be a *haji*; he has ceased to be Javanese — he is a *haji*. By means of the pilgrimage, Islam has turned him into a citizen of the world."[118]

Sufism

In addition to the continuing defenders of the Javanese mystic synthesis and the *shari'a*-oriented reformers, Sufi *tarekats* also played an important role in nineteenth-century Java. What *hajis* brought back from Mecca and what found a receptive soil in Java was not only the law but also Islamic mysticism. While much of what went on in Sufi circles is obscure, it is clear that the Naqshabandiyya order was of particular significance. There were two Sufi orders that represented the

---

[116] Nico Kaptein (ed.), *The Muhimmât al-Nafâ'is: A bilingual Meccan fatwa collection for Indonesian Muslims from the end of the nineteenth century* (Seri INIS 32; Jakarta: INIS, 1997), pp. 3, 161, 199.

[117] Robson, *Wedhatama*, pp. 36–7 (with minor variation to Robson's translation).

[118] C. Poensen, *Brieven over den Islām uit de binnenlanden van Java* (Leiden: E.J. Brill, 1886), p. 68.

Naqshabandiyya in Java in the nineteenth century. The first was the Naqshabandiyya proper of the Khalidiyya branch, introduced to the Indonesian archipelago by the Sumatran Shaikh Isma'il Minangkabawi, who returned there from Mecca in the 1850s. He based himself mainly in Riau and Singapore, but had considerable influence throughout the archipelago. Amongst his students and followers were many Javanese.[119] The second was a new Sufi order that combined Naqshabandiyya and Qadiriyya techniques, and was thus called Qadiriyya wa Naqshabandiyya. This was the creation of Shaikh Ahmad Khatib (d.c. 1875 in Mecca)[120] of Sambas, West Kalimantan. It also spread throughout the archipelago and is still a major force today.

Both Naqshabandiyya and Qadiriyya wa Naqshabandiyya gave greater emphasis to observing the five pillars of Islamic orthodoxy than was true of the previously dominant order, the Shattariyya. Consequently, conflicts between them and the Shattariyya were not uncommon. Leaders of these orders were also more anti-Christian and, to varying degrees, thus more opposed to Dutch colonial rule. Nevertheless, the Shattariyya could also produce anti-colonial movements, as happened in at least one minor case in Madiun in 1886.[121] In the late 1880s, it was reported that in Banyumas and Bagĕlen, Shattariyya was still the larger order, but Naqshabandiyya was next in size of following. Its foremost leader there was one Muhammad Ilyas, who had a personal following of a thousand adherents. His sole purpose was reportedly "to stimulate better fulfillment of the Islamic religious obligations" and the practice of *dhikr*. The Shattariyya, by contrast, was said to be "not of such a mystical character as Naqshabandiyya" and "not so strict in its demands as the other sect".[122]

---

[119] Consul-General G. Lavino, Singapore, to GG, 6 Dec. 1889, in MR 1889 no. 866/ 18 Dec.; Martin van Bruinessen, "The origins and development of the Naqshabandi order in Indonesia", *Der Islam* 67, no. 1 (1990): 161–4, 169–73; idem, *Tarekat Naqsyabandiyah di Indonesia: Survei historis, geografis, dan sosiologis* (Bandung: Penerbit Mizan, 1992), pp. 98–101.

[120] I am grateful for the advice of Dr Werner Kraus concerning the year of Ahmad Khatib's death.

[121] MR 1886, nos. 759/1 Dec. and 812/24 Dec. The leader was one Ky. Ngali Muhammad, who reportedly emphasised the importance of the five daily prayers and *dhikr* of the Shattariyya order. He was arrested and given 20 days hard labour.

[122] MR 1889, no. 41/26 Jan. See also van Bruinessen, *Tarekat Naqsyabandiyah*, pp. 163–4.

Both the Naqshabandiyya and the Qadiriyya wa Naqshabandiyya should thus be seen as part of the Islamic reformist movements of the nineteenth century. The principle difference in their social impact was that the Naqshabandiyya tended to gain adherents among the elite of Javanese society, while the Qadiriyya wa Naqshabandiyya found supporters more among the common people. While mystical in orientation, they sought greater observance of the obligations of the faith, as those obligations were set out in Islamic sources, known in Mecca and increasingly being emphasised in Java. Sufi *tarekats* had long been known in Java but, in the pre-colonial era, they had evidently coexisted comfortably with the dominant mystic synthesis of Javanese Islam. The Naqshabandiyya and Qadiriyya wa Naqshabandiyya of the nineteenth century were no longer, it seems, prepared to make such compromises. There was no room for the Goddess of the Southern Ocean in their spiritual life.

Because both *tarekats* initially spread among Javanese in a way that was invisible to the Dutch, it is not clear when they first became a significant force. When the colonial regime became worried about the anti-colonial potential of these *tarekats* in the 1880s, the reports that were gathered then indicated that, in most places in Java, Naqshabandiyya had been introduced c. 1850–60.[123]

The role of Arabs is less clear in the case of Sufi *tarekats* in Java than is true of the *shari'a*-oriented reform movements. But there can be no doubt that there were Sufis among Arabs in Java, just as was true anywhere else in the Islamic world. For example, when two Indian *sheikhs* and an Arab named Sayid Abdullah visited Pasuruan in 1873, some 500 locals — both Javanese and Chinese — flocked to them for blessing and healing. They asked for no money, neither slept nor ate (so *Bramartani* reported) and spent their entire time in Sufi *dhikr* (recitation of pious formulae as a mystic exercise), asking only for food which was then distributed to the people who were present.[124]

The most prominent Javanese *sheikh* of the Naqshabandiyya Khalidiyya in the 1880s was H. Abdul Kadir of Sĕmarang. He was

---

[123] Pelzer, Resident of Priangan, to GG, Bandung 29 Sept. 1885, in MR 1885, no. 642a/9 Oct. L.W.C. van den Berg, "Over de devotie der Naqsjibendîjah in den Indischen archipel", *TBG* 28 (1883): 163; N.D. Schuurmans, "De tariqah Naqsjibendijjah op Java", *Nederlandsch Zendingstijdschrift* 2 (1890): 265.

[124] *BM* 17 Apr. 1873. Most Arab Sufis would presumably have been associated with the Alawiyya *tarekat* rather than the *tarekats* which Javanese joined.

initated into the Naqshabandiyya in Mecca by the head of the order, Sulaiman al-Zuhdi. He returned to Sěmarang and attempted to promote the Naqshabandiyya there, but found that most people still preferred the Shattariyya order. In 1881 he was said to have promoted "a serious movement in the religious field" in the interior of Java. The elderly *pangulu* (head of the mosque) in the Yogyakarta subsidiary principality of the Pakualaman fell under Naqshabandiyya influence. Behind closed doors at night, Naqshabandiyya *dhikr* was being taught in the Pakualaman mosque. This *dhikr* was so exhausting, with its large number of repetitions of the confession of faith that there is no God but God (*La ilaha illa 'llah*), that two devotees in Surakarta and one in Kota Gěde had perished of exhaustion, the Dutch were told.[125] The growth of followers in Yogyakarta proceeded so secretly that neither prince Pakualam V (r. 1878–1900) nor Sultan Haměngkubuwana VII (r. 1877–1921) knew of this until told by the Resident of Yogyakarta, or at least so the Dutch claimed. The old *pangulu* of the Pakualaman was consequently dismissed and Abdul Kadir's pupils who were promoting his teachings were expelled from Yogyakarta. The chief *pangulu* of the Sultan's mosque in Yogyakarta condemned the new teachings. Abdul Kadir also visited Surakarta and there gained influence over three princes who were sons of Susuhunan Pakubuwana IX (r. 1861–93) and — more ominously — over the prince who was the commander of the Mangkunagaran Legion. These four were admonished to mend their ways and Abdul Kadir was prohibited from entering the city. His movement also won a significant following — this time among commoners — in Kědu. All of this seemed too much of a threat to the established order, both that of the Dutch and of the Javanese monarchs in Surakarta and Yogyakarta. So H. Abdul Kadir was arrested and exiled from Java.[126] This provoked at least one angry protest, from one Purwasastra who wrote to the Resident of Sěmarang demanding to know on what grounds Abdul Kadir had been arrested, Muslims engaged in *dhikr* had been expelled from the mosque of Surakarta upon the orders of the Resident and Naqshabandiyya

---

[125] On Naqshabandiyya *dhikr*, see van Bruinessen, *Tarekat Naqsyabandiyah*, pp. 80–1.

[126] MR 1881 nos. 981/31 Oct., 1007/4 Nov., 1041/9 Nov., 1102/28 Nov.; van den Berg "Naqsjibendîjah", pp. 162–5; Michael F. Laffan, " 'A watchful eye': The Meccan plot of 1881 and changing Dutch perceptions of Islam in Indonesia", *Archipel*, no. 63 (2002): 101–5 (note that Laffan refers to Abdul Kadir as Abdul Karim, a name that appears in Dutch archival sources).

teachings had been denounced.[127] The colonial regime was, of course, unmoved.

In Bantěn in West Java, Qadiriyya wa Naqshabandiyya became a powerful social and political, as well as religious, force. Its leaders gained widespread influence and by the 1880s had begun to plot a rebellion against the Dutch colonial regime and its local representatives, both indigenous and European. In July 1888 a significant insurrection broke out in Cilěgon under the leadership of these Sufis. Both European and indigenous people were killed and wounded before the rebellion was put down.[128] Similarly, a major rebellion of Muslim Sasaks against their Hindu Balinese overlords on the island of Lombok in 1891–94 was led by a local Naqshabandiyya leader. This precipitated Dutch military intervention there.[129] Nothing comparable occurred in the Javanese heartlands of Central and East Java, but the Cilěgon and Lombok uprisings made the Dutch all the more nervous of the influence of *tarekat* leaders throughout their Indonesian territories.

At the turn of the century, Ky. H. M. Muhammad Shaleh bin Haji 'Umar al-Samarani (c. 1820–1903) or Ky. Shaleh Darat, as he was known,[130] played a leading role in communicating orthodox Sufi teachings of the kind associated with al-Ghazali to Javanese audiences. His greatest work — among the thirteen or more he wrote — was the first Javanese-language interpretation of the *Qur'an* done from a Sufi perspective, *Tafsir faidl al-rahman fi tarjamah tafsir kalam malik al-dayyan*. Ky. Shaleh Darat had studied with various gurus in Java, including a grandson of H. Amad Mutamakin, a controversial Islamic teacher of the earlier eighteenth century.[131] He went on to study Qur'anic interpretation in Mecca and, upon his return to Sěmarang, set up a *pěsantren* where he taught Sufism within the context of Islamic reform, that is, mysticism in harmony with observation of the *shari'a*. Among those who are said to have studied with Ky. Shaleh Darat were several major figures of the early twentieth century, including K.H. Hasyim Asy'ari (one of the founders of Nahdlatul Ulama), K.H. Ahmad Dahlan (the founder of

---

[127] Poerwosastro to Resident Sěmarang, 20 Oct. 1881, in MR 1881 no. 1041/9 Nov.; Laffan, "Watchful eye", p. 105.

[128] Kartodirdjo, *Peasants' revolt*, chs. 5–8. Note that Kartodirdjo refers to the Qadiriyya wa Naqshabandiyya *tarekat* simply as "Kadiriah".

[129] Van Bruinessen, *Naqsyabandiyah*, p. 28.

[130] After his home in Kampung Mělayu Darat, Sěmarang.

[131] Ricklefs, *Seen and unseen worlds*, Ch. 4.

Muhammadiyah) and R.A. Kartini (who will be discussed in Chapter 6 below). Ky. Shaleh Darat's writings were published in Javanese using Arabic script by lithograph presses in Bombay, Singapore and Cirěbon, and can still be found in bookshops and *pěsantrens*.[132]

Islamic Messianism for the New Islamic Century

In the 1880s, there was messianism abroad in the Islamic world. As noted above, this was fed by the impending turning of the Islamic centuries. AH 1300 began in November 1882. Many Muslims expected a renewer of the faith, or indeed a messiah, to arrive with the new century. In this *fin-de-siècle* atmosphere, Dutch colonial authorities in Indonesia were particularly concerned about two developments far from Indonesia's shores. The first was an alleged anti-Christian plot in Mecca in 1881 under the famously anti-Christian Sharif of Mecca 'Abd al-Muttalib (d. 1886), a plot that supposedly involved Javanese.[133] The second was the progress of the Mahdi movement in Sudan. In 1881 Muhammad Ahmad b. Abd Allah declared himself to be the Mahdi — the Islamic messiah — in Sudan and in 1883 he defeated the Egyptian army there. Although the Mahdi died in 1885, not until Kitchener's defeat of the army at Omdurman in 1898 was the Mahdist movement finally crushed. In the mid-1880s the affairs of the Mahdi were discussed in the archipelago among both Arabs and local people. On the part of some people, there was reportedly a tendency to exaggerate the significance of Mahdism's achievements and a refusal to believe that the Mahdi had died.[134]

Such developments may have encouraged the spread of millennial and messianic ideas within pious Islamic circles in Java. We have already seen above that messianic ideas, inspired as much by the turning of the Javanese (AJ) century in 1871, were found in Akhmad Ngisa's messianic Ratu Adil movement in Banyumas in 1871 and in the Akmaliyah ideas

---

[132] M. Muchoyyar (ed. and transl.), *Tafsîr Faidl al-Raḥmân fî tarjamah tafsîr kalâm mâlik al-dayyân, karya K.H.M. Shaleh al-Samârani (suntingan teks, terjemahan dan analisis metodologi)* (Doctoral thesis, IAIN Sunan Kalijaga, Yogyakarta, 2002), pp. xv–xxiii, 1–17, 71, 78–9. It is not clear into which *tarekat* or *tarekats* Shaleh Darat had been initiated.

[133] Laffan, "Watchful eye", pp. 85–101.

[134] B., "Godsdienstige beweging", p. 741; G. Lavino, Consul-General, Singapore, to GG, 25 Sept. 1885, in MR 1885, no. 638/13 Nov.

taught by Ky. Hasan Maulani, M. Malangyuda and Ky. Nurhakim from the 1840s to the 1880s. There was a more orthodox Islamic variant of such ideas as well.

From the 1860s, the Dutch became familiar with a Javanese text about the *akhir ing jaman*, the end of times. This prophesied a final, bloody war in which successively the Dutch, the English and the French would be defeated by the king of all Muslims and then would convert to Islam.[135] A variant of this was a letter which was dated (in the Javanese, not Arabic, calendar) at a time equivalent to AD 1865. It claimed to be sent by the king of Mecca to warn people that the day of resurrection was near, so they must mend their sinful ways. They must observe the five daily prayers and fast for three days.[136] In 1881, as the end of the Islamic century approached, in Sundanese-speaking West Java prophecies were spread that the end of times was near and the rule of the Dutch was about to end. The Ratu Adil would come but this Ratu Adil was said to be the emissary of the Prophet Muhammad. The purveyor of these prophecies was, of course, soon in Dutch custody.[137]

In the 1880s a Javanese text called *Pralambange tanah Jawa* (prophesy of the land of Java) or similar titles was distributed around Java. The version preserved in a manuscript in Leiden University library, which was confiscated from a *haji* in Sidayu, prophesied the appearance in Java of "the Lord Ratu Adil, the Imam Mahdi" who would give birth to a son Raden Rakhmadi, who would become king of Mecca, appearing after 330 years of meditation in Java in AH 1299 (AD 1881). In that year also the Javanese would be attacked by an army of spirits. Only those who prayed five times a day and who fasted for three days would be spared.[138] Javanese were told that these were the final admonitions of the Prophet Muhammad to his community. The missionary Hoezoo, based in Sĕmarang, reported that while this seemed to mean fasting for

---

[135] W. Hoezoo, Sĕmarang, to Bestuurders NZG, Rotterdam, 9 Sept. 1864, in ARZ 210.

[136] C. Poensen, "Een mohammadaansche traktaatje", Kĕdiri, Jan. 1887, in ARZ 261; also in *MNZG* 32 (1888): 1–23.

[137] Van Vleuten, Resident of Priangan, Ciamis, to GG, 24 May 1881, in MR 1881 no. 487/3 June; idem, 16 June 1881, in MR 1881 no. 559/24 June.

[138] LOr 6536 *Pralambange tanah Jawa*. The original MS from which this was copied is LOr 7175; see Th.G.Th. Pigeaud, *Literature of Java: Catalogue raisonné of Javanese manuscripts in the library of the University of Leiden and other public collections in the Netherlands* (4 vols.; The Hague: Martinus Nijhoff; Leiden: Bibliotheca Universitatis Lugduni Batavorum; Leiden: Leiden University Press, 1967–80), vol. II, p. 391.

three days in total, some people were fasting for three days every week. There was great pressure placed on people to pray five times daily. The version being distributed in Java in 1884 said also that the bodies of those who had mocked the faith should be left unburied, but in Sĕmarang that had evidently been done to some who had only failed to pray five times a day, thus constituting complete rejection from the community.[139]

Four Ways to Pray

As this chapter has shown, from roughly the middle of the nineteenth century to its end, the world of pious Javanese believers grew polarised into differing, often contending, camps. We can capture a sense of that difference by thinking of these groups in terms of their approach to prayer.

Among the adherents of the Javanese mystic synthesis, those who practiced the "everlasting *salat* [prayer]" did not see a need to perform "the (ordinary) *salat* with ablutions".[140] Or, as Ronggawarsita's prose *Sĕrat Maklumat Jati* explained the "true five pillars of Islam":

> The pillars of Islam are said to be five: (1) the confession of faith (*sahadat*) ... (2) fasting (*siyam*) ... (3) paying the tax (*jakat*) ... (4) ritual prayer (*salat*) ... (5) the pilgrimage (*kaji*).

> [But:] (1) a silent mouth, (2) a closed nose, (3) unseeing eyes, (4) unhearing ears, (5) a dead body: indeed it is these which provide what is necessary as pillars of the true Islam, for this means that we can die within life.[141]

Ritual prayer was, in the eyes of some, a matter for the uninitiated, for those whom Mangkunagara IV's *Wedhatama* described as youths "obsessed with taking as their model and example the Prophet". Mangkunagara IV reminded Javanese princes that

> If you insist on imitating
> the example of the Prophet,
> O, my boys, you overreach yourself.
> As a rule you will not hold out long:

---

[139] B., "Godsdienstige beweging", pp. 739–40. See also *BM* 8 May 1884.
[140] Zoetmulder, *Pantheism and monism*, pp. 145–7.
[141] SOAS 310763(D), ff. 17v.–18r.

seeing that you are Javanese,
just a little is enough.[142]

For *shari'a*-oriented reformers and their following, by contrast, the
five daily prayers were an essential part of God's commands to humankind.
Along with the other pillars of Islam, prayer was essential to the good
religious life. Poensen observed that, for the *putihan*, "the fulfillment of
the five daily prayers and joining in the Friday religious observance ...
has become a distinguishing characteristic".[143] The "true *salat*" for these
believers was carried out five times a day, after ritual ablutions, at
prescribed times and in prescribed fashion. The idea that this was a
matter merely for the uninitiated, for those who lacked real understanding, was anathema. Such reformers carried back from their
experiences of the *hajj* a sense of a better, purer form of religious life that
they had perceived in Mecca and that they brought to their fellow
Javanese, in the hope both of a better society and eternal reward. Some
of them at least were opposed to the Sufi *tarekats*. The *kyai* of Sidasrĕma
said that he had forbidden Sufism and admonished Natarata, "Oh, my
son, do not persist in searching for secret knowledge and then cast off
the *shari'a* of God's Emissary."[144]

Followers of the reformed Sufi *tarekats*, the Naqshabandiyya and
Qadiriyya wa Naqshabandiyya, had yet another approach to prayer.
For them, as for their *shari'a*-oriented fellows, the orthodox commitment
to the five daily prayers remained important. But there were also mystical
doctrines to be pursued and gnosis to be sought. For these Sufis, as for
the followers of the mystic synthesis, observation of the daily ritual
prayer was among the first steps on the mystic path to enlightenment
through spiritual guidance and secret doctrines. But, unlike some followers
of the mystic synthesis, these Sufis did not leave ritual prayer or the rest
of the *shari'a* behind. The five pillars of Islam remained essential to
upholding their religious life.

Finally, those who adhered to messianic ideas were prepared to
believe that their prayers for a just world, for the expulsion of their
Christian rulers and for the arrival of a messiah were about to be
answered. Always, of course, about to be, and never in fact answered.

---

[142] Robson, *Wedhatama.*, pp. 28–31, with a few minor departures from Robson's
translation.
[143] Poensen, *Brieven*, p. 163
[144] Tanaya, *R. Natarata*, p. 2.

If the daily prayers were important, they were so because they had been commanded as a way to distinguish those who would be saved from those who would not when the final cataclysm came.

But this diverging world of pious Muslims was only part of the story in nineteenth-century Javanese society. As will be seen in the following chapters, there were small communities emerging who, although they were praying, were doing so as Christians. There were also Javanese — and they were probably the majority of the society — who had spiritual concerns but weren't praying to a transcendent God very often, or indeed at all.

4

The Birth of the *Abangan*

From about the middle of the nineteenth century, there emerged in Javanese society a category of people who were defined by their failure — in the eyes of the more pious — to behave as proper Muslims. These were the *abangan*, the nominal or non-practising Muslims. This term derives from the "Low Javanese" (*ngoko*) word *abang*, meaning the colour red or brown. At the time, the usual terms were *bangsa abangan* (the red/brown sort) or *wong abangan* (the red/brown people). In "High Javanese" (*krama*) the word was *abrit* and these people were thus also called *tiyang abritan*, *tiyang* being the *krama* equivalent of *wong* (people, person). As we shall see below, *abangan* originated as a term of derision employed by the pious *putihan*, the "white ones".[1]

---

[1] There is a folk etymology which claims that *abangan* derived from the name of one of the semi-legendary *walis* of Javanese Islam, Seh Lĕmah Abang, who was martyred for disclosing secret doctrines to the uninitiated. But there is no evidence to support this. However unorthodox his methods, as a saint of Islam Lĕmah Abang would certainly have been regarded as one of the *putihan*. To confirm the irrelevance of this etymology, we may note that in *krama* Javanese his name is given as Seh Siti Jĕnar, yet the *abangan* were never called *jĕnaran* in *krama*, but rather *abritan*.

More recently, an Islamised etymology has been suggested. This posits that *abangan* derives from *aba'an*, derived from the Arabic verb *aba* (to reject, refuse). This etymology is unacceptable on 3 grounds: (1) It is grammatically unsound. (2) At the time the term emerged, contemporary sources describe it as meaning "red", not "rejectors, refusers". (3) Again, in *krama* Javanese the term is *abritan*, whereas if it were from the Arabic, then we would expect the Arabic word to be used in both *ngoko* and *krama*.

It is important to emphasise that no evidence has come to light of a group known as the *abangan* in Java before the mid-nineteenth century. It is always risky to argue on the basis of something that is not seen in the historical evidence, for there is a chance that the phenomenon in question existed but went unrecorded, or that the evidence is limited and has not been noticed by historians. In this case, however, we may proceed with some confidence. Pre-nineteenth century Javanese history is recorded in many thousands of pages of (mainly) Javanese- and Dutch-language literary works and archives. During the past century, these sources have been subjected to scrutiny by philologists and historians, although only a few of the latter. I have been studying these sources myself for 40 years and have read large volumes of both Dutch and Javanese sources over that time. As is true of anyone who began the study of Java, or Indonesia more generally, in the 1960s, I was much impressed by Clifford Geertz's book *The religion of Java*.[2] Geertz divided Javanese society into three variants, the *santri* (those who in this book are called the *putihan*), the *abangan* and the *priyayi*. When Geertz and his colleagues did their fieldwork and *The religion of Java* was published, these categories were thought of as an abiding way of classifying Javanese society with roots deep in the ancient past. So I set off on my study of Javanese history expecting to see the *abangan* everywhere and curious to learn what could be known of them in earlier times. But they never appeared. Not until my research touched sources from the mid-nineteenth century did I encounter any sign of the *abangan* existing as a social category. The term used for the opposite category, the *putihan*, was well attested in earlier sources as a collective term for the professionally religious, also known as the *kaum*. But there was no sign of the *abangan* in earlier sources.

The first edition of the standard Javanese-Dutch dictionary by J.F.C. Gericke and T. Roorda, published in 1847, does not contain a definition for a social group called *abangan* or *abritan*. It has an entry for *abang* (red), with subentries for *abang tuwa/abrit sĕpuh* (crimson) and *ngabangake/ngabritakĕn* (make red, paint red), but no entry for a social group.[3] By the time of the final edition of 1901, however, we find what had become the meaning by then:

---

[2] Clifford Geertz, *The religion of Java* (Glencoe: The Free Press, 1964); first published in 1960.

[3] J.F.C. Gericke & T. Roorda, *Javaansch-Nederduitsch woordenboek* (Amsterdam: Johannes Müller, 1847), p. 79.

> In the red, *which is what the santris call an ungodly person who does not carry out his religious obligations (probably from the red or colourful clothing and the red lips from chewing betel), in contrast to the* wong putihan, *as the santris call themselves.*[4]

It is reasonable to conclude therefore that this social category either did not exist at all before the mid-nineteenth century or, if it did, was of such marginal significance that there are insufficient references in the historical record for anyone to have noticed them. I argued in my book *Mystic synthesis in Java* — summarised in Chapter 1 above — that by the early nineteenth century the synthesis of firm Islamic identity, observation of Islam's five pillars and acceptance of indigenous spiritual forces, all within the capacious boundaries of what Javanese understood Sufism to be, was found not only among the elite but also — so far as we can see from the very limited evidence — among Javanese commoners.[5] There does not seem to have been a social category of people who rejected Islam's pillars who were called *abangan* or anything else. Yet by late in the nineteenth century, as will be seen below, it seems that such *abangan* constituted the majority of Javanese. This was a significant social change with major consequences, calling for explanation. Thus, in this chapter we are considering the emergence of both (a) a new group within Javanese society — those who began to distance themselves from what seems to have been a previously widespread commitment to Islamic identity and orthopraxy — and (b) a new term to describe them — the *abangan*.

It is interesting to note, *en passant*, how fortuitous patterns of scholarship have shaped views of Javanese society on the part of both Javanese themselves and external observers. It seems that the dichotomy between *abangan* and *putihan* emerged around the mid-nineteenth century and it is one of the purposes of this book to show how those categories became clearer and harder down to the early twentieth century. By the time that Geertz and his colleagues did their research in the 1950s, those categories — only a century old in some places, and probably much less than that where the Geertz team worked — seemed to be so profound that they must be very old, deeply rooted and enduring. And so they

[4] J.F.C. Gericke & T. Roorda, *Javaansch-ederlandsch handoordenboek* (revised ed.; ed. A.C. Vreede and H. Gunning; 2 vols.; Amsterdam: Johannes Müller; Leiden: E.J. Brill, 1901), vol. I, pp. 197–8.
[5] Ricklefs, *Mystic synthesis*, pp. 204–5, 214–7.

came to be regarded, ironically just when (as I hope to show in a later book) the categories were approaching their final, violent culmination, thereafter to diminish as ways of organising Javanese society. A fluid, contingent social reality was perceived as fixed because no one had yet done the historical research to show that it was not so. The anthropological interest in social structures and relationships gave insufficient attention to historical contingencies and a view of Javanese society was born that implied that there was little change. This idea was often extended more generally, and frequently inappropriately, to the rest of Indonesian society. On the basis of this illusory — sometimes called "traditional" — society, scholarly analyses, political strategies and social policies alike were erected.

A note on the historical sources that are used in this chapter is needed, for they are dominated by a type of evidence that some readers may find surprising, the reports of Dutch Christian missionaries. Christian missions were first allowed to operate among Javanese society in the nineteenth century. Below we will use evidence from men such as W. Hoezoo who lived in Sĕmarang from 1849 until his death in 1896, Samuel Eliza Harthoorn and D.J. ten Zeldam Ganswijk who arrived in Java in 1854 and both of whom eventually resigned because they could no longer support the approach of the Netherlands Missionary Society (NZG), and Carel Poensen who came in 1860 and spent over 30 years in Java. Because they came as pioneers of the Christian missions, such men inherited little background knowledge about Javanese society. They had much to learn and no doubt often misunderstood what they saw. Their aim was to convert Javanese to Christianity and they therefore often saw Islam as an opponent. The missionaries, in other words, often arrived in Java bearing piety, ignorance and prejudice. Harthoorn's 1865 book on education in Indonesia, for example, reflected his animosity towards all things Arabic, Islamic or superstitious, and his view of the Javanese as a people of a low level of civilisation who were readily shaped by outside influences.[6] When the missionaries' accounts were intended for publication in their journal *Mededeelingen van wege het Nederlandsche Zendelinggenootschap*, they no doubt wrote fully aware that they would mainly be read by a devout Christian readership, which presumably influenced the content of their writing.

Despite their limitations, however, mission records have advantages as sources for the study of history. The missionaries often lived for a

---

[6] S.E. Harthoorn, *De toestand en de behoeften van het onderwijs bij de volken van Neêrlands Oost-Indie* (Haarlem: A.C. Kruseman, 1865).

significant period in Java and commanded the language to a reasonable standard. They communicated with each other both by correspondence and by publication in the mission journal *MNZG* and in other outlets. They had contact with other Europeans and Indo-Europeans with scholarly expertise about Java and Javanese. For example, when Hoezoo made a trip to Surakarta in 1851, he met J.F.C. Gericke (1799–1857), C.F. Winter Sr (1799–1859), J.A. Wilkens (1813–80) and A.B. Cohen Stuart (d. 1876) there, all of them significant figures in the early study of Javanese.[7] The missionaries had an interest in observing Javanese society as accurately as they could, for only on the basis of such observation could a successful mission strategy be conceived. Most were, thus, relatively educated, direct observers of Javanese society with a professional interest in religious matters, local experience, Javanese informants, and a command of Javanese. If their evidence is approached with caution, as historians should approach all evidence, it constitutes a treasure house of social history.

While we will refer to several missionaries in this chapter, particular importance attaches to Carel Poensen, who spent almost all of 30 years in Kĕdiri in East Java. It was also to the Kĕdiri area that Geertz and his colleagues would go for fieldwork 60 years after Poensen left, so that we have more information about the dichotomy between *putihan* and *abangan* in Kĕdiri than anywhere else in Java. Poensen was born in Amsterdam in 1836 but received little education in his youth. In 1855, at the age of 19, he was accepted as a trainee by the NZG. He was put on a ship to Java in 1860. In 1862 he was dispatched to Kĕdiri to replace Hendrik Smeding, who had been there since 1858 but had to be repatriated for health reasons. Poensen stayed in Kĕdiri until 1889 in the first instance. He was strongly committed to the local Christian community and declined an offer to take up a teaching post at the Gymnasium Willem III in Batavia in 1875. His views of Islam and of Muslim Javanese were balanced for his time, without overt prejudice. In 1889 Poensen repatriated to the Netherlands for health reasons and then, upon recovery, returned to Kĕdiri in 1890. But this time he stayed only until 1891, when he left to take up a position as Professor of Javanese at the Koninklijke Akademie for training Indies civil servants in Delft.[8] He published several scholarly works before his death in 1919. Thus,

---

[7] W. Hoezoo, Sĕmarang, to Bestuurders NZG, Rotterdam, 20 Sept. 1851 in ARZ 210.
[8] Biographical note in ARZ 261.

Poensen was an unusually well-informed and scholarly observer of Javanese society. But it must be said that he was not of the intellectual standard of the scholarly giant of his generation, Christiaan Snouck Hurgronje (1857–1936) who, indeed, did not hold Poensen's work in high regard. Poensen's letters in the Utrecht mission archive show that his prose was often rewritten before publication in *MNZG*. His scholarly publications are useful but somewhat pedestrian. His lack of early education and the long years of intellectual isolation in Kĕdiri probably limited his analytical capacities. His writings are thus a resource of great value for the purposes of this book but they are not to be regarded as authoritative in all respects.

The First References

The earliest references I have found to the *abangan* are from 1855. One is in a Christian tract that Hoezoo translated from Javanese into Dutch in that year in Sĕmarang. He treated the term *abangan* here as meaning people who were profane or secular. The tract depicted people who held communal meals (*slamĕtan*) but did not gain well-being (*slamĕt*), who got distressed when things went wrong, who couldn't get along with their neighbours or their families "and don't think that this just happens among the profane (*tiang abangan*, actually the reds); even among my friends who are religious (*tiang poetian*, actually the whites) it is so". Hoezoo's tract of course recommended Jesus as the cure for such woes.[9] A second reference from that year is in a report by Harthoorn from Majawarna, near Jombang in East Java. He wrote of the activities of a minority of Javanese who were pious Muslims; "the holy people, the *bangsa putihan*, while the others belong to the red people, the *bangsa abangan*".[10]

The following year Ganswijk reported from Kĕdiri, where he was then posted. He perceived a generally lax approach among Javanese to Islamic prohibitions, yet asserted that Islam was nevertheless a significant presence in their lives. And he reported on the emerging social division:

> Whoever among ordinary Javanese is, for whatever reason, attracted
> to religion, then takes himself to a school where an aged Javanese

---

[9] W. Hoezoo, Sĕmarang, 16 Feb. 1855, in ARZ 210.
[10] S.E. Harthoorn, "Iets over den Javaanschen Mohammedaaan en den Javaanschen Christen", *MNZG* 1 (1857): 192.

teaches reading, praying, singing, etc. in Arabic. Then he goes to the mosque and no longer belongs to the lay "red population" (*bangsa abangan*), "the stupid multitude who don't know the law", but rather to the *bangsa putihan* (the white stock, the holy ones).

Through the influence of the *pěsantrens* and their *santri* students, Ganswijk wrote, "Islam ever more penetrates the spirit of the population".[11] It will be seen below, however, that it was many years before Poensen reported on an *abangan-putihan* distinction in Kědiri, so it is possible that Ganswijk was reporting on what he understood to be the case in some other places in Java, rather than specifically about Kědiri.

In his annual report from Malang for the year 1856, Harthoorn reported a different, but related, distinction among Javanese. He said that learned Muslims drew a contrast between *ilmu santrian* (mystical science of the students of religion), which was true Islam, and *ilmu pasek* (non-Islamic mystical science), which was not.[12] In fact, the former was mixed with the latter, noted Harthoorn, and what really distinguished the devotees of *ilmu santrian* was that they observed the five daily prayers. "In the ... village religious school they learn Arabic formulas and a few other things connected with Islam, from the *wayang*..., from a guru and from reading indigenous Javanese works they learn the tenets of the old faith of the Javanese, Buddhism." Thus, Harthoorn was describing what here we call the mystic synthesis of Java. But he also observed in Malang the emerging challenge to this synthesis. "This wavering between the old (Buddhist) and new (Mohammedan) belief is the source of much dispute and discord."[13] So while he did not then report the existence of an *abangan-putihan* categorisation in Malang, as he had with regard to Majawarna the year before, he saw the roots of it there.

In 1860, Harthoorn published an article particularly concerning Malang, in which he described the *abangan-putihan* distinction as an

---

[11] D.J. ten Zeldam Ganswijk, "Beantwoording der jaarvragen" for 1856, Kědiri [early 1857], in ARZ 209.

[12] From Arabic *fasiq*, defined in Hans Wehr, *A dictionary of modern written Arabic*, ed. Milton J. Cowan (Ithaca, NY: Cornell University Press, 1961), p. 713, as "godless, sinful, dissolute, wanton, licentious, profligate, vicious, iniquitous, nefarious; trespasser, offender, sinner; fornicator, adulterer; a person not meeting the legal requirements of righteousness".

[13] S.E. Harthoorn, annual report for 1856, Malang n.d. (received Rotterdam 10 April 1857), in ARZ 259.

emerging phenomenon, in response to the spread of Islamic revivalism. He wrote,

> The number of *santris* (fancy and dilettante theologians) is great and constantly grows. That is understandable, for ... they are freed of compulsory services, which has greatly helped the spread of Muhammad's ideas.... These *santris* and all who observe the prayer times are called "the white people", "the holy people", in contrast to the great multitude, who take no part in this and therefore are scornfully called "the red people".

The editor of the *MNZG*, where the article was published, added a footnote saying, "This expression concerning the white people and the red people is also common in the same sense in the Sĕmarang area, as is clear from the reports of the missionary Hoezoo."[14] That footnote seems to confirm the view taken in this chapter that this was new information in the 1850s, not something known to exist widely in Java at that time.

In these early years, the meanings of *abangan* and *putihan*, and the social realities that attached to these terms, were still fluid. When in 1861 Hoezoo went to Majawarna, the site of one of the earliest Christian communities, he found this to be so. By this time Hoezoo had been over twelve years in Java and was a seasoned observer, familiar with the *abangan-putihan* distinction as he had seen it in Sĕmarang. He found that in Majawarna the Javanese Christians were calling their Muslim fellows — however pious — both *wong abangan* and *wong kapir* (infidels), while they named themselves *wong putihan*. This was, said Hoezoo, "stupid vainglory".[15]

A report in the Javanese newspaper *Jurumatani* in 1867 also seems to reflect social fluidity or fluidity of terminology. The story concerned a conflict — not about religious issues — between a village religious, a *kaum dhusun* who was a *kyai*, and his son-in-law who was an *abangan* (*tiyang abritan*) named Pun Diman, himself the son of another *kyai*.[16] Given that the term *kaum dhusun* — so far as I am aware — can only have applied to a member of the Islamic *putihan*, this suggests surprising family circumstances in which an *abangan* was both the son of a *kyai*

---

[14] Harthoorn, "Zending op Java", p. 237.
[15] W. Hoezoo, "Verslag mijner werkzaamheden en bevindingen over het jaar 1861", Majawarna, 21 Mar. 1862, in ARZ 210; also in *MNZG* 7 (1863): 178.
[16] *BM* 13 June 1867.

and the son-in-law of another. This raises considerable questions about
the social reality, or perhaps the meaning of the term *abangan*, then to
be found in Java. When social categories and their labels became
more fixed in Java, it became almost inconceivable that the son of a *kyai*
and the son-in-law of a *kyai* could be anything other than a member of
the *putihan*. A similarly interesting story was printed over several issues
of *Bramartani* in 1879. This was a long poem in Javanese verse in which
one "former *kaum* Nur Yakimbalaka" told how he had been a *santri* for
eight years, then "became *abangan* (*abritan*) again".[17] This suggests
social fluidity but at least clarity of terminology as of 1879. Nur Yakimbalaka's poem will be discussed at greater length in Chapter 6 below.

Despite the evident fluidity in this matter, some missionaries were
confident of their understanding of the *abangan-putihan* distinction.
"The *santris* call themselves *bangsa putihan*, the whites, the consecrated.
The great multitude they curse as the *bangsa abangan*, the reds, the
impure", wrote Harthoorn in 1865.[18] Thus the *putihan* were the minority,
indeed the minority we saw in the previous chapter who were pressing
for more Islamic orthodoxy and orthopraxy, as they understood them.
Abangan was a term of derision used by that minority to characterise the
majority, who did not share their enthusiasm for more fastidious forms
of Islam.

In 1869 Poensen wrote from Kĕdiri about Javanese name-giving
practices. In the course of that discussion, he commented that "the
Javanese divide themselves into *bangsa putihan* and *bangsa abangan*,
although they are all Mohammedans".[19] No further details followed
except a footnote comment that the pious were a small minority in
Javanese society, as was true in all societies. This was Poensen's earliest
reference to the *abangan*, so far as I am aware. It is curious that in his
voluminous, detailed writings on Javanese society over the coming years
based on his own observations, he did not again refer to the existence
of the *abangan* until the early 1880s. This raises the suspicion that in
1869 he knew of these categories from the observations of other
missionaries, but had not yet seen it himself in Kĕdiri so could not yet
describe it in detail.

---

[17] *BM* 1 May, 8 May, 15 May, 29 May 1879. There was presumably more of this
in the issue of 22 May, and there was more to follow after 29 May, but those issues
are missing from the set in PNRI.
[18] Harthoorn, *Onderwijs*, p. 40.
[19] C. Poensen, "Iets over Javaansche naamgeving en eigennamen", *MNZG* 14 (1870):
312 (dd. Kĕdiri, 1869).

Curious Silences

Not all missionaries seem to have noted the *abangan* and *putihan* categories described by some in the 1850s and 1860s. The missionaries knew each other and corresponded directly and the reports of people like Hoezoo and Harthoorn were published in the *MNZG*, where they were read by other missionaries. That being so, failure to report this phenomenon on the part of some missionaries cannot be explained by them being unaware that such a distinction might exist.

In his annual report for 1863, when he had been in Kĕdiri for little over a year, Poensen wrote at length on the religious life of the Javanese.[20] They had little understanding of the principles of Islam, he wrote, and were still influenced by Hindu-Buddhist ideas. Javanese recognised multiple spiritual beings in their lives, including local spirits and demons and major figures such as the Goddess of the Southern Ocean, Rara Kidul. There were multiple sects within Javanese Islam, following various mystical sciences (*ngelmu*). These *ngelmus* were distinguished from religion proper, which Javanese called *agama*. Christianity had at first been seen as just another *ngelmu*, Poensen reported. The serious followers of *agama Islam* were characterised by circumcising their children, holding *slamĕtans*, rejecting pork, and so on. There were many professional Islamic religious, a number that Poensen put at 60,000 men, "the standing army of Islam".

> Although the *santris* and other religious must be regarded as the champions, maintainers and truest followers of Islam, one must not, however, regard them together as a precisely exclusive caste or think that they agree in all things or punctiliously observe Islamic religious obligations. That is far from the case.

Not a few of these religious, said Poensen, even neglected the five daily prayers and insisted that God only cared about one's inner spiritual state, not one's outward conduct. But these circumstances were changing:

> Yes, we have already come to the conclusion that the Javanese heart is still inclined towards paganism, not yet penetrated by Moham-medanism. We should not readily assert that it will always remain so, for Mohammedanism is a power in itself which ... will more and more

---

[20] C. Poensen, annual report for 1863, Kĕdiri, Jan. 1864, in ARZ 261; also "Een en ander over den godsdienstigen toestand van den Javaan (uit een verslag over 1863, van C. Poensen, zendeling te Kediri)", *MNZG* 8 (1864): 214–63; 9 (1865): 161–202.

influence, and is influencing, the Javanese world, until it entirely penetrates the organism of the moral and spiritual life of the Javanese
world.

In this report, Poensen — who would have known of the accounts of
the other missionaries quoted above — did not report on an *abangan-
putihan* distinction. As noted above, he specifically denied that "the
santris and other religious" should be regarded as "as a precisely exclusive
caste".

This silence about an *abangan-putihan* distinction is notable in
other documents from the 1850s to 1870s. One of the most famous
books of the time was a description of four trips around Java, from
Batavia in the west to many destinations in Central and East Java,
undertaken c. 1858 by the *Bupati* of Kudus Condranĕgara V (c. 1836–
85). Under the pseudonym Purwalĕlana (the first traveler), his accounts
were first published in 1865. He described many groups and classes
across the island but, to the best of my knowledge, he did not report
the existence of a category known as *abangan* among his fellow Javanese.[21]
When Samuel Keijzer, then professor at the Koninklijke Akademie in
Delft, published a book in 1860 emphasising Islamic matters, he nowhere
referred to an *abangan-putihan* distinction amongst Javanese.[22] In a
typically long-winded account written in 1870, Poensen again refered
to *santris* as religious students, but made no mention of a distinction
between *abangan* and *putihan*.[23] In his three-volume study of Java
published between 1875 and 1882, P.J. Veth relied heavily on missionary
reports in *MNZG*, "among which above all stand out the communications
of Mr Harthoorn, who later withdrew from the mission enterprise, and
of Mr Poensen, who remained faithful to it with heartfelt love".[24] But
Veth did not mention a category called *abangan*. And, as will be seen
below, he shortly changed his estimate of Poensen, too.

It would be wrong to conclude from these curious silences that the
observers who reported an *abangan-putihan* distinction were misinformed,

---

[21] Purwalĕlana, *Lampah-lampahipun*. I have not read all of Purwalĕlana. Rather, I
rely on Bonneff, *Pérégrinations*, who does not refer to a social category called *abangan*
in his translation. Using Bonneff as a guide, I have also searched parts of the original
Javanese text where the *abangan* category might be found and encountered nothing.
[22] Keijzer, *Onze tijd in Indië*.
[23] C. Poensen, "De Javanen en het evangelie", Kĕdiri, Jan. 1870, in ARZ 261; also
in *MNZG* 14 (1870): 123–216.
[24] Veth, *Java*, vol. I (published 1875), p. 312.

or that the writers who did not were unobservant. Rather, two other conclusions seem more attractive. The first is that the *abangan-putihan* distinction was still developing in this period and was a noteworthy social reality in some places and not in others. It is interesting in this regard that the earliest reports came from Sěmarang, where Islamic reform and revival movements were particularly prominent at the time, as was noted in the previous chapter. Since it seems clear that *abangan* was initially a pejorative term used by those who prided themselves on their superior piety and purity, it would not be surprising if this categorisation emerged earliest where Islamic reform movements were strongest. It is not clear, however, why Malang should also make an early appearance in this regard. The second conclusion is safer. That is, that dividing Javanese society into *putihan* and *abangan* was not yet a universal, normal, or even very common way of describing that society. It was to become so, but as of the 1870s it was not yet.

The 1880s

In the preceding chapter, the 1880s were seen as a period of ferment in pious Islamic circles. The *hajj* continued to supply large numbers of Javanese who had been exposed to developments in the Middle East; the *hajj akbar* years of 1880, 1885 and 1888 doing so particularly. The number of *pěsantrens* and of *santris* studying in them grew and remained high. The Naqshabandiyya and Qadiriyya wa Naqshabandiyya were spreading. In 1881 an alleged anti-Christian plot of 'Abd al-Muttalib in Mecca and the rise of the Mahdist movement in Sudan gave impetus to messianic ideas, as did the new Islamic century beginning in 1882 and the eruption of Krakatau in 1883. It would be consistent with the hypothesis of this book if this growing pressure for reform and revival from Islamic circles generated an opposite reaction, a social response like Newton's third law of physics. We should thus perhaps not be surprised if, as reform and revival movements became more apparent, so did Javanese who were not prepared to embrace them. At the village level, these were the *abangan*. In subsequent chapters we will see that some villagers went beyond this to become Christians, while the *priyayi* elite embraced a new world of discovery which was distant from, and largely hostile to, the demands of Islamic reformers.

In the 1880s Poensen reported on the *abangan-putihan* distinction, evidently on the basis of what he had by then observed in Kědiri. In 1883 he published anonymously a series of "letters from a villager" in the newspaper *Soerabajasche Handelsblad* concerning Islam in the interior of Java. Poensen provided this material to the Leiden publisher E.J. Brill intending that it be published anonymously as a book with the same title. But Brill brought the volume out in 1886 employing the title "letters concerning Islam from the interior of Java" (*Brieven over den Islām uit de binnenlanden van Java*), with Poensen named as the author. Poensen's *Brieven* are a valuable resource, but they provoked criticism that he found distressing. He wrote to the head of the mission house in Rotterdam,

> Dr Snouck Hurgronje has led me to feel, certainly in a more charitable fashion than did Prof. Veth, but not thereby any less clearly, that this is not "my field". And Prof. Veth adds to that that I write the Dutch language far too poorly to be able to contribute anything to scholarship. Was not my writing "even for epistolary style rather too disjointed"? And what followed after that! ... *Sudah!* [Enough!] ... But *I* will never do such a thing again.[25]

However distressing the publication experience was for Poensen, the information in his *Brieven* from the early 1880s remains valuable as first-hand observation from Kĕdiri, if not as deep analytical scholarship. He described a dynamic situation, with the reforming impulse of Islam gaining ground. His description of this merits quoting at some length:

> We have already noted that the *pĕsantren* and the pilgrimage constantly spread true concepts about the spirit and the essence of Islam among the populace.... The "great majority" ... living in ignorance, error and poverty, especially in the eastern and southern parts of the island, indeed know little more about Islam than that circumcision of children,

---

[25] C. Poensen, Kĕdiri, to J.C. Neurdenburg, Rotterdam, 14 Dec. 1886, in ARZ 148. Two years before, Poensen had written to Neurdenburg to express respect for Snouck Hurgronje's scholarship but dismay at his style of expression. The occasion was Snouck's criticism of Van den Berg's 1882 article on "De Mohammedaansche geestelijkheid". Poensen wrote, "I don't know the man personally.... I have learned *much* from his writings.... But I am not actually alone in feeling that his tone of writing is rather unpleasant, not to use a stronger word.... He is in any case still too young, and ought to be too courteous, to write in such a fashion. What he says about Christianity and missions I leave unmentioned! But how I, as a Christian and a missionary, should look upon him on the basis of his writings, I do not know. His scholarship and learning cannot cover up *everything*"; C. Poensen, Kĕdiri, to J.C. Neurdenburg, Rotterdam, 18 Sept. 1884, in ARZ 148.

fasting, and eating no pork are a part of Islam, that there are a *Garĕbĕg Bĕsar* and a *Garĕbĕg Mulud*[26] and a couple of other festivals, that everything *priyayi* is Mohammedan, as is self-evidently so, and that all Christians are *kapir-londo* [Dutch infidels]....

The consequence of these circumstances must necessarily be that Islam becomes progressively firmer among "the great majority", and its teachings progressively better known: the populace will become progressively better Mohammedans.... In the meantime it is clear that the more Islam is fostered and cared for, and everything in public and official life is given an Islamic color from the top, the *inner* life must also come under its influence....

In connection with the pilgrimage becoming ever easier and the rapidly increasing communications with Arabia, Islam is striking ever-firmer roots in Java.... Indeed, all members of the *bangsa putihan* circles feel themselves from the beginning at one with the Arabs — even though the latter cheat the natives!.... The religiously Islamic Javanese feels himself to be one *ummah* [community] with the Arabs and all other Muslim peoples.... That is constantly strengthened by the arrival of Arabs and their residence in Java, by circumcision and its associated festivals, by the *langgars* [prayer houses] and *pĕsantrens*, and by the pilgrimage to Mecca not least!...

The title *haji* is very highly regarded and valued in the circle of *bangsa putihan*. A common villager will step aside for a *haji*.... He feels himself to be a *haji*; he has ceased to be Javanese — he is a *haji*! By means of the pilgrimage, Islam has turned him into a citizen of the world....

A Muslim should pray! ... In Java the ... *salat* [prayer] in general, the fulfilling of the five daily prayers, and joining in with the Friday service ... are distinguishing characteristics of the *bangsa putihan*.... The great majority, the *bangsa abangan* ... never pray; indeed they would not be able to do it. For if a Muslim wishes to pray properly, he must have learned a good deal by heart and have practiced the kneeling and bowing. The great majority of Javanese never pray.... That is, not as Mohammedans.[27]

Thus, Poensen depicted the Javanese society with which he was familiar as one in which the reforming and revivalist forces of Islam held

---

[26] Two of the three annual Javanese Islamic festivals. *Garĕbĕg Bĕsar* commemorates Abraham's willingness to sacrifice his son and the pilgrimage to Mecca and *Garĕbĕg Mulud* celebrates the birth of the Prophet. The third, *Garĕbĕg Puasa*, celebrates the end of the fasting month.

[27] Poensen, *Brieven*, pp. 4–6, 8, 9, 65–6, 68, 163, 172.

the initiative — a picture already familiar from the preceding chapter. The followers of this more pious Islam were, however, a minority. And Poensen saw them as distancing themselves from the majority of Javanese society. That majority, for whom Poensen now used the term *abangan*, was progressively being influenced by reformed Islam's message but amongst them were also many who were ignorant of, and indifferent to, that message.

Poensen's *Brieven* and other writings of the 1880s went into detail on the *abangan-putihan* division. It is again worth reading some of his observations directly:

> The population divides itself into two classes, the *bangsa putihan* and the *bangsa abangan*. The first of these consists of a relatively small number of persons, whom we may call "the pious", the orthodox Mohamamedans, although one may dispute their orthodoxy. The other are the great majority, who do not think or live in a Mohammedan-religious fashion, but rather as they have learned from their forefathers.[28]
>
> Indeed the ordinary villager passes by the mosque without dropping in or thinking of Allah; he lets the *bangsa putihan* worship Allah and visit the mosque…. Praying and going to the mosque and reading the *Qur'an* are religious duties for a particular class of people indicated with the term *bangsa putihan* — *santris*, *hajis*, those who are attached to services at the mosque — they have to observe all of that! And all other Javanese, that is to say the great majority of the people, are together termed the *bangsa abangan*.[29]

Poensen's most extensive accounts of this social dichotomy — indeed the most important accounts from any source in the nineteenth century — were his descriptions of "the Javanese as a person" and "the Javanese family" written in Kĕdiri in 1884 and 1886. Poensen wrote at excessive length, as always — a function perhaps of there being few other diversions in 1880s Kĕdiri. Only the key passages for our purpose are quoted below.

In describing "the Javanese as a person", Poensen importantly depicted a dynamic process, as the Javanese society around him changed.

> The influence of Islam is active in ever greater degree, at the cost of the previous religious life…. The truth is that, indeed, very many people are ever more penetrated by Arabic or Islamic concepts in a

---

[28] Ibid., p. 7.
[29] C. Poensen, "Iets over den Javaan als mensch", Kĕdiri, July 1884, in ARZ 261; also in *MNZG* 29 (1885): 49, 137.

more or less unrecognised way. But among the great majority there flows another current[30] which, under the influence of present circumstances, causes the previous — in many ways naïve — religion more and more to be lost to the people. Basically, people are beginning to become less religious and pious....

There are many influences to be noted. For example, those associated with interaction with European society; the activities of the European government; the many native lower schools;[31] these are all to be regarded as so many forces working without interruption to pull down and destroy religious life. The congenial — one might say convivial — aspects of the old religion can neither be carried on nor developed by Islam. For that, it has become too official for the Javanese soul. It concerns itself, for example, with marriage, divorce, inheritance, jurisprudence, etc. — too much with the material life of the natives.... *Ngelmu*, especially the higher, mystical *ngelmu*, disappears more and more, and with it the *ngelmu*-seekers. ... But the new *ngelmu-sarengat*[32] hasn't as a result yet replaced the old. It is unlike it. The new *ngelmu* is much too burdensome, too bookish, and that in a foreign language! The higher *ngelmu* they [the Muslims] have never been able to imitate or to replace; not even Sufism with its own mysticism and formulae [has been able to do this].... The newer *ngelmus* have only fostered a superficial, vapid superstition, but they will also find their death in the general irreligious current of our time....

In Mohammedan religious circles, among the *bangsa putihan*, ... the children already display the type of environment that is called *ngibadah* [pious]. They usually go every day to *ngaji* [recite the *Qur'an*] with a guru. If the education is successful, they'll be able to read a book in *pegon* [Javanese written in Arabic script], but not a purely Javanese book [in Javanese script]. Above all, Javanese *maca* [reading, especially verse] has fallen into disdain there. In these circles one hears many Arabic words used and one can see the influence of Islam in all respects — not only clothing and personal names.[33]

Thus, this was a society in the midst of drawing apart. As the devout Muslims became more pious, the *abangan* were "beginning to become

---

[30] Poensen's term is *stroom*, which in modern Indonesian would be translated as *aliran*, the term that was indeed used for these political-social-religious categories in the twentieth century.

[31] Discussed in Chapter 6 below.

[32] Islam is meant, the term *ngelmu sarengat* literally meaning the science of *shari'a*.

[33] C. Poensen, "Iets over den Javaan als mensch", Kědiri, July 1884, in ARZ 261; also in *MNZG* 29 (1885): 117–9, 139.

less religious and pious". Education was, as always, part of this. The young *putihan* were learning to read the *Qur'an* and, if successful, would be able to read a work in Arabic script but not one in Javanese script. As will be seen in Chapter 6 below, at the same time non-*putihan* schools were educating children who could read Javanese but not Arabic script. A society drawing apart on religious grounds was also producing children who literally could not communicate with each other, at least in writing, and probably in more profoundly cultural ways as well.

Regarding the Javanese family, Poensen observed,

> The moral and religious life of the native family is not the same everywhere. First, we have to think of the families whose members wish to be reckoned to belong to the *bangsa putihan*. To a greater or lesser extent, these all stand under Arabic or Muslim influences, genially mixed with a great deal left over from the previous Hinduism. Then we have the families of the *bangsa abangan*, that is, the great majority, who certainly do not live outside the influence of Islam, but who more or less completely neglect the rituals of Islam and who practice, so to speak, a household religion. And finally there is a class whose families may also be counted among the *bangsa abangan*, where all morality and religion are as good as expelled....
>
> In the *bangsa putihan* families there reigns a not-to-be-denied religious tone. The older members of the family practice more or less meticulously the prescriptions of Islam. They receive people of a similar persuasion in their homes, read and discuss Mohammedan texts and discuss among one another the affairs of the Mohammedan world. Household festivals and ceremonies are maintained in the company of the like-minded, and they invite *santris* to celebrate the functions in a religious way. They are in every way religious, right down to their superstitions, which acquire a peculiar Mohammedan tint via Arabic formulas and actions. In their clothing, amulets, speech, in practicing or avoiding this or that, in a word in their entire type, there reigns something Javanese-Mohammedan, just as at heart they entertain far more superstitions than others.
>
> In many of these families there reigns a certain prosperity, or they attempt at least to maintain their standing respectably. Thus, they readily engage in trade, lend money, buy the harvest of the fields of the "little man" by advance payment and, if nothing else can be done, manage to see to their needs in various other remarkable ways. So a certain refinement in their houses, clothing and manners immediately strikes one and very, very many of these use no opium and do not gamble. But they make a great deal of festivals and religious proceedings

and of circumcisions and marriages — sometimes too much, even leading to extravagance.

The child in these families ... grows up under the influence of these conditions.... As an adult, it is just as much a member of the *bangsa putihan* as Dutch people are Christians by birth, baptism and upbringing.... Discipline in these families is often very strict, although naturally that varies according to the personality and character of the various parents....

Morally they undoubtedly stand, generally speaking, far above the great majority. But their manner of living, their environment, a certain worldly wisdom, greater intellectual development and a natural aptitude or inclination to calculating transactions, which also becomes shrewdness and deftness, naturally give them a certain ascendancy over the "little man". Thus, for the village population many of these can become in a certain sense the same sort of blood-suckers as the Chinese often are. That also explains the unfavorable opinion of this class on the part of the European world, sometimes correct and well grounded, often without foundation and resting upon the prattle of others, or on a personal unfavorable experience. That all of them [the *putihan*] reveal a strongly pronounced antagonism towards the European-Christian world is true, and naturally so....

Fortunately we can say that the greater part of the population far and away does not belong to this class. The great majority indeed lives under the influence of Islam ... but they lack the *bangsa putihan* type; they are called the *bangsa abangan*. In the families of the *bangsa abangan* the child is also born and raised under religious-superstitious influences, to which Mohammedanism is certainly not foreign, but that which is typical of the *bangsa putihan* is completely absent. ...

Of Mohammedan-religious proceedings, such as the prayer, there is nothing to be seen in family life. The to and fro of society lead to all boys being circumcised, many observe the fast and every bridegroom ... memorises the formula he must know if he wants to be married in the *surambi*.[34] Where the custom of the village requires it, on the first of the month Sawal a father and his brood will go to pay his *pitrah* [religious tax] to his *kyai-modin* or guru, and in the fasting month the youths and their mates will happily follow their elders to join the five *malĕmans*[35] at the house of the village head.... In this way people show themselves to be Muslims. Their social environment, with the village head at the top, would take it much amiss if someone wished to withdraw from that....

---

[34] The front gallery of a mosque, where a legal court held sessions.
[35] The communal meals (*sidhĕkah malĕman*) on certain nights of the fasting month.

After all, here people think and act more in an old Hindu-Javanese spirit. Among them are found those who uphold the *ngelmu gunungan* [mountain mystical knowledge], also called *ngelmu pasek* [non-Islamic mystical knowledge], who are to be found only and exclusively in this class....

Catechetic or religious education is never given to the members of these families. As opportunity arises and as if by chance the child is told and explained what is allowed or not allowed.... But the hearing of much that is immoral, or in general downright evil, in the discourse of a *dhalang* [puppeteer] in a *wayang* performance and attending parties such as *tandhakan, nayuban* and *ludrukan*[36] etc. ... destroy again much of the good that they may have heard in the home, where they are in general not always cautious and fastidious about dealing with sexual matters in the presence of children....

One can grasp what we are intending to say here: in all these families there is an absence of any profound, religious-moral tone in daily intercourse.[37]

So the differences in approach to Islam mirrored more general social differences. The *putihan* were wealthier, active in business, better dressed, had better homes, seemed more refined in manners, avoided opium and gambling, observed the pillars of Islam, gave their children more education and disciplined them more. The *abangan* differed on these same points. They were poorer, were not involved in trade and did not provide their children with education. *Abangan* still observed some religious activities, but did so in the name of village solidarity. Whereas the *putihan* read Arabic works and discussed the Islamic world's affairs, the *abangan* watched *wayang* performances and attended lascivious entertainments. In the *wayang* in particular, Javanese spiritual forces were at work. The two groups mixed only with the like-minded. We might note, without surprise, that it was not only the Christian missionary Poensen who disapproved of the influence of such performances in the 1880s. Correspondence in *Bramartani* concerned *putihan* rejection of the *gamělan* as something forbidden (*karam*) in Islamic law.[38]

These were worlds far apart from one another and becoming more so. They were distinguished by social class, income, employment, dress,

---

[36] Performances by dancing women who were also prostitutes and comic folk theatre.
[37] C. Poensen, "Iets over het Javaansche gezin", Kědiri, Dec. 1886, in ARZ 161; also in *MNZG* 31 (1887): 252–60.
[38] *BM* 8 Nov. and 13 Dec. 1883, 17 Feb. 1891.

education, manners, cultural life and the mode of raising children. Insofar as commerce, money-lending, indebtedness and interpretations of piety provided the principle modes of interaction between these two worlds, their inherently conflicting interests could easily give rise to dislike and conflict. In the early twentieth century, this mix would be made more volatile by the addition of political competition.

The *Abangan* and the Pious *Putihan* Middle Class

The evidence of Poensen and others cited above enables us to draw some conclusions, despite the uncertainty and obscurity that necessarily surrounds the topic of this chapter. We are dealing with subtle but significant social changes that took place over several decades, probably at varying speeds in different parts of Java, with only a few really informative sources available. So we are bound to be left with many questions. Nevertheless, the sources that we do have can tell us much that is of interest.

We may reasonably conclude that the new middle class who emerged as beneficiaries of the economic developments described in Chapter 2, who drove the Islamic reform movements seen in Chapter 3, were not able to sweep all Javanese along with their dreams of a more Islamic society. While many Javanese were becoming more orthodox and pious in a variety of ways, far larger numbers were indifferent to the call of the reformers. But it is not only that they were failing to respond to the stricter demands of the reform movements. It seems that they were also abandoning their previous levels of Islamic observance. If the evidence from before 1830 is to be relied upon — and we must remember its limited nature — then prior to the nineteenth-century reform movements in Java, observance of the five pillars of Islam was common throughout Javanese society. Most Javanese, it seems, recited the confession of faith, fasted in Ramadan, paid the religious tax (*jakat*), and prayed. A small number who could afford to do so undertook the *hajj*. This observance of the ritual life of Islam was combined with a strong sense of Islam as the religious element in Javanese social identity and with acceptance of multiple local spiritual forces as real. This was the mystic synthesis of Java.

From the mid-nineteenth century onwards, significant change occurred. Of the main elements in the mystic synthesis — Islamic identity, observation of the five pillars, and acceptance of local spiritual powers, all within the context of Sufism — definition of the first, Islamic identity, was becoming a claimed monopoly on the part of the *putihan*. The second, observation of the five pillars, was their claimed ritual territory. In response, and in the context of a more general social differentiation, it seems that some Javanese — eventually the majority — began to abandon Islamic prayer and only observed other Islamic rituals in the name of community solidarity. In coming decades, even their commitment to these rituals would grow more attenuated.[39] The reformers held these people in contempt and castigated them as *abangan*. As these categories developed, the third element in the mystic synthesis, belief in local spiritual powers, was becoming the territory of the *abangan* alone.

But for most *abangan*, Islam was still the faith to which they adhered, however nominally, reluctantly or ignorantly. For a few, however, there was a new religion — at first conceived as a new *ngelmu*, said Poensen — that began to attract them. For the first time in history, some Javanese who were part of the community of Islam abandoned that faith altogether and embraced Christianity, as will be seen in the following chapter. Thus came about another element in the polarisation of Javanese society.

---

[39] Note the data cited in B.J. Boland, *The struggle of Islam in modern Indonesia* (*VKI* vol. 59; The Hague: Martinus Nijhoff, 1971), p. 186, that in the 1960s, in Central Javanese villages 0–15 per cent prayed; in 1967 only 14 per cent of the people of Yogyakarta paid *jakat* and only 2 per cent observed the fast.

5

Javanese Christian Communities

Until the middle years of the nineteenth century, there was no significant Christian mission effort in Java and there were no Javanese Christian communities. Then the first Javanese embraced Christianity. This was in the context of Dutch colonial rule, of course, so it might be tempting to presume that these first converts were embracing the religion of their rulers, with the implications carried by such an observation. It will be seen below, however, that while no doubt some Javanese were attracted to Christianity because it was the religion of their overlords, many also chose Christianity for a quite different reason: because it accommodated itself to Javanese identity and culture.

There was a notable contrast in the degree of success won by two different groups of Christian proselytisers. On the one hand were the European missionaries sent out by various Dutch mission societies. Some of these were collectively — and perhaps not always admiringly — dubbed "the saints of Surabaya". They won few converts, even after many years of effort. On the other hand were both pious Indo-European lay persons, who had personal roots in Javanese society and were bilingual, and some remarkable indigenous Javanese religious leaders. They won converts in large numbers, sometimes in the thousands. There is a message about culture and identity in this contrast and in that already seen in the previous two chapters. At this time, some versions of pious Islam were distancing themselves from Javanese culture, "denying their Javaneseness and at all costs bending their steps to Mecca in search of knowledge" as it was put in *Wedhatama*.[1] As a consequence, other Javanese — the emerging *abangan* majority — were distancing themselves from Islamic religious practices. On the Christian side, most European missionaries saw Javanese culture as a heathen legacy to be reformed or abolished. But the Indo-European and Javanese proselytisers, often looked down upon as insufficiently pure by the Europeans, embraced much of Javanese culture. As a result, there was sometimes a distinction drawn by Javanese between Christians who had been converted by European missionaries, who were called *Kristen Londo* (Dutch Christians), and those who were converted by Javanese proselytisers, who were called *Kristen Jawa* (Javanese Christians).[2] Thus, in the polarising society of nineteenth-century Java, not even the new and tiny groups of Christians were a single community.

The European missionaries, whose reports proved so valuable in the previous chapter, did not find Java an easy place to achieve their Christianising objectives. Christian missions have normally achieved little in Islamic societies, so perhaps it was remarkable that these missionaries converted anyone. They found the language extremely difficult and devoted much of the first stages of their time to attempting to master it. Javanese was "appallingly difficult", said Jellesma: "Mr Gericke speaks of at least twenty years being needed to know the language *well*."[3] Gottlob Brückner, the first translator of the Bible into Javanese, wrote of "the difficult Javanese language" in 1850, after 36 years in Java.[4] In 1863, Poensen was still reporting that learning Javanese was "the principal work to which I give my time. And not the easiest. Ach, what trouble and hassle! What frequent insuperable difficulties — words, sentences, forms that are impossible to grasp."[5] Modern students of Javanese will empathise with these comments. Eventually, however, many of the missionaries did master Javanese quite well, yet still conversions were few.

---

[1] Robson, *Wedhatama*, pp. 36–7.

[2] C. Guillot, *L'affaire Sadrach: Un essai de christianisation à Java au XIXe siècle* (Paris: Editions de la maison des sciences de l'homme, 1981), p. 94.

[3] J.E. Jellesma, Surabaya, to Bestuurders NZG, Rotterdam, 31 Dec. 1846, in ARZ 509.

[4] G. Brückner, Sěmarang, to Bestuurders NZG, Rotterdam, 12 Jan. 1850, in ARZ 511. On his life and work, see J.L. Swellengrebel, *In Leijdeckers voetspoor: Anderhalve eeuw Bijbelvertaling en taalkunde in de Indonesische talen* (2 vols.; VKI, vols. 68, 82; 's-Gravenhage: Martinus Nijhoff, 1974, 1978), vol. I, pp. 39–49.

[5] C. Poensen, Kědiri, to Bestuurders NZG, Rotterdam, Mar. 1863, in ARZ 261.

The missionaries founded schools, which were as important to the Christianisers as to the Islamic reformers of Chapter 3. They taught reading and writing in the Javanese and Malay languages, significantly teaching the latter in roman, not Arabic, script. There were attempts to introduce geography, but evidently this did not go well, although it is not clear why that should have been so. Javanese was the language of instruction. Typically these schools had only a few pupils, many of them non-Christians. Some missionaries reported that they had 10 pupils, others 20 to 30, occasionally one reported nearing the 50 mark. In the Christian community at Majawarna, J. Kruyt had over 169 students registered in his school in 1867, most of whom attended.[6]

The resistance to European Christian missions was strong and the missionaries were few in number. In 1843, the pioneer G. Brückner lamented that there was nothing very encouraging to say about the missions in Java. "I've been here pretty much alone all the time. The other brothers who were supposed to help in the work were either cut off by death or rendered incapable because of illness before they could understand the local language."[7] In 1874, when he had been over a decade in Java, Poensen turned to Old Testament metaphor to reflect on 25 years of missionising in Java. "The practical and greatly experienced Jellesma came to Java, courageous as a hero, ready to see the walls of this Javanese Jericho tumble down at the sound of the trumpet. But it didn't happen! The walls still stand, stronger than ever!"[8]

We have already seen in Chapter 3 that Javanese as well as Arabs were found among the opponents to missionaries. Javanese resistance was partly on grounds of cultural identity. In 1856 Jansz was asked by ordinary villagers whether converting to Christianity meant the abandoning of *slamětans,* visiting the graves of ancestors, playing the *gamělan,* visiting sacred places (*pundhen*) and inviting Javanese dancing-girls to their houses. Jansz said that this was indeed so, given the "unseemly things" that normally attended *gamělan* and *wayang* performances and the "improper company" of dancing-girls.[9] On another occasion he was asked whether it was true that Javanese who became Christians were shipped to the Netherlands to serve as soldiers there, and whether

---

[6] Anon., "De inlandsche school op Java", *MNZG* 11 (1867): 101, 105, 119–20.
[7] G. Brückner, Sěmarang, 1 Sept. 1843, to B. Ledeboer, Secretaris NZG, Rotterdam, in ARZ 511.
[8] C. Poensen, Zending methode op Java, Kědiri, 31 Dec. 1874, in ARZ 261.
[9] Jansz, *Tot heil,* p. 118.

Christians were not in fact heathen, since they did not practise circumcision. The discussion then embraced the idea of a distinction between those who knew much and those who knew little of Christian teachings, referring to the teaching of Jesus (Luke 12: 48) that "for everyone to whom much is given, of him shall much be required". The Javanese enquirers asked whether, in that case, it would not be better to know little.[10]

Poensen was given a series of reasons why Javanese refused to convert, most of them related to cultural identity. He listed the fear of falling under the supernatural power of Christians; the claims of *tiyang pasek* (followers of non-Islamic mystical sciences) that the Christians were like Islamic students of religion (*santris*), always seeking the truth, but in fact stumbling about blindly, for the truth was within oneself; that Christianity was the religion of the Prophet Moses (Nabi Musa), consisting of the Torah and the Psalms, which were superseded by Islam; that if one died as a Christian, one would not join one's family and ancestors on the Day of Resurrection; that one would not rest in peace if the *talqin* (prayer for the dead) was not said; that one would have to abandon all Javanese customs: circumcision, the *Qur'an*, the religious tax, pious donations (*sidhĕkah*), exorcisms (*ruwatan*), *slamĕtans* invoking the Prophet (*rasulan*), the communal meals (*sidhĕkah malĕman*) on certain nights of the fasting month, public dance performances, *wayang*, planning secret revenge (*ĕndhĕm-ĕndhĕman*), giving *slamĕtans* and so on, and would thus be ridiculed.[11] Even when the missionaries managed to convert and baptise small numbers of Javanese, sometimes social pressures and the commands of their superiors led them to revert to Islam.[12]

While the missionaries from Europe laboured to master Javanese, to understand the society around them and to win their first converts, remarkable locally domiciled lay persons began to plant Christianity more firmly in Java. It is hard to know which of these characters is the more extraordinary. They all operated on cultural and religious boundaries in remarkable, sometimes outlandish, ways. They negotiated these boundaries with the aid of their spirituality and reputed command of mystical knowledge and supernatural powers that made sense to local

---

[10] Ibid., p. 128.

[11] C. Poensen, annual report for 1863, Kĕdiri, Jan. 1864, in ARZ 261; also *MNZG* 9 (1865): 193–6.

[12] C. Poensen, Kĕdiri, to Bestuurders NZG, Rotterdam, Mar. 1863; idem, annual report for 1865, Kĕdiri Jan. 1866; idem, annual report for 1873, Kĕdiri, Jan. 1874, all in ARZ 261. See also Jansz, *Tot heil*, pp. 111, 126.

Javanese. We might imagine that, five hundred years before, the first Islamic proselytisers in Java must have behaved in similar ways. European missionaries and colonial administrators alike commonly mistrusted the influence of these Christianisers, the former fearing that they were creating only superficial or indeed heretical Christians, the latter that by introducing Christianity they would disturb social harmony within Javanese society. But these proselytisers carried on and established Javanese Christian communities that remain today. With this development, Islam ceased to be the only conceivable religious element in Javanese cultural identity — a development unthinkable only a few years before. Thereby another element in the previous mystic synthesis came under challenge.

One of the first, and certainly one of the most extraordinary, of the Christianisers was the larger-than-life Conrad Laurens Coolen.[13] Coolen was born in Sěmarang to a Russian father and a Javanese mother, said to be of aristocratic origin from Surakarta, c. 1773. He grew up and married in the European community and had five children by his European wife. At the age of 43 he became a committed Christian. He was then appointed to the government forestry service in Majaagung in the interior of Java, near the remains of the pre-Islamic kingdom of Majapahit, an area full of historical significance and supernatural potency to Javanese. But Coolen's wife and family stayed behind in Surabaya. In Majaagung he married a Javanese wife in the mosque and subsequently had six children by her. Some sources indicate that he had two Javanese wives. His previous European marriage had not been dissolved, so to the "saints of Surabaya", his personal life was scandalous.

In the late 1820s Coolen moved to Ngara, south of Majaagung. He sought out this land, which had once been settled but had then been abandoned, in part because he believed that his eldest son by his Javanese wife was a reincarnation of the original settler of Ngara, one Ki Gědhe. In March 1829 the government gave Coolen a long-term lease on this land. C. 1830 he, his wife and others moved to Ngara. As he cleared the land for settlement and for agriculture, Coolen also built a church. As an example of how to make the countryside fruitful, Coolen's estate was a model. Work was well organised and the estate prospered. As an example of how to spread Christianity, Coolen's work was also a remarkable success.

---

[13] The description of Coolen here rests upon Philip van Akkeren, *Sri and Christ: A study of the indigenous church in East Java* (London: Lutterworth Press, 1970), pp. 53–82; Guillot, *Sadrach*, pp. 71–87.

Population began to flow to Ngara from other, more heavily populated, surroundings. By 1844 the population of Ngara was 986. At the heart of the community was Coolen, towering over his Javanese tenants, conveying his Christian faith to all who would embrace it. But Coolen did not require conversion to Christianity before allowing Javanese to settle in Ngara. Muslims also came and Coolen saw to it that there was an *imam* (leader) for the Muslim community there.

In 1848 occurred a natural disaster that enhanced Coolen's supernatural reputation. Mount Kĕlut erupted to the south of Ngara. As was common during such eruptions, a blanket of ash and hot lava struck surrounding villages and caused alarm widely. Coolen gathered his flock around him, told them to kneel and pray and assured them that Ngara would be safe. The stream of lava passed Ngara by, leaving it unharmed. When famine struck the area in 1852, Ngara continued to enjoy abundance. When conflict arose with the government, Coolen took the side of his tenants, even objecting to them being required to perform the compulsory services levied on other Javanese. Under his leadership, Ngara was reportedly free of opium usage, tragically common in surrounding areas. As van Akkeren observes, Coolen "was known in a wide circle for his supernatural powers and great wisdom, and even as a spiritual father and teacher".[14] In 1850, however, the colonial government refused to renew Coolen's lease. The old man — now in his late 70s — was crushed. His tenants became landowners and Coolen retired to die in his 90s.

Coolen embraced Javanese culture with style. He spoke Javanese perfectly, we are told, although it is possible that it was defective in some measure, as was his Dutch. He led the Sunday service in Ngara himself, in which his charismatic personality held worshippers spellbound. He performed *wayang* and *gamĕlan*, which most European missionaries thought to be heathenish things best wiped out. He was acknowledged as a *kyai*, but a Christian one, the first such in Javanese history. He solved riddles and had visions. He refused to let his converts be baptised, regarding that as a European cultural invention. When several of his converts nevertheless went to Surabaya and were baptized there, Coolen expelled them from Ngara. In 1854, Coolen relented on this point and 200 of his people were then baptised, but they insisted on not cutting their hair or changing their names, as was customary for other Javanese who were baptised.

---

[14] Van Akkeren, *Sri and Christ*, p. 56.

Coolen translated basic doctrines into Javanese, not only in a linguistic but also in a cultural sense. He took over the Javanese custom of a leader ritually ploughing the soil while singing an invocation in Javanese verse of the rice-goddess Dewi Sri and her brother Sĕdana, whose union promised fertility. A prayer by Coolen has been preserved that shows how he Christianised this Javanese tradition, employing the Islamic profession that there is no God but God (*La ilaha illa 'llah*) and presenting the Christian idea of the Trinity of Father, Son and Holy Spirit in a way that would, indeed, have made European missionaries uncomfortable:

Mount Sumeru we sing of,
the sign of the land of Java:
may my farming endure
in the pleasures of Sri and Sĕdana,
who take the form of rice.
Who gives me leave is Allah the Most Pure.
Yea, there is no God but God (*ilaha ilĕlah*) and Jesus Christ
is the Spirit of God.[15]

Coolen's version of the Christian creed was also close to the Islamic confession and dubiously Trinitarian:

I believe in Allah the One:
There is no God but God (*la illah la illolah*);
Jesus Christ is the Spirit of God
who excels in his power.
There is no God but God (*la illah la illolah*);
Jesus Christ is the Spirit of God.[16]

This creed was sung like Sufi *dhikr*, the phrases being repeated over and over with associated movements of the head, in search of mystic transport.

Guillot appositely observes that "mysticism, egocentricity and megalomania seem to have contended for Coolen's soul".[17] It is worth

---

[15] Javanese text in van Akkeren, *Sri and Christ*, p. 92. My translation differs from van Akkeren's. It may be noted that in the *Qur'an* (4: 171), Jesus is called the Spirit of God.
[16] Sutarman Soediman Partonadi, *Sadrach's community and its contextual roots: A nineteenth century Javanese expression of Christianity* (Amsterdam & Atlanta: Rodopi, 1990), p. 135. My translation differs slightly from Sutarman's.
[17] Guillot, *Sadrach*, p. 76.

observing, however, that Europe and Java seem not to have done so to any significant degree. When Coolen left Surabaya, his European wife and his European children behind at an age when his contemporaries were considering retiring, he was making a choice for the Javanese side of his inheritance over the European for his remaining years. There is no evidence to suggest that, from that time onward, there was any contest at all. Christianity went with him into the interior of East Java but there was no cultural choice to be made in his mind, so far as we can judge. For him it was possible to be a Christian and a venerable Javanese *kyai*. He persuaded hundreds of Javanese followers that for them, too, there was no conflict of identity involved in conversion to Christianity. In this way the foundations of Javanese Christianity were laid in East Java.

Among Coolen's assistants were Paulus Tosari and Abisai Ditatruna,[18] who earned their *kyai*'s displeasure by being among those who went to Surabaya in 1844 to be baptised, against Coolen's instructions. In 1846 Abisai and others left Ngara and founded Majawarna, a few kilometres away. Paulus Tosari eventually joined them and became the leading figure in the community. He was of Madurese descent, like an increasing number of the inhabitants of East Java, and a dynamic preacher with significant leadership qualities. Both Christians and Muslims settled in Majawarna. The Christians made contact with the European missionaries and invited J.E. Jellesma to settle there as their preacher, which he did in 1854, remaining until he died in 1858. But he did not displace Paulus Tosari, who remained the leader of the Christian community. In 1860 Hoezoo arrived to replace Jellesma and found the Christians still too much in the grip of older Javanese supernatural concepts for his liking. Indeed, in 1857 Abisai had fallen to temptation by organising a *tayuban* dance party. Paulus Tosari denounced him and Jellesma excluded him from communion, a breach in the community that was not subsequently healed. Paulus Tosari died in 1881.[19]

---

[18] The account of Paulus Tosari and Abisai Ditatruna is based upon van Akkeren, *Sri and Christ*, pp. 97–105; Guillot, *Sadrach*, pp. 96–9.

[19] See further Edwin Wieringa, "Het Christendom als het ware inzicht: Hendrik Kraemers uitgave van Paulus Tosari's *Rasa sejati*", pp. 56–88 in Willem van der Molen and Bernard Arps (eds.), *Woord en schrift in de Oost: De betekenis van zending en missie voor de studie van taal and literatuur in Zuidost-Azië* (*Semaian* 19; Leiden: Opleiding Talen en Culturen van Zuidoost-Azië en Oceanië, Universiteit Leiden, 2000).

Perhaps the most colourful of all of these remarkable characters was Kyai Ibrahim Tunggul Wulung.[20] He was from Jĕpara on the *pasisir*, but in the course of his spiritual seeking he had become a hermit on Mount Kĕlut, along with his wife. Legend had it that a copy of the Ten Commandments miraculously came to him in his hermitage. There were indeed Christian tracts circulating in Java and presumably one of these reached Tunggul Wulung. He was persuaded that he had been called supernaturally to become a Christian. So he came down from his mountain hermitage to Ngara, where he met Coolen. He went on to meet European missionaries as well. Jellesma was so persuaded of Tunggul Wulung's sincerity and calling that he baptised him in 1857, at which time Ibrahim was added to his name.

Ibrahim Tunggul Wulung was tall and imposing, with long hair and a wispy beard under his chin. He spoke in riddles and allusions in the Javanese style, conveying the charisma and supernatural authority that was associated with a Javanese hermit and *kyai*. Jansz, who deeply distrusted him, claimed that he still taught various *ngelmus*.[21] As for Coolen, even more so for Tunggul Wulung, Christianity was not in conflict with Javanese identity. He wandered around East Java, particularly around the Malang area, winning converts to Christianity. He founded three new Christian villages north of Jĕpara. His were the *Kristen Jawa*, as opposed to the "Dutch Christians", the *Kristen Londo* who followed the European missionaries.

Pieter Jansz was based in Jĕpara as a missionary and saw Ibrahim Tunggul Wulung as a competitor, whose Christianity he thought to be impure at best, scandalous at worst. In 1854, Tunggul Wulung told Jansz personally another version of his magical conversion involving a disembodied voice ordering him to go to Jellesma. He also related his defiance of tigers who roamed near his hermitage and how he had thrice leapt into the sea only to be thrown back to shore. All of this Jansz thought to be not miracles but richly embroidered tales from a charlatan.[22] Javanese, however, believed in such tales. One missionary was told by Javanese Christians that Ibrahim Tunggul Wulung could run at amazing speeds, but before he became a Christian he had been able

---

[20] Unless otherwise noted, the account of Tunggul Wulung is based on van Akkeren, *Sri and Christ*, pp. 154–6; Guillot, *Sadrach*, pp. 88–95.

[21] See the descriptions in Jansz, *Tot heil*, pp. 112–3, 136, 142.

[22] Ibid., p. 71.

to fly at infinite speed so that he could appear in two places at once. This was, however, a devilish art that he had abandoned on conversion.[23] The outcome of the competition between Jansz and Tunggul Wulung, if measured in terms of numbers of converts, was clear. Whereas Ibrahim Tunggul Wulung created Christian communities totaling over a thousand members by the time of his death in 1885, Jansz's converts were less than 200 over a similar period.

Ibrahim Tunggul Wulung was not the only Javanese hermit to be interested in the new *ngelmu* offered by Christianity. In 1856 one Kyai Trawulan, from near the ruins of Majapahit, came to Jellesma to seek baptism. He was regarded as a *pandhita* (wise man) of the non-Islamic *ngelmu pasek* and had great local influence. He had first come into contact with Christians four or five years before. As with Tunggul Wulung, so also with Ky. Trawulan, Jellesma was persuaded of the sincerity of this conversion and baptised the *kyai* and his wife. Ky. Trawulan now became Johannes.[24] Not all *pandhitas*, however, decided that Christianity was the answer to their search for truths. In 1864, a *pandhita* from Blitar encountered one of Poensen's Javanese helpers. He claimed to live in the mountains with many students and to have had previous contact with Coolen. He knew the Ten Commandments, Lord's Prayer and the Twelve Articles of Faith, albeit with some peculiarities. But neither Christianity nor Islam satisfied him, so he was teaching his own unique *ngelmu*.[25]

Among the Javanese Christians of this time, probably the most influential in the longer term was Kyai Sadrach Surapranata (c. 1835–1924), who was instrumental in the establishment of Christianity in Central Java.[26] There three pious Indo-European women also played crucial roles. Christina P. Stevens-Philips (1824–76), her sister-in-law J.C. Philips-van Oostrom (1815–77) and E.J. de Wildt-le Jolle (1824–1906) all spoke Javanese and proselytised Christianity among their

[23] Th.F. van der Valk, Dagboek May–Nov. 1854 (under date 19 June), dd. Sidakari, 4 Nov. 1854, in ARZ 259.

[24] J.E. Jellesma, Dagverhaal 1 July–31 Dec. 1856 (under dates 15 July & 31 July), dd. Mojowarno 20 Jan. 1857, in ARZ 509.

[25] C. Poensen, annual report for 1864, Kĕdiri, Jan. 1865, in ARZ 261.

[26] Unless otherwise indicated, the account of Sadrach and his times rests upon Sutarman, *Sadrach's community*, especially pp. 55–107; and Guillot, *Sadrach*, especially pp. 110–283. See also Adriaanse, *Sadrach's kring*; and Lydia Herwanto, *Pikiran dan aksi Kiai Sadrach: Gerakan jemaat Kristen Jawa Merdeka* (Jogjakarta: Matabángsa, 2002).

Javanese servants, thereby laying early foundations of Christian communities in the areas of Purwarĕja, Banyumas and Salatiga, before Sadrach appeared.

Sadrach (the name he adopted only after his conversion to Christianity) was born on the *pasisir* c. 1835. As a young man, he became a *santri* at several *pĕsantrens,* then returned to live in the *kauman*, where pious Muslims lived, in Sĕmarang. On his return, however, he found that his former guru there was no longer a Muslim but now a Christian, having been defeated in debate and thus converted by Ky. Ibrahim Tunggul Wulung. Sadrach met Tunggul Wulung and was also won over by him, for here was a man who was both Christian and Javanese. Sadrach began attending Hoezoo's services. Not yet baptised, Sadrach travelled to Batavia with Tunggul Wulung, where they met F.L. Anthing (1820–83), a pious Christian lawyer who had supported missionising during his previous work in Sĕmarang and was now a senior government official in the capital. Inspired further by Anthing, Sadrach took Christian instruction and was baptised in Batavia in April 1867. The following year he returned to work with Tunggul Wulung, but a parting of the ways followed after about a year, the reasons for which are not clear, but may have had to do with Tunggul Wulung taking a second wife. Sadrach went to Purwarĕja and there began working with Mrs Stevens-Philips.

Sadrach was a powerful evangeliser. He challenged Javanese gurus to public debate and, upon defeating them, accepted their conversion to Christianity along with their followers. With such skills, he produced a significant expansion in the Christian community already founded by Stevens-Philips. After about a year, he struck out on his own, moving some 25 kilometres from Purwarĕja to a village called Karangjasa, where he created a Christian community. He continued converting *kyais* and their followers through public debates and gained a reputation for being able to control malign spiritual forces. In other ways, too, his version of Christianity preserved Javanese customs as far as possible. Jesus was presented as the Ratu Adil. Circumcision was not abolished. *Slamĕtans* were held. The church was called a *mĕsjid* (mosque) and the church at Karangjasa was built to look like one. Men and women sat in separate places, as in an Islamic mosque. But *tayuban* dances, opium usage and polygamy were condemned.[27]

Sadrach's methods produced dramatic results. In the space of only three years, from 1870 to 1873, he built five churches and is said to have

---

[27] Sutarman, *Sadrach's community*, pp. 138, 147–54, 209–10.

converted almost 2,500 Javanese to Christianity, the most remarkable record yet for any Christianiser. As of 1874, there were reckoned to be about 6,200 Javanese Christians in Java, almost all of the growth since 1870 being that achieved by Sadrach.[28] Such numbers are not, however, very reliable and tend to jump about wildly. A decade later, in 1883, Poensen reckoned there to be about 4,400 indigenous Christians in Javanese-speaking areas, 3,500 of them in Sadrach's area of Bagĕlen.[29] Whatever the figures, it is clear that Ky. Sadrach was the most effective proselytiser Christianity had ever seen in Java.

Initially Sadrach's relations with European missions were less confrontational than was the case with Coolen or Tunggul Wulung. Although his identity and style were clearly Javanese, he sent his converts to the European mission at Puwarĕja for baptism and Christina Stevens-Philips visited Karangjasa regularly. But the dramatic growth of his following led to jealousy and competition for the attention of ordained ministers between Sadrach's community and Europeans. A breach followed, with the consequence that European ministers no longer served Sadrach's Christians, so sacraments such as Communion, baptisms and marriages could no longer be administered. It was several years before Sadrach achieved a solution to this problem. The colonial government also looked on Sadrach's influence and independence as a potential threat. Whereas a Muslim leader of similar stature might have been arrested and exiled, however, it was difficult for this to be done in the case of a Christian. So a series of attempts were made to undermine Sadrach's influence and place his community under the control of European missionaries, all of which failed.

The greatest *cause célèbre* of Sadrach's life occurred in 1882. A smallpox epidemic broke out and the colonial government ordered a vaccination campaign. Sadrach, however, ordered his Christians to refuse vaccination. This was based upon his understanding of two passages of the Bible, I Timothy 5 : 6–7 and II Corinthians 6 : 3. Neither of these seems relevant in the Dutch (or English) versions, but both seemed so to Sadrach in the Javanese translation of the Bible then in use.[30] In the English Revised Standard Version, the first reads, "Command this, so that they may be without reproach" and the second, "We put no obstacle

---

[28] De Waal, *Indische financien*, vol. I, pp. 256–7. This source gives 1509 Christians for Bagĕlen in 1874, which seems to have been already an out-of-date figure.

[29] C. Poensen, annual report for 1883, Kĕdiri, Jan. 1884, in ARZ 261.

[30] The RSV and Javanese texts are in Sutarman, *Sadrach's community*, p. 74.

in anyone's way, so that no fault may be found with our ministry." In Javanese, the first read, "In all these matters, let there indeed be no blemish (*cacad*) in all the people" and the second, "We have caused no offence in any matter, so that our service will be unblemished (*dicĕla*)." Both *cacad* and *cĕla* mean blemish, flaw or imperfection in a physical as well as spiritual sense. Since smallpox vaccinations left a scar on the body, Sadrach understood I Timothy 5:6–7 and II Corinthians 6:3 to prohibit them. For European missionaries and administrators seeking grounds to bring Sadrach's community under their control this was, so to speak, a godsend. Sadrach was arrested in March 1882 for resisting government orders and was jailed for three weeks, and was thereafter held for almost three months in the house of the hostile European missionary Ph. Bieger.[31] Bieger told the Javanese congregations that he was now their leader. But there was insufficient evidence against Sadrach to justify his arrest and detention, so he was freed on the authority of the Governor-General. Bieger shortly left the area.

Sadrach returned to leadership of his community in mid-1882. A year later, his church took a new and significant name. Now the Christians called themselves *Golongane Wong Kristen kang Mardika*: the Group of Independent Christians. They invited a European, J. Wilhelm, as their preacher but were clear that this was at their choice, not on the orders of any European mission. Their number was now over three thousand. By 1890, these independent Javanese Christians numbered nearly seven thousand, settled in over four hundred individual villages. Never before had Christianity seen such success among the Javanese.

Between 1893 and 1899 an irreconcilable split finally developed between Sadrach and the missionaries of the *Nederlandse Gereformeerde Zendings Vereniging* (NGZV), the society active in his area. Once again accusations were made that Sadrach's teachings were false, so an investigation was ordered by the Dutch mission authorities. That investigation decided against continuing to recognise Sadrach as a Christian proselytiser. Further difficulties followed. Finally Sadrach went to Batavia in 1899 and there joined the Apostolic Church, in which his old mentor F.L. Anthing had become active late in his life.[32] Sadrach was ordained as

---

[31] On Bieger, see Coolsma, *Zendingseeuw*, pp. 158–9, 172–3.
[32] Sutarman, *Sadrach's community*, p. 43, notes that as an Apostle, Anthing formed churches in the area of Batavia that were free of affiliation with any specific denomination and were known as *Anthingsche Christen-Inlandsche Gemeenten* (Anthingese Christian-Native Congregations).

an Apostle in this idiosyncratic branch of Christianity, which meant that for the first time he regarded himself as able to administer the sacraments. The vast majority of Sadrach's flock stayed with him, so the effect of this breach was to bring the NGZV mission in Central Java to an end.

Sadrach died in 1924, leaving behind the largest Javanese Christian community to be found in the island, totaling in the thousands.[33] His coffin was draped with a *bathik* in the pattern Parang Rusak, normally reserved for Javanese monarchs. Some years after his death, the split with the Dutch mission society was healed by Sadrach's successor. In 1933, about half of the 7,500 Sadrach Christians were reincorporated into the successor mission society to the NGZV. Of the remainder, some stayed with the Apostolic Church, others formed a new group and a few joined the Catholic church.

Not only Europeans opposed Sadrach and his Christians. Muslims sometimes attacked them as well. In the 1880s, Sunday services were harassed, churches were burned, and Christians were driven out of villages. In two years, between 1882 and 1884, almost all the churches of Sadrach's community were burned. But thereafter incidents diminished.[34] That Javanese could be both Christians and Javanese at the same time was perhaps becoming conceivable to Javanese Muslims. As early as 1871, Hoezoo commented, presumably with specific regard to the Sĕmarang area, that the jibe that had been common in his first years that Christians were *Landa wurung Jawa tanggung* (failed Dutchmen and half-baked Javanese) had fallen out of fashion.[35]

The stories told above can hardly capture what it meant for ordinary individuals or families to be among the first to join the new Christian *ngelmu*. There is, however, one published autobiographical account that gives a sense of what it meant for a member of the *priyayi* elite. This was written by one Kartawidjaja at the request of a missionary c. 1914, and

---

[33] Sutarman, *Sadrach's community*, p. 129, cites J.C. Rutgers as putting the total at 20,000. But there are problems with this. Sutarman says that Rutgers writes of numbers "in the year of Sadrach's death" (i.e. 1924) but gives the date of her book as 1912. There is an edition by Jacqueline C. van Andel-Rutgers published in 1921, which was still 3 years before Sadrach's death, but must be the work intended by Sutarman. The figure of 20,000, however, cannot be reconciled with figures given in other sources.

[34] Guillot, *Sadrach*, pp. 234–6.

[35] W. Hoezoo, fragment from a longer document dd. 18 Sept. 1871, in ARZ 210.

tells of his conversion to Christianity in the 1890s.[36] This is a valuable insight into the memories of one individual, although it is of course a defence of the conversion written for the edification of a devout Christian audience. Kartawidjaja's name suggests that he was of Sundanese rather than Javanese background. He was from Indramayu, on the coast northwest of the Javanese *kraton* town of Cirĕbon. This region is the boundary between Javanese and Sundanese cultural areas. Kartawidjaja had a command of Javanese and Malay as well as Sundanese and evidently lived in the Javanese world as well as the Sundanese.

Kartawidjaja was born c. 1851. His grandfather was a *haji* and from his youth Kartawidjaja was taught to read the *Qur'an* by his grandfather and father. He studied at a *pĕsantren* where he became literate in Arabic script, but not in Javanese or roman scripts, which he subsequently mastered through his own efforts, along with arithmetic. He was, he said, devout and prayed five times daily. He became a junior government official and climbed through the ranks until retiring in 1891, burdened with guilt that he had become so absorbed in his work that he had ceased to observe the daily prayers and fast. With his wife, he returned to Indramayu, settled in the Arab quarter and resumed a life of piety. He became a follower of the Naqshabandiyya and considered undertaking the *hajj*. But he became irritated by the incessant pressure upon him from local Arabs and decided not to go to Mecca after all. His reading of the *Qur'an* meanwhile failed to satisfy him: "However often I read it, I became no wiser."[37]

One day an acquaintance, the son of an indigenous senior official in Indramayu, told Kartawidjaja that Muhammad was no prophet and that the true word of God was to be found in the Bible. Kartawidjaja drove this friend furiously from his house. He turned to the *Qur'an,* but found there in *Qur'an* 3 : 3 exhortations to believe in the law of Moses and the Gospel of Jesus. After further reading, he began to believe that the Mosaic law and the Gospels were truly the word of God and that Muhammad had used them to concoct the *Qur'an.* So he began to believe in Jesus, he said, and to attend church services in Indramayu, abandoning Islamic prayer. This produced a storm of protest from his family and local Arab notables. Karawidjaja feared that the Arabs would

---

[36] Kartawidjaja, *Van Koran tot Bijbel, uit het Maleisch vertaald* (Rotterdam: Nederlandsche Zendingsvereeniging, n.d. [c. 1914]). I am grateful to Michael Laffan, who found this book in a Dutch bookshop, for providing me with a copy.
[37] Ibid., p. 8.

inspire his murder, and particularly feared that this might happen before he could become a Christian through baptism. So he left Indramayu and wandered about, preaching the Gospel. Yet he dared not seek baptism because of the absolute objections of his mother and wife. The latter's father was a *haji* and a great hater of Christians. His mother threatened to disown him. When both his mother and wife died in 1896, however, Kartawidjaja concluded that their deaths were "willed by God to remove all objections to me asking to be baptised".[38] Still his baptism was delayed because he wanted another wife and felt that he would have to get one before his conversion, for he would be unable to do so after it. In 1898, he married a new wife who then refused to convert with him and left him when he was baptised on Christmas day 1899. Arabs gave her refuge and made ready to attack him physically. There was shock in Indramayu at his apostasy. Local officials ordered everyone to carry out Islam's five pillars strictly. Women were ordered again to wear the veil like women who had completed the *hajj*, which had apparently fallen into desuetude. Some, however, refused to do this, particularly among the elite. Kartawidjaja carried on as an evangelist for his new faith but found Indramayu uncongenial. The Arabs were hostile and "there was actually much quarrelling and conflict among the Christians"; so "I decided to seclude myself from them both".[39] In 1902 he moved away and lived in the town of Bangoduwa until his death in October 1914. Kartawidjaja's story thus reflected the profound social and personal conflicts that sometimes attended conversion.

The Catholic Church was a late entrant to this competition for Javanese souls among the various versions of pious Islam, multiple Protestant mission societies, the Apostolic Church and independent Javanese churches. Not until the 1890s did the Catholic Church give serious attention to proselytising among the Javanese.[40] In Yogyakarta, Catholicism even won two sons of a prince of the house of Pakualam, who were baptised in 1897. With the arrival of the Jesuit father Franciscus van Lith (1863–1926) in Batavia in 1896, serious Catholic conversions were about to begin. Van Lith and the Jesuits who followed him often became real experts in Javanese. The most outstanding of these would

---

[38] Ibid., p. 36.
[39] Ibid., p. 47.
[40] The following account, down to the discussion of Ganjuran, relies upon Karel Steenbrink, *Catholics in Indonesia, 1801–1942: A documented history*, vol.I: *A modest recovery 1801–1903* (*VKI* vol. 196; Leiden: KITLV Press, 2003), pp. 203–18.

Music lesson at Xavier College, Muntilan, c. 1925 (Collection of KITLV, Leiden)

one day be Professor P.J. Zoetmulder, S.J. (1906–95), one of the twentieth century's greatest scholars of both Javanese Islamic mysticism and Old Javanese language and literature. The Jesuits had a gift for studying Javanese society and reconciling Catholicism with it. Not for them the frontal assault on Javanese customs that marked so much of the Dutch Protestant missionising.

In 1897 van Lith opened a Jesuit post in Muntilan. In 1904 a teacher training college was opened there, after 1910 called Xavier College, which was to become a key to the advance of Catholicism in Java. From 1907 the colonial government began to open village schools throughout Java, which produced a great demand for graduate teachers from the Jesuit normal school in Muntilan, all of whom, according to Karel Steenbrink, went in as Muslims and came out as Catholics. Through them Catholic influence was spread widely in Java. Some graduates of Xavier College went on to the priesthood. One of these early converts was Sugiyopranoto, who would be ordained in 1940 as the first Indonesian Bishop.

The Catholic accommodation of Javanese culture and identity was sometimes reflected in church architecture and practices, perhaps most dramatically in the case of the church at Ganjuran, south of Yogyakarta.

In the early twentieth century, a sugar factory in the area was run by Dr. Joseph Schmutzer and Mr Julius Schmutzer, who were devout Catholics. They and Joseph's wife Caroline established elementary schools for boys and girls, a health clinic (later a hospital) at Ganjuran and what was to become Panti Rapih hospital in Yogyakarta. In 1924 they founded the Church of the Sacred Heart in Ganjuran.

At Ganjuran Javanese culture and Catholicism are entwined. On the altar of the church sit angels depicted like dancers of the *wayang wong* (dance drama). The *gamělan* is used in church services. In 1927 the Schmutzers began constructing a temple at Ganjuran that closely copies the style of a pre-Islamic, Old Javanese temple (*candhi*). The seated statue of Christ the king with his sacred heart is modeled on Old Javanese statuary. When the Schmutzers left for the Netherlands in 1934, the church and *candhi* were led by Father Sugiyopranoto, SJ, already referred to above as the future Bishop. In 1997 bas-relief panels of the stations of the Way of the Cross in Hindu-Javanese style were eventually added, as originally intended by the Schmutzers. Church festivals continue to be held there in which participants dress in *kraton* style, with the priest celebrating Mass attired like a court official (*abdi-dalěm*). Water believed to have healing powers may be gathered from the base of the *candhi*.[41] At Puh Sarang, in the mountains above Kědiri, another Catholic church emulating Old Javanese styles was built in 1936 by the Dutch architect Henricus Maclaine Pont, who was also responsible for building the museum at Trawulan, near the ruins of Majapahit.[42]

By 1900 there were reportedly around 10,000 Javanese Christians in East Java.[43] The figures for Central Java would probably not have been much different. If one works with a very rough estimate of 20,000 in total, then it is clear that the Christians were a tiny minority, under 0.1 per cent of Javanese. But they represented a new element in definitions of Javanese cultural identity. The cultural-historical lesson that the Protestant missionaries found difficult to learn, that came instinctively to Coolen, Ibrahim Tunggul Wulung and Sadrach, and that was made

---

[41] Information supplied by Alex Sudewa, and contained in a pamphlet entitled *The church of the Sacred Heart of Jesus at Ganjuran: Her concerns and hopes* (n.p., n.d. [c. 1999]).

[42] Information from a booklet available there: J. Hadiwikarta, *Gua Maria Lourdes Puh Sarang, Kediri, Keuskupan Surabaya* (Kediri: Sekretariat Keuskupan Surabaya, 2001).

[43] Van Akkeren, *Sri and Christ*, p. 120.

Ganjuran Catholic church:
(a) The *candhi*
(b) The image of Christ in the *candhi* (with the Javanese royal titles *Sampeyan-dalĕm Maha Prabu Yesus Kristus*)
(c) Altar angel in *wayang* style

Puh Sarang Catholic church

a principle by the Jesuit fathers, was that there was resilience in Javanese culture and strength in Javanese identity. If one introduced a new religious idea and insisted that the cost of embracing it was to abandon Javanese identity, then the probabilities of successful conversions were small. Islamic revivalists might draw the same lesson, as was seen in the previous chapter. Of course there were some Javanese who did wish to make such a cultural transition — just as there were Indians who felt more at home in London than in Bombay or Vietnamese who felt more at home in Paris than in Hanoi. But for every Javanese who sought such a change of identity there were thousands who did not. Among the missionaries, however, whether Christian or Muslim, such cultural questions may ultimately have been of little consequence. For they were doing what they understood God to command.

The discussion in Chapters 4 and 5 has mainly focused on ordinary Javanese villagers. They were the majority of Javanese and their choices of culture and identity mattered. But this was still a strongly hierarchical society, headed by an elite, the *priyayi*, who had the most direct contact with the Dutch colonial regime. Many of these shared the views expressed in Kartawidjaja's memoirs c. 1914:

> The Dutch teach the Mohammedans arithmetic and writing with Javanese and Dutch script. Throughout the whole of the Netherlands Indies the government has appointed teachers for native children. One can get beautiful clothing, all sorts of furniture and decorations for the house, various implements. One has machines, telegraph, telephone, steam ships, railways, money of gold, silver, copper and paper. One can very easily undertake the pilgrimage to Mecca. The government does all this.... May God let the Mohammedans feel and understand well that there is no blessing to be gained except through the Dutch, who are indeed blessed by Him.[44]

While Islamic reformers and Christian missionaries brought revolutionary new ideas, so did the Dutch, including all the dramatic advances of nineteenth-century science associated with Western civilisation, several of them mentioned by Kartawidjaja above. Thus, the elite were faced with an even broader choice of new ideas than was true of most other Javanese. How they responded is the subject of the next chapter, as the *priyayi* provided yet another pole of difference in this polarising society.

---

[44] Kartawidjaja, *Van Koran tot Bijbel*, p. 54.

6

The Elite's New Horizons

We have seen in Chapter 2 that the *priyayi* elite were essential to the functioning of the colonial state in nineteenth-century Java. For the Dutch, if the social prestige of the *priyayi* could be combined with sufficient administrative skills to make the administration work acceptably, then the Javanese elite provided a cheap means of running Java in the interest of the Netherlands. For many *priyayi* this meant increased scrutiny of their activities by Europeans but also enhanced personal status, good incomes and security of employment for themselves and their descendants, while lesser members of Javanese society bore the indisputably heavy costs of the colonial state. Thus, as was pointed out in that chapter, Javanese society began to be increasingly differentiated because of the unprecedented circumstances of colonial rule. The royal elite of the Central Javanese principalities of Surakarta and Yogyakarta (the *Vorstenlanden*) also faced new circumstances, notably demilitarisation (except to some extent for the Mangkanagaran)[1] and much restricted room for political manoeuvre on the one hand, with greater dynastic stability and personal security on the other.

---

[1] As noted in Chapter 3 above, G.G. Daendels established the Mangkunagaran Legion in 1808 with 1,150 men. By the mid-nineteenth century, the Legion was a serious military force of infantry, cavalry and artillery which served the Dutch colonial regime in several combat theatres. A much smaller Pakualaman Legion was also established, but was never of much significance and was disbanded in 1892.

In previous chapters, we have explored the ways in which cultural and religious orientations of the nascent middle class and ordinary villagers in Java changed in the nineteenth century in response both to Islamic revival movements and to colonial conditions. The changes for the *priyayi* were no less profound. Their cultural and intellectual horizons expanded dramatically, for association with Dutch colonial rule brought with it the ideas and styles of industrialising Europe, which were very different from older ways of doing and seeing things in Java.

A survey of Javanese elite culture from before colonial times, as evidenced in its literature and other surviving cultural artifacts, would concern itself with matters quite foreign to nineteenth-century Dutch ways. It would focus upon literary works concerning Javanese history and mythologised historical traditions, Islamic works of the mystic synthesis style, interlinear translations of and commentaries on Islamic religious texts, admonitory and didactic works, adventures in war and romance of which some were set in pre-Islamic times, Modern Javanese versions of Old Javanese works and such like. Wonderful works of art in *wayang* puppets and *bathik* also reflected this vibrant pre-colonial culture, as did the palaces, mosques and pleasure-gardens of the elite. But this was not a world of newspapers, of regular reports of events from around the world or even around the Indonesian archipelago. It was a world of punctilious distinctions of status and of competition — sometimes fierce and bloody — for place, power and wealth. But it was not one of formal bureaucratic rules, form-filling and paper-shuffling, a branch of civilisation in which the Dutch nation excelled, as indeed it does today. It was a world in which commoners were exploited for the benefit of the elite, but not one in which that was achieved through the grinding routines of nineteenth-century colonialism.

In essence, two contending forms of modernity were offered to the *priyayi* in the nineteenth century: that brought by Europeans and that brought by Islamic reformers. Only the former offered them also employment, salaries, status and security. Islamic reform was mainly associated with the merchant middle class, whom the elite generally seem to have held in disdain. If one were to ask a Javanese *priyayi* whether he preferred to be a pious Muslim merchant competing in the market place or a petty — sometimes a great — lord over his people, backed by the colonial state, it would have been a rare *priyayi* who would have chosen the former. In other words, as between these choices of modernity, in the minds of the Javanese elite there was never really much of a contest, so far as can be told from the surviving evidence.

The great German naturalist Franz Junghuhn (1809 or 1812–64)
published a description of Surakarta in 1844 in his monumental work
Reizen door Java that probably captures reasonably well some of the
styles, preoccupations and priorities of the elite of the *Vorstenlanden*
before dramatic changes took place and, by contrast, the circumstances
of the general population. He was in Surakarta to observe a tiger-buffalo
fight and tiger-sticking on the great square (*alun-alun*) before the *kraton*.

> The massed population of Javanese in their national dress, with
> the upper body usually uncovered, the glittering lances, the *waringin*
> trees spreading their thick, shadowed crowns to the side of the square
> [of people], the *pĕndhapas* (open houses or shelters) which stand all
> about on the sides of the *alun-alun*, the noble state of the emperor
> [Pakubuwana VII] and his extraordinary entourage, the playing of the
> *gamĕlan* and the melodies of its music — these are all particularities
> that give a characteristic colour to this whole spectacle, which is too
> splendid, too rich in variegations, for my poor pen to be able to
> compose a true picture of it....
>
> The (general) population is more indolent, recalcitrant and morally
> more decadent than any other in the whole of Java. If one thinks of
> the meaningless magnificence, of the decked-out but empty-handed
> masses, of the drums and trumpets and of the licentious pleasures in
> which the Javanese kings spend their time, while ten *palen* [approx
> 15 kms]² away from their *kraton* everything is in dilapidation and not
> a single road is maintained, so the wish must come to everyone that
> the [colonial] government should also take these *Vorstenlanden* under
> its direct administration.³

Junghuhn's description is valuable. It may not be free of hyperbole
and his suggestion that colonial rule was the answer to the woes of Java's
masses would not find wide acceptance today. Nevertheless, Junghuhn
captured the pageantry and magnificence that were central features of
court life and the distance between that and the poverty in the lives of
ordinary villagers. This gap between royal splendour and ordinary life
would not diminish as the nineteenth century progressed. Nor did the
Dutch wish it to do so. For the status of the courts as cultural axioms,

---

² A *paal* was 1.507 kms.
³ Fr. Junghuhn, *Reizen door Java, vooramelijk door het oosterlijk gedeelte van dit eiland,
opgenomen en beschreven in het jaar 1844* (2 vols.; Amsterdam: P.N. van Kampen,
1852), vol. I, pp. 116, 118–9.

exemplified in their grandeur, and the wish of lesser aristocrats who served the Dutch as *Bupatis* and lower officials to emulate that style, were among the keys to cheap administration.

The Dutch thus found no cause for concern when the cultural styles that they now brought to Java enhanced rather than diminished the difference between the *priyayi* on whom they relied on the one hand and the general populace and Islamic reformers on the other. Anything that might contribute to a sense of awe when ordinary villagers regarded Javanese *priyayi* and royalty would be of assistance to the colonial regime in keeping Java under control. Anything that might enhance the commitment of the royal elite and broader *priyayi* to European-style modernity would bind their interests and aspirations closer to the colonial regime and distance them from pious Islamic styles. Such objectives were achieved in part by the increasing professionalisation of the *priyayi* as an administrative elite.[4] The key to that was education, a matter that will be discussed below. While it is does not seem that, in the mid-nineteenth century, the Dutch had a clearly formulated cultural policy about the *priyayi*, nevertheless they went on to transform *priyayi* culture dramatically and, in doing so, increased the distance between the elite and the rest of their society.

What was even more remarkable about this cultural transformation was that it enabled the *priyayi* at the same time to be more modern and to be more traditional, at least as they defined that tradition. European culture seemed to open a door to modern inventions and modern cosmopolitanism and yet at the same time to a more glorious, more authentically Javanese cultural identity. That vision of a more authentic Javaneseness was, importantly, uncongenial to the reformist Islam then spreading in Java. The older-style mystic synthesis, however, seemed readily accommodated.

The New Literary Culture

To gain a sense of the cultural transformation of the Javanese elite, and consequently of that elite's increasing distance from other members of

---

[4] See particularly Heather Sutherland, *The making of a bureaucratic elite: The colonial transformation of the Javanese priyayi* (Singapore: Heinemann Educational Books (Asia) Ltd., 1979). Concerning the *kraton* elite, see Vincent J.H. Houben, *Kraton and Kumpeni: Surakarta and Yogyakarta 1830–1870* (*VKI* vol. 164; Leiden: KITLV Press, 1994).

Javanese society, we may turn to the first Javanese-language newspaper to be published in Java, a rich source for the widening *Weltanschauung* of the *priyayi*. This was first published in Surakarta in 1855 under the title *Bramartani*. It was in fact the first vernacular-language newspaper to appear anywhere in the Netherlands Indies. The paper came out weekly under the initial editorship of C.F. Winter Sr (d. 1859) and one of his sons. The Winter family were of mixed European and Javanese ancestry and had worked in Surakarta as translators and cultural mediators between Dutch and Javanese since the late eighteenth century. Later there were also Javanese editors. In 1873 F.L. Winter handed the editorship to the local school teacher Surana.[5] *Bramartani* failed as a business enterprise at the end of 1856 and ceased printing.[6] In 1864, however, it was brought back to life under the title *Jurumartani*, later changed again to *Bramartani*, and it was then published weekly, and sometimes biweekly, until 1932, a remarkable record in the history of indigenous journalism in Indonesia.

Surakarta was the site of important cross-cultural educational innovations. An Institute for the Javanese Language, where future Dutch administrators were taught Javanese, was opened there in 1832. There were also early if small starts in involving Javanese in European education. In 1833 there were reported to be several Javanese among the 100 pupils in the European primary school there, which had been opened in 1820. Multilingualism and cross-culturality were unavoidable for many Europeans living in places like Surakarta — where European women were rare and the partners of European men and the mothers of their children were frequently Javanese. Not infrequently Javanese was the language of the household and sometimes even the only tongue in which children were fluent. Thus, in the 1840s the primary school at Surakarta was open to the children of "needy parents, who frequently reside in the villages, in the midst of the Javanese population, whereby the children

---

[5] *BM* 1 May 1873, 3 July 1873. Surana was a teacher at the teacher-training school in Surakarta and was sent to the Netherlands for further education in 1874; *BM* 12 Mar. 1874.

[6] Ahmat B. Adam, *The vernacular press and the emergence of modern Indonesian consciousness (1855–1913)* (Ithaca, New York: Cornell University Southeast Asia Program, 1995), pp. 16–9. Adam is wrong to treat *Bramartani* and *Jurumartani* as if they were different publications when he says (p. 19) that "the paper did not reappear until 1871". Except for the change of masthead — which actually took place in 1870, not 1871 — they were the same newspaper, as will be seen in the discussion about its title below.

Bramartani (10 February 1887)

only understand the Javanese language and frequently have no understanding at all of Malay".[7] But it was not only poor Europeans who lived
so. J. Dezentjé was the greatest lease-holder in Surakarta, with about
one-third of all of Surakarta's coffee production and a work force of
38,717 people under his control in 1837. He was married to a Raden
Ayu of the Surakarta aristocracy and lived in a grand house in the
mountains built like a princely residence. Said a contemporary, "Time
and again one thought oneself in the presence of a native ruler or regent,
and not that of a Christian landowner."[8]

In 1848 it was decided to open a teacher-training school to provide
indigenous teachers for the government schools then being opened
across Java. That school was finally opened in Surakarta in 1852 and

---

[7] I.J. Brugmans, *Geschiedenis van het onderwijs in Nederlandsch-Indië* (Groningen &
Batavia: J.B. Wolters' Uitgevers-maatschappij, 1938), pp. 81, 97, 100, 103. In 1842
the Institute in Surakarta was closed and the training of future civil servants was
taken over by the newly established Delft Academy in the Netherlands.

[8] Houben, *Kraton and Kumpeni*, p. 262. The quote is from S.A. Buddingh in 1838.

was to take "Javanese of the respectable class" as pupils.[9] Given such initiatives and the general Dutch view that Surakarta was the centre of Javanese civilisation, where the purest form of the Javanese language was to be found, it is not surprising that many of the notable figures in early Dutch scholarship about Java resided there in the 1850s: men such J.F.C. Gericke, J.A. Wilkens, A.B. Cohen Stuart and, of course, the Winter family. Notable Javanese literary figures were also prominent there, as will be seen below. In Chapter 3, we have already referred to figures such as Mangkunagara IV and Ronggawarsita. Local Chinese and Arabs, too, necessarily commanded Javanese.

Thus, in Surakarta *Bramartani* had a multiethnic Javanese-literate elite readership available. It was also distributed widely throughout Java, although I have not encountered any figures on the number of its subscribers. One of its readers was R.M. Suteja, an assistant at the observatory in Batavia,[10] who in 1867 described the paper's readers as being, "aside from the Europeans (*para tuwan-tuwan*), Javanese elite and officials (*amtěnar*, Dutch *ambtenaar*), ... writers and such like".[11] Poensen reported that the paper survived mainly on subscriptions by "eminent natives and some Chinese and Europeans.... No villager reads the paper".[12] *Bramartani*'s frequently repeated admonitions to its subscribers to pay their subscriptions suggest that its survival was not always easy. The paper's advertisements were probably a more reliable source of income.

It is important to recognise that literacy was the preserve of a tiny elite in Java. The devout Muslims discussed in Chapter 3, some of the Christians described in Chapter 5, and the *priyayi* of interest in this Chapter were the only people who could read. The first group, the devout Muslims, undoubtedly included some — perhaps many — whose literacy was restricted to the Arabic script. They could not therefore read *Bramartani*, which was published in the Javanese script; when *Bramarartani* began to publish sections in Malay in 1886, it employed roman script rather than Arabic. We do not have figures for literacy from the nineteenth century. We may, however, note that in the census of 1930 — after decades of increasing educational opportunities pro-

[9] Brugmans, *Onderwijs*, pp. 128–9.
[10] On the history of astronomy in the Netherlands East Indies, see Lewis Pyenson, *Empire of Reason: Exact sciences in Indonesia, 1840–1940* (Leiden: E.J. Brill, 1989), ch. 2.
[11] *BM* 14 Nov. 1867.
[12] C. Poensen, Kědiri, to Bestuurders NZG, Rotterdam, 31 Jan 1881, in ARZ 261.

vided by the colonial government, Christian missions and Islamic organisations — the literacy rate in Central Java was only 5.9 per cent, in the principality of Yogyakarta only 4.4 per cent and in the principality of Surakarta only 3.6 per cent. Even in the cities of Surakarta and Yogyakarta, by then full of new schools of all sorts, the literacy rate reached only 19.7 per cent in the former and 17.9 per cent in the latter in 1930.[13] So nearly a century before such figures were achieved, we may safely assume, literacy was found in only a tiny percentage of the Javanese-speaking population. Of literacy in the Dutch language there was hardly any. Groeneboer estimates that in 1900 there were only some 3,300 indigenous speakers of Dutch in Java, about 0.012 per cent of the indigenous population at that time.[14]

In comparison with the usual reading material available to the elite of Java before the appearance of *Bramartani*, the newspaper represented a revolution. Common items of report included the following (some of which will be pursued further later in this chapter):

- announcements of official appointments, transfers, furloughs, resignations and deaths, among both Europeans and Javanese;
- major colonial ceremonials and events, such as travels by the Governor-General;
- lotteries and the subsequent winners of them;
- local news from throughout Java, including prominently highway robbery and other crimes, local resistance and rebellion movements, opium smuggling, droughts, crop failures, epidemics, burnings of cane-fields and tobacco barns, other fires, great storms, volcanic eruptions, attacks by animals including tigers and snakes, unusual or bizarre events such as the birth of quadruplets to a human mother or of mutant animals;
- descriptions, ridicule and denunciations of the ignorant superstitions of Javanese commoners;
- reports (usually lacking ridicule or denunciations) of superstitious ideas and observations of the Javanese elite;
- births, deaths and marriages of the royal elite and senior *priyayi* families;

---

[13] Departement van Landbouw, Nijverheid en Handel & Departement van Economische Zaken, *Volkstelling 1930 / Census of 1930 in Netherlands India* (8 vols.; Batavia: Landsdrukkerij, 1933–36), vol. II, pp. 67–8.

[14] Kees Groeneboer, *Weg tot het Westen: Nederlands voor Indië 1600–1950; Een taalpolitieke geschiedenis* (*VKI* vol. 158; Leiden: KITLV Uitgeverij, 1993), p. 383.

- legal disputes and criminal trials;
- Javanese social and ritual occasions, from *kraton* celebrations of the great Garĕbĕgs to European-style or hybrid receptions (*rĕsepsi*), parties (*pistha, pista*) or dances (*dhansah*);
- events from around the Indonesian archipelago, including colonial wars of conquest;
- reports on other Indonesian cultures, such as the Tĕnggĕrese or the Hinduism of Bali;
- world events, from European wars and colonial conflicts to the Boxer Rebellion, and great occasions such as the Paris Exhibition of 1878;
- improvements in communications such as railways, telegraph and steamships;
- scientific inventions of all kinds, such as smokeless gunpowder, early-model machineguns or other military technology, photography, electric lighting and much else;
- oddities from across the world, from the behaviour of idiosyncratic Europeans to the birth of a two-headed child, vicious crimes or natural disasters;
- correspondence columns with letters from Javanese readers on any and all topics, often feisty and at times downright rude in style;
- riddles sent in by readers and replies from others;
- reports of entertainments, including amateur theatricals, visiting magicians, performing theatrical troupes and fireworks displays;
- serializations of Javanese literature — in most cases also advertised for sale in *Bramartani* — whether of pre-Islamic or Islamic inspiration, and sometimes Javanese translations of European works;
- auction notices for deceased estates and departing officials; and
- advertisements for local businesses, mostly European- and Chinese-owned, often featuring goods recently imported from Europe.

A substantial part of the news content was taken from Dutch-language papers available in the colony, particularly from *De Locomotief,* published in Sĕmarang from 1852.[15] By the 1870s, items were also being taken

---

[15] Originally with the title *Samarangsche Advertentieblad,* but changing its title to *De Locomotief, Samarangsche Handels- en Advertentieblad* in 1863; Gerard Termorshuizen, with the collaboration of Anneke Scholte, *Journalisten en heethoofden: Een geschiedenis van de Indisch-Nederlandse dagbladpers 1744–1905* (Amsterdam: Nijgh & van Ditmar; Leiden: KITLV Uitgeverij, 2001), p. 816.

from Malay-language papers such as *Slompret Melajoe*, which began to be published in Sěmarang in 1860. Religion was only infrequently discussed.

As noted above, the style of correspondence was often feisty and combative. Anyone enamoured of the stereotype that social interaction amongst Javanese *priyayi* was always refined (*halus*) in style would be challenged by the correspondence columns of *Bramartani*. In this combative style, the paper reflected contemporary Dutch-language newspapers. In his authoritative study of the Netherlands Indies press, Termorshuizen comments on the "tropical style":

> Engagement and combativeness characterised the leading Indies papers. A specific sort of language went along with this. This being often very emotional, the press developed a specific "tropical style". This vigorous and animated style of writing also sat well with the life style of the colony. A journalist once characterised the influence of the Indies environment on the *totoks* [pure-bloods] just arrived from Europe by saying, "The climate requires rather more *sans gêne* [disregard for convention] in daily life, consisting of people going around bare-footed and one's casual attire being made of little and thin clothing."[16]

The missionary Carel Poensen indeed complained about the negative impression that the lively Dutch-language press in Java gave "of the Christian world or of Christian religious teachers or of religion in general — that is at least to be regarded as very careless, not to say that it should make us blush with shame".[17]

How far Javanese society was already removed from the day when kings presumed that they could crush, exile or kill those who disagreed with them was exemplified by the matter of the newspaper's title. In January 1867, three years into the paper's second life, it received a royal command (which it published) from Susuhunan Pakubuwana IX, conveyed by Ronggawarsita. It was commanded that *Jurumartani*, the title then being used, be changed back to *Bramartani*, because the ruler intended to bestow the name Jurumartani on princes in the future. The editor, F.W. Winter, explained that because the large characters for the

---

[16] Termorshuizen, *Journalisten*, p. 21.
[17] Poensen, "Iets over de Javaan als mensch", Kědiri, July 1884; also in *MNZG* 29 (1885): 120.

newspaper masthead had to be specially made, the change of name had to await the arrival of that new masthead.[18] In fact, it took well over three years, suggesting little haste in the matter. The first issue to use the title *Bramartani* again came out on 18 August 1870. To mark that change, the editor — now F.L. Winter — published a four-stanza poem in classical Javanese verse to say that the publishers were of course obeying the royal command of the Susuhunan.[19]

There was often criticism and ridicule of the superstitions of commoners in *Bramartani*. This reflected the increasingly visible intellectual and social distance separating the newspaper's editors and contributors from ordinary Javanese and probably also reflected current Dutch stereotypes. One contributor wrote of his visit to a supposedly miraculous cave at Panaraga where, in fact, he found nothing miraculous.[20] The newspaper denounced two charlatans who visited Surakarta, who claimed to be Arabs and attracted hundreds of locals wanting to see their performance, which was perhaps some sort of conjuring. *Bramartani* added a warning to those who sought enlightenment not to be carried away by such superstition.[21] In 1873 *Bramartani* published newly promulgated police regulations which included fines or forced labour for anyone selling amulets (*jimat*) for which supernatural powers were claimed.[22] For at least some contributors, European learning was the key to superstitions disappearing, for "it has now been proved that, when European learning has spread more and more in Java, certainly there will remain only [a few] traces of superstition".[23] The Javanese term used for European learning was *kawruh Eropah*. *Kawruh* was consistently used for European knowledge in this period; in the following chapter it will be seen that it was a central concept in anti-Islamic polemical works.

When *Bramartani* reported popular messianic movements of the kind described in Chapter 3 above, they were dismissed as another form of superstition. In Kĕdiri the police arrested a young man who deceived commoners by calling himself Sunan Waliyollah Imam Sampurna and other grand and notionally Islamic titles. He said that he was a spirit, and that he had the power to command tigers and to create a child to

---

[18] *BM* 3 Jan. 1867.
[19] *BM* 18 Aug. 1870.
[20] *BM* 22 Aug. 1867.
[21] *BM* 8 Jan. 1874.
[22] *BM* 13 Feb. 1873.
[23] *BM* 29 Jan. 1874.

replace lost children.[24] A man who peddled superstitions about his dreams and his *jimats* was sentenced to four years of forced labour.[25] Another R. Surya who tried to declare himself the Ratu Adil was arrested in 1879.[26] The paper made an interesting comment in its report (received by telegraph) of the 1864 uprising in Tĕgal by some 60 people led by Raden Haji (Mas Cilik). As noted in Chapter 3 above, this caused the death of one Dutchman and several Javanese officials and troops. The paper reported, "to judge from their conduct in pausing at a graveyard and from their all-white clothing, what moved those who joined the violence seems to be an excessive commitment to religion".[27]

In 1869 the paper denounced those who looked forward to the coming of the Ratu Adil as being merely bad-intentioned folk who did not trust the justice of the rulers of Yogyakarta and Surakarta. Those who claimed to be Ratu Adil were just seeking to profit from the ignorance and superstition of the people. How could they not know that only the descendants of kings could become kings, asked the paper rhetorically?[28] In fact, however, many members of the court elite remained just as susceptible to the superstitious claims of holy men, even if some among the *priyayi* sought to rise above such beliefs. One such character gained a reputation for supernatural powers among the aristocrats of Surakarta in 1869 but was soon arrested. The Dutch commented on "the superstition that still prevails even among the higher Javanese aristocracy".[29]

Royal or *priyayi* superstitions were, it seems, a different matter to *Bramartani* and its readers. In 1876 the *kris* Tunggul Wulung, one of the holy regalia (*pusaka*) of the Sultanate, was paraded ceremoniously around Yogyakarta to ward off disease. Even in the twentieth century such efforts to mobilise the supernatural powers of royal *pusakas* continued. *Bramartani*'s report said, with perhaps just the gentlest hint of criticism, "May the lord Allah deign to listen to the laments of the people, although those laments are by means of a weapon being carried about."[30] In 1877, emissaries from the Yogyakarta *kraton* went to the

---

[24] *BM* 8 & 29 Aug. 1867.
[25] *BM* 22 Aug. 1867.
[26] *BM* 13 Feb. 1879.
[27] *BM* 17 Nov. 1864.
[28] *BM* 20 May 1869.
[29] MR 1869 no. 66; MR 1870 no. 196.
[30] *BM* 13 July 1876.

south coast and to Mount Lawu to make offerings to the Goddess
of the Southern Ocean and to the god Hyang Brama. The newspaper
report conveyed no hint of criticism.[31] Such offerings, too, continue to
the present day. In 1880 *Bramartani* reported on the haunted forest
Krĕndhawahana, north of Surakarta, where the demonic goddess Bathari
Durga was to be found. This site was important in the supernatural life
of the *kraton* and the Mangkunagaran principality of Surakarta. In
previous times, it was said that "if a person goes in, that person will die;
if an animal goes in, the animal will die". But now, said the report, a
large village had settled there and only certain antiquities remained to
be seen in the centre of the forest, yet that was still said to be haunted.
So change was reported, but not that all of this might be rank superstition.[32] A contributor in 1878 found all of this rather confusing, or
so he claimed — perhaps disingenuously. He said that many Javanese
still believed in the Goddess of the Southern Ocean who had originally
come from the Pajajaran royal house, or in Prabu Mayanggada from
the same house who became the god of the spirits on Mount Mĕrapi.
But white-skinned people, he said, did not believe that such beings
existed. "I hope there will be experts in *Bramartani* who can clarify this
truly."[33]

The indigenous cultural referents that were reflected in the pages of
Bramartani derived from Javanese elite traditions of the mystic synthesis
kind, with their combination of older pre-Islamic ideas and Islamised
Modern Javanese literature, not the more exclusive world of nineteenth-
century Islamic reformers. Among the many works of literature that were
serialised in the paper were chronicles (*babad*), the legends of Sultan
Ibrahim Ibnu Adam, stories of the Prophet's shaving (*paras Nabi*),
wayang scenarios and such like. Non-indigenous works were also serialised,
such as an account of the marriage of Willem III in the Netherlands (in
1879) and a story of the holy site *Santah Mariyah dhel Nofah*, presumably
the Franciscan monastery Santa Maria La Nova in Venice. It will be seen
in the following chapter that, at least by the 1870s, interpretations of
Javanese history would become a battle-ground for those who objected

---

[31] *BM* 29 Nov. 1877.
[32] On Krĕndhawahana and the *maesa lawung* buffalo-sacrifice ritual carried out
there, see Stephen C. Headley, *Durga's mosque: Cosmology, conversion and community
in Central Javanese Islam* (Singapore: Institute of Southeast Asian Studies, 2004),
particularly pp. 227–30.
[33] *BM* 7 Feb. 1878.

to the advancing Islamisation of Javanese society, some of the first skirmishes being found in serialised literature and correspondence in *Bramartani*.

There was much literary activity in court circles in the middle and later nineteenth century, as reflected in *Bramartani*. Some of the notable authors of Surakarta have already been mentioned in Chapter 3 above, and will be discussed further here. In Yogyakarta there was a particular issue, for at the conquest of the court in 1812 the British forces had looted the royal library. Most of those treasures are now preserved in the collections of the India Office, the British Library and the Royal Asiatic Society in London.[34] During the subsequent troubled years down to the end of the Java War (1825–30) there had been little opportunity to restore that library. It seems that in the second reign of Sultan Haměngkubuwana V (r. 1822–6, 1828–55) effort was put into rebuilding that collection. The works which were written then show the expected combination of Islamic and pre-Islamic mystical works, histories, admonitory literature, works of divination and exorcism, and classics of Modern Javanese, including works derived from Old Javanese literature. Alex Sudewa's analysis shows that in the years 1846–51 were written *Sěrat Cariyos Nabi, Sěrat Jatipusaka, Sěrat Menak, Sěrat Menak Malebari, Sěrat Purwacampur, Sěrat Rama, Sěrat Ngabdulsuka, Sěrat Pawukon, Sěrat Sittin, Sěrat Arjunawiwaha, Sěrat Bratayuda, Sěrat Wulang Brata, Sěrat Kandha ringgit tiyang, Sěrat Arjunasasrabau kawi miring, Sěrat Rama kawi miring, Sěrat Purwakandha, Babad Ngayogyakarta, Babad Mětaram, Sěrat Banjar Rětna, Sěrat Suryaraja, Sěrat Primbon, Sěrat Pangruwatan, Sěrat Wuruk Rěspati, Sěrat Jatiswara* and *Sěrat Suluk warni-warni*.[35]

In the literary world of Central Java, however, there could also be seen what Behrend has called "the accommodation of Dutch science, or

---

[34] See M.C. Ricklefs and P. Voorhoeve, *Indonesian manuscripts in Great Britain: A catalogue of manuscripts in Indonesian languages in British public collections* (London Oriental Bibliographies, 5; Oxford: Oxford University Press, 1977).

[35] Alex Sudewa, "Sultan Hamengku Buwana V: Strategi sastra budaya menghadapi perubahan sosial" (unpublished paper presented to Seminar Sastra dan Budaya, Pusat Kajian Bahasa dan Kebudayaan Indonesia, Universitas Sanata Dharma Yogyakarta, 14 Juli 1997), pp. 9–10. On the production of new Javanese MSS at this time, see T.E. Behrend, "Manuscript production in nineteenth-century Java: Codicology and the writing of Javanese literary history", *BKI* 149, no. 3 (1993): 407–37, esp. pp. 416–21.

perhaps better, the incorporation of certain European ways of thinking, within the larger world of Javanese thought".[36] Behrend's comment is made in the context of the writings of the Yogyakarta prince Suryanagara (b. 1822, d. c. 1886). He was a prolific author, mainly active in the period 1845–76, who produced something like 50 works. He was one of the few Javanese to become a member of the Batavian Society of Arts and Sciences, although he became embroiled in conflict with the Society over the question of whether or not he needed to pay a subscription like others. His works included "studies of language and literature and the associated arts of manuscript decoration, encyclopedic compendia of facts, *belles-lettres*, history and didactic/moralistic *piwulang*". Probably inspired by the lexicographical work of C.F. Winter Sr. and J.A. Wilkens in Surakarta, aficionados of Javanese literature were taking a more scientific approach to their own language. Behrend notes that, in this spirit, Suryanagara's works often include glossaries of obscure words, something never found in the older literature, thereby "in a sense desacralising the language of priest-poets and their fellow purveyors of secret meanings, the puppet masters".[37] Thus, although Poensen observed from Kĕdiri in 1869 that Javanese who could read classical poetry (*macapat*) preferred manuscripts to printed books and were uninterested in more modern, less fabulous literature,[38] in fact in the court cities of Central Java change was well under way.

Bramartani contributors sometimes composed edifying works in *macapat* verse for publication, the very fact that such works were being printed in a weekly newspaper being a major change from the past. Png. Cakradiningrat of Surakarta composed such a work based on teachings found in the *Bratayuda* and *Arjunawijaya*, the Modern Javanese versions of Old Javanese pre-Islamic works. Reflecting his interest in the wider world of European learning, however, Cakradiningrat exemplified his point that kings rarely have true friends by pointing to Henry IV of France (r. 1589–1610).[39]

---

[36] T.E. Behrend, "The writings of K.P.H. Suryanagara: Shifting paradigms in nineteenth-century Javanese thought and letters", *BKI* 155, no. 3 (1999): 404.

[37] Ibid., pp. 390, 393, 406, 410.

[38] C. Poensen, "Bijdragen tot de kennis van den godsdienstigen en zedelijken toestand der Javanen: Eene beschouwing van den inhoud der Javaaansche litteratuur", ARZ 261; also in *MNZG* (with slightly different title) 13 (1869): 153–236 (esp. p. 154), 313–56; 14 (1870): 259–90.

[39] *BM* 5 & 12 Jan. 1865.

But this was not enough for another contributor, one Mas Ngabei Wedapaekarma, a person clearly of lesser aristocratic rank than Cakradiningrat. Wedapaekarma criticised Cakradiningrat for just repeating old lessons from books accessible to anyone who was able to read *Bramartani*. It was easy to teach such ideas, he said, but hard to carry them out. He added,

> It is more appropriate for princes and lower or younger officials to be obliged to go every day to the Javanese and Dutch schools that have been created by the Honoured Government in all of our towns large and small, which teach all branches of knowledge (*kawruh*) aspired to by humankind. That is better than printing passages from good teachings in the paper [*Bramartani*].[40]

A week after Wedapaekarma's criticism was published, another contributor sent in a *macapat* poem that also privileged European over Javanese learning. The poem questioned the value of works such as *Asthabrata, Sruti, Nagarakrama* and *Mĕkutha Raja* and concluded,

> The Dutch people are different,
> for immeasurable are their capabilities
> and truly of great usefulness,
> growing ever greater
> in committing themselves to learning,
> aiming to advance
> towards higher wisdom.[41]

Edifying literature, emphasising the moral requirements of a *priyayi* — invariably including loyalty to the Dutch colonial government — continued to appear in *Bramartani*.[42] One was by Prince Pakualam III himself, addressed to "my friends, the Europeans (*tuwan-tuwan*) and the upper *priyayi* of Java".[43]

---

[40] *BM* 19 Jan. 1865.
[41] *BM* 26 Jan. 1865.
[42] E.g. *BM* 26 Jan. & 2 Feb. 1865.
[43] *BM* 2 Feb. 1865. The author is called Kangjĕng Gusti Pangeran Adipati Surya Sasraningrat, who was in fact Pakualam III (r. 1858–64). Because he died before his 40th birthday, he had not yet formally been given the title Pakualam. The poem was published posthumously. Pakualam III was the author of several works; see Ki Hadjar Dewantara, *Beoefening van letteren en kunst in het Pakoe-Alamsche geslacht* (Djokjakarta: H. Buning, 1931), pp. 16–7.

The printing and publication of Javanese literature was not, of course, limited to the pages of *Bramartani*. Several publishers in Surakarta, Yogyakarta, Sĕmarang, Kĕdiri, Batavia, elsewhere in Java, Singapore and even in the Netherlands published works in Javanese.[44] A sample taken from the bibliography of published Javanese works held in the library of the Batavian Society of Arts and Sciences[45] can illustrate how dramatic and wide-ranging was the impact of the new world of printing in Java. Among the many entries in the catalogue, one finds works such as the prose edition of *Sĕrat Bratayuda* by C.F. Winter Sr. (Amsterdam, 1845), the thousand-and-one nights by the Winters (Netherlands, Sĕmarang, Surakarta, 1847, 1894), "strange stories" taken from Dutch by C.F. Winter Sr. (Netherlands, 1849; another such published in the Netherlands in 1855 and Batavia in 1878), edifying tales (*Tutuge dongeng isi wĕwulang bĕcik*; Netherlands, 1854), *Prĕgiwa* by R.M. Sasradiwirya (Yogyakarta, 1830, 1880), Pakubuwana IV's *Wulang reh* (Batavia, 1858; Sĕmarang, 1884), *Tapĕl Adam* (Batavia, 1859; Surakarta, 1903), extracts from *Tapĕl Adam* (Batavia,1874), *Anggĕr nĕgari* (Sĕmarang, 1871), *Arjuna Sasrabau* (Batavia, 1868; Sĕmarang, 1872, 1873, 1883), *Nitisastra kawi* (Batavia, 1871), the Javanese translation of the *Qur'an* (Batavia, 1858), *Sĕkar kawi* (Batavia, 1870, 1879), *Angling Darma* (Batavia, 1853; Sĕmarang, 1884), *Sĕrat Rama* by Yasadipura I (*Verhandelingen van het Bataviaasch Genootschap van Kunsten Wetenschappen*, Batavia, 1846; Sĕmarang, 1872, 1884), *Sĕrat Bratayuda* by Yasadipura I (*Verhandelingen van het Bataviaasch Genootschap van Kunsten Wetenschappen*, Batavia, 1860); *wayang* scenarios (e.g. *Lampahan obong-obong bale si Gala-gala* by H. Kern, Amsterdam, 1876; and *Suksma-lĕmbara* by R.Tg. Purbanĕgara, Yogyakarta, 1898), Ronggawarsita's *Paramayoga* (Surakarta, 1884) and *Pustaka Raja* (Yogyakarta, 1884, 1885, 1887, 1888, 1892), *Sĕrat Tajusalatin* (Semarang, n.d.), *Dewa Ruci* by M. Bei Kramaprawira (Sĕmarang, 1873, 1880, 1890), admonitions of Pakubuwana IV (*Piwulang-dalĕm Ingkang Sinuwun Pakubuwana kaping IV*; Surakarta, 1876), *Nawawi* (Surakarta, 1877), *Babad Pĕcina* (Batavia, 1874), *Sultan Ibrahim* turned into Javanese by

---

[44] A complete set of Javanese printing typefaces was made in the Netherlands in 1839; E.M. Uhlenbeck, *A critical survey of studies on the languages of Java and Madura* ('s-Gravenhage: Martinus Nijhoff, 1964), p. 46.
[45] Poerwasoewignja and Wirawangsa, *Pratélan*. This wonderful catalogue not only lists works, but also includes abstracts of them, often very lengthy, in Javanese. Readers seeking more information on the individual works listed here may locate them by using the indices in *Pratélan*.

C.F. Winter (Yogyakarta, 1881; Batavia, 1882, 1908), *Umul Brahim* (a work of Sufism produced in Javanese verse by R. Panji Jayasubrata; Sĕmarang, 1884), *Johar Manik* (Sĕmarang, 1886), *Carios Nabi Rasul* (Sĕmarang, 1891), *Suluks* (Sĕmarang, 1905), *Mikradipun Gusti Rasul* (Yogyakarta, 1910), Mangkunagara IV's *Wedhatama* (Surakarta, 1897), *Sĕrat Cĕnthini* (Batavia, 1912, 1914, 1915) and many, many more such publications.

Some works in the Batavia collection reflected the purifying work of Islamic reformers, including translations of the works of Sayid Uthman bin Aqil bin Yahya al-Alawi (1822–1913), as already pointed out in Chapter 3. One such work was published in Javanese verse (*Nasehat*, turned into Javanese verse by R. Astra Sutadiningrat; Pandegĕlang, 1903). The book *Bab sarat rukuning agami Islam* (Surakarta, 1897) taught the obligations of all Muslims under *shari'a* law. *Manasik Haji* (Yogyakarta, 1899) advised how to conduct the *hajj*. We have already noted that the Javanese translation of the *Qur'an* was published in Batavia in 1858. Christianity was also, of course, represented in print. The Javanese translation of the Bible had a complicated history. A version of the New Testament was printed in 1831 that the Dutch government banned, but nevertheless some copies seem to have found their way into circulation in Java. A translation was allowed to be published in 1848.[46] In the library of the Batavian Society of Arts and Sciences were found works of Christian teaching such as *Wĕwulang Kristen* (Rotterdam, 1889) and books on prayer in Protestantism (*Pĕdupan kĕncana*, n.d.) and Catholicism (*Wose agama Kristen Katolik*; Magĕlang, n.d., Yogyakarta, 1915). The New Testament (*Prajanjian anyar*) was also published in Singapore in 1911.

More utilitarian literature was also published, such as textbooks for Javanese schools on arithmetic (*Bĕbukaning kawruh itung*; Surakarta, 1855), the proper use of the Javanese language (*Ukara sarta tĕmbung ingkang kadamĕl lĕpat*; Batavia, 1865), surveying (*Elmu ukur bumi* by W. Palmer van den Broek; Batavia, 1865, 1875*)*, the responsibilities of teachers (*Wulang guru*; Batavia, 1865, 1872, 1897) and of students (*Wulang murid*; n.d.), the geography of the Netherlands East Indies (*Kapuloan Indie wetan* by T.A.F. van der Valk; Batavia, 1863, 1890), a thick volume on astronomical and meteorological phenomena and Western, Arab, Javanese and Chinese calendars (translated from Dutch

---

[46] Swellengrebel, *Leijdeckers voetspoor*, vol. I, pp. 42–3, 62.

by M.Ar. Candranagara; Sěmarang, 1876), the geography of Java (*Pěthikan elmu bumi*; Batavia, 1871), a work by F.W. Winter on how to compose and sing classical Javanese verse (*Těmbang Jawa nganggo musik*; Batavia, 1874, 1899), Ki Padmasusastra's instructions on Javanese script and words (*Parama basa*; Batavia, 1897, 1898) and his book on the language of Surakarta (*Basa Sala*; Batavia, 1911), children's stories (*Kitab akan dibaca anak-anak*, translated into Javanese by R. Ng. Sasrakusuma; Sěmarang, 1872), advice on personal hygiene and other matters (*Pělajaran běcik*; Batavia, 1880), measures against influenza (*Lělara influenza*; Weltevreden, 1920) and so on.

The world of the Europeans, whether in Java or overseas, was also represented in print. C.F. Winter published an account of the Napoleonic Wars (*Pěrang ing něgari Neděrland*; Yogyakarta, 1879). A presumably Catholic writer named Benedictus Sastrawiarja published an account of medieval Belgium (*Singaning Vlaanderen*; Magělang, 1916). One might also purchase an account of the Batavia exhibition of 1865 (*Tentoonstelling Bětawi taun 1865* by Jatmika; Batavia, 1867) or of the city of Batavia more generally (*Carios něgari Bětawi* by R. Arya Sastradarma; Batavia, 1867, 1869, 1877), a poem in Javanese verse about the horse-drawn trams of Batavia (*Tramweg kareta gěrbong*; Batavia, 1869), or a description of the Dutch-style celebration of the new year in Surakarta (*Pasamuan taun baru ing Surakarta* by R. Atmadikara; Surakarta, 1870). The life of the *Patih* Sasraněgara of Surakarta and the bestowing of the star of the Lion of the Netherlands on him was also published (*Laksitarja*; Surakarta 1885, 1894). In this hybrid Dutch-Javanese world of the *priyayi* who served the Dutch government, fine points of status were important. Government rules on public displays of status by *priyayi* from *bupatis* down to lowly scribes were published in 1870 (*Prěnatan agěm-agěmanipun pameran priantun Jawi*; Surakarta 1870).

Among the most innovative works of the time were the travels of R.M. Condranagara V, writing under the pseudonym Purwalělana. These *Lampah-lampahipun R.M.A. Purwalělana* were published in Batavia in 1865–66, in Sěmarang in 1877 and again in Batavia in 1880. Condranagara V (b.c. 1836, d. 1885) was *Bupati* of Kudus (1858–80) and of Brěběs (1880–85). Around 1858 he travelled across much of Java, from Batavia in the west to Banyuwangi at the eastern extremity of the island, a total of some 5,000 kms of travel. His journals of these trips were written or substantially revised in 1864 and first published by the government printing office (Landsdrukkerij) in Batavia in 1865–66. Purwalělana's travels represented an important new prose genre of

R.M. Condranagara V (Purwalĕlana),
c. 1867 (Photo by Woodbury & Page;
Collection of KITLV, Leiden)

realistic reportage in Javanese. He described the countryside, the population, the towns, officials he encountered, and so on. Not surprisingly Purwalĕlana was among the readers of *Bramartani*, which published a letter from him in its issue of 7 October 1869 about a visit he had made to the Gunung Kidul area, where he found multiple pre-Islamic (called *Buda*) antiquities and heard local stories of their supernatural endowments.[47] The following year he became a member of the Batavian Society of Arts and Sciences.[48]

Other travel accounts similar to *Purwalĕlana* were also published, and were to be found in the library of the Batavian Society. These included the work *Purwa carita Bali*, which described the circumstances of each of the Balinese kingdoms, Balinese religion and Balinese customs, written by R. Sasrawijaya and published in Batavia in 1875. *Carios nĕgari Padhang* described west Sumatra and Nias. Raden Ngabdullah Ibnu Sabar bin Arkebah's account of travelling from Batavia to the Netherlands (*Carios nĕgari Nederland*) was published in Batavia in 1876. The

---

[47] *BM* 7 Oct. 1869.
[48] Bonneff, *Pérégrinations*, p. 25. Bonneff's study is the authoritative work on Purwalĕlana's travels; interested readers should seek further details there. The original Javanese text is to be found in Purwalĕlana, *Lampah-lampahipun*.

Malay-language travels of Munshi Abdullah were published in Javanese translation in Batavia in 1883 (*Ngabdullah bin Ngabdulkadir Munsi*, translated by Jaka Mubtadi). In 1916 R.M.Ar. Suryasuparta published his account of travel to the Netherlands, *Carios kĕkesahan saking tanah Jawi dhatĕng nĕgari Wĕlandi* (Weltevreden, 1916) followed three years later by the account of M. Yitnasastra's travel to Papua (*Kesah layaran dhatĕng pulo Papuah*, Weltevreden 1919).

While such publications were coming out in large volumes, Europeans' interest in the pre-Islamic past in Java was growing, supported by increasing Dutch connections with Bali, where Old Javanese literature was preserved in greater volume and accuracy than in Java. In Bali, Old and Middle Javanese literature were part of a living Hindu literary culture. Europeans began to publish Old Javanese works from the middle of the nineteenth century. The first such publications were by R. Friederich, who brought out editions of Old Javanese works based on manuscripts from Bali beginning in 1850. J.L.A. Brandes published the Middle Javanese *Pararaton* in 1897 and the *Deśawarṇana* (then entitled *Nāgarakṛtāgama*) in 1904, providing accounts of Java's pre-Islamic kingdoms. A major watershed occurred in 1900 when H. Kern published a scholarly edition of the Old Javanese *Rāmāyaṇa*. This was followed by the publication of the Old Javanese *Bhāratayuddha* by J.G.H. Gunning in 1903. These publications were emblematic of the way in which Dutch scholarship was opening a way to the Javanese pre-Islamic past, a theme we will consider further in the following chapter.

Among the new literary works of mid-nineteenth century Java, those by Mangkunagara IV (r. 1853–81) and Ronggawarsita (1802–73) are probably best known. The latter is commonly described as the last of Java's great poets (*pujangga*), although — as will be seen below — there was less unanimity on that at the time than later.[49] His grave remains today a place of pilgrimage among devotees, who seek mystical experiences there. Among the works ascribed to Ronggawarsita, *Paramayoga* (The exalted age[?]) and *Pustakaraja Purwa* (Book of the kings of ancient times) were the most ambitious. These constituted a legendary or pseudo-history of pre-Islamic times in Java. They were structured chronologically in a way that reflected the influence of Western

---

[49] On Ronggawarsita's place in Javanese literary history, see also Nancy Florida, "Reading the unread in traditional Javanese literature", *Indonesia* no. 44 (Oct. 1987): 1–15, or Nancy Florida, *Writing the past, inscribing the future: History as prophecy in colonial Java* (Durham [N.C.] & London: Duke University Press, 1995), pp. 37–50.

styles of scholarship, for they employed a fake dual calendrical system, using both a solar and a lunar year. Javanese literati knew that the European calendar of 365–66 days rested on a solar year, whereas their *Anno Javanico* was a lunar year of 354–55 days. As a consequence, every lunar century is three years shorter than a solar century. In the nineteenth century these two calendars marched in their incommensurate way ever forward. What *Paramayoga* and *Pustakaraja Purwa* did was to make them also march backward, to the year 1 in Java's legendary past. From then on, *Paramayoga* and *Pustakaraja Purwa* provided a chronology of the supposed history of Java dated in the two calendars. This innovation was matched by the innovative use of prose. Indeed, it was probably the fact that these works were in prose rather than verse that raised questions in the minds of contemporary literati as to whether they should be regarded as proper works of literature at all.

Ronggawarsita and Mangkunagara IV were collaborators and the earliest version of *Pustakaraja Purwa* that we can date with any confidence is in fact ascribed to the latter, who was himself undoubtedly one of the major literary figures of his age.[50] This is a manuscript that "tells of the sequence of all events in the whole of the island of Java" from the year 1 to 1400. It is described as the royal creation (*yasa-dalĕm*) of Png.Ad.Ar. Mangkunagara IV, done in agreement with the royal wish (*karsa-dalĕm*) of Susuhunan Pakubuwana VII.[51] Since Pakubuwana VII reigned from 1830 to 1858 and Mangkunagara IV from 1853 to 1881, this work must have been composed in the overlapping years 1853–58. Enthusiasm for earlier Javanese history is exemplified in the opening invocation of the text, which is not Islamic but rather a version of the formula found in Old Javanese Hindu-Buddhist works, *O I laeng ong mangarcana mataya awignam astu nama siddhim.*[52]

Thus, *Pustakaraja Purwa* seems to be a work of the mid-nineteenth century, although it is not known when Ronggawarsita wrote his version. Day believes it to have been in the 1850s, on the grounds that the earliest reference is from 1855, when "a lady courtier recomposed or copied an unpublished section of the *Pustaka Raja* in verse".[53] This could, however,

---

[50] See the works published in Mangkunagara IV, *Sĕrat-sĕrat.*
[51] *Sĕrat Pustakaraja* by Mangkunagara IV, written at the wish of Pakubuawana VII (for details, see the bibliography below), pp. [i], 1.
[52] Ibid., p. 1.
[53] John Anthony Day, "Meanings of change in the poetry of nineteenth-century Java", PhD dissertation, Cornell University, 1981, pp. 221–2.

Grave of Ronggawarsita, Palar

have been the version ascribed to Mangkunagara IV described in the previous paragraph. As noted above, Ronggawarsita's *Paramayoga* was first published in Surakarta and his *Pustaka Raja* in Yogyakarta, both in 1884. In the later published editions that I have been able to study, the former consists of 3 thin volumes and the latter of 29.[54] These are not, in other words, small works of literature.

Paramayoga begins with Adam who, in this work of wonderful imagination, becomes the ancestor of the Hindu gods. His son Sis marries a heavenly nymph (*widadari*), begets Said Anwar who begets the Hindu-Buddhist deity Sang Hyang Nurasa. From then on the transition to the age of gods and legendary heroes of Javanese myth is easily made. *Pustakaraja Purwa* then tells of Java, Sumatra, Madura and Bali from when the first people appeared there. The stories of the early legendary parts of *babads* and the great epics of the *wayang* theatre are here fitted into Ronggawarsita's grand theme as if they were part of a real history.

[54] Ronggawarsita, *Sěrat Paramayoga* (3 vols.; Djokja: Kolff-Buning, 1941) and *Sěrat Pustakaraja Purwa* (29 vols.; Djokja: Kolff-Buning, 1938–39). Invaluable Javanese summaries of these works may be found in Poerwasoewignja and Wirawangsa, *Pratélan* vol. I, pp. 345–8, 439–74.

How are we to understand this strange pseudo-history of the ancient past in prose, tied together by a dual calendrical framework that lent it an entirely false air of historical precision, written in a society that had never before seen such a work? Day suggests that one approach is to "see the work as an imitation of and response to Dutch philological scholarship on ancient Java in the nineteenth century".[55] This is consistent with a general theme in this chapter, the response of the *priyayi* of Java to the new world brought by the Europeans. The application of what may have been intended to look like a more modern and analytical methodology to Java's most ancient, pre-Islamic history was also emblematic of the way in which, for the Javanese elite, European-style modernity was a means to embracing pre-Islamic culture.

For some Javanese *priyayi*, however, Ronggawarsita's contribution was not exemplary of a new age, but rather in contrast to it. In 1873, the year of Ronggawarsita's death, there occurred a debate in *Bramartani* about the value of his contribution. One writer said that if Ronggawarsita were compared with "the students at the teacher-training school who can understand arithmetic, Javanese, Malay and some Dutch, geography, natural history, astronomy and other things that are useful to the government, ... then truly the Raden Ngabei [Ronggawarsita] will be left with his standing as *pujangga* rather shaky". He also compared the progress of the Japanese, who had been in contact with Europeans for less than 200 years, with the Javanese had been in contact for 400.[56] This was historically erroneous, but the claim had a cultural pointedness in the wake of the Meiji restoration of 1868 and subsequent rapid changes in Japan — knowable through the pages of *Bramartani*.

In *Paramayoga, Pustakaraja Purwa* and the vast range of published works listed above, as in the pages of *Bramartani*, there could be found that "incorporation of certain European ways of thinking, within the larger world of Javanese thought" suggested by Behrend, as we noted above. Javanese language and literature were not only being enriched by new ideas and insights, but were themselves becoming objects of a more scholarly approach. *Bramartani* frequently published correspondence about the meaning of words. It was noted above that the Malay-language travels of Munshi Abdullah were translated into Javanese by Jaka Mubtadi and published in Batavia in 1883. Three years before, Jaka Mubtadi

---

[55] Day, "Meanings", p. 227.
[56] *BM* 4 Sept. 1873. Other correspondence follows in subsequent issues of *BM*.

Grave of C.F. Winter Sr adjacent to that of Ronggawarsita, Palar. The remains were identified in Surakarta by "paranormal" means and moved to Palar in recent years

wrote to *Bramartani* at length expressing concern that the great variety in Javanese usage in various places in Java meant that there was no standard for the language. Even those regarded as great literati (*pujongga agĕng*) frequently disagreed with one another on such matters, he said.[57] Other contributors took an interest in the dialect of Banyuwangi: "the people are Javanese, the words are indeed Javanese, but in an ancient form" said one Dwijawara, who said that he intended to write a book on this subject.[58]

Throughout 1880 in particular there was a steady stream of correspondence on the meanings of Javanese words, or the titles of Javanese works of literature. Sometimes this lexicographical correspondence concerned Arabic religious terms. One writer wanted to know who had invented the *gamĕlan*.[59] Female contributors named Widawati and Kusumaningrum queried the meaning of terms such as *suksma* and

[57] *BM* 20 May 1880.
[58] *BM* 25 Dec. 1879 & 4 Mar. 1880.
[59] *BM* 4 Nov. 1880.

nyawa.[60] These were central concepts in Javanese Sufism, with *suksma* meaning immateriality, the soul, or, in the combination *Hyang Suksma*, God, while *nyawa* might mean the immaterial soul but also conveyed the idea of the life principle. It was an innovation in Java for such abstruse matters regarding the unseen world to be discussed openly in a weekly newspaper. We cannot, however, know whether it was unusual for women to be the discussants. We know of very few women literati in Javanese history, but then we know the names of very few writers of either gender. It is clear that in the eighteenth century there were elite women who were active in literary endeavour.[61] There were probably many more of whom we are ignorant. Nor can we know how many of the contributors in *Bramartani* who used noms de plume were female. But we may be confident that Widawati and Kusumaningrum were not the only women joining the intellectual exchanges in the paper's columns, for there were others who can also be identified by their names.

Priyayi Loyalty

This more analytical, more — we may say — European approach to learning was combined with strong *priyayi* loyalty to those who had brought that new approach to Java. Praise of the colonial government and its wisdom was common in *Bramartani*. For example, when there was a formal brick-laying for a new *Bupati*'s residence in Ciamis (Cirĕbon residency), the *Bupati* made a speech in which he emphasised that this exemplified the goodness of the government for which the common folk (*tiyang alit*) should be grateful. The Islamic scholars (*ngulama*) should be strong in their thanks, said he, for this was a sign that the government took to heart the welfare of the common folk, who were now more prosperous than when ruled by Javanese kings.[62] The evidence discussed in Chapter 2 above suggests that this claim may have been of greater rhetorical than analytical weight, of course.

The greatest example of *priyayi* loyalty — one that illustrates the immense distance between nineteenth-century Java and the twentieth-century world of Indonesian nationalism — was found in their reaction to the Aceh War. In March 1873 the Dutch colonial forces attacked

---

[60] E.g. *BM* 11 Nov. & 9 Dec. 1880.
[61] E.g. see the references to Ratu Pakubuwana and Ny.M. Kaduwang in Ricklefs, *Seen and unseen worlds.*
[62] *BM* 16 Feb. 1865.

the independent state of Aceh, thereby initiating the longest war in Dutch colonial history, indeed the longest war in colonial history anywhere.[63] That first Dutch expedition was repulsed by the Acehnese and its commander, Major General J.H.R. Köhler, was killed. *Bramartani's* coverage of this disastrous expedition and the subsequent war was marked by two things: unquestioning loyalty to the government side and pride that Javanese soldiers were amongst those fighting to conquer Aceh for the colonial state. The paper reported how Köhler was killed in the mosque in Aceh. When the fighting was over, the bodies of the enemy were buried; there were 80 of these, many of them *hajis*, said *Bramartani*. Although eventual victory for the colonial side was certain, it editorialised, the Acehnese were capable and well-armed fighters who had no fear of death.[64] Soon thereafter, the paper reported proudly that the Mangkunagaran and Pakualaman legions were about to be dispatched to Aceh and had been entrusted with new breech-loading rifles. It expressed the hope that the Javanese troops would fight bravely and that they might "repay the love of the Honoured Government that governs and defends the island of Java, amen".[65] It may have been no coincidence that as *Bramartani* reported on the Aceh War throughout 1873, it also serialised *Babad Mataram*, much of it devoted to Javanese wars and heroic martial exploits of pre-colonial times.

Government Schools

Fascination with European learning and loyalty to the colonial government were combined above all in the *priyayi* enthusiasm for modern schools. As with the Islamic reformers, education was at the centre of the new *priyayi* world.

Before the middle years of the nineteenth century, there was little provision of formal education in Java other than the *pĕsantrens* discussed in Chapter 3, and there do not seem to have been many even of them. In 1845 J.F.C. Gericke lamented the absence of schools where the youth of Java could learn "reading and writing and other useful skills", except

---

[63] For a brief account, see Ricklefs, *History of modern Indonesia*, pp. 186–9. For a detailed scholarly analysis of the background to the war and its progress, see Anthony Reid, *The contest for North Sumatra: Atjeh, the Netherlands and Britain, 1858–1898* (London: Oxford University Press, 1969).

[64] *BM* 1 May 1873.

[65] *BM* 17 July 1873.

where *priyayi* managed to send their children to the few elementary schools set up by the government for Europeans.[66]

In 1865, Purwalĕlana published in *Bramartani* a survey of education in Java, based on responses to the 1819 colonial survey mentioned in Chapter 3 above. He pointed out that there was then hardly any education beyond religious matters and that levels of literacy among the *priyayi* were low. In various places the local religious (*kaum*) taught recitation of the *Qur'an* (often without understanding the meaning of the text) to the children of *priyayi* but rarely anything else. Those who wanted to attain higher levels of religious understanding — presumably Sufism was meant — must go to the famous schools of Madiun or Panaraga. In Tĕgal, *kaum* also taught children to read and write Javanese, to speak Malay and some arithmetic. Yet out of 850 village heads in the area, only three or four could even write their names. In Jipang, among village heads only ten could read and write Javanese. In Kĕdu, the sons of *priyayi* were taught to read and write Javanese by their parents, relatives or educated servants. In Grĕsik, all of the sons of *priyayi* were said to be literate in Javanese, having been taught by a scribe employed by their parents. In Surabaya, reading, writing and arithmetic were taught by family members or friends of the *priyayi*. Only the sons of the most senior *priyayi* on the *pasisir* could speak Malay. In Pasuruan reading and writing in Javanese was taught by the scribes of the *priyayis*. In Banyuwangi, even the *Bupatis* could not read or write well in their own language.[67]

The data published by Purwalĕlana was already out of date by 1865, for from 1848 the government began to open schools in Java where Javanese could learn skills useful to the administration. Javanese was the language of instruction but Malay was also taught, along with practical skills such as arithmetic, geography and surveying.[68] The Javanese elite embraced these schools with enthusiasm, led by the example of royalty. The *Babad Mangkunagaran* notes that in 1859 Mangkunagara IV became both a knight of the Netherlands Lion and chairman of the commission for the Javanese teacher–training school set up in Surakarta in 1852.[69]

---

[66] J.F.C. Gericke, "Iets omtrent de oprigting van scholen op Java", Surakarta 27 Sept. 1845, in ARZ 512.

[67] *BM* 13 & 27 Apr., 11 May 1865, Purwalĕlana here identifies himself as R.M.Tg. Ar. Surya Condranagara, *Bupati* of Kudus (the position held by Condranagara V/ Purwalĕlana from 1858 to 1880).

[68] Brugmans, *Onderwijs*, p. 128 *et seqq.*

[69] LOr 6781, p. 96; this reference from notes by Soegiarto in LOr 10,867c, no. 43, p. 7.

In 1865 other contributors to *Bramartani* responded to Purwalĕlana's articles to say how much educational improvement there already was in the Central Javanese principalities. In the Pakualaman there was a school with a government-paid Javanese teacher and 28 students from *priyayi* families. They were taught Javanese and Dutch literature, arithmetic and Malay or other languages. The Pakualaman *Pangulu* and his colleagues taught the *Qur'an* and Arabic literacy to 22 pupils. In the *Patih's* residence were taught Javanese script, poetic metres and classical literary form (*krama kawi*), as well as *priyayi* etiquette and Dutch literature.[70] From Surakarta, a European resident praised Mangkunagara IV's provision of education in useful knowledge (*kawruh*) by employing teachers of Javanese, Malay and Arabic.[71] During his third trip around Java c. 1858, Purwalĕlana himself visited the teacher-training school in Surakarta. There he found three European teachers (*tuwan-tuwan*) offering eight subjects: writing in the Javanese script, writing Malay in the Western alphabet, arithmetic, geography, surveying, Javanese language, some Madurese and some Sundanese. Many of the students were from outside the principalities. He was of the view, however, that the Javanese language did not seem to be well taught.[72] These subjects were those commonly found in post-1848 government schools in Java. It is notable that the Malay that was taught did not employ the Arabic script, while in the *pĕsantrens* discussed in Chapter 2, the students were not taught the Javanese script. So these two school systems were producing students who could literally not write a letter to each other. And whereas religion was central to the Islamic schools, it was expressly excluded from the government schools, which was why earlier ideas about seeking the help of the Netherlands mission societies in education went nowhere.[73] Educational polarisation was thus paralleling social differentiation in Java.

Everywhere in Java the opening of these modern schools was the subject of celebration. The new school at Kudus opened in 1864 with speeches by the Dutch Assistant Resident and the *Bupati*, who was of course Purwalĕlana. He spoke in *krama* Javanese and Malay, addressed himself in Dutch to the Europeans present, then used *ngoko* Javanese to the Javanese officials. The pupils, of whom there were already 53, sang

---

[70] *BM* 8 June 1865.
[71] *BM* 15 June 1865. The writer signed himself Tuwan Kondhestu and said he was a 42-year-old native of Surakarta who had always lived there.
[72] Purwalĕlana, *Lampah-lampahipun*, vol. II, pp. 22–3.
[73] Harthoorn, *Onderwijs*, p. 104.

a Javanese song composed for the occasion and the Dutch national anthem in Javanese translation.[74] Purwalĕlana would drop into the school to observe the lessons on a daily basis when he was present at his Regency office.[75] Harthoorn expressed the view in 1865 that the *priyayi* only supported these schools in order to remain in favour with the government, not out of any genuine enthusiasm on their part.[76] He seems to have been wrong in this judgment. His colleague Jellesma noted how the local *priyayi* at Majawarna sent their sons to his mission school, particularly to learn literacy in Javanese and Malay and arithmetic. "They distinguish themselves in their diligence and ambition", he wrote. He had had to turn away other *priyayi* children who could not pay for their own maintenance while at school, for he could not support them himself.[77] Some *Bupatis* took their own initiatives, such as the *Bupati* of Magĕtan who set up his own private schools.[78] Other examples will be seen below.

Public examinations of pupils at these schools became major events which the *Bupati*, local Dutch officials, *priyayi* and parents usually attended. Students demonstrated their competencies and prizes were awarded to the best. Sometimes they were then treated to entertainments, to horse-riding or *wayang* for example.[79] The pupils took part in the developing *priyayi* hybrid intellectual culture and could be found among letter-writers to *Bramartani*.[80] Consistent with the idea that European education was also the key to Javanese culture, one writer said that he was grateful to the government because the teacher-training school in Surakarta would be the means to preserve the proper formation of Javanese script, which might otherwise disappear.[81] In 1873 and again in 1877, three students were selected for further study in the Netherlands,

---

[74] Anon., "Oordeel van een Javaansch regent over het inlandsche onderwijs", *Koloniale jaarboeken* 4 (1864): 319–21.

[75] *BM* 4 Jan. 1866.

[76] Harthoorn, *Onderwijs*, pp. 168–9.

[77] Hoezoo, "Verslag 1861", pp. 196–7.

[78] *BM* 27 Nov. & 11 Dec. 1873.

[79] E.g. see *BM* 4 Jan. 1866, 7 July 1870, 14 July 1870 (noting that one of the sons of Mangkunagara IV was among those who demonstrated their competence), 21 Nov. 1872, 30 Oct. 1873, 15 Jan. 1874, 31 Dec. 1874, 23 Nov. 1876, 29 Nov. 1877, 9 May 1878, 5 Sept. 1878, 13 Nov. 1879. Such reports continued in subsequent years; for a later example, see *BM* 26 July 1883.

[80] E.g. see *BM* 27 Sept. 1866, 27 Nov. 1873.

[81] *BM* 26 Sept. 1867.

one each from the teacher-training schools in Java (Surakarta), Sunda (Bandung) and Sumatra (Padang).[82] A teacher at the school in Magĕtan hoped to be selected to go to Amsterdam in 1873 and was studying Dutch from a dictionary, but *Bramartani*'s editor, Surana, advised him that this was unlikely to give him command of the language.[83] In 1851 the government opened a school for indigenous health professionals — called *dhoktĕr Jawa* — attached to the military hospital in Weltevreden (Batavia, now the Gambir district of Jakarta).[84] Graduates of this elite school were also reported in *Bramartani*.[85]

Praise of the schools was part of the general praise of European learning. In 1865, Raden Panji Puspawilaga wrote to *Bramartani* of his life experience. He commenced by saying that "our Prophet the Messenger of God, Muhammad" commanded that all of his community should become enlightened (*binudiya*, from *budi*, a term that will be seen in the following chapter to be of significance). Puspawilaga had been poor as a child, but Europeans adopted him and taught him Dutch and other useful skills such as mathematics and surveying. At the age of 27 he went to work in the government's General Secretariat in Batavia. Later he worked with Png. Surya Sasraningrat (i.e. Pakualam III) in Yogyakarta. For all of this he blessed King Willem III.[86] Another writer expressed thanks first to God, then to Muhammad, then to the government of the Netherlands Indies for what children could now learn in the government schools. He went on to describe an inspection trip to the schools of Purwakĕrta.[87]

One of *Bramartani*'s many poetically inclined contributors, Mangunkaswasih from Madiun, wrote in classical Javanese verse in 1886 to praise the government and its schools:

> Truly beneficent is the Dutch government
> towards all its subjects,
> striving for their welfare.

---

[82] *BM* 6 Nov. 1873, 28 Apr. 1877.

[83] *BM* 27 Nov. 1873.

[84] Brugmans, *Onderwijs*, p. 285. The *dhoktĕr Jawa* course initially lasted two years. Training of indigenous vaccinators went back to 1811. From 1875 the *dhoktĕr Jawa* course was extended to five or six years and was taught in Dutch.

[85] *BM* 20 Nov. 1873.

[86] *BM* 2 Mar. 1865. On Pakualam III, see n. 43 above.

[87] *BM* 10 Oct. 1872.

Everywhere one goes, it has given
schools which educate
all the youth
without selecting on the basis of their descent.
Even if they are sons of commoners,
all are given education most elevated
so as to fulfill their futures.

When they become adults,
their path is eased in seeking
their food and clothing,
coming from doing what is good,
constantly engaged in superior endeavour,[88]
doing no wrong
to others,
compassionate towards their fellow beings,
certainly bringing peace and order to the state;
burdensome for them is any evil deed.[89]

Although the students at the government schools in Java were boys, education for girls also received some attention. In the early 1870s, the *Bupati* of Madiun, R.M.Ad. Sasranagara, opened a school for girls on his own initiative. They were taught Javanese and Arabic script, *shari'a* law concerning the duties of women, their obligation of homage to parents, teachers and the ruler, and useful skills such as sewing, weaving and cooking. Cooking was taught in both Dutch and Javanese styles. Girls from the age of 8 upwards were admitted and 60 to 80 reportedly attended.[90] A decade later *Bramartani* published an article on education in the United States — a nation admired by the paper and its readers for its advances in science and industry — where there were a great many schools. It was a regulation there, said *Bramartani*, that all boys and girls attend school, where they received the same education. Able graduates, including women, were employed by the government. An estimated 4,000 women worked for the American government in post offices and elsewhere. There were approximately 20,000 girls in education in

---

[88] The words translated as "superior endeavour" are *utameng budi*. This "superior *budi*" was also later captured in the name of the *priyayi* organisation Budi Utomo, founded in 1908 (see Chapter 8 below).
[89] *BM* 4 Mar. 1886.
[90] *BM* 9 Oct. 1873.

the city of New York. Three hundred very bright women were educated at Wellesley College. There were even women lawyers. Concluded *Bramartani*, "What is amazing is that people in America are regarded as equally distinguished in intelligence without treating men separately, for women are treated just the same."[91] Female education in Java, however, was still a minority interest in either Dutch or Javanese circles.

By 1861 there were 44 government schools in Java with 1931 pupils.[92] These numbers were small when compared with those of the Islamic schools seen in Chapter 3. Table 4 there records nearly 94,000 students in religious schools in 1863. But the students of the government schools were on their way to being the *priyayi* elite of Java and their numbers were growing. By 1877 there were over 600 students in the six schools in the Regency of Madiun.[93] In 1892 there were 35,495 pupils in government schools in Java and Madura and 14,801 in private (some of them mission) schools, for a total of 50,296. A decade later those numbers had grown to 50,734 and 35,098 respectively, for a total of 85,832. About 2.2 per cent of the students were girls in 1892, about 4.6 per cent in 1902. There were, however, high rates of absenteeism and in the light of the total population of Java and Madura — some 29 million in 1902 — these numbers remained derisory.[94]

European Science and European Ways

Although the readers of *Bramartani* were in awe of the scientific advances of the United States — "America, that land whose inventions of all kinds are ever greater and more amazing"[95] — the principle cultural reference was to the Netherlands, represented directly in Java by the colonial regime. For European science and the Dutch language there was much enthusiasm.

One Abdulatip of Sěmarang — unknown to me except as a frequent contributor to *Bramartani* — wrote in 1867 about natural history and

---

[91] *BM* 4 Jan. 1883 (a misprint in the masthead gives the date erroneously as 4 Jan. 1882). Wellesley was founded (chartered) in 1870.

[92] Harthoorn, *Onderwijs*, p. 116. For a general account of the development of these schools from 1848 to the mid-1860s (when the book was published), see ibid., pp. 104–22.

[93] *BM* 18 Apr. 1877.

[94] Van Deventer, *Overzicht*, pp. 196–7.

[95] *BM* 18 Oct. 1866.

said that the Dutch word *atoom* was the same as Sanskrit *anu* (both meaning atom).[96] This provoked a poem in *macapat* verse from one Mangunjarwa in praise of Dutch learning. In part, the poem read,

> In literature is it Javanese or Dutch words
> that promise clarification?
> Now, Dutch ideas are completely sufficient.

He went on to discuss the appearance of lights in the sky that were variously interpreted in superstitious ways.

> Javanese *priyayi* call it
> the luminous revelation of status,
> and even the *kaum*,
> as Ramadan approaches,
> tell of awaiting the descent
> of the *Laylat al-Qadr*.[97] ...
> The *tuwans* who together
> write and run
> the publication of *Jurumartani*,
> give news to the confused,
> inform the ignorant.[98]

Another contributor followed up the issue of the so-called "mysterious appearance that radiates like a star" by discussing meteors found in the Himalayas, the Cordilleras of the Americas, in Bohemia, Italy and China. "Nowadays", the contributor wrote, "Europeans all pursue knowledge (*kawruh*), so the breath of superstition is in the process of disappearing."[99] Abdulatip wrote to dismiss the views of a writer less impressed than he with European advances: "I ask you to note who was the first to invent printing of literature, who was the first to invent projection of pictures [i.e. the 'magic lantern'], the telegraph, hot air balloons and such like."[100] Such correspondence recurred with some frequency. In 1876 C.F. Winter's proposal to publish a Javanese translation of a Dutch history of the world[101] was greeted by a contributor

---

[96] *BM* 7 Mar. 1867.
[97] Observed on 27 Ramadan, when the *Qur'an* was sent down.
[98] *BM* 31 Oct. 1867.
[99] *BM* 14 Nov. 1867.
[100] *BM* 21 Nov. 1867.
[101] I have not been able to identify this work.

with praise for its usefulness. "If the Javanese and their compatriots are involved with knowledge (*kawruh*) from Europe, then our understanding will increase greatly of natural phenomena that are consistent and those that are not, with the result that superstition will begin to disappear."[102] In 1877 there was a series of letters concerning the utility of natural history (*ngelmu kodrat*).[103]

New inventions were frequently reported. There was great interest in the extension of the railway network in Java. The first link from Sěmarang to Surakarta was completed in 1870, as noted in Chapter 1. Thereafter the rail network spread further. In 1884 the Surakarta-Surabaya line was completed and the following year the link from Surabaya *via* the Javanese principalities to Batavia was opened.[104] The completion of the telegraph network in Java in 1870 along with its link to Singapore and thence to Europe was a major breakthrough. Now one could sit in Surakarta, Yogyakarta, Kědiri, Banyuwangi, Banyumas or anywhere else of any size in Java and have a direct link to the rest of the island and to Europe.[105]

Along with European science, European ways were attractive to the *priyayi*. In the 1850s some were already furnishing their houses in European fashion.[106] A scribe in Yogyakarta acquired Dutch and set up a private school there in 1865 teaching Dutch, arithmetic and other subjects to *priyayi* children.[107] By then several Yogyakarta *kraton* servants could perform Dutch-style theatricals, played the piano and harmonium and could perform Dutch tunes on the *gamělan*.[108] Another contributor said that such things were also done in Surakarta.[109] From the *Vorstenlanden* to the *pasisir* to the eastern tip of Java, *priyayi* held European-style receptions (*rěsepsi*), parties (*pista*), dances (*dhansah*) and costume balls (*bal kustim*) attended both by the Javanese elite and by local Europeans.[110] In Těgal, the *priyayi* set up a reading club "copying

---

[102] *BM* 15 June 1876.
[103] E.g. *BM* 8 Nov. 1877.
[104] C.Ch. van den Haspel, *Overwicht in overleg: hervormingen van justitie, grondgebruiken en bestuur in de Vorstenlanden op Java 1880–1930* (*VKI* vol. 111; Dordrecht & Cinnaminson: Foris Publications, 1985), p. 13.
[105] *BM* 1 Dec. 1870.
[106] J.L.V. "Bijdragen", p. 9.
[107] *BM* 29 June 1865.
[108] *BM* 29 June 1865.
[109] *BM* 6 July 1865.
[110] E.g. *BM* 8 Dec. 1870, 4 Jan. 1872, 18 July 1872, 19 Dec. 1872, 12 Mar. 1874, 2 Aug. 1877.

Radyapustaka museum, Surakarta

the custom of Dutch gentlemen", with a president, secretary, commissioner, and treasurer. Each member contributed 50 cents per month to buy Javanese and Malay newspapers and books. Once a year the materials that had been read were auctioned and the proceeds used to buy more books.[111] In Pĕkalongan they established a library "following the style of Dutch gentlemen".[112] In 1890 the *Patih* of Surakarta, R. Ad. Sasradiningrat IV, took the lead in establishing the Radyapustaka Museum, at first housed in his own official complex. In 1913 it moved to its present building. Radyapustaka, even in its present sadly under-funded condition, is still the home of interesting collections and a valuable library of Javanese manuscripts. Around the turn of the century, the Surakarta *priyayi* established an organisation called Abipraya to support the cause of progress for the Javanese.[113]

 Priyayi were also attracted to both Freemasonry and Theosophy. In 1871 the future Pakualam V joined the Masonic lodge "De Vriendschap" (established in Surabaya in 1809). The lodge "Mataram" was established

[111] *BM* 13 Feb. 1873.
[112] *BM* 10 July 1873.
[113] Kuntowijoyo, *Raja, priyayi dan kawula: Surakarta, 1900–1915* (Jogjakarta: Ombak, 2004), pp. 45–7.

Grave of Mangkunagara IV
(d. 1881)

in Yogyakarta in 1870 and Sultan Haměngkubuwana VI provided a
building on the city's main street, which the Masons occupied until the
Javanese invasion of 1942. In 1878, Pakualam V became "Head of
House" of the Mataram lodge.[114] The genteel idiosyncracy of Theosophy,
combining supposed ancient wisdom of the East with the modernity of
the West, attracted the Javanese elite from the early twentieth century,
just as it attracted many Indians. Here ideas such as found in the mystic
synthesis version of Islam could be combined with an embrace of
European styles.[115]

---

[114] Th. Stevens, *Vrijmetselarij en samenleving in Nederlands-Indië en Indonesië 1764–
1962* (Hilversum: Verloren, 1994), pp. 209, 377, 378.
[115] See H.A.O. de Tollenaere, *The politics of divine wisdom: Theosophy and labour,
national and women's movements in Indonesia and South Asia, 1875–1947* (Nijmegen:
Uitgeverij Katholieke Universiteit Nijmegen, 1996), pp. 107, 115 *et seqq.*; Iskandar
P. Nugraha, *Mengikis batas timur dan barat: Gerakan theosofi & nasionalisme Indonesia*
(Jakarta: Komunitas Bambu, 2001), pp. 13–4.

Grave of Mangkunagara V (d. 1896)

Depiction of uterus, fifteenth-century Candhi Sukuh, on which Mangkunagara V's gravestone is modeled

Kartini with her husband
R. Ad. Jayaadiningrat, 1903
(Photo by Tee Han Sioe;
Collection of KITLV, Leiden)

The graves of the two leading Mangkunagaran princes of the nineteenth century at Girilayu, high on Mount Lawu, reflect their enthusiasm
for the new world of the nineteenth century, but also for Javanese
cultural identity. These two matters were evidently not in conflict for
them. Mangkunagara IV (r. 1853–81) — great moderniser and Javanese
poet that he was, the author of *Wedhatama* and reformer of the
administration and economy of the Mangkunagaran — decided to have
a European mausoleum in which to find his eternal rest. So he imported
a large cast-iron mausoleum from Germany. Its arrival in 1874 is reported
in a Leiden university manuscript.[116] This is a splendid, silver-coloured
building with ornate cast-iron lattice door and windows. Knowing that
this was intended for royalty, the German manufacturers of course
adorned it with a crown on the top in the European fashion, despite the
fact that Javanese royal attire did not include crowns. Mangkunagara V

---

[116] Soegiarto notes, LOr 10,867c, pp. 8, 9, referring to LOr 6781 *Babad
Mangkunagaran*, pp. 111, 117.

(r. 1881–96) lived in an age when European archaeologists and philologists were revealing much about the glories of Java's pre-Islamic past. His grave and that of his main queen (d. 1888) are adorned with a stylised version of the bas-relief of a uterus from the fifteenth-century Hindu temple Candhi Sukuh, also located on Mount Lawu. This was a potent pre-Islamic symbol of procreative powers. For both of these princes, the modern world brought by Europeans was also a doorway to Javanese civilisation, one in which more puritanical forms of Islam had no place.

The best-known figure among turn-of-the-century Javanese who were attracted to European learning was undoubtedly R.A. Kartini (1879–1904), who remains an honoured symbol of female leadership in Indonesia today.[117] Her father, the *Bupati* of Jĕpara R.M.Ad.Ar. Sasraningrat, was regarded as one of the most forward-looking of the *priyayi*. Kartini married the *Bupati* of Rĕmbang, also regarded as progressive, but died tragically young in childbirth, before being able to implement her dreams. She and her sisters had been educated at the European primary school in Jĕpara. We noted above that there were others who took an interest in female education even before this time. By 1873 the *Bupati* of Madiun, Sasranagara, had opened a school for girls that taught literacy and practical skills of a kind thought specific to the roles of women, rather than the more general education to be found in the European elementary school.[118] *Bramartani* published an admiring article on women's education, including higher education, in the United States in 1883.[119] But the enthusiasm displayed by Javanese *priyayi* for the education of boys only rarely extended to the education of girls. Kartini hoped to change this. The letters she exchanged with

---

[117] There is much published on Kartini. Her letters (originally written in Dutch) are available in several published collections and translations. See Kartini, *Door duisternis tot licht: Gedachten over en voor het Javaanse volk* (compiled by J.H. Abendanon; revised ed., ed. Elisabeth Allard; Amsterdam: Gé Nabrink & Zn, 1976); Kartini, *Brieven aan Mevrouuw R.M. Abendanon-Mandri en haar echtegenoot met andere documenten* (Ed. F.G.P. Jaquet; Dordrecht & Providence: Foris Publications, 1987); Kartini, *Letters from Kartini, an Indonesian feminist, 1900–1904* (transl. Joost Coté; Clayton: Monash Asia Institute in association with Hyland House, 1992); Kartini, *Letters of a Javanese princess* (ed. Hildred Geertz; trans. Agnes Louise Symmers; New York: W.W. Norton & Company, 1964). For a biography, see Sitisoemandari Soeroto, *Kartini: Sebuah biografi* (Jakarta: Gunung Agung, 1986).

[118] *BM* 9 Oct. 1873.

[119] *BM* 4 Jan. 1883 (a misprint in the masthead gives this erroneously as 4 Jan. 1882).

Dutch correspondents were published after her death and inspired others to act in the cause of women's education and emancipation.[120]

In May 1899, 20-year-old Kartini wrote — we might say, gushed — to the radical Dutch feminist Stella Zeehandelaar,

> I have *so* longed to make the acquaintance of a "modern girl", a proud, independent girl who would have my full sympathy, who with swift and firm step makes her way through life, happy and cheerful, full of enthusiasm and warm feelings, working not for her own welfare and happiness alone, but also giving herself to the greater society, working for the welfare of many fellow human beings.[121]

As was characteristic of the progressive *priyayi* of her time, Kartini's admiration for what was modern and European was combined with a love for Javanese tradition. She attempted to find words to capture the sound of the *gamělan* orchestra: "How movingly beautiful it is!" she wrote.[122] Her letters are infused with the sense of *noblesse oblige* of the *priyayi* for their lesser fellows. She also engaged in modern scholarship. At the age of twenty she wrote an article on "marriage among the *Kojas* [local Indian Muslims]". This was published in the prestigious *Bijdragen tot de Taal-, Land- en Volkenkunde van Nederlandsch-Indië* but — given her age, her sex and the expectations of the age — the paper was published under the name of her father Sasraningrat. Kartini was not only the first Indonesian woman to contribute to *Bijdragen* but still the youngest author ever to have been published in its august pages.[123]

The New *Priyayi* Culture and Islam

One of Kartini's letters to Zeehandelaar illustrated how detached Kartini, a young turn-of-the-century woman of a modernising *priyayi* family, felt from Islam.

---

[120] See also Kartini's memorial to the Dutch government on education, entitled "Give the Javanese education!", published in Kartini, *Door duisternis tot licht*, pp. 390–410 and in English translation in Kartini, "Educate the Javanese!" (ed. and trans. Jean Taylor), *Indonesia*, no. 17 (Apr. 1974): 83–98.

[121] Kartini, *Door duisternis tot licht*, p. 1.

[122] 12 Jan. 1900, in ibid., pp. 28–9.

[123] Maarten Kuitenbrouwer, *Tussen oriëntalisme en wetenschap: Het Koninklijk Instituut voor Taal,- Land en Volkenkunde in historisch verband, 1851–2001* (Leiden: KITLV Uitgeverij, 2001), p. 96.

I cannot tell you about Islam's teachings, Stella. It forbids its believers to speak of it to the believers of other religions. And, in truth, I am a Muslim because my ancestors were. How can I love my religion if I don't know it — am not allowed to know it? The *Qur'an* is too holy to be translated into any language at all. Here no one knows Arabic.[124]

Kartini's letter reflected ignorance as well as distance. Manuscripts of the *Qur'an* with Javanese translations had long been available in Java and a Javanese translation of the *Qur'an* was printed 20 years before Kartini was born. There were many thousands of Javanese who knew Arabic well enough to read the *Qur'an* and other Arabic works and many among them had genuine mastery of the language. But few such people were to be found among the *priyayi* class. Kartini's statement to Zeehandelaar is also at odds with the claim, referred to in Chapter 3 above, that she was among those who studied with Ky. Shaleh Darat, the author of *Tafsir faidl al-rahman fi tarjamah tafsir kalam malik al-dayya*, a Javanese interpretation of the *Qur'an* from a Sufi perspective. It is possible, of course, that she and her siblings spent some time with that major figure of Islam, but not enough to embrace his teachings. Although surely Kartini and her family must have been readers of *Bramartani*, it seems that she had not absorbed even what could be learned about Islam from that source, limited as it was. Or perhaps she was posturing for Stella Zeehandelaar.

It is important to note that, despite the generally secular content of *Bramartani*, there was normally no anti-religious tone. When Islamic identity arose it was usually in a positive light if it was of the mystic synthesis variety as espoused by the Javanese elite. An account of the life of Ki Bĕstam/Ky.Ng. Kĕrtabasa (d. 1762) a major figure in the eighteenth century, emphasised both that he was loyal to the Dutch and that he was "a person of ability and strong in his Islamic piety".[125] The paper reported the visit of the *Bupati* of Grobogan to pay respects at the graves of his ancestors and holy figures, and his donations of money to "the mendicants, *santris*, and the *hajis*". Because of the blessing power (*bĕrkah*) of such graves, it reported, those who cared for them regarded themselves as being blessed in their lives. At the grave of the Mataram dynasty

---

[124] Letter of 6 Nov. 1899 in Kartini, *Door duisternis tot licht*, p. 20.
[125] *BM* 30 June 1864. Kĕrtabasa worked as a translator for the VOC; see M.C. Ricklefs, *Jogjakarta under Sultan Mangkubumi 1749–1792: A History of the division of Java* (London Oriental Series 10; London: Oxford University Press, 1974), p. 153n37.

ancestor Ky. Agĕng Sĕsela, the *Bupati* engaged in *dhikr*.[126] When a prince of Yogyakarta died suddenly, it was reported that in his last hours he recited memorised passages from the *Qur'an* and did *dhikr*. This was noteworthy because in his life he had not previously wanted to *dhikr* or "carry out the Islamic faith". Only as he neared death did he "wish to mention the name of Allah".[127] When the elderly wife of the *Bupati* of Bangil died, it was reported that she bequeathed nearly half her estate to the local mosque.[128] New mosques that had been built at Madiun and Panaraga were said to "honour the Lord Prophet Muhammad", while other new mosques were reportedly to be built at Magĕlang and Ngawi.[129]

There were several reports about the refurbishing of the mosque at Sĕmarang. In 1876 it was rumoured that money collected for this purpose had secretly been diverted to support the Acehnese resistance to the Dutch, so a commission was established to oversee the funds.[130] The *Bupati* gathered all the Arabs, Malays and Indian Muslims and, first setting an example himself, got them to contribute money for the mosque rebuilding.[131] The paper similarly reported Mangkunagara IV's decision to build a mosque[132] and Pakubuwana IX's attendance at the mosque as usual at the celebration of Garĕbĕg Mulud Dal.[133] When Sultan Hamĕngkubuwana VII sent four persons on the *hajj* on his behalf and to build lodgings in Mecca where pilgrims could stay free of cost, *Bramartani* reported that.[134] A contributor said that many Muslims did not know the names of the Prophet and therefore sent in ten such names.[135] There was a report on the restoration of the mosque at the holy grave of Muryapada that had reportedly burned down many years before. In 1879 it was restored as the result of leadership by one

---

[126] *BM* 8 June 1865.

[127] *BM* 27 July 1865.

[128] *BM* 3 Oct. 1867.

[129] *BM* 18 Feb. 1869.

[130] The commission consisted of one Ĕncik Akowan (presumably a Chinese Muslim), two *hajis* and two Arabs; *BM* 25 May 1876.

[131] *BM* 13 Sept. 1877.

[132] *BM* 14 Mar. 1878.

[133] *BM* 16 Apr. 1878.

[134] *BM* 28 Aug. 1879.

[135] *BM* 19 Dec. 1878. The author gave Akyan satitah, adam mukim, adam ilapi, roh ilapi, kaspidultiyah, khakekatulkaji, badrulngalam, maklumat, rasullullah, roh rambani.

H. Muhammad Saleh of Kudus and the contributions of many people. Thereafter the site was visited by hundreds, at times thousands, of people.[136]

Bramartani published discussions about the obligations and prohibitions of Islamic life. People discussed the meaning of the five pillars of the faith, what foods were forbidden (*haram*), the prohibition on usury (*riba*) and Islamic rules for inheritance.[137] As the number of *hajis* grew in Java, the newspaper took a greater interest in the pilgrimage. In 1870 it published practical advice about preparing for the *hajj*, including the information that the best coffee of all was to be found in Arabia.[138] Other information about rules and costs of the pilgrimage appeared from time to time, as did warnings about the risks of cholera in Mecca and Wahhabi attacks.[139] The examination of returning *hajis* and the discovery of fraudulent claims of having done the pilgrimage were also reported.[140] As was at least one conflict in interpretation of Islamic law between the returning *hajis* and established Islamic authority, in this case over inheritance rules.[141]

A view of Islam at odds with the mystic synthesis style and more consistent with Islamic reform movements was occasionally seen. Some examples were noted in Chapter 3 above: the contributor who objected to the communal meal (the *sidhĕkah malĕman*) on certain nights of the fasting month, on the grounds that this lacked any foundation in Islam;[142] "the mendicant" (*tiyang pĕkir*) who approved of greater religious practice by many, but objected to young people who were still raising dogs, playing cards and watching dancing-girls;[143] and the contributor who merely signed as "D", complaining about villagers" superstitions such as the veneration of holy sites and faith in hidden powers and spirits.[144] A further example similar to the last concerned the building of a new mosque in the district of Wirasari, reported in 1879. The

---

[136] *BM* 13 May 1880.
[137] *BM* 8 July 1869, 18 Aug. 1869, 14 July 1870, 4 Aug. 1870, 1 Sept. 1870, 25 Jan. 1872, 11 July 1872.
[138] *BM* 6 Oct. 1870.
[139] E.g. *BM* 12 July 1877, 1 May 1879, 19 Aug. 1880, 20 Apr. 1882.
[140] *BM* 10 July 1873, 26 Jan. 1882.
[141] *BM* 5 Oct. 1876. The report was taken from *De Locomotief.*
[142] *BM* 25 Feb. 1869.
[143] *BM* 7 Oct. 1869.
[144] *BM* 17 Apr. 1879.

mosque's frame was of teak, with each of four great pillars receiving an honorific name: Ky. Panji, Ky. Sela Gĕndhana, Ky. Rĕmĕng, and Saka Tatal. These pillars were prayed to and flowers and incense were presented to them by devotees seeking boons, including Chinese. Such practices were nothing unusual in Java and indeed have continued into contemporary times. But "Juru Gabah", evidently the editor of the paper, added after this report: "How many years has it been since the lives of the Lord Prophets Jesus and Muhammad, who both taught the saying 'in the name of God', down to the present, yet there are still people who pay obeisance to wood."[145]

Criticism of the religious sometimes appeared in *Bramartani*. In Chapter 3, we noted the exchange that took place in *Jurumartani* in 1868. Then one Kramaruci from Krawang, who identified himself as "a true Muslim", criticised religious folk (*kaum*) who could only read out religious books but could not explain the inventions and discoveries being published in newspapers. A Cirĕbon *kyai* responded that the newspaper was not a suitable venue for religious teachings.[146] Abdulatip of Sĕmarang, whom we have met above, criticized the conduct of *santris* and of *hajis* who, among other things, escaped the compulsory labour duties of their neighbours.[147]

A lengthy denunciation of the *putihan* was published in 1879, when a contributor named Nur Yakimbalaka wrote of having been one of the *putihan* for eight years, after which he returned to being an *abangan*. He sent in a lengthy poem in *macapat* verse denouncing the hypocrisy of the students of religion. It began,

> When I became one of the *kaum*,
> already unlike that of normal people
> was the conduct of those who became *santris*.
> What I sought was to be rewarded with understanding.

> Now I've become *abangan* again,
> having received divine inspiration,
> for my understanding has increased
> about the secrets of all the *kaum*.

---

[145] *BM* 27 March 1879.
[146] *BM* 2 Jan. & 16 Jan. 1868. Kramaruci described himself as *tiyang agami Islam kang khak* in a letter to *BM* 26 Dec. 1867.
[147] *BM* 18 Feb. 1869. There is much much more to Abdulatip's criticisms than summarised here.

Not like usual are the wishes of the *kaum,*
or the story of their doctrine.
My lad, be warned about the *kaum.*
Usually the *kaum* teach *shari'a.*

(But) the *shari'a* of God's Messenger is rendered shameless, virtueless,
by the *kaum,*
abandoning that which is right, all the way to the foundations,
deviations frequently deviating.
The root of this is that the *kaum* enjoy compulsion
but their language of authority is sloppy when it comes to law,
for they break the law,
extremely shameless, even shaming,
exerting themselves in their determination to be paid for their services.

Nur Yakimbalaka went on to tell how *santris* would flock to wherever
someone was sick or dead to say prayers in return for payment. It didn't
matter whether a sick person lived or died: either way the *santris* got
rewarded for their prayers. They would count out the days for the
observations of a death at three, seven, forty and one hundred days, two
years and a thousand days, and again flock to the occasion.[148] This was
not, then, a rejection of Islam or of religion, but a protest at pious
hypocrisies.

A wry observation in a similar vein was published in *Bramartani* in
1892. A contributor had noticed a circumcision ceremony for a youth
where *santris* were singing religious songs. Afterwards, however, they
went off to get drunk on Dutch gin and dance, "exceeding their *abangan*
fellows. But after all, [the difference] between *abangan* and *putihan* is
just a name, yes?"[149]

The two contending modernisms of Java — those of purifying Islam
and of modernising Europe — were finding it difficult to communicate
with each other. We have already noted above how the Islamic and
government school systems, with their very different syllabuses, were
producing students who did not share a language and script in which
they might write a letter to each other. This gap of intellectual universes
was also exemplified by an exchange of correspondence in *Bramartani*
in 1880. One reader wrote in to ask the meaning of several Arabic

---

[148] *BM* 1, 8, 15, 29 May 1879. The issue of 22 May is missing from the PNRI
collection.
[149] *BM* 24 Dec. 1892.

religious terms. Another replied with explanations and asked, in turn, for explanations of Javanese verse forms and social levels.[150]

The gap between *putihan* and *priyayi* at the level of school children was also exemplified by the experience of Achmad Djajadiningrat. He was from one of the most distinguished *priyayi* families of Bantĕn, and was a protégé of Snouck Hurgronje, as was his brother Hoesein, who went on to become the first Indonesian to gain a doctorate from Leiden University in 1913. Achmad Djajadinigrat rose to be *Bupati* of Batavia itself (1924–29). In his youth in the 1880s, he was sent to a *pĕsantren* to study. There he found that his fellow *santris* were utterly contemptuous of the *priyayi* officials of the day. "The native officials from high to low were in general made objects of mockery" he recalled. The *santris* expressed their dislike of everything to do with government. For their part, village youths who were not *santris* held the latter in contempt. "Dumb santri" (*santri bodho*) was a popular cliché and anyone who was stupid, slow or clumsy was said to be like a *santri*.[151]

Priyayi interest in the wider world also encouraged some discussion of other religions, not always to Islam's advantage. In 1873 *Bramartani* reported on Buddhism in Siam and its ten precepts — not to kill, steal, commit adultery, lie, and so on. These were said to be "ten types of lessons the value of which exceeds that of the twenty attributes [of Islam]".[152] The paper also published a part of a Javanese *macapat* translation of St Mark's Gospel.[153] It extracted a translation from a Dutch work on the pre-Islamic period in Java's history[154] and a report on the religion of the Tĕnggĕr region of East Java, a pocket of pre-Islamic faith.[155]

This accompanied an increasing interest in Java's pre-Islamic past, encouraged by the Europeans' fascination with that age. We have already noted that by mid-century, the works *Paramayoga* and *Pustakaraja Purwa*, with their mythologised past and fake calendrical system, probably

---

[150] *BM* 4 & 18 Mar. 1880, 8 Apr. 1880. Further correspondence on these issues in *BM* 22 & 29 Apr. 1880.

[151] Achmad Djajadiningrat, *Herinneringen* (Amsterdam & Batavia: G. Kolff & Col, [1936]), p. 23; A. Djajadiningrat, "Het leven in een pasantren", *Tijdschrift voor het Binnenlandsch Bestuur* 34 (1908): 6–17, 18.

[152] *BM* 9 Oct. 1873.

[153] *BM* 23 Mar. 1876.

[154] *BM* 16 Mar. 1876.

[155] *BM* 16 Mar. 1882.

already represented a response to Dutch philological and archaeological interests in that ancient period. Similarly, in 1882 *Bramartani* published an account of antiquities on the north coast that were said to be associated with the characters of the *Bratayuda*[156] — even though in fact those characters were based on prototypes originally from India. Sears proposed in her study of *wayang* theatre that a cultural accommodation between Islam and the *wayang* — an accommodation that we may say was rooted in the prior mystic synthesis — began to fracture in the later nineteenth century because of the influence of Islamic reformers on the one hand and that of Dutch scholarly privileging of pre-Islamic Java on the other.[157] The evidence considered in this book is consistent with that interpretation.

Because education was so central both to the Islamic reformers and to the *priyayi* supporters of the government-sponsored version of modernity, it is perhaps not surprising that disputes about education arose early. In the 1860s there were already signs of conflict that presaged the bitter animosity to be discussed in the following chapter. Abdulatip — whom we have already met in the correspondence columns of *Bramartani* — directed his fire at the *pĕsantrens* in 1867. He praised the government schools for the utility of their subject matter and as the key to wiping out superstition and enhancing prosperity. The teachers in *pĕsantrens*, however, had no command of useful knowledge (*kawruh*) such as arithmetic, geography, astronomy and such like. They were ignorant people who could only teach Islam and were mostly incapable of clear thinking even about religion. They could only memorise Arabic words without even understanding their meaning. "Now I ask all my people [the Javanese], are such schools beneficial? Are they useful? Certainly not." In the government schools, by contrast, the teachers gained their *kawruh* from the teacher-training school in Surakarta. He went on to draw a contrast between the aristocratic schooling of Java, however, with that in Europe, where even commoners sought education and were capable of clear thinking.[158] A contributor identified as Pandhita Sura Sajati Kyai Sukamulya (i.e. a learned person whose titles suggest a link with pre-Islamic ideas) agreed but asked whether Abdulatip was Javanese or an Arab or indeed a Muslim, since he was so critical of

---

[156] *BM* 13 Apr. 1882.
[157] Laurie J. Sears, *Shadows of empire: Colonial discourse and Javanese tales* (Durham [N.C.] & London: Duke University Press, 1996), pp. 25–6.
[158] *BM* 4 Apr. 1867.

"schools that come from Arabia". Sukamulya argued that these schools were of value to Muslims.[159] Abdulatip responded that he was both a Muslim and Javanese, "but it seems that we differ somewhat in our views on education and religion". In a remarkable early defense of the comparative study of religion, Abdulatip said that in the *pĕsantrens* the superiority of Islam was taught, but it was never compared with the faiths of other peoples. "so with regard to Islam, people think: I'll believe what is good, but I'll also believe what is bad". He said that he was concerned about the common Javanese, who had no understanding of their faith and were Muslims only in name, merely because it was the faith of their ancestors. If religious schools were useful, he asked, what was that use?[160]

Yet, it was evidently possible for the two contending modernities to meet in the field of education. This was evidenced when Susuhunan Pakubuwana X ordered the foundation of the first modern Islamic school in Java, the *Manba' al-'Ulum* school in Surakarta, in 1905. The *Pangulu* of Surakarta took the initiative in proposing this school after seeing what Dutch schools had achieved. Some of the local *kaum* opposed it on the grounds that it was an imitation of infidel education, but the school was opened nevertheless. It was both Islamic and modern in the European style. It developed a system of graded classes, fixed periods of study and certificates upon graduation. *Manba' al-'Ulum* taught reading of the *Qur'an*, Arabic, arithmetic, astronomy, algebra and logic in a course that lasted for eleven years. After four years of study students could become low-level religious officials; after eight they could be appointed to higher posts, after eleven they could become *pangulu*. The school was open to the children of the religious establishment, the aristocracy and court officials of Surakarta. Students also came from outside the principality. Some major religious figures were among its graduates.[161]

For most of the Javanese elite, there does not seem to have been any questioning of their religious identity. They were Muslims as their ancestors had been for centuries. Although the *priyayi* embrace of European-style modernity distanced them from the purifying activities of the pious *putihan*, most of the Javanese elite, we may presume, could

---

[159] *BM* 23 May 1867.
[160] *BM* 6 June 1867.
[161] Muhamad Hisyam, *Caught between three fires: The Javanese pangulu under the Dutch colonial administration 1882–1942* (Jakarta: INIS, 2001), pp. 141–6.

not imagine themselves as anything other than Muslims, however nominally so. They may have been offended by the style of the Islamic reformers, they may have been contemptuous of the hypocrisies, as they judged them to be, of the *putihan*, but this constituted a difference of opinion, at times a conflict, over what was the true Islam. It was not a conflict over whether one should be a Muslim at all.

Around 1870, a *Bupati* put his continuing commitment as a Muslim in entertainingly instrumentalist terms. This gentleman reportedly expressed his enthusiasm for all things Dutch — an enthusiasm we have seen above in many of his peers — saying that he wanted to be like the Dutch in all ways. So, his interlocutor asked, did this mean that he wished to become a Christian? He replied, "Ah, ... to tell the truth, I would rather have four wives and a single God, than one wife and three Gods."[162] There were, it seems, some things upon which the Europeans could not improve.

But there were some *priyayi* in the second half of the nineteenth century who were beginning to question their Islamic identity. In the modern *kawruh* of European science, in the modern education of the Dutch schools, in the renewed interest in Java's pre-Islamic past, some saw reasons to question whether Islam was after all the right religion for Javanese. They gave rise to an anti-Islamic interpretation of history and a new vision of what the future might hold. In the intellectualism (*budi*) of European learning, they perceived a door opening to a pre-Islamic (*Buda*) and more genuinely Javanese identity. As this anti-Islamic vision developed, the last element in the nineteenth-century polarising of Javanese society emerged. This is the subject of the following chapter.

---

[162] Keesteren, "Koran", p. 46.

7

Anti-Islamic Reaction: Budi and Buda

In 1866 a scientific discussion in *Bramartani* led to the suggestion for the first time (so far as I am aware) that the age of Islam might come to an end in Java. Raden Saleh Sharif Bustaman (1811–80), the great painter and a prominent figure of this hybrid age, had discovered megafauna fossils near Yogyakarta — the first palaeontological excavations to be done in Java, which was later to play such a prominent role in world palaeontology with the discovery there of *homo erectus* by Eugène Dubois in the 1890s.[1] Raden Saleh's discoveries prompted discussion of the most ancient past in Java. One Ratukusya from Yogyakarta was inspired to write to *Bramartani* to describe Java's history as a progression of epochs. After the age of water (*jaman tirta*), he wrote, Asians knew how to make boats. Hindus came to Java and the Javanese all embraced Hinduism. Then Aji Saka's people came and the Javanese embraced what he called Siamese religion (*agama Siyam*). This was when they began to write inscriptions on stone as found in the *batu tulis* (written stone) at Bogor, in the government museum in Batavia and at the great temple of Borobudur. Then came Seh Molana Maghribi and some thirty Arabs. These Arabs were able to employ "magical means, ruses and lies" so that

---

[1] Raden Saleh's excavations were at Banyunganti and Kalisana, both in the area of Sĕntolo, west of Yogyakarta. I am grateful for this information and for Raden Saleh's date of birth to Dr Werner Kraus, who is completing a detailed study of Raden Saleh. On Dubois' work, see Paulus *et al.*, *Encyc. Ned. Ind.*, vol. III, p. 413 (*sub* Pithecanthropus Erectus).

the Javanese embraced "Arab religion" and read Arabic literature. Siamese literature was also still read but with many changes. If the lies of an Arab were discovered by the Javanese, then that man was called a *wali*, said Ratukusya iconoclastically. But in the future the Javanese would change their religion yet again, he said, for in Batavia there were already some 200 people who had become Christians.[2]

Ratukusya's thinking was, however, only partly a harbinger of what was to come. He was wrong on two points. First, his Christian numbers were inaccurate. Already when he wrote to *Bramartani* in 1866, the total number of Christians in the Javanese-speaking heartland was greater than he knew. At Ngara, Majawarna and elsewhere there were hundreds more than he imagined, and Java was about to see the dramatic results achieved by Ky. Sadrach's methods, which would shortly mean that there were thousands of Javanese Christians. This was an important development, for the *Kristen Jawa* accommodation of Christianity with Javanese culture and identity was an element in questioning the previously unquestionable amalgamation of Javanese and Islamic identities. But the Christians remained a tiny proportion of the Javanese population. It was not Christianisation that seemed to most dissatisfied *priyayi* to offer an alternative to Islam, despite Christianity's links with the Europeans whose science many *priyayi* admired. This was Ratukusya's second error. For *priyayi* who found Islam in its more puritanical form unattractive and the older mystic synthesis inadequate, the alternative lay not in Christianity but in Java's own pre-Islamic heritage, a heritage that Europeans were helping to disclose through archaeological and philological research.

The historical episode which became the focus of controversy in the later nineteenth and earlier twentieth centuries was not the ancient past of megafauna or early Hinduisation, but rather the fall of Majapahit to the first Islamic states four hundred years before. Summarised very briefly, Javanese historical traditions had it that the last king of Majapahit, named Brawijaya, impregnated his queen, a Chinese princess, but then sent her away from the court before the child's birth. The king and his court were, according to historical traditions, still *Buda* (i.e. Hindu-Buddhist) at this time. The king's son, named Raden Patah, however, was raised as a Muslim in Palembang. On reaching maturity he returned to Java and was recognised by his father. The king gave him land to

---

[2] *BM* 5 July 1866.

govern at the place that was later known as Dĕmak, destined to become the first Islamic state in Java, ruled over by Raden Patah as the first Sultan.[3] In the end, Raden Patah constructed a coalition of Islamic *pasisir* states that marched on Majapahit and conquered it in the year Śaka 1400, equivalent to AD 1478–9.[4]

For Javanese literati of the nineteenth century, AJ 1400/AD 1478–79 was the most important turning-point in the history of the Javanese, for it marked the victory of Islam. We have already seen how the turning of the Javanese and Islamic centuries in AJ 1800/AD 1871–72 and AH 1300/AD 1882–83 respectively were important to others in Java. The turn of the century seems to have mattered to some disgruntled *priyayi*, too. But this group seems to have done its calculations in the old solar Śaka calendar, rather than the lunar AJ calendar, so that the century turned for them at yet a third time: Śaka 1800/AD 1878–79. It will be seen below why this year appears to have mattered so much. In Javanese, the Hindu-Buddhist age was called *jaman Buda*, the latter word clearly being derived from the word Buddha but probably not to be taken literally as meaning Buddhist. Rather, it stood more generally for the hybrid Hindu-Buddhist religion of Java of which the nineteenth-century *priyayi* were progressively learning more.

When *Babad Pajajaran* (the chronicle of Pajajaran, a pre-Islamic kingdom of West Java) was serialised in *Bramartani* in 1870, it presented a view of the fall of Majapahit and Islamisation of the Javanese that was implicitly hostile to Islam. So far as I am aware, this was the first time that such a version had been published. But this was not yet the fully elabourated denunciation of Islam that we will see in other texts to be discussed below.

In the *Babad Pajajaran* account, the future Sunan Giri (one of the nine *walis*) becomes proficient in esoteric knowledge and is regarded as a son by Sunan Ngampel (a more senior *wali*). He travels to Malacca and meets Seh Aluliman there, and tells him that he and his companion are from Java and are going to Mecca as pilgrims. Seh Aluliman says,

---

[3] According to the tradition. There is, however, no actual evidence of the Sultan title being used by Javanese kings before the seventeenth century.

[4] For extracts from late eighteenth- and early nineteenth-century versions of these traditions, see M.C. Ricklefs, "A consideration of three versions of the *Babad Tanah Djawi*, with excerpts on the fall of Majapahit", *Bulletin of the School of Oriental and African Studies* 35, pt. 2 (1972): 285–315. In fact, the state of Majapahit, or at least a branch of the ruling family, seems to have survived in Kĕdiri until c. 1527, but that was not known in the nineteenth century.

"I don't agree:
what are you going to Mecca for?
Only to worship a stone?
You won't get much out of that."

He advises them instead to return to Java and save the Javanese, a task that would be pleasing to God. So they returned to Java.[5] In dismissing the *hajj* as being nothing more than a trip "only to worship a stone" (i.e. the holy black stone of the Ka'ba in Mecca), the text belittled one of the central pillars of the faith.

In subsequent instalments, the Islamisation of Pajajaran and of the Javanese are described. In this version,[6] Raden Patah of Děmak demands of his father that he become a Muslim or face attack. On receiving this threat, Brawijaya laments that the Muslims have forgotten his goodness towards them, for he has given them freedom and land. Before being defeated by his treacherous son, Brawijaya makes a statement that links the people of the *jaman Buda* directly with the Europeans. He says,

"If it comes to that which is determined
and the Muslims are victorious in battle,
certainly in the future reparation will be demanded
by the *Buda* people who are defeated,
who will incarnate in the traders who arrive
in Jakarta, that will be their place."[7]

In the end, the Muslims win in bloody battle and Brawijaya ascends to heaven. The *walis* enter the court and find it empty.[8]

In implicitly depicting Raden Patah's victory over his good-hearted father as treacherous and establishing a direct link between the Dutch and the pre-Islamic civilisation of Java, this *Babad Pajajaran* presaged two core ideas of the anti-Islamic literature of the 1870s.

Another contributor to *Bramartani* in 1873 also thought in terms of consecutive ages in Java and this time linked those ages to educational issues. In ancient times (*jaman kina*), said the writer, Javanese lived like animals, naked and without homes. Then came the Hindus (*tiyang*

---

[5] *BM* 15 Sept. 1870.
[6] *BM* 22 Sept. 1870, 6 Oct. 1870. The serialisation continues to the end of 1870; *Bramartani* for 1871 is missing from the collection in PNRI.
[7] *BM* 16 Oct. 1870.
[8] *BM* 20 Oct. 1870.

Hindhu) who taught Javanese the ways of humans, such as wearing clothing, building houses and engaging in agriculture. The Hindus taught religion such as praying to the sun, fire, stones and wood, and knowledge (*kawruh*) such as literature. Then came the Islamic religion and Hinduism lost out, because Islam promised much about the hereafter. At this time, Javanese were still very superstitious so Islam could strike roots and grow in Java, indeed in almost all of the Netherlands Indies (*Hindu Nedĕrlan*). Javanese praised the name of Allah and became more intelligent. Although Islam had been present in Java for some five hundred years, nevertheless Hinduism had not entirely disappeared because Javanese remembered having once been Hindus. Then Java was flooded by European education. Both of the previously mentioned religions — i.e. Hinduism and Islam — at first resisted this but in the end they had to recognise that they were bested. For 20 years European knowledge (*kawruh*) had been present in Java and already this new *kawruh* was defeating superstition. Idol-worshippers had almost disappeared and many people had awakened from darkness into light.[9] Children were flocking to schools and no longer hanging around or going from one *pĕsantren* to another. Java now worshipped and deified the honoured government of the Netherlands Indies that was spreading *kawruh* without considering the costs.[10] So in this version of history, Islam partially replaced Hinduism but European education was in the process of entirely displacing both.

Four key ideas may be seen in these views published in *Bramartani*. They were:

- Javanese history consisted of a series of stages, each associated with a particular religion or a particular set of ideas, brought to the Javanese by outsiders. This form of sequential history had not come to an end, the latest outsiders to come to Java being the Europeans.
- Islam's age in Java was implicitly lacking in legitimacy, for Islam had succeeded through "magical means, ruses and lies", by treachery of

---

[9] One encounters this metaphor from time to time in this period, and of course it was used later when Kartini's letters were published under the title *Door duisternis tot licht*. I do not know whether writers were consciously quoting 1 Peter 2:9 (or, perhaps less likely, Acts 26:18) or whether the similarity with Christian scripture was coincidental.

[10] *BM* 14 Aug. 1873. This ends with a comment about the Chinese who, the writer said, only came to Java to teach how to fill one's pockets (with money) but the Javanese weren't yet able to do that.

a son against his good-hearted father, or because Javanese were still very superstitious so that Islam could strike roots and grow in Java.[11]

- A new age was dawning, in which the Europeans were bringing new knowledge (usually called *kawruh*).
- There were links between this new age of European learning and the pre-Islamic past, captured in Brawijaya's prophecy that "the *Buda* people who are defeated ... will incarnate in the traders who arrive in Jakarta".

As we will see below, the links between European learning and the pre-Islamic past came to be expressed in a word-play that established equivalence between the words *buda* and *budi*. *Buda* referred to the pre-Islamic age of Java's history. Its partner, *budi*, is one of those crucial but nearly untranslatable terms one sometimes encounters in cross-cultural research. It covers a range of meanings for which in English we use terms like mind, intellect, reason, genius, wit, discretion, judgment, wisdom, aptitude, character, disposition, sense, and also desire, longing, and so on.[12] So *budi* was a very positive concept associated with intellect, elevated character and striving; we will leave it untranslated when we encounter it in the texts below.

Three Books

Three related works of literature formulated the anti-Islamic argument in the 1870s and remained famous long after. They were entitled *Babad Kědhiri*, *Suluk Gatholoco* and *Sěrat Děrmagandhul*. Shared content and characters confirm that they were related to each other, but it has

---

[11] In 1888 *Bramartani* again serialised a history of Java, including the Islamic conquests of Majapahit and Pajajaran. The sections discussing the fall of Majapahit (*BM* 16 Aug., 30 Aug., 6 Sept., 20 Sept., 27 Sept. 1888) do not criticise Raden Patah as severely as do the versions discussed in this chapter. But Patah is still presented as being ungrateful and disloyal to his father Brawijaya, disregarding the latter's generosity to the Muslims despite remaining "Hindu" himself. After their victory, the Muslims are depicted as destroying Majapahit and all its treasures. This version is said to be from *Suluh Pangajar* (the teacher's torch). I imagine this to be a Malay-language publication for indigenous school teachers, but have been unable to confirm that. Adam, *Vernacular press*, p. 199, lists a *Soeloeh Pelajar*, but gives only 1910 and 1913 as years of publication; this may be a different publication.

[12] See Gericke and Roorda, *Handwoordenboek* (1901), vol. II, p. 694.

never been possible to clarify with certainty in what order they were written or which borrowed from which. Van Akkeren thought that *Babad Kĕdhiri* was adapted from *Sĕrat Dĕrmagandhul*, whereas Drewes was of the view that the borrowing occurred in the opposite direction.[13] In my judgment, Drewes was probably correct in this. In any case, these works are to be taken together as evidence of a bitter *priyayi* rejection of Islam. Drewes commented that *Sĕrat Dĕrmagandhul* "breathes rejection of Islam as being a religion foreign to Java and the Javanese; moreover a religion which had come to power as a result of the utterly reprehensible conduct of the *walis*".[14] As we will see, this theme runs throughout all three books.[15]

Suluk Gatholoco clearly existed in manuscript form by the early 1870s. In February 1872 Poensen discussed it with some of his Christian Javanese assistants. "In the original", said Poensen, "this work has expressions and discussions that are worse than vulgar and since some of them had a copy of this book, I felt that I had to bring certain matters to their attention which must restrain them from giving this book to others to read".[16] While much remains uncertain about the interrelation-ships between these works, we may reasonably regard all three as coming from the 1870s, *Suluk Gatholoco* because of Poensen's information, *Babad Kĕdhiri* because of the dating discussed in the following section, and *Sĕrat Dĕrmagandhul* because of the reference to the opening of the *Hoofdenschool* at Prabalingga that will be seen below.

The fact that, in 1872, *Gatholoco* was in the hands of Poensen's Christian assistants in Kĕdiri may be significant. As will be seen below, the rejection of Islam and the embrace of European learning that is a theme in these books, in *Sĕrat Dĕrmagandhul* also extended to the clear implication that Christianity might be the right choice for Javanese,

---

[13] Philippus van Akkeren (ed. & transl.), *Een gedrocht en toch de volmaakte mens: De Javaanse Suluk Gaṭolotjo, uitgegeven, vertaald en toegelicht* ('s-Gravenhage: "Excelsior", 1951), p. 11; G.W.J. Drewes, "The struggle between Javanism and Islam as illustrated by the Sĕrat Dĕrmagandul", *BKI* 122, no. 3 (1966): 328.

[14] Drewes, "Struggle", p. 310.

[15] See also E.P. Wieringa, "Ketzer oder wahre Gläubige? Der Kampf zwischen Javanismus und Islam in *Suluk Lebé Lonthang*", *Der Islam* 78 (2001): 129–46, on another text using bawdy humour to criticise Islam that may also be from the nineteenth century.

[16] C. Poensen, report on meeting of medehelpers and annual report for 1871, Kĕdiri, March 1872, in ARZ 261. Poensen summarised the text in his article "Gaṭo-lotjo (Een javaansch geschrift)", *MNZG* 17 (1873): 227–65.

for it would be the same as their *Buda* religion. This rather echoed the ideas of Ratukusya as expressed in *Bramartani* in 1866, as noted above.[17] In *Děrmagandhul* we will also find a spirit who lives on Mount Kělut named Tunggul Wulung, the same as the name borne by the Christian *kyai* of Chapter 5 who had indeed begun as a hermit on Kědiri's Mount Kělut. We may, therefore, suspect that *Děrmagandhul* may have been written by a Christian, or at least by someone familiar with and attracted to Christianity as part of the package of European government and learning.

Babad Kĕdhiri

Babad Kĕdhiri (The chronicle of Kědiri) is the only one of these texts to describe and date its own origins, but readers will quickly recognise that this information is not to be taken at face value. According to the book's opening passages, in 1832 the colonial government asked for information about the historical past of Kědiri from one M.Ng. Purbawijaya, a descendant of the local princely line. Purbawijaya called upon an elderly *wayang* master named Děrmakondha. The latter, however, said that he needed to call upon the knowledge of his friend Ky. Butalocaya, who lived in a cave and was the king of all the spirits. On an agreed day, Děrmakondha returned to Purbawijaya, bringing with him another *wayang* master who was said to be Butalocaya's incarnation. *Babad Kĕdhiri* was thus presented as an account the authority of which rested upon information given by the local king of the spirits.

The introduction crediting the book's content to the king of spirits of the Kĕdhiri area probably tells us nothing about who first composed it, or when. It is worth noting, however, that Butalocaya may have been a real person, or at least that this name was evidently used by someone who was a real person. For in 1883, a contributor to *Bramartani* identified himself as "Butalocaya Kadhiri". He wrote to ask for clarification of the *astha guna*, the eight attributes of a holy ascetic.[18] But I know nothing more about him.

---

[17] *BM* 5 July 1866.

[18] *BM* 29 Mar. 1883. The eight attributes he asked about were *widayaka* (learned), *Kesawa* (a name for Wisnu or Krěsna), *Wisnu* (the god of that name), *sudibya* (outstanding), *pujongga* (learned, a poet), *sujana* (virtuous), *sarjana* (shrewd, a philosopher), and *gunawan* (consummate, beautiful).

At the end of the book, the author of this redaction of *Babad Kĕdhiri*
identifies himself as Mas Sumasĕntika, the retired *wĕdana*[19] of the
district Lengkong, who wrote the book in 1873; his description of how
he did this will be quoted below. If *Suluk Gatholoco* borrowed from
Babad Kĕdhiri, or possibly the reverse, then the fact that Poensen knew
of a manuscript of *Gatholoco* in early 1872 gives us a consistent picture
of one or more *priyayi* in Kĕdhiri composing a new and iconoclastic view
of Java's Islamisation in the early 1870s. This was expressed in a version
of *Gatholoco* known in early 1872 and in *Babad Kĕdhiri* written down
by Sumasĕntika the following year. After the main text of *Babad Kĕdhiri*
are found historical notes setting out 18 historical ages (*jaman*), each
100 years long, from the age before there were kings to the *jaman Buda*
and thence to Raden Patah's reign in Dĕmak and on to the age of
Surakarta. It is said that these notes were written by Ky. Ng. Rĕksadiwirya
of the Kĕdiri area in 1885.[20] It is not impossible that this information
is meant to refer to the *Babad Kĕdhiri* text as well. Again there is a
chronological comparability with *Gatholoco*, which was certainly in
circulation as a manuscript in 1883 — for a contributor to *Bramartani*
referred to riddles he found while reading it[21] — and was first published
as a printed book in Surabaya in 1889.[22] Given the evidence discussed
above suggesting that *Dĕrmagandhul* could have been written by a
Christian, it is important to emphasise that *Babad Kĕdiri* was not. Both
M. Sumasĕntika and Ky. Ng. Rĕksadiwirya must have been Muslims,
however nominally, for neither had a Christian given name as was the
normal practice with Javanese converts.

　　Babad Kĕdhiri was published in Javanese with a Dutch translation
in 1902. The Dutch editor and translator, P.W. van der Broek, reported
that the manuscript he worked from was not the original, but rather a
copy. He had not been able to locate the original, owned by one of the

---

[19] An official just below the *Bupati*, the head of a district.

[20] P.W. van der Broek (ed. & transl.), *De geschiedenis van het rijk Kĕdiri, opgeteekend
in het jaar 1873 door Mas Soemâ-Sĕntikâ, gepensioneerd Wĕdânâ van het district
Lèngkong* (Leiden: E.J. Brill, 1902), text pp. 155–7. Lengkong district is in the
Kabupaten of Nganjuk, Kĕdiri. The summary of the text given here rests upon Van
der Broek's edition. Quotations from the Javanese are my own translations, which
sometimes differ significantly from Van der Broek's.

[21] *BM* 5 July 1883. The writer referred to riddles employed by Gatholoco in his
confrontration with *kyais*, about which came first amongst *dhalang* (puppeteer),
wayang (puppets), *gamĕlan* (orchestra) and *blencong* (lamp).

[22] Drewes, "Struggle", p. 314.

Bupatis of Kědiri. The text is in prose and Van der Broek commented that, "while it is written in *krama*, the writer often makes use of *ngoko* words or *ngoko* suffixes".[23] This was common practice in Javanese verse, suggesting that Sumasěntika's work might have been a prose version of a text originally in verse, or a work that borrowed passages from previous verse texts.

Babad Kědhiri's account of the Islamisation of Java is of central interest to us here. Ky. Butalocaya, the cave-dwelling king of the spirits, says that after Majapahit fell to the forces of "[Brawijaya's] son, the Islamic king", the new ruler sought to destroy all traces of the *Buda* religion. So the old books, which contained all the true information, were burned. All Javanese were compelled to embrace the new religion and did so out of fear. All the old images were destroyed or thrown away in the forest. Now the dead had to be buried rather than cremated. The successor Sultan of Pajang also had no regard at all for the old books. In the time of the king of Mataram, however, the old books were again respected, but they had already been burned by the Sultan of Děmak. The king gathered all that he could find from the books still in the hands of villagers, but knowledge of history was already corrupted, so the books contradicted each other.[24]

Later in *Babad Kědhiri*, Butalocaya tells the true account of the fall of Majapahit. As the forces of Islam gather to attack Majapahit, its last king Brawijaya summons his *Patih* Gajah Mada and says to him,

> "What is it that Raden Patah [his son, the future Sultan of Děmak] wants? I can't understand. Javanese can embrace Islam as they wish. I have even intended to become a Muslim myself.... If Patah wants to become king and succeed me, if he asked respectfully I would agree.... I don't want the trouble of war.... Because his religion is the religion of the Arabs, he regards me as a stranger although I am his father, because our religions are different.... It is best to write this down in the books, so that later whoever among my descendants become great persons should all know.... Do not forget your father and his goodness and secondly, do not render homage and put into practice the religion of foreigners. Put into practice your own religion, the heritage of

---

[23] Van den Broek, *Geschedenis van Kědiri*, p. vii.
[24] Ibid., text pp. 99–100, transl. pp. 81–2. The ruler of Mataram referred to here is almost surely Sultan Agung (r. 1613–46); on his role, see Ricklefs, *Mystic synthesis*, esp. Ch. 2.

ancient times, the religion of the ancestors that has been carried out; don't change it."[25]

Brawijaya decides not to oppose the Islamic armies but to go instead to Bali. There he will gather a coalition of the not-yet-Islamic kingdoms of eastern Indonesia to reconquer Java. He laments again, "The character of those who follow the religion of the Messenger is generally bad, like that of mice. I gave them land and I gave them abundance."[26] Brawijaya leaves, Gajah Mada puts up token resistance to the advancing Islamic armies, and then Majapahit falls. After their victory, Raden Patah and his allies go to see the Nyai Agĕng of Ngampel (a woman of great spiritual authority) who, rather than congratulating him, denounces Raden Patah for treason against his own father. After lengthy denunciations of the conduct of those who conquered Majapahit, she orders one of the *walis*, Sunan Kalijaga, to seek out the fleeing king.

Sunan Kalijaga catches up with Brawijaya and asks him to return to Majapahit and to forgive his son for his treachery. Brawijaya, however, says that he will leave his kingdom to Raden Patah, become a Muslim himself and live at Ngampel. Kalijaga teaches him "the highest mystical science (*ngelmi*) of the *walis* and the Confession of Faith".[27]

Brawijaya asks his companion, Sĕbdapalon Nayagenggong — who in fact soon proves to be a supernatural being[28] — also to embrace Islam. The latter objects that the king had not consulted him before changing his own religion and, had Brawijaya done so, he would have prevented him from converting. The king says that he has entered Islam and pronounced the name of Allah, the true God. But Sĕbdapalon Nayagenggong responds,

> "Those who call that true are those who are of that religion themselves, who are devoted to it. But I call it not yet the truth and I am not yet

[25] Van der Broek, *Geschiedenis van Kĕdiri*, text pp. 112–4, transl. pp. 91–4.

[26] Ibid., text p. 118, transl. p. 96.

[27] Ibid., text p. 131, transl. p. 107.

[28] Van der Broek treats the name Sĕbdapalon Nayagenggong as if it referred to two companions: Sĕbdapalon and Nayagenggong. I believe that this lengthy name is meant to refer to a single figure, who later turns out to be the supreme god-clown Sĕmar, as will be seen below. Companions who are clowns but also divinities, in the case of the character Sĕmar indeed the highest of gods, are a feature of the Javanese *wayang* theatre. Sĕbdapalon Nayagenggong means something like "words hammered out, like crickets".

devoted. I am devoted to the old religion, the *Buda* religion. The
meaning of the *Buda* religion is the religion of *budi*. The meaning of
budi is the being of Yang Latawaluja,[29] who envelops my human
body, who has the power to move the world. The duty of humans is
to be faithful to their *budi*, which is true, bright and clear."[30]

After further such discussion, Brawijaya comes to see that he has
made a mistake in converting to Islam. But as a king he will not change
his word, so he must persist in his conversion. Sunan Kalijaga reassures
him by giving him a sign. He magically converts unpotable water to
sweet water, as a proof that Islam is the true religion. Sĕbdapalon
Nayagenggong dismisses this trick, and declares that he is the creator of
heaven and earth. Brawijaya decides to go his separate way, whereupon
Sĕbdapalon Nayagenggong says,

> "I will serve you in secret then, wherever you go. I'll not leave nor will
> I stay, enveloping all that is hidden (*samar*), consistent with my name
> Kyai Sĕmar.... The land of Java I will make to prosper. I will bring
> foreigners to Java and the people of Java who are bad I'll exile overseas.
> Foreign things that are good, I'll bring to Java. Javanese junk I'll send
> overseas. Even if it is you, if you are bad I'll drive you overseas. I won't
> stop instructing your descendants until they know the way to drink
> alcohol and eat pork, as in the age of Majapahit, and know profit and
> loss."[31]

Subsequently Brawijaya dies and is buried at Majapahit, at his
request. The story-teller, the king of all the spirits Ky. Butalocaya, then
discusses the significance of all of this history further. He responds to
a question about whether it is not so that, whenever there is a drought
in Java, Javanese Muslims pray with the help of *santris* for rain and that
these prayers are answered. He says,

> "If the followers of the Arab religion could make rain fall, it would rain
> 300 times a year in Mecca. Dĕmak has tens of thousands of *santris* and
> there is a mosque built by the *walis*; if these were transplanted to
> Mecca, every year wet-rice fields would still fail there because there

---

[29] Presumably a term for God, but I know of it in no other source and see no obvious
meaning in it.
[30] Ibid., text p. 133, transl. pp. 108–9.
[31] Ibid., text pp. 137–9, transl. pp. 113–4.

would be a shortage of rain water in Mecca. What's the reason? Because the *santris* can't bring rain."[32]

The work ends with an afterword by M. Sumasĕntika, who tells how he wrote down the text in 1873 upon his retirement as *wĕdana*.

> Badly without anything to do, I searched my memory rather than snoozing in the afternoon. To console my unhappy heart, I composed this book. I added a few lies in the interest of the elegance of the words. May this be enjoyable to readers or listeners. Whether they believe it to be lies or the truth, I leave to the feelings of readers and listeners. But all of the antiquities that are mentioned above exist.[33]

Thus, *Babad Kĕdhiri* asserted that there was a secret history of the Islamisation of Java, a story that the first saints of Islam sought to conceal by burning all the old books. The conversion itself was ascribed to the treachery of a son against his father, so egregious that a revered Islamic figure such as Nyai Agĕng Ngampel was outraged. The last king of Majapahit, Brawijaya, had been generous to the Muslims and had been repaid with treachery, led by his own son. He drew the lesson from this that his descendants should practice their own religion, the *Buda* religion of the ancestors. That *Buda* religion was, said the king's companion, the same as *budi*.

Brawijaya's companion, who revealed himself as the god-clown Sĕmar, promised to remain after the king's conversion to Islam to make Java prosper. He would bring about the things that any reader of *Babad Kĕdhiri* would recognise as being what the Dutch were doing in the 1870s: outsiders came to Java and Javanese miscreants were exiled overseas. Foreign goods were imported and Javanese goods ("Javanese junk", said Sĕmar) were exported. He would not stop instructing the Javanese "until they know the way to drink alcohol and eat pork, as in the age of Majapahit, and know profit and loss". As we have seen in previous discussions in this book, here the modern ways of the Europeans — drinking alcohol and eating pork — were equated with the ways of pre–Islamic Majapahit. And the business style of the Dutch — calculating profit and loss — would be a part of this new-yet-old age that Sĕmar would bring, the age that was both *Buda* and *budi*. Islam was given short

---

[32] Ibid., text p. 148, transl. p. 121.
[33] Ibid., text pp. 154–5, transl. p. 125.

shrift here. It was a religion of Arabs, from a barren land where it never rained. In Java it rained, but not because of the prayers of *santris*. "If the followers of the Arab religion could make rain fall, it would rain 300 times a year in Mecca", said Butalocaya.

Thus did Sumasĕntika's *babad* portray Islamisation as a tragedy for Javanese. At the end, perhaps out of a sense of caution that was not shared by the authors of the two other books we will discuss shortly, he said that he had "added a few lies in the interest of the elegance of the words". Readers could believe what they liked of the story, he wrote, but as if to ask that it not be dismissed out of hand, he added, "But all of the antiquities that are mentioned above exist." He did not go so far as to suggest that Java's Islamic age was about to end. Other writers were, however, prepared to do so. As will be seen below, the anonymous author of the bitterly anti-Islamic text *Sĕrat Dĕrmagandhul* adapted the story of Sunan Kalijaga's magic water from *Babad Kĕdhiri* to show that Islam's time in Java was about to end. But first we turn to the extraordinary *Suluk Gatholoco*.

Suluk Gatholoco

As noted above, *Suluk Gatholoco* was known to Carel Poensen by February 1872. He was concerned about the impact on readers of a work with "expressions and discussions that are worse than vulgar".[34] Of vulgarity there was plenty, but it is more significant that this vulgarity was used to pillory Islam, those who brought it to Java and the *putihan* who by the 1870s were promoting a more demanding reformed version of the faith.

The story[35] begins in the kingdom Jajar where the king is concerned about the weird appearance of his only son. He has a shriveled body, no eyes, nose or ears and he sleeps most of the day. The description continues, leaving the reader in no doubt that this son, Gatholoco — the name means literally "polished ploughshare" — is a penis, which

---

[34] C. Poensen, report on meeting of medehelpers and annual report for 1871, Kĕdiri, March 1872, in ARZ 261.

[35] The summary here rests upon the Javanese text edition in van Akkeren, *Gedrocht*. That edition includes a Dutch translation. Direct quotations are my own translations. The work has also been translated into English in Benedict Anderson (ed. & transl.), "The Suluk Gaṭoloco", *Indonesia*, no. 32 (Oct. 1981): 109–50; no. 33 (Apr. 1982): 31–88.

is confirmed later in the story. Gatholoco receives his father's permission to set off on his adventures, but the king warns him to beware of an opponent he'll encounter named Pĕrjitawati who lives in the cave Tĕrusan. The audience for this story would have recognised that Pĕrjitawati means "having sex with her genitals". As the story develops, it becomes unmistakably clear that she represents the female sex organs. So off goes Gatholoco for a life of opium, drinking and gambling,[36] accompanied by his companion named Dĕrmagandhul (whose name means "has the task of dangling", i.e. the scrotum). They encounter three *pĕsantren* gurus called Ngabdul Jabar, Ngabdul Manab and Amat Ngarib, who have many students. These *Kyais*, who are also refered to as *santris*, speak disparagingly of Gatholoco's strange appearance.

Gatholoco says to the three *Kyais*,

> "My name is Gatholoco,
> the name of the True Man,
> my home is in the centre of the earth....
> Do not laugh at me,
> for my name is a name superior.
> The meaning of Gatho is the head of the penis
> and Loco is a rubbing-post."[37]

The *Kyais* are consumed with hilarity and admonish Gatholoco to learn the ways of Islam to escape going to hell.

> Gatholoco replied calmly,
> "The reason I am so very clever
> is that I adhere to the wishes
> of the honoured Prophet Emissary:
> Every day day I follow them
> by going to the opium-shop
> and buying left-over opium
> and buying prepared opium at the opium-shop,
> which I eat and smoke.
> It is Allah who gives me this knowledge.

---

[36] *Madat minum lan main*, 3 of the so-called "5 *ma*" (*ma lima*) of Javanese anti-Islamic tradition: *madat* (opium, nowadays marijuana), *minum* (drinking alcohol), *main* (gambling), *madon* (womanising), and *maling* (thievery).
[37] Van Akkeren, *Gedrocht*, p. 71; cf. ibid., pp. 112–3; cf. Anderson, "Gaṭoloco", p. 127.

"If I did not obey,
he would be very angry with me,
great would be his chastisement
and all night long I would get no sleep
and my body would be as if it had been pulled out of a fire."
The three *santris* spoke,
"There you go again,
the Holy Emissary in an opium-shop!
The Lord Emissary is honoured by the people of all the world
In the city of Mecca."

Gatholoco said angrily,
"The Emissary of Mecca whom you honour
exists no more.
He died a thousand years ago.
His place was in Arabia,
which takes seven months to reach
and is hidden by the sea.
Only his grave remains.
Every day you pray standing on your heads,
and you imagine you can reach him!

"so your praying is fruitless.
To know your own body,
pray to your own Emissary,
indeed to your own life.
Praying to the Emissary who is outside yourselves
with all the (prescribed) words
is improper.
You call upon Allah unreasonably,
shouting at each other so Allah can't concentrate on sleeping
for being disturbed by your voices."[38]

This diatribe against the Prophet and Islam continues to infuriate
the three *kyais*. Gatholoco then sets a riddle for them to answer, which
leads to mystical teachings from him and further debate. Gatholoco
eventually demands of them,

"What sort of people are you,
with your snipped [penis-]head all soaking wet.

---

[38] Van Akkeren, *Gedrocht*, p. 73; cf. ibid., p. 116; cf. Anderson, "Gatoloco", p. 132.

Are you Dutch or Chinese or Indians?

"Are you Bengalese?"
The three *santri* replied,
"We are Javanese
and Muhammad is our religion."
Gatholoco spoke,
"You are really like infidels (*kapir*)
of the Christian religion.
If you are Javanese,
Why don't you call upon the [Hindu-Buddhist] gods?

"That religion of Muhammad
is a religion of the Arabs.
You call upon a foreigner.
You are thieves
calling upon a different kind.
Because your sin in life
is that your knowledge (*kawruh*) is imperfect.
and you don't hold fast to anything
so destroyed is your faithfulness, shocking.

"Since ancient times
down to the age of Majapahit,
Javanese called upon the [Hindu-Buddhist] gods.
That changed with the age of Děmak.
(Javanese) began to call upon the Emissary of God,
as he is called by the Arabs.
Now you've changed over
and have left your original religion.
That makes you Javanese gone astray and unbelieving infidels."[39]

As the debate continues, the *santris* insist that Mecca is the centre of the world and that the Ka'ba is the navel of the world, towards which all Muslims prostrate themselves. Again, Gatholoco dismisses this idea:

"You all misunderstand.
Mecca has been cursed by Allah.

"Because what the people of Mecca
prostrate themselves before
is not the true Lord.

---

[39] Van Akkeren, *Gedrocht*, p. 77; cf. ibid., pp. 121–2; cf. Anderson, "Gaṭoloco", p. 141.

So the people of Mecca
earned the wrath of God.
Unreasonable was their calling upon
the word of God,
morning and evening screaming everywhere,
moving their heads back and forth like incense that's been splattered
    by rain.[40]

"Great is the anger of God,
as shown by that country
where it rains just once a year
and it is unbearably hot
so that nothing can grow from
whatever is planted.
Food and clothing are expensive.
The reason that the people of Mecca
all — men and women — throughout their lives

"if they urinate or defecate,
rarely wash their genitals
is because water is very scarce.
So they wipe with dirt instead.
That's why of the prophets
none had their homes there
but they moved to another country,
to Medina or Egypt,
because Mecca is a place of unfortunate people.

"All of that is clear,
yet you dare to call (Mecca)
the navel of the world!
How do you know that,
that you go along in calling it so?
Have you surveyed it?"
The three *santris* replied,
"It says so in our books."[41]

---

[40] Van Akkeren, *Gedrocht*, p. 126, translates "as if they had chicken disease because rain had got in"; Anderson, "Gaṭoloco", p. 147, follows him in translating "like rain-soaked fowl brought down with chicken-cholera". I don't see how they arrived at this.

[41] Van Akkeren, *Gedrocht*, pp. 79–80; cf. ibid., pp. 125–6; cf. Anderson, "Gaṭoloco", p. 147.

The debate carries on extensively. In response to one of his opponents' points, Gatholoco says, "If that is so, your Allah is stupid and has no *budi*."[42] Consuming opium as he goes, Gatholoco proceeds to tackle other *pěsantrens* and everywhere defeats the devout Muslims with his arguments.

Gatholoco climbs the mythical Mount Endragiri and bests all of the hermits and holy men. Eventually he encounters the female ascetic Pěrjitawati, she whom his father had warned him about as his greatest opponent. She sets him a series of riddles which he solves. So in the end he is invited to enter her cave, that is, to have sex with her via the metaphorical genius of the poem. Gatholoco is transported by passion and delight. He declares that at that moment he becomes a king whose title is Kalammulah. A word-play of the kind found throughout the text is then based on *kalam*. Kalammullah (Arabic *Kalam Allah*) means the word of God and is one of the terms used for the *Qur'an*. It is also the standard Arabic term for theology (Arabic *'ilm al-kalam*). *Kalam* also means pen (Arabic *qalam*), and — crucially for the word-play — in Javanese it also means penis. Gatholoco explains to the attendants who are present that Kalammullah means, not the word of God, but the penis of *budi* that enters. And when that happens in Pěrjitawati's "cave", Gatholoco will become *Buda*:

"Let all of you witness
that at this moment I become king
and my title is
Lord King Kalammulah.
The word 'king' means the top's been cut off.
That's the meaning of 'king'
and that means to enter.

"The meaning of *kalam* is penis,
and the word *mulah* means *budi*,
If your understanding is insufficient
I'll explicate it all together:
When Gatholoco has entered the cave
he will immediately become a *Buda* person."[43]

Flamboyant metaphorical intercourse follows.

---

[42] Van Akkeren, *Gedrocht*, p. 85; cf. ibid., p. 134; cf. Anderson, "Gaţoloco", p. 41.
[43] Van Akkeren, *Gedrocht*, p. 99; cf. ibid., p. 150; cf. Anderson, "Gaţoloco", p. 73.

Finally *Suluk Gatholoco* ends with a sexual interpretation of the *Shahada*, the Confession of Faith that "there is no God but God and Muhammad was the Messenger of God" (*La ilaha illa 'llah Muhammad Rasul Allah*). This is often opened with the words *ashadu* (I testify) and is sometimes described as the two sentences (connected by "and"). Were there any devout *putihan* among the readers of *Gatholoco*, they would probably have found this passage to be the culminating offence:

> "The formula *ashadu*
> means the origin of my body,
> because our parents
> contested with their (bodily) openings.
> *Allah* means
> something that is exceedingly bad (*ala*).
>
> "*Ilaha ilaha*,
> (means) that there are no others
> that are the same in form.
> *Washadu anna* means
> that woman confesses that she has
> something that is equally bad (*ala*).
>
> "*Muhkamad Rasullolah*
> indeed is the certain place
> of the secret essence that is manifest.
> As for the two sentences:
> man and woman are their places,
> they are called the two sentences."[44]

Like *Babad Kědhiri*, *Suluk Gatholoco* rejected Islam but used ribald humour more than historical reinterpretation. Many of the ideas in *Gatholoco* have already been seen in the discussion of the *babad*. Islam was depicted as a religion of Arabs and Arabia as a terribly hot, rainless place cursed by God. Muslims were not true Javanese but rather foreigners of some sort — Dutch, Chinese, Indians or Christians — or at best "Javanese gone astray and unbelieving infidels". "Down to the age of Majapahit," *Gatholoco* said, "Javanese called upon the [Hindu-Buddhist] gods", implying that this *Buda* age was what was truly Javanese. Gatholoco asserted that "Allah is stupid and has no *budi*". Throughout the text,

---

[44] Van Akkeren, *Gedrocht*, p. 105; cf. ibid., p. 157; cf. Anderson, "Gaṭoloco", p. 85.

bawdy sexuality was used to ridicule Islam. The phrase *Kalamullah*, meaning the word of God, in *Gatholoco* became *Kalam-mulah*, which was explained as the penis of *budi* that enters. And when that sexual entry took place, Gatholoco would become "a *Buda* person". Even the *Shahada* was treated to sexual reinterpretation. It requires no imagination to see the deep rejection of Islam behind the ridicule, word play and bawdiness in *Suluk Gatholoco*.

As noted above, *Gatholoco* was in circulation as a manuscript in the 1880s, being referred to by a *Bramartani* contributor in 1883,[45] and was printed in Surabaya in 1889.[46] *Babad Kĕdhiri* was published in Leiden in 1902, but must also have been available in Java. In neither case was there any hostile public reaction, so far as I am aware. It will be seen in the next chapter that there was a very different outcome when *Sĕrat Dĕrmagandhul,* was published in the early twentieth century.

Sĕrat Dĕrmagandhul

Sĕrat Dĕrmagandhul brought together the historical revisionism of *Babad Kĕdhiri* and the bawdy humour of *Suluk Gatholoco* and thus, in a sense, was the culminating text. It also seems to have been the last to be written. As will be seen below, it seems to refer specifically to the opening of the *Hoofdenschool* at Prabalingga in 1879 and was evidently written at about that time.[47]

Sĕrat Dĕrmagandhul opens[48] with the teacher Kalamwadi (meaning "secret penis") giving instructions about the past to his pupil Dĕrmagandhul (meaning "has the task of dangling", i.e. the scrotum), whom we have already met as the companion of Gatholoco. We will also meet again Kalamwadi's wife Pĕrjitawati ("having sex with her genitals") and

---

[45] *BM* 5 July 1883.

[46] Drewes, "Struggle", p. 314.

[47] The *hoofdenscholen* at Bandung, Magĕlang and Prabalingga were established as a result of a decision taken by the colonial government in 1878; Brugmans, *Onderwijs*, p. 183. They actually opened in 1879–80; Paulus *et al.*, *Encyc. Ned. Ind.*, vol. III, p. 104.

[48] The summary here follows the précis in Drewes, "Struggle", pp. 334–65, which has been checked at many points with the printed text in *Sĕrat Dĕrmagandhul, anyariosakĕn rĕringkĕsanipun babad bĕdah ing karaton Majapahit, sarta bantahipun Prabu Brawijaya kalayan Sabdapalon bab kawontĕnanipun agami Buda lan Eslam, sarta dunungipun carakan sastra Jawi* (Kediri: Boekhandel Tan Khoen Swie, 1921). All direct translations are my own.

Sabdapalon (the same as Sĕbdapalon, "words hammered out") from *Suluk Gatholoco*, and Butalocaya (or Budalocaya) from *Babad Kĕdhiri*. In its first stanza, *Dĕrmagandhul* asserts that the history of Java has been corrupted:

> That which has been written is not all the same,
> for certain people [who recorded the past]
> each discovered their own distinct knowledge (*kawruh*).
> Therefore the books that tell of the land of Java
> don't follow a single standard
> but present two or three versions.[49]

The equivalence between *Buda* and *budi* was established early in the text, as was the significance of the new European schools of the time and the inappropriateness of the Javanese being Muslims. Moreover, it was implied that the new ruler of Java — the European government — was bringing a new religion that Javanese might follow:

> Dĕrmagandhul said sweetly,
> ... "According to the source [of information],
> *Buda-budi* is called a religion
> and it calls upon the [Hindu-Buddhist] gods.
> If you want to eat the fruit of the tree of knowledge (*kawruh*),
>
> "then call upon the name of the Honoured Prophet
> Jesus, the famed,
> and change your religion.
> If you want to eat the fruit of the tree of immortality,[50]
> then call upon the Honoured Prophet,
> Muhammad our Emissary.
>
> "If you like (only) the leaves of knowledge (*kawruh*) and *budi*,
> then pray to Pik Kong

---

[49] *Dĕrmagandhul* (1921), p. 3; cf. Drewes, "Struggle", p. 320. Drewes believed (p. 327) that *kawruh* meant Christianity, but readers of this book have already seen multiple examples that demonstrate that *kawruh*, an old term used widely in Javanese mysticism, in the late nineteenth century was used also generally for European learning and science. At the same time, as noted above, it is possible that the author of *Dĕrmagandhul* was a Christian.

[50] *Wit kuldi*. As explained in Drewes, "Struggle", p. 334n3, "the forbidden fruit of the Islamic paradise-story is called *woh kuldi* in Javanese (from Arabic *khuld*, eternity, immortality)".

and follow the religion of the Chinese,
following the law of the king Li Sin Bin.[51]

... "To follow the ruler in religion is not to be an infidel (*kapir*),
for what is true or false
is possessed by the ruler.

"For the ruler has provided (what is needed)
for all his subjects, young and old,
who are ordered to request all knowledge (*kawruh*).
So that they may know the true from the false
in all the cities
schools (*sĕkolah*) are being built.

"If one does not join in eating
the fruit of the tree of knowledge (*kawruh*),
following the law of the Prophet Jesus,
that is a sign that a person does not know about trees.
Anyone who knows about trees
follows the religion of the king.

"Anyone who does not follow the religion of the king
is a half-baked person,
unripe both inside and outside.
To follow the king is to seek advantage,
inwardly standing up to
those of a different belief....

"If you adhere to the religion of the *walis*,
You should go far away
to Arabia and join the people there.
If you follow the command of the ruler,
the Sultan of Dĕmak,
you should go to a grave.

"Such scoundrels should just be driven away.
Don't let them mix with the ancestors and their king

---

[51] Pik Kong is also known as (Toa) Pek Kong in Indonesia, meaning the gods who are honoured in Chinese religion. Li Sin Bin probably refers to the Tang Emperor Li Shi-min (in Hokkien: Lee Si Bin), otherwise known as Tang Tai-zong. His reign was marked by many reforms, including in the legal realm. I am grateful for the advice of Dr Geoffrey Wade on this matter.

in Java, for their knowledge (*kawruh*) will disturb
the proper order of the commoners
and the regulations of the king.

"Nowadays Arabic books
should not be used;
they turn to chaos (distinctions among) injustice, justice and the law.
What should be used to settle legal matters
are the books of the Honoured Prophet
Jesus, the Spirit of God.

"The Dutch ruler indeed holds firm to Dutch
customs and ways of doing things,
of how to run the country and of religion.
So the fruit hangs securely on the tree,
a firm foundation in life,
the possession of the king.

"Even though you ask for two forms of knowledge (*kawruh*),
the inner and the outer truths,
adhere to the ancestors and the ruler.
The ancestors are empowered to teach and educate.
The ruler has greater responsibilities,
having to teach the law."[52]

The book moves on to the story of the fall of Majapahit.

At the time of Sultan Bintara [Raden Patah],
with his *kraton* at Děmak,
so says the book *Surya Ngalam*,
[Majapahit] was attacked by the *walis*
and two matters got mixed up:
infidels (*kapir*) and Muslims have different laws.
For robbery and plunder
[Muslims] cut off hands and cut off feet,
an unjust law like the law of Arabia. ...

From the time of Děmak there arrived
foreigners from right and left of Java
who did not pay obeisance to Java.
Because the firm foundations were destroyed,

---

[52] *Děrmagandhul* (1921), pp. 4–9. In summarising this passage, Drewes, "Struggle", refers to "Government" but the text does not use the term *gupremen*. It refers to "the king" with the standard terms *Něrpati* and *ratu*.

[Javanese] left the *Budi* religion
and changed to the religion of the Emissary.
[The ruler] was weak, not strong enough to give orders
overseas, to the right and left of Java,
because insufficiently distinguished
was the king.[53]

Děrmagandhul wants to know why the Javanese changed their religion and Kalamwadi, after initial reluctance, reveals what he knows. Brawijaya made a mistake in marrying a Muslim princess, the Putri Cěmpa. Many Muslim teachers were then allowed to settle in Java. Kalamwadi tells particularly of the brutal conduct of the *wali* Sunan Bonang. He also introduces two spirits of the Kědiri area named Butalocaya (or Budalocaya) and Kyai Gung Tunggul Wulung who, in life, had served the legendary king Jayabaya of Kědiri. Budalocaya lives in a cave, while Tunggul Wulung lives on Mount Kělut. Readers will recognise the latter as bearing the same name as Ibrahim Tunggul Wulung (d. 1885), the Christian *kyai* of Chapter 5 who had in fact been a hermit on Mount Kělut, which overshadows Kědiri. Budalocaya threatens Sunan Bonang that he will enlist the aid of the Goddess of the Southern Ocean and slaughter all the Javanese who have converted to Islam unless Bonang makes amends for his actions. In the end, Bonang agrees.

Budalocaya denounces Sunan Bonang and his Arab religion when he sees Bonang vandalise a Hindu-Buddhist image.

Budalocaya snapped,
"You are a troublesome character!

"That was the creation of an exalted ruler,
the Honoured king Jayabaya,
beloved of the All-Seeing,
who was granted an exalted revelation,
who was learned and rich in understanding.
Even in Arabia, he would have been a king.
He knew to write down things which had not yet occurred,

"and, sir, the rules for writing
and the rules of the Javanese in literature
are an esteemed inheritance from the ancestors.
All believed the reports,

---

[53] Ibid., pp. 23–4.

great their reverence for
the written reports of old.
The antiquities could be examined.

"People who revere Arab reports,
don't know how things are here.
They believe both lies and truths.
They believe what they're told by wanderers.
So you came to Java
to peddle boasting tales
about the grandeur of Mecca,

"Only people without *budi*,
with cattle-shit for brains,
who smell like a split-open coconut
believe what you say.
While people like me,
Who've retained
their *budi* and knowledge (*kawruh*),
we regard this as the prattle of a child.

"For I know
how things are in Mecca.
The people there rarely wash their genitals,
The land is stony and water is rare,
whatever you plant fails to grow,
it's dreadfully hot and it rarely rains.
People with sound understanding

"call Mecca a land
that has been cursed by Allah,
an unfortunate place it is called.
People call arbitrarily
upon the name of Allah.
Many sell their own people,
turned into bought slaves,

"with whom they have illicit sex without marrying.
Treated just like animals
are people of other religions,
for they forget that they are also human beings,
all descendants of Adam.
Sir, leave here immediately,
for you are a sinful person."[54]

---

[54] Ibid., pp. 45–6.

The history of the fall of Majapahit now becomes the focus of the story, in which it echoes — indeed almost surely borrows from — *Babad Kĕdhiri*. *Patih* Gajah Mada informs king Brawijaya of the activities of the Arabs on the coast.

> The king spoke angrily,
> "*Patih*, those Arab *ulama*
> are untrustworthy in their aims.
> Egg-saints is what they are:
> white on the outside but yellow on the inside.
> They're not satisfied to settle here but also ring-bark the fenced *waringin*
>   trees.[55]
> Heh, *Patih*, you drive away
> the Arabs who are in Java,
> who try to cause troubles for the kingdom.
>
> "Only at Dĕmak and in Ngampel
> will I allow them to stay in Java
> and to carry on their religion."[56]

The *walis* now press Raden Patah to attack his father, destroy Majapahit and thereby convert Java to Islam, for which God will bless him. Eventually Patah agrees to do this. The war begins, to the dismay of Brawijaya, who asks Gajah Mada,

> "*Patih*, what is the reason
> that Patah and the *Bupatis* of the *pasisir*
> have gone along with destroying Majapahit,
> without regard for my goodness?"
> *Patih* Gajah Mada made the *sĕmbah* and said,
> "I am at my wit's end
> and cannot explain this to you, my lord,
>
> "for this is far from my ability to understand.
> The good that has been done to them they repay with harm.
> They are treacherous towards what is said in the books,
> the firm foundation of the Javanese people.

---

[55] The *waringin kurung* still stand on the great squares at the front of *kratons* in Java. They are revered objects of great supernatural potency, conveying the presence and potency of royalty. To ring-bark and kill these trees would be a direct assault on the standing of royalty.

[56] *Dĕrmagandhul* (1921), p. 49.

Javanese-Javanese who know the difference between coarse and smooth:
their obligation if treated with goodness
is truly to repay with goodness.

"But the people of Islam are different.
If they are done good they repay with harm,
maintaining what is said when
they call upon the name of Allah.
So the people of Islam are bad inside.
Their sweetness is merely on the outside,
inside they are bitter through and through."

"What is called upon by the *Buda* people is different.
They call upon the exalted realm of the great gods,
the realm that is their bodies,
the gods of *budi* and desire.
The intention of calling upon the essence of *budi*
is to rise up to the name of being,
there praising the most excellent (*utami*).

"If one calls upon the Prophet Muhammad
the Emissary of God, the seal of the prophets,
"Muhammad" means a revered grave (*makaman*);
that grave is the wrong essence.
So they crazily bend this way and that in the morning and at sunset,
with their hands on their breasts muttering softly,
standing on their heads and kissing the ground.

"All sorts of foods they condemn...." [57]

Readers might note *en passant* the connection in this passage among *Buda, budi*, and a third term, *utami*, the most excellent. We will encounter this connection again in the next chapter when we see how in 1908 Javanese *priyayi* who were little impressed by reformed Islam established an organisation which they named *Budi Utama*.

The story of *Dĕrmagandhul* continues to the fall of Majapahit. Again, as in *Babad Kĕdhiri*, the old books, "the honoured *Buda* heirlooms", are burned. "There remained not a single one of these foundations of the *Buda* religion."[58] After the victory over Majapahit, Raden Patah is denounced by the Nyai Agĕng of Ngampel.

---

[57] Ibid., p. 61.
[58] Ibid., p. 71. Drewes, "Struggle", p. 346, misreads the text in summarising it as "Only one is left".

"And how about you,
attacking your own father without cause!"

"Truly this is a great disaster,
for on your death you'll go to hell,
according to God's law.
People like you
are ignorant of divine law...."

"And you have lost your royal father.
You are called no good,
who destroyed the order of humankind.
You will be ridiculed and shamed before the world;
for as long as you live
you will be called a bad person,
for you aimed at victory in battle,
attacking your own old father.
Just calculate and add up
all of your faults!"[59]

Sunan Kalijaga then sets off in search of Brawijaya while Raden Patah returns to Dĕmak and tells Sunan Bonang of what has happened.

"The books that were *Buda* heirlooms
I collected together
and I burned them all
so that all the foundations would disappear of the *Budi*[60] religion."
Sunan Bonang laughed,

"You did the right thing, my lad.
If there remained books of *Buda* law,
the Javanese would remain infidels (*kapir*)
for a thousand years.
There is no way that they would decide to change their religion,
to follow the law of the Emissary of God.
There's no way that they would decide to recall,
to call upon the name of Allah
and to call upon the name of the Honoured Prophet,
Muhammad the Emissary of God.

"There's no way they would decide to pray, to praise and to *dhikr*."[61]

---

[59] Ibid., p. 79.

[60] Sic. But since this is the end of the line of verse, the metre required final *i* even if the author intended *buda* rather than *budi*.

[61] *Dĕrmagandhul* (1921), p. 92.

Meanwhile, Brawijaya has reached the eastern tip of Java, accompanied by Sabdapalon and Nayagenggong.[62] There Kalijaga catches up with him and comes to feel remorse at the injustice that he has had a hand in committing against the old king. A discussion about Islam follows in the course of which Kalijaga gives a sexual interpretation of the Islamic concepts, as we have seen previously in *Gatholoco*. This time it concerns prayer and the four stages of the Sufi path to enlightenment: the law (*sarengat*, i.e. *shari'a*), the mystical way (*tarekat*), reality (*hakekat*) and gnosis (*makrifat*). This involves plays on words, some of which can be reflected in the translation below.

" ... *la ilaha illu llahi,*
indeed Muhammad is the true Messenger of God.

"That is the *Shahada* of Islamic law (*sarengat*).
The meaning of *sarengat*
is that when you sleep (*sare*) the penis arises.
Tarekat (mystical brotherhood) (means)
to ask (*taren*) a woman (whether she wants to).
Kakekat means to have the same intention (*kapti*)
for women and men must (*kĕdah*) agree (*rukuk*).
Makripat means to know women,
the confession of faith and law of men and women (*sarak sarat laki-rabi*),
permitted to make preparations to be father and mother,
secondly with the permission of the king
and thirdly with witnesses together.

"Therefore there are directions for prayer (*keblat*, i.e. *qibla*): to the east (*wetan*)
is the origin (*wiwitane*) of human form,
to the west (*kulon*) the man cuddles up (*kĕlonan*),
to the south (*kidul*) the penis opens (*kalam dudul*) the vagina
and it is dark in the middle of heaven,
to the north (*lor*) is where the essence originated (*lair rasa*)."[63]

Further word-playing explications of Islamic concepts follow. At the end of this discussion, Brawijaya announces that he wishes to convert to Islam.

---

[62] In this version, these are clearly two separate characters. On ibid., p. 100, they are referred to as "two servants".
[63] *Dĕrmagandhul* (1921), pp. 107–8.

Sabdapalon and Nayagenggong, however, refuse to join Brawijaya in becoming Muslims. Sabdapalon tells Brawijaya that he is the first king in the 8,300 years that Sabdapalon has been looking after Javanese kings who has changed his religion. All have maintained the *Budi* religion.[64]

> "Only you yourself
> have abandoned the foundations of Javanese custom.
> Javanese means understanding.
> To accept (the new faith) means to go astray...."[65]

Sabdapalon's denunciation of Islam continues at length. The crude bawdiness seen in *Gatholoco* is also evident here.[66] He speaks of the reincarnations of various types of prominent Muslims as animals:

> "Frogs enjoy praising,
> rumbling together in the water:
> they are the reincarnation of *santris* who've gone astray,
> who arbitrarily call upon the name of God,
> reincarnated bowing over like frogs.

> "Grasshoppers are the reincarnations of *hajis*,
> their (Arab-style) robes double the usual length,
> their heads in a thick turban,
> with small, thin arms."[67]

Nevertheless, Brawijaya feels that he cannot withdraw his word and must carry through with his promise to become a Muslim. As in *Babad Kĕdhiri*, here, too, Kalijaga magically turns bad water into sweet water to demonstrate the superiority of Islam. Sabdapalon dismisses this as a cheap trick and reveals himself to be Sĕmar. He admonishes Brawijaya,

> "My lord, know well,
> if you have changed your religion,

> "abandoning the *Buda* religion,
> indeed weak will be your descendants in the future,
> for they will have abandoned Javaneseness.

---

[64] Sic. But again this is at the end of the line of verse, so the metre required final *i* even if the author intended *buda* rather than *budi*.

[65] *Dĕrmagandhul* (1921), p. 125.

[66] E.g. ibid., p. 155: "If your knowledge (*kawruh*) is unclear, then your spirit enters your anus and mixes with shit."

[67] Ibid., p. 158.

Their Javanese-Javaneseness disappeared,
They'll want to go along with foreigners.
Certainly in the future they will be less
than Javanese-Javanese of understanding....

"Javanese who change religion,
who abandon the religion of the ancestors,
in the future, if they should regret this
and recall the religion of *Buda-budi*
and want to eat the fruit of knowledge (*kawruh*),
then the gods will forgive.
The fruit will again be as in the age of *Buda*."[68]

The book's most important prophecies soon follow. After four days, Brawijaya reaches Prabalingga. There Kalijaga's magically sweet water is tested:

The fragrant water was examined
and it smelled stinking, rotten,
tasting bitter like a camel.
The water was thrown away.
The king said sweetly,
"Heh, Kalijaga, know
that this land of Prabalingga in the future

"will have two names,
the people of Prabalingga of the stinking water.
In the future, here will be a place
where will gather all the peoples
of (the Netherlands) Indies
in order to devote themselves to knowledge (*kawruh*)
and proficiency in external matters.
Their devotion to *budi*

"is how they will learn to become Javanese,
Javanese-Javanese who understand with one eye.
When their eye has become one,
all the people of Java
will recall the religion of *budi* and knowledge (*kawruh*).
The meaning of Prabalingga
Is the magical power (*prabawa*) of the Javanese

"who will recall the fame of its miraculous power (*prabawa*).
The law of the Emissary

---

[68] Ibid., pp. 175–7.

will be for the Javanese for four hundred years,
during four *kratons.*
When it comes to the fifth *kraton* their religion will change.
The religion of knowledge (*kawruh*) will be adopted
and a sign of this is that the smell of the water

"was fragrant for only four days."[69]

The "one eye", the four centuries and the five *kratons* of this passage were important. The first would have reminded any of its audience familiar with older Javanese Sufism — i.e. with the mystic synthesis version of Islam — of a doctrine found in that school. In the teachings of Pakubuwana II (1749–88) (*Sĕrat wulang Pakubuwana II*), Arabic and Javanese literature are compared to the right and left eyes, respectively. The work says,

> For Arabic literature is
> a vision of the True Immaterial (God);
> Javanese literature is a vision of the (material) self.
> If you do not know them both,
> if you understand neither Javanese nor Arabic,
> you will make no use at all of the teachings
> and instructions of your father and grandfathers.[70]

But whereas *Sĕrat wulang Pakubuwana II* insisted on the necessity of these two eyes to comprehend life fully, *Sĕrat Dĕrmagandhul* insisted that only one eye — a Javanese one — was needed.

A sequence of *kratons* after Majapahit was known in Javanese tradition. Each was usually regarded as having prevailed for a century, even though from the eighteenth century on, real history did a poor job of fitting the pattern. The first of these *kratons* was Dĕmak, which according to tradition lasted from Śaka 1403 to Śaka 1500. The second was the combined age of Pajang and Mataram, evidently regarded in Javanese tradition as a single period because it was thought to have occupied a single century, from Śaka 1503 to AJ 1600. The third was Kartasura, founded in AJ 1603 (AD 1677). It did not fall — as it should have, according to the tradition — in AJ 1700 (AD 1774) but rather over 30 years earlier. Surakarta (est. AD 1746) seems to have been regarded as being of one age with Kartasura. That would make Yogyakarta

---

[69] Ibid., p. 183.
[70] Ricklefs, *Seen and unseen worlds*, pp. 218–20.

(est. 1755) *kraton* number four. Or, alternatively, Surakarta and Yogyakarta were together the fourth of these ages. In either case, that would make Dutch Batavia *kraton* number five, the one that would usher in the new age with a restoration of the religion of knowledge (*kawruh*), otherwise identified as the religion of *Buda* and *budi*.[71]

The reference to four centuries as the age of Islam in Java was linked to Prabalingga as the "place where will gather all the peoples of (the Netherlands) Indies in order to devote themselves to knowledge (*kawruh*) and proficiency in external matters" — a "devotion to *budi*" which "is how they will learn to become Javanese, Javanese-Javanese who understand with one eye". In the 1870s, Dutch educational efforts were extending to setting up schools to give more professional education to the sons of *priyayi* who were destined for careers as colonial officials. The first of these "heads" schools" (*hoofdenscholen*) were established in 1878 in Bandung, Magĕlang and Prabalingga.[72] For a writer in Kĕdiri, the Prabalingga *hoofdenschool* was of most immediate interest. The dating of this is, however, somewhat unexpected. In the hybrid lunar Javanese AJ calendar, four centuries after the fall of Majapahit in Śaka 1400 was AJ 1800 (AD 1871–72). We have noted, however, that the *Pustakaraja Purwa* shows that the Javanese were aware of the differences between the solar and lunar calendrical systems and were playing historical games with that difference. Consistent with that, it seems that the author of *Dĕrmagandhul* calculated his four centuries in the solar calendar, so that the 400th anniversary of the fall of Majapahit in Śaka 1400/AD 1478 became AD 1878, the year of the establishment of the Prabalingga *hoofdenschool.*

To return to the text of *Sĕrat Dĕrmagandhul,* after Brawijaya has delivered his prophecy of the end of the Islamic age in Java, the text explains why the history of Majapahit is not properly known.

> The reason that the story of Majapahit
> is not as great as was that kingdom,
> as broad as were its dependencies,

---

[71] Rĕksadiwirya's historical notes at the end of *Babad Kĕdhiri* give a different sequence. The four ages since the fall of Majapahit in his list are (1) the age of Raden Patah of Demak or Pajang, (2) the age of Sultan [Agung] of Mataram, (3) the age of Kartasura and (4) the age of Surakarta. See Van den Broek, *Geschedenis van Kĕdiri*, p. 157. Van den Broek did not include this part of the text in his translation.

[72] Brugmans, *Onderwijs*, p. 183.

is because the story was cut short.
Because it would open up a royal secret
of a son who went to war against his father.
That is a low tale,
(re)written by the poets
who only hint at the fall of Majapahit
as they set it down in the chronicles.[73]

The pro-Christian sentiments of the author become clear as the
lengthy work marches to its close.

The *sunans* who were also *walis*
destroyed their own religion.
Their law is that people to whom good has been done
actually should avenge that goodness.
In the meantime arrived
the Christian religion of Ngarbun.[74]
Its character is sweet, as beautiful as brass.
....
From the first time it set foot in Java,
it has contributed to three matters:
its first contribution is
budi, understanding, faithfulness and prosperity;
its second goods and money;
its third
a wounded breast and cut-through neck.[75]
From the beginning down to the present,
(Christians) have deployed much wealth.

I believe that in the future,
salt will again turn to water.
Javanese will hold firm
to the religion of Ngarbun:[76]
they will all convert to Christianity.[77]

---

[73] *Děrmagandhul* (1921), p. 189.

[74] Ngarbun is a mystery to me. Readers will see that it also occurs below. Prof. Karel Steenbrink suggests that perhaps it is meant to be a variant name for Ngara, Coolen's Christian settlement. I cannot suggest any better explanation.

[75] This line is not clear to me. Perhaps it is meant to refer to the wounds of Christ on the cross, or to Dutchmen suffering personal injuries in Java.

[76] See n. 74.

[77] *Děrmagandhul* (1921), pp. 192–3.

Finally, *Sĕrat Dĕrmagandhul* concludes with a passage that ties the entire text back to the sort of speculations that were common in Javanese mysticism, regardless of the pro-Christian sections of the poem.

> Praise the true reality of knowledge (*kawruh*)
> and know the true reality of life.
> Life is the shadow
> of the being of God.
> What are the capacities of humankind?
> If human thoughts are to be carried out,
> it is *budi* that does the moving.
>
> Words derive from thoughts,
> thoughts derive from concepts,
> concepts derive,
> they derive from our wishes,
> wishes derive from *budi*
> and *budi* is the being of God
> who is most high.
> His greatness is complete,
> without shortcoming or increase or excess,
> without direction and without place.
>
> It is not the moon that illumines
> and not the sun that makes light.
> It is none other than the one who possesses,
> who possesses the void,
> the void that certainly spreads before us.
> Ponder this.
> In truth, it is knowledge (*kawruh*),
> knowledge (*kawruh*) that is truly exalted,
> exaltation from life until death,
> that replaces the light of the moon.[78]

More than Four Ways to Pray

It will be clear to readers that we have come a very long way from Chapter 3. There we saw the world of pious Javanese Muslims polarising into differing, often contending, camps. We discussed this in terms of four different approaches to prayer. There were followers of the older

---

[78] Ibid., pp. 201–2.

Javanese mystic synthesis who practiced the "everlasting *salat* [prayer]" and saw no need to perform "the (ordinary) *salat* with ablutions".[79] For them, ritual prayer was for the uninitiated. There were also the reformist *putihan* for whom the five daily prayers were an integral part of God's law, not a topic for mystical speculations. The "true *salat*" for these believers was carried out five times a day, after ritual ablutions. Followers of reformed Sufi *tarekats*, the Naqshabandiyya and Qadiriyya wa Naqshabandiyya, too, accepted the orthodox commitment to the five daily prayers and included mystical doctrines and practices in their religious life. Across Java there were also messianic leaders and followers who looked to a millennial solution for their woes, including in their prayers the expulsion of their Christian rulers.

In Chapter 4 we saw that many — almost surely a large majority — of the Javanese were distancing themselves from Islamic identity and religious practice, as the *abangan* emerged as a recognised and named part of Javanese society. It seems that they weren't praying much at all, at least not to a god as defined by a world religion. In Chapter 5 we saw the first small Christian Javanese communities emerge, with their own understanding of prayer — an amalgamation, in many cases, of Christian and indigenous concepts. In Chapter 6 we saw *priyayi* who embraced European learning and life styles with enthusiasm, but who still regarded themselves as Muslims. In about 1870, we encountered a *Bupati* who was, like many of his fellows, an enthusiast for all things Dutch. But when asked whether that meant he would convert to Christianity, he replied, "Ah, ... to tell the truth, I would rather have four wives and a single God, than one wife and three Gods".[80]

And now we have seen the work of *priyayi* who rejected Islam altogether and wanted to return to the *Buda*. For them the Islamisation of Javanese society was a great civilisational mistake. It had been achieved by a treacherous assault on a goodly king of Majapahit, led by his own evil son. For them the Dutch government of Java was not a thing to be expelled but an opportunity to restore the Javanese to their true Javaneseness. To do this they would embrace the *budi* and *kawruh* of the Dutch-transmitted age of European progress. And that would be the key to restoring the pre-Islamic religion of Java, the *Buda* age that represented the true character of the Javanese people. For the author of

---

[79] Zoetmulder, *Pantheism and monism*, pp. 145–7.
[80] Keesteren, "Koran", p. 46.

Sĕrat Dĕrmagandhul, conversion to Christianity might be part of this package. But for her or him, that, too, was all to do with *budi, kawruh,* and *Buda.*

Javanese society had drawn far apart already by the 1870s and 1880s. The circumstances of the early twentieth century would allow those divisions to become more institutionalised, more politicised. As they did so, they also became harder, deeper and more conflictual. It is to that period that we turn in the following chapter.

8

Polarities Politicised, c. 1908–30

Into the increasingly polarised society that we have seen emerging in nineteenth-century Java there came, in the early twentieth century, more modern forms of organising and mobilising people and of distributing ideas. Social categories that had previously been seen in such matters as religious and cultural practices, educational style, place of residence, cultural tastes and social class thus came also to be defined by formal organisations. They began to be political. This would render them more readily identifiable and less readily bridgeable.

The *hajj*

Many of the phenomena we have seen in preceding chapters carried on into the early twentieth century. Increasing numbers of Javanese undertook the *hajj*, as can be seen from the figures in Table 8.[1]

These Javanese and Madurese pilgrims were part of a wider Indonesian pattern. In the years before the Depression of 1930, some 30 to 50

---

[1] Vredenbregt, "Haddj", pp. 143–4. There are some gaps in Vredenbregt's data; only years for which the data is complete are reported here. It should be noted also that World War I caused such disruption to shipping patterns that between 1915 and 1919 almost no Indonesians were able to undertake the pilgrimage. This caused higher than usual numbers when shipping was restored after the war. Martin van Bruinessen, "Muslims of the Dutch East Indies and the caliphate question", *La question du califat* (Les Annales de l'autre Islam no. 2; Paris: Publication de l'ERISM, 1994), pp. 264–5.

TABLE 8: *Hajj* departures from Javanese-speaking areas and Madura, selected years, 1912–30

Year	*hajis*
1912	4,915
1913	8,759
1914	10,006
1920	7,455
1921	15,036
1922	8,512
1923	7,719
1924	10,318
1927	6,025
1928	7,768
1929	7,326
1930	7,031

thousand *hajis* from across the Indonesian archipelago travelled to Mecca each year, usually representing around 40 per cent of all pilgrims there.[2]

Educational Modernisation

As the twentieth century opened, the Dutch colonial regime made an increased commitment to providing education for Indonesians as a part of its new "ethical" policy.[3] The number of Javanese and other Indonesians receiving a more modern education consequently grew. From 1907 to 1930, the number of three-year primary schools across the archipelago grew from 122 to 16,605 with 1,229,666 pupils registered. The number of Indonesians studying at Dutch-Indonesian secondary schools (*Hollands-Inlandse scholen*), which played an important role in the education of the first generation of Indonesian nationalists, grew from 19,577 in 1915 to 37,453 in 1930.[4] In the light of Indonesia's large and rapidly growing

[2] D. van der Meulen, "De Mekka-bedevaart en Nederlansch-Indië's belang darbij", *Indisch Genootschap: Verslag van de algemeene vergadering gehouden den 10 Nov. 1938*, p. 22.
[3] For an overview of this matter, see Ricklefs, *History of modern Indonesia*, ch. 14.
[4] S.L. van der Wal (ed.), *Het onderwijsbeleid in Nederlands-Indië: Een bronnenpublikatie* (Groningen: J.B. Wolters, 1963), pp. 691, 696.

Village school in Java c. 1920 (Collection of KITLV, Leiden)

population — 59.1 million indigenous Indonesians in 1930 — this was
a very poor performance on the part of the colonial power. But it contributed to the creation of a tiny educated elite who played a decisive role
in anti-colonial movements. As will be seen below, Islamic organisations
also expanded their educational activity in those decades.

Among the identifiable socio-cultural groups in Javanese society at
the turn of the century, the first to embrace more modern forms of
organisation were the *priyayi* elite, particularly those who were seeking
advancement through the vocational qualifications offered by the
Dutch. In 1900 the old *hoofdenscholen* at Prabalingga, Bandung and
Magĕlang — whose opening had been so welcomed by the author of
Sĕrat Dĕrmagandhul, as was seen in the preceding chapter — were
upgraded and converted to "training schools for native officials" (OSVIA:
Opleidingscholen voor inlandsche ambtenaren). The *dhoktĕr Jawa* school
at Weltevreden was similarly turned into STOVIA (*School tot opleiding
van inlandsche artsen*, school for training native doctors) in 1900–1902.
These two institutions had tiny numbers of students but were important
sources for the intellectual leadership of the new century.

Budi Utomo

In May 1908 the medical students at STOVIA created the first modern-type organisation in Indonesia, which they called Budi Utama — usually spelled Budi Utomo to reflect Javanese pronunciation of the last two vowels.[5] They officially translated this Javanese title into Dutch as meaning *het schoone streven* (the beautiful endeavour), but readers will know from the discussion of *budi* and *Buda* in the preceding chapter that this was a heavily loaded title in contemporary Java. Budi Utomo could as well mean elevated or superior mind, intellect, reason, genius, wit, discretion, judgment, wisdom, aptitude, character, disposition, or sense. It conveyed that its members were superior — as indeed they were confident that they were as a fruit of their education — and that they were not claiming devout Islam as the grounds of that superiority. They were, in fact as well as in their view of themselves, the holders of the keys to Dutch-conveyed *budi* and, implicitly, to the resurrection of the *Buda* age.

Several senior figures who inspired the creation of Budi Utomo made their cultural allegiances clear. Dr Wahidin Soedirohoesodo (1857–1917) looked upon Javanese civilisation as being principally of Hindu-Buddhist inspiration. To him, Dutch education was the key to revitalising Javanese society.[6] Another leading figure was Dr Radjiman Wediodiningrat (1879–1951), who embraced classical Javanese art forms, Theosophy and various contemporary European philosophical trends.

In 1911 Dr Radjiman addressed the prestigious *Indisch Genootschap* (Indies Society) in the Hague — the first Javanese ever to do so. His subject was "the psychological life of the Javanese people". He made it clear that he was a child of the modernising elite that sought to embrace modern learning on the basis of a restored Hindu-Buddhist past: *budi* and *Buda*. Readers will readily recognise themes from the preceding chapter:

> It is a firm fact [he said] that Hindu culture has been of great influence on Javanese national life.... Hindu civilisation has struck roots in

---

[5] On the history of Budi Utomo, see particularly Akira Nagazumi, *The Dawn of Indonesian nationalism: The early years of the Budi Utomo, 1908–1918* (Tokyo: Institute of Developing Economies, 1972); Robert Van Niel, *The Emergence of the modern Indonesian elite* (The Hague & Bandung: W. van Hoeve, Ltd., 1960); or, more briefly, Ricklefs, *History of modern Indonesia*, pp. 207–9.

[6] Nagazumi, *Dawn*, pp. 29–30.

Javanese society.... Literature, art and the character of the people betray their Hindu origin....

When in the beginning of the fifteenth century (AD) the Mohammedan religion gained a foothold in Java and the great Javanese empire of Majapahit was laid waste by the Javanese lords who had converted to Islam, Javanese developments began to experience the influence of that religion.

[With regard to literature] we must immediately admit that the change was detrimental. After the reworkings of Hindu literature, we no longer encounter the previous clarity in expression and command of the language in Javanese–Mohammedan literature.

It is clear that this coincided with the splitting–up of the Javanese empire of Majapahit and the incessant wars and conflicting claims of the contemporary Javanese lords.[7]

Nine years later Radjiman again addressed the *Indisch Genootschap*, this time on "the social course of the Javanese (Indonesian) population". By now he had read the fourteenth-century Old Javanese poem *Deśawarṇana* (then called *Nāgarakṛtāgama*) which had been published in 1919 by H. Kern and N.J. Krom. Radjiman quoted repeatedly from the *Deśawarṇana* in praise of the Hindu-Buddhist kingdom of Majapahit. He insisted that there was "a profound bond between society and religion in that glorious and powerful age of the Javanese people. The references to the many religious foundations, both Buddhist and Siwaite, and the many village societies attached to them, is proof of that." But the religious ideas of the age of Majapahit were distorted "by the invasion of the Mohammedan religion", he told his audience. This was not, however, a fundamental change, for there was still room for expressing Javanese syncretism.[8]

Dr R. Soetomo (1888–1938) was another major *priyayi* figure and leader of Budi Utomo. He studied in the Netherlands, qualified there as a doctor in 1923 and married a Dutch woman. He was a syncretic mystic at heart who was more devoted to meditation than to prayer. He was inspired (as were many others) by Hindu civilisation and particularly by Gandhi, Rabindranath Tagore and Swami Vivekenanda. When he made a world tour in 1936–37, however, he was to be disappointed by

---

[7] Radjiman, "Het psychisch leven van het Javaansch volk", *Indisch Genootschap: Algemeene vergadering van 14 February 1911*, pp. 153–5.
[8] Radjiman, "De maatschappelijke loop van de Javaansche (Indonesische) bevolking", *Indisch Genootschap: vergadering van 27 February 1920*, pp. 60–1, 64.

his experience of India.[9] In 1918, on the occasion of the first Congress for Javanese Cultural Development held in Surakarta, Soetomo reassured those who had written to him expressing concern "that the restoration of Old Javanese culture would bring with it the pernicious domination of the aristocracy over the common people; arbitrariness and suppression of individual freedom would be the outcome of this." Soetomo said that such views were erroneous, arising from the one-sided education that young Javanese had received, for they couldn't read Javanese script, let alone understand Javanese literature and history.[10]

Such views were widely shared among the modernising *priyayi* elite of early twentieth-century Java. Only a few were explicitly anti-Islamic, but there were also, it seems, only a few who were pious Muslims. The educated younger *priyayi* who took the initiative with new ideas and organisations in this period commonly saw Majapahit as the apogee of Javanese civilisation and Dutch education as the key to restoring a Javanese culture that was both more modern and more authentic. An implicit indifference, and sometimes hostility, towards Islam as an element of Javanese culture was widespread.[11] Yet the categories we are discussing were still rather porous at the edges. It is a token of this that the pious founder of Muhammadiyah — to be discussed below — Ky.H. Ahmad Dahlan, joined Budi Utomo in the early years and remained a member until his death in 1923. But he soon found more supportive environments in which to do his religious work.

Amongst the *priyayi*, only a few seem to have considered the *hajj* to be a desirable — let alone obligatory — undertaking. And of those who did, not all seem to have found the experience uplifting. Such at least is suggested by the memoirs of the *hajj* by the Sundanese OSVIA graduate and *Bupati* of Bandung, Wiranatakusuma, written in the 1920s. This was a lengthy account in Dutch of how awful the entire experience had been. He wrote of the exploitation and extortion of pilgrims by

[9] Savitri Prastiti Scherer, "Harmony and dissonance: Early nationalist thought in Java", MA thesis, Cornell University, 1975, pp. 183–247; Paul van der Veur in Soetomo, *Toward a glorious Indonesia: Reminiscences and observations*, ed. Paul W. van der Veur; transl. Suharni Soemarmo & Paul van der Veur (Athens, Ohio: Ohio University Center for International Studies, Center for Southeast Asian Studies, Southeast Asia Monograph Series no. 81, 1987), pp. liii–liv, lviii.
[10] *Wederopbouw* 10 Oct. 1918, in IPO no. 45/1918.
[11] For a fine study of these movements, see Hans van Miert, *Een koel hoofd en een warm hart: Nationalisme, Javanisme en jeugdbeweging in Nederlands-Indië, 1918–1930* (Amsterdam: De Bataafsche Leeuw, 1995); see esp. ch. 4.

local Arabs, of the threat of highwaymen and murderers and, when the *hajis* reached Mecca, of finding there — in Islam's holiest place — "people who unscrupulously sin against the holy prescriptions". "The filthiness of Jeddah may be called proverbial", he said, as were Arab eating habits. But nevertheless Wiranatakusuma found himself moved by the experience of Islam's universal reach. Ever the European-educated sophisticate, however, he commented that the *fatiha* — the opening verses of the *Qur'an* — sounded particularly beautiful in French.[12]

Islamic Modernism

Yet as we know from preceding chapters, there were also many pious Muslims in Java, the people who called themselves the *putihan*. Their world was becoming more complex, too, for into the polarising mix there came a new category, that of Modernist Islam. Modernism in Indonesian Islam had roots in both Middle Eastern developments and Indonesian circumstances. Some Middle Eastern religious reformers sought to solve or to ameliorate problems that were found also in Indonesia — Western colonial dominance, perceptions of Islamic backwardness amongst Muslims as well as Westerners and the manifest superiority of Western science and other forms of learning.[13] So the answers that they came up with made sense also to Indonesian thinkers. Modernism was in essence a conservative intellectual revolution, an attempt to embrace the future by restoring the past. It was, in that sense, like the Protestant Reformation in Christian history. Modernists sought to rid their faith of the obscurantism and formalism of the medieval schools of Islamic law so as to return to the pristine truths of the original revelations to the Prophet Muhammad. This was the conservative, indeed puritan, aspect of Modernism. Then they would embrace the modern learning of the West and regain both self-respect and agency in facing their colonial overlords. Here lay the modernity. Readers will immediately notice the similarity in principle to the anti-Islamic writers of the preceding chapter, who also thought that returning to a former pristine belief — in their case, that of the *Buda* past — would be a key to

---

[12] G.A. van Bovene, *Mijn reis naar Mekka: Naar het dagboek van den Regent van Bandoeng Raden Adipati Aria Wiranatakoesoema* (Bandoeng: N.V. Mij. Vorkink, n.d. [c. 1925]); quotation from p. 8. It is worth noting in the context of colonial cultural politics that this work was also translated into Indonesian and published by the colonial government's publishing house, the Kantoor voor de Volkslectuur.

[13] The classic study remains Hourani, *Arabic thought*.

embracing modern learning: the *budi* brought by the Dutch colonisers. In fact such principles underlay many of the modernising movements of Asia, whether the Meiji restoration of Japan, the self-strengthening movement of China, or the reforms of king Mongkut in Siam.

Modernism entered Javanese religious life in the opening years of the twentieth century and achieved its most important organisational expression with the foundation of Muhammadiyah in Yogyakarta in 1912 by Ky. H. Ahmad Dahlan (1868–1923). In seeking to abolish unlawful innovations (*bid'a*) in Java, Modernism faced deeply rooted cultural traditions, such as the *wayang* theatre with its stories derived from Hindu-Buddhist classics, *gamělan* music, belief in local spirits and the power of holy places, people and animals with supernatural powers and multiple local customs and art forms. Its targets for reform were not, however, only the *priyayi* and the *abangan* who embraced such aspects of Javanese culture. Many practices of pious Javanese Muslims were also unacceptable to Modernist purifiers. Muhammadiyah was thus part of the purifying trend visible since the middle years of the nineteenth century, but it added a new layer of reform and social conflict within pious communities themselves.

Dr Mohamad Roem (1908–83), one of the leading nationalist figures of twentieth-century Indonesia, was born on Java's *pasisir*. He and his family were among the first to embrace Islamic Modernism. He later reminisced,

> I was a school boy at that time and my older brothers and my brother-in-law were Muhammadiyah....
>
> At that time the Muhammadiyah began to say to the people that the Friday sermon must not be conducted for 100 per cent in Arabic because it must be understood so it is sufficient to say just a few *Qur'an* verses but after that you have to explain that in the language which is understood by the audience, so that's Malay or Javanese.... So after a couple of months our neighbours looked at us in a different way because they do not want that religion should be changed.... They got hostile.... My brother used to sing the *azan* [call to prayer] during the *maghrib* [sunset prayer] and he was not invited any more.
>
> I remember one day I was in Kudus, there was a celebration of the Muhammadiyah and there was also a boy scout movement of Muhammadiyah taking part in that and on a Friday the boy scout movement went to the mosque marching with a drum and we are dressed in a boy scout uniform.... Nothing happens and then the *khatib* [sermon-giver] when he delivers his sermon — it was a famous Kyai, Kyai Asnawi from Kudus — he make a criticism: what the hell

are we now? Going to the mosque in costume with a drum! Where are we going?... We lived in the city of Pekalongan so we are forced to move to another *kampung.*

Muhammadiyah *kampungs* became the *kampungs* where the *hajis* do not live.... We lived in a *kampong* where the *hajis* lived ... so we moved to the outskirts, to the boundary of the city.[14]

Another major figure of the twentieth century, Dr Ruslan Abdulgani (1914–2005), also recalled the early conflicts engendered by Modernism, in this case in Surabaya, looking back from the 1970s.

Next door ... lived Pak Achmad Djais, the famous tailor. He was known not only for his many Dutch clients, but for his daring opposition to what he thought was old-fashioned Islam.... Once, in the middle of a Friday sermon being given at the mosque ... he pulled out his red handkerchief and waved it about, demanding that the sermon be given in Javanese rather than Arabic, so that everyone might understand it. The incident caused quite an uproar among the orthodox![15]

Ruslan also recalled the difference in social identity between devout Muslims and those who were thought to be authentically Javanese at that time:

Nothing in my *kampong* environment encouraged me to learn about, let alone love, *wayang.* I have never really had the opportunity to study and understand the philosophy behind this art form.... Perhaps the reason can be found in the "marginal" character of my family, which lived between cultures. We were not fully Javanese, for we were in the Islamic fold. Yet we were not fully Moslem in culture either.[16]

Ky. H. Ahmad Dahlan himself was not afraid of controversy. He had gained notoriety before the establishment of Muhammadiyah by pointing out that the *qibla* (the direction of Mecca) was wrongly reflected in the siting of the great mosque of his home town of Yogyakarta. The ensuing controversy became very bitter, until Sultan Hamĕngkubuwana VII removed Dahlan from the fray by dispatching him back to Mecca in

---

[14] Interview with Mohamad Roem, Jakarta, 3 August 1977. Ky. Asnawi was one of Muhammadiyah's strongest opponents and was later one of the founders of Nahdlatul Ulama; Hisyam, *Caught between three fires,* p. 172.
[15] Ruslan Abdulgani, "My childhood world" (ed. & transl. William H. Frederick), *Indonesia* 17 (April 1974): 116.
[16] Ibid., pp. 131–2.

1903. When he founded Muhammadiyah in 1912, Dahlan generated serious initial conflict within the *putihan* community of Yogyakarta, who lived in the area known as the *kauman*. He was opposed by the chief *pangulu* of the Sultanate, Haji Cholil Kamaludiningrat, and others. Dahlan was accused of being a "false *kyai*" and his organisation was denounced as being *Kristen alus* (glib Christianity).[17] Eventually, however, Muhammadiyah won the allegiance of the *kauman* community.

Despite the existence of such conflicts, in its early years, while still under the influence of its Javanese founder Dahlan, Muhammadiyah was more tolerant and incremental in its approach to local customs than it later became. A more hard-line style was visible after Muhammadiyah's leadership was taken over by Minangkabau reformers after Dahlan's death in 1923, and particularly after 1930.[18]

Muhammadiyah remained an organisation committed to religious, social and educational activism. Its schools introduced modern educational methods and content, rather than the learning by rote which dominated older Islamic schools. By 1925 it had 4,000 members (mainly in Java) and ran a significant number of schools that adopted the Dutch colonial government's curriculum and standards: eight Dutch-Indonesian secondary schools (*Hollands-Inlandse scholen*), a teacher training college in Yogyakarta, 32 elementary schools and a "link school" (*schakelschool*) as well as 14 modern religious schools (*madrasah*). These employed 119 teachers and had 4,000 students. Muhammadiyah also had a clinic in Yogyakarta and another in Surabaya, a poor house and two orphanages.[19] Muhammadiyah was also, of course, active in proselytising. The Dutch Resident of Kĕdu, for example, reported in 1927 that Muhammadiyah had responded to Father van Lith's activities in Muntilan with enhanced religious activism "so that attendance at the mosques and in the village mosques has increased greatly, because of the propaganda put out by Muhammadiyah".[20] But the organisation avoided direct political action

---

[17] Ahmad Adaby Darban, *Sejarah kauman: Menguak identitas kampung Muhammadiyah* (Yogyakarta: Tarawang, 2000), pp. 23, 37, 39–40. See also Hisyam, *Caught between three fires*, pp. 168–9.

[18] Ahmad Najib Burhani, "The Muhammadiyah's attitude to Javanese culture in 1912–30: Appreciation and tension", MA thesis, Leiden University, 2004.

[19] Deliar Noer, *The Modernist Muslim movement in Indonesia, 1900–1942* (Singapore: Oxford University Press, 1973), p. 83.

[20] M.B. van der Jagt, *Memorie van overgave*, 23 May 1927, in Arsip Nasional Republik Indonesia, *Memori serah jabatan 1921–30 (Jawa Tengah)* (Jakarta: Arsip Nasional Republik Indonesia, 1977), p. 249.

and indeed cooperated with the colonial government in its educational and welfare roles.

Taman Siswa

There was also a *priyayi* response to the educational initiatives of the government, of Muhammadiyah and of other, less prominent Modernist organisations. This was the Taman Siswa school system founded by Ki Hajar Dewantara (1889–1959). He was a member of the Yogyakarta princely house of Pakualam, which produced several prominent leaders of the early twentieth century. Under his previous name of Suwardi Suryaningrat, he studied at STOVIA but did not finish his degree there. He became involved in the radical Indies Party and was exiled to the Netherlands in 1913, along with his colleagues Tjipto Mangunkusuma (1885–1943) and E.F.E. Douwes Dekker (1879–1950). On his return to Indonesia in 1919, he joined a mystical group in Yogyakarta that felt the need for a more authentically Javanese educational system. That is, one that was less self-consciously Islamic yet did not just copy the Dutch. So Dewantara turned to educational reform rather than political action.

Dewantara established Taman Siswa (Garden of pupils, inspired by the German — and now universal — term *Kindergarten*) in 1922.[21] Here modern educational styles and content were combined with Javanese language and art forms. Because Taman Siswa refused to conform to the colonial curriculum it operated without a government subsidy, unlike the Muhammadiyah schools. Subsequently Taman Siswa produced many leaders of the Indonesian anti-colonial movements and in later years found itself particularly aligned with more radical, *abangan*-oriented political elements. By 1932 Taman Siswa had 166 schools with 11,000 students.

In 1935 Dewantara explained some of his views on national education and the role of Taman Siswa. It will be seen here that his views were consistent with those of *priyayi* who were reluctant to embrace Islamic reform. Readers will note a significant omission: the cultural or national question for Dewantara was about Javanese identity on the one hand and Dutch on the other: Islam played no role in the balance and, when

---

[21] For valuable analyses of Taman Siswa, see Ruth T. McVey, "Taman Siswa and the Indonesian national awakening", *Indonesia*, no. 4 (Oct. 1967): 128–49; Abdurrahman Surjomihardjo, *Ki Hadjar Dewantara dan Taman Siswa dalam sejarah Indonesia modern* (Jakarta: Penerbit Sinar Harapan, 1986).

Dewantara addressed the question of languages, Arabic did not appear. But now such ideas were set in the context of the anti-colonial movements of the time, which embraced the idea of an Indonesia-wide identity. Hence Taman Siswa was open to the use of Malay/Indonesian, as indeed Budi Utomo also had been from its inception. But not for Dewantara was the embrace of the Dutch displayed by many *priyayi* in previous chapters.

> It is not easy to go through a period of transition, and it becomes even harder when extraneous factors intervene in the renovation process.... Dissatisfaction has thus befallen us, and worse: slowly but surely we have become alienated from our own people and our own environment. This alienation would have been bearable had it not been that in our case the abandonment of our own culture did not at the same time bring access to another civilisation.... We have lost our world, but we have not entered another.
>
> Who is to blame? Our answer is that it is our own fault.... We have added much new cultural material, the value of which cannot be discounted; however, it often fits so ill with our own style ... that we can use it at best as a decoration and not as material to build with....
>
> Because of the great inferiority complex which we derived from our particular governmental experience, we were easily satisfied with anything that made us look a bit Dutch....
>
> When the Taman Siswa leaders ordered, "Return from western to national principles", one of the consequences was the use of the native tongue as the medium of instruction and another the replacement of Dutch children's games and songs by national ones.... The rule for introducing languages in our curriculum is as follows: the native tongue [i.e. Javanese] as the general vehicle of instruction, particularly for the lower grades; instruction in Dutch and Malay for the higher grades of the primary school, and English for secondary school.[22]

Sarekat Islam

While Muhammadiyah and Taman Siswa sought to avoid overt political activism this was not true of Sarekat Islam (SI), which was founded in 1912 and became Indonesia's first mass-based political party. This organisation is the subject of much scholarly analysis of high quality

---

[22] Ki Hadjar Dewantara, "Some aspects of national education and the Taman Siswa Institute at Jogjakarta", *Indonesia*, no. 4 (Oct. 1967): 150–68.

which we need not review in detail here.[23] Readers should, however, be aware of three salient points about SI. Firstly, it was overtly political, gathered a large and generally unruly following and was the precursor of the anti-colonial and nationalist movements that succeeded it and brought the nation eventually to independence. By 1919 SI was claiming a membership of two million, although it presumably had no way of knowing how many followers it really had and the numbers probably did not exceed one-half million. Secondly, its appeal in Java was partly based on messianism rather than its ostensibly more modern political ideology and organisation. Indeed, its charismatic Javanese leader, H.O.S. Tjokroaminoto (1882–1934), was taken by uneducated Javanese peasants to be the Ratu Adil, who would be named Erucakra, in part because "tjokro" and *cakra* are the same word. Secret oaths were taken and membership cards were sometimes regarded as powerful amulets. Thirdly, while at the beginning the "Islam" of its title was mainly a form of ethnic identification — it proclaimed itself thereby Indonesian and not Dutch, Chinese or regionalist as were many other associations — its spread often stimulated increased religious observance and over time it became more self-consciously religious in inspiration. SI thus became the political vehicle of Javanese *putihan*. In many branches, for example, its leadership was in the hands of local *hajis*, many of whom were also traders.[24] It will immediately be obvious that this was a potentially volatile mixture of elements.

In its early years, much of the hostility and violence that was channeled into SI was expressed in anti-Chinese actions. In 1913–14 there was a particularly severe wave of anti-Chinese riots across Java. The last major outbreak occurred in Kudus in 1918. Readers of this book will not be surprised to learn that SI was also anti-*priyayi*. SI objected to *priyayi* demands for gestures of obeisance from commoners. The *priyayi* elite, for their part, saw SI as a threat to their authority and status

---

[23] See particularly Van Niel, *Emergence of the modern Indonesian elite*; Ruth T. McVey, *The Rise of Indonesian Communism* (Ithaca: Cornell University Press, 1965); A.P.E. Korver, *Sarekat Islam 1912–1916: Opkomst, bloei en structuur van Indonesië's eerste massabeweging* (Amsterdam: Historisch Seminarium van de Universiteit van Amsterdam, 1982).

[24] One occasionally also finds *kyais* listed among SI leaders, but they are rarer than the *hajis*. See the various local Dutch reports in Arsip Nasional Republik Indonesia, *Sarekat Islam local* (Jakarta: [Arsip Nasional RI], 1975); Kartodirdjo, *Protest movements*, ch. 5. A valuable local study is Farinia Fianto, "The Sarekat Islam Kudus: The rise, development and demise", MA thesis, Leiden University, 2002.

Foundation meeting of the Sarekat Islam branch in Blitar, 1914 (Collection of KITLV, Leiden)

and were deeply suspicious of it.[25] Of course, many Dutch colonial officials and private businessmen also perceived SI as a major threat.

Javanist Activism

In the years immediately after World War I, the level of political activism and polarisation grew in Java[26] and — given the history set out in preceding chapters of this book — not surprisingly issues of religious identity became involved. In 1917–18 a Comité voor het Javaansch Nationalisme (Committee for Javanese nationalism) was established by *priyayi* in Surakarta with Mangkunagara VII (r. 1916–44) as its patron and main inspirer. It aimed for a renaissance of Javanese *priyayi* culture, in opposition both to the radicals' anti-aristocratic views and the antagonism of Islamic activists to Javanese cultural forms. Under the influence of Theosophy, the leaders of this Comité were confident that

---

[25] See various reports in Arsip Nasional, *Sarekat Islam local*; Fianto, "Sarekat Islam Kudus", pp. 69–70; Hisyam, *Caught between three fires*, p. 155.

[26] For an overview of some of the issues, see Ricklefs, *History of modern Indonesia*, pp. 216 *et seqq.*

their "Eastern" culture was spiritually superior to that of the materialist West, so that a restored Javanese culture need not abandon its cultural moorings. The West had science and technology to offer, not culture. This Comité, says van Miert, "made the restoration of Majapahit more concrete and believable".[27] It published its own newspaper entitled *Wederopbouw* (Reconstruction). Despite all of these *priyayis'* commitment to Javanese culture and language, however, *Wederopbouw* was published entirely in Dutch. The year 1918 also saw the first Congress for Javanese Cultural Development held in Surakarta. Out of this came the following year a new Java Institute — the membership of which was elite Javanese and Europeans sympathetic to Javanese culture — which produced the important scholarly journal *Djåwå*, also written in Dutch. In its pages were published the fruits of research that was doing so much to inspire Javanese *priyayis'* pride in their "classical" — i.e. pre-Islamic — past.[28]

The anti-Islamic side of *priyayi* thought drew a sharp response when in January 1918 the Surakarta Javanese newspaper *Djawi Hisworo* published an article slandering the Prophet Muhammad as a gin-drinker and opium-smoker, based on passages in *Suluk Gatholoco*. So far as is known, there had been no hostile public response when *Babad Kĕdhiri*, *Suluk Gatholoco* and *Sĕrat Dĕrmagandhul* were written in the 1870s, when *Gatholoco* was published in Surabaya in 1889 or when *Babad Kĕdhiri* was published in Javanese with a Dutch translation in 1902. But by 1918 the public atmosphere was different and the *Djawi Hisworo* article produced much anger. Islamic activists led by Tjokroaminoto founded an "Army of the Lord Prophet Muhammad" (*Tĕntara Kangjĕng Nabi Muhammad*) to protest such slanders. Indeed for Tjokroaminoto this was an opportunity to attack some opponents of long standing. There was much condemnation of the *Djawi Hisworo* article in the indigenous press, protest rallies in Surabaya and then in 42 locations across Java and a demand to the colonial government that it prosecute the offending editor Martodharsono and the author of the article Djojodikoro.[29] But the controversy instead died down, to be replaced by others.

---

[27] See Van Miert, *Koel hoofd*, passim; this Comité is one of the principle organisations studied. Quotation from p. 62.

[28] Ibid., p. 95.

[29] Drewes, "Struggle", pp. 313–5; Takashi Shiraishi, *An age in motion: Popular radicalism in Java, 1912–1926* (Ithaca & London: Cornell University Press, 1990), pp. 106–7.

The Committee for Javanese Cultural Development, Surakarta, 1918. (Front row, left to right: R.M.A. Woerjoningrat, Png. Hadiwidjojo, R. Sastro Widjono, Dr. Radjiman Wediodiningrat, Png.Ad.Ar. Prangwadana, Sam Koperberg. Back row: Dr. Satiman Wirjosandjojo, Z. Stokvis, D. van Hinloopen Labberton, Dr. Tjipto Mangunkusuma, J. Rottier, A. Mühlenfeld, R.M.S. Soeriokoesomo) (Collection of KITLV, Leiden)

In December of that year *Djawi Hisworo* published an analysis of the views of *putihan* and *abangan*, with an implicit endorsement of the latter. *Putihan*, it said, believed everything literally while *abangan* looked at the meaning of things. For example, *putihan* believed that God exists as a being with a specific form and often said "That is God's will." *Abangan* also believed in a god but one that was non-existent, without colour or form. *Putihan* believed in prophets but *abangan* asked how and from where did the power of the prophets come. *Putihan* believed in angels, but *abangan* were unable to do so, for they had never seen any.[30] The article — to judge from the summary in the government's analysis of the indigenous press — did not pursue the very many superstitions in fact associated with *abangan* beliefs. In the pages of *Bramartani*

---

[30] *Djawi Hisworo* 20 Dec. 1918, in IPO no. 51/1918.

in the nineteenth century, *priyayi* writers often did that. But now was an age in which masses were being mobilised, so at least some activist *priyayi* sought to associate themselves with *abangan* villagers, not distance themselves from them.

From a different perspective, *Islam bergerak* (Islam on the move) also joined the controversies of 1918. This was the newspaper of Haji Misbach of Surakarta, who gained both fame and arrest as a proponent of Islamic Communism. (The Indonesian Communist Party will be discussed shortly.) *Islam bergerak* attacked the Hinduism that was praised by those *priyayi* who sought in some way to restore the age of Majapahit. Social classes were the fruit of contact with the Hindus, the paper claimed, for they had introduced the caste system. This was diametrically opposed to the democratic principle of equality, said the writer.[31]

Among the multiple movements emerging at village level around 1920 were several that were dubiously Islamic or indeed clearly anti-Islamic. In Klaten an "Islam-*abangan*" movement was established that claimed 120,000 members. Its leader had links with Tjokroaminoto, Tjipto Mangunkusumo and H. Misbach. The Igama Jawa-Pasundan (Java-Sundalands religion) was anti-Islamic and clashed with devout Muslims in 1925. It was led by an aristocrat of princely status from Cirebon and viewed Islam as a religion of Arabs, unsuited to Javanese — a theme familiar from the anti-Islamic literature of the preceding chapter. Another anti-Islamic movement emerged in Banyumas in 1920. An organisation called Hardapusara (fervent bond) counted Yogyakarta and Surakarta princes among its members and was anti-Islamic, denying the existence of God. Ilmu Sejati (true knowledge) was founded in Yogyakarta and advocated abandoning ritual prayer, saying one only needed to believe in God.[32]

Communism

By this time all of the actors so far discussed in this chapter — Dutch colonials, Javanese *putihan* of whatever allegiance, *priyayi* whether officials or private individuals and *abangan* villagers — were becoming acquainted with the most politically radical movement of all in the form of the Indonesian Communist Party (PKI). Here radical young *priyayi* combined

---

[31] *Islam bergerak* 20 Nov. 1918, in IPO no. 50/1918.
[32] Kartodirdjo, *Protest movements*, pp. 127–33.

with a nascent urban proletariat and an unruly rural base to become the leaders of extreme *abangan* anti-colonialism. The Party could trace its roots to the Indische Sociaal-Democratische Vereeniging founded in 1914 by Hendrik Sneevliet (1883–1942), who later played a role in the founding of the Chinese Communist Party under his Comintern alias G. Maring. Sneevliet and most of the other Dutch leaders were exiled in 1918–19 after a wave of radical actions by urban workers. Thereupon leadership fell into the hands of young Indonesian activists, most of them in Java of course being Javanese. The most prominent among these was Semaun (1899–1971), a young railway employee from the Surabaya area who was drawn into union activism and political radicalism in Surabaya and Sĕmarang. By 1916, at the age of 17, he was vice-chairman of the Surabaya branch of the ISDV. When ISDV was converted into PKI in 1920, Semaun was its chairman.[33] Until 1920 the Communists attempted to work in alliance with Sarekat Islam, thereby avoiding a clash between the two competing parties, obscuring the differences between Communism and Islam, and bridging the already substantial *abangan-putihan* divide. This strategy was to fail.

PKI propaganda in the hands of its young Indonesian leaders introduced ideas from Marxism and sought to portray the Bolshevik Revolution in Russia positively, but also linked Communist aspirations with local ideas and traditions. The main problem for PKI was how to define its relationship to Islam. There were three main approaches. One was to assert that there was a natural synthesis between Islam and Communism since both sought justice and equality. From this strain was born the Islamic Communism of H. Misbach, versions of which were also found in Banten and in West Sumatra.[34] A second was that

---

[33] Initially PKI was called Perserikatan Kommunist di India (Communist Association in the Indies); in 1924 it changed its name to Partai Komunis Indonesia (Indonesian Communist Party). The most authoritative work on the PKI remains McVey, *Rise of Indonesian Communism.*

[34] A valuable study concerning the PKI in Banten, West Java, is to be found in Michael Charles Williams, *Communism, religion and revolt in Banten* (Athens, Ohio: Ohio University Center for International Studies Monographs in International Studies, Southeast Asia Series number 86, 1990). On West Sumatra, see B.J.O. Schrieke, *Indonesian sociological studies: Selected writings of B. Schrieke* (2 vols.; The Hague & Bandung: W. van Hoeve Ltd., 1955–57), vol. I, pp. 83–166; Audrey R. Kahin, "The 1927 Communist uprising in Sumatra: A reappraisal", *Indonesia*, no. 62 (Oct. 1996): 19–36.

Semaun (from J. Th. Petrus Blumberger, *De communistische beweging in Nederlandsch-Indië*, Haarlem: Tjeenk Willink, 1928)

Communism was neutral with regard to religion but had the same objectives as all religions. A third theme reflected the anti-Islamic legacy we have seen in the previous chapter and in Budi Utomo. In this variant, Java's past — especially its pre-Islamic past — was invoked as a golden age that Communism sought to restore. Majapahit as a classless society and Hinduism as an egalitarian ideology of course would have strained the credulity of anyone who knew Java's past, but few of PKI's adherents knew much of that. Thus, PKI sought to justify itself in terms of Javanese history. PKI's enemies — in the hot-house, intensely personalised conflicts of this era — sought to condemn it by referring to the contemporary reality of Communism in Europe. They were determined to depict the Party as anti-Islamic and eventually succeeded in doing so.

  Semaun spoke often of history to demonstrate that Dutch colonialism had brought enslavement and poverty to Indonesia.[35] Others did the same, sometimes specifically emphasising the merits of pre-Islamic as well as pre-colonial Java. One "Kromotoelan"[36] said that people should adhere to the communistic principles of the Hindu ancestors.[37] "Sparta"

---

[35] E.g. *SH* 7 Jan., 8 July, 12 July and 28 Sept. 1920, in IPO no. 2/1920, no. 28/1920, no. 29/1920, no. 40/1920.

[36] Probably Kromotulen, "genuine proletarian", obviously a *nom de plume*.

[37] *SH* 2 Nov. 1920, in IPO no. 45/1920.

wrote of the fall of Majapahit which, he said, had led to the decline of Java and her colonial conquest.[38] Like the anti-Islamic writers of the previous chapter, "Sparta" was implicitly pointing to the conversion of Java to Islam as the core problem. A prominent PKI leader was Darsono, a young Javanese aristocrat, who had studied his Marxism seriously and much admired the Bolshevik Revolution.[39] But the view of Java's pre-colonial past that he presented was considerably idealised. Before European domination, he told readers of the PKI newspaper *Soeara ra'jat*, villagers prospered and *priyayi* and their people were bonded in friendship. Communism would replace the social competition that capitalism brought with such cooperation, he wrote.[40]

PKI sought to appropriate Javanese historical figures in its support. At its Sĕmarang congress of 1921, portraits of the rebel prince Dipanagara and of his lieutenants Kyai Maja and Sĕntot were displayed alongside Marx, Lenin, Trotsky and Rosa Luxemburg.[41] Dipanagara was also on the walls of the meeting of the Madiun section of the PKI in 1924, along with Sneevliet and others.[42]

Perhaps the most remarkable appropriation of the Javanese past — remarkable because it was not done by a Javanese leader at all — was in a 1922 book by Tan Malaka (1897–1949). He was a member of the Minangkabau gentry from West Sumatra who had received a Western education there and went on to study in the Netherlands, where he was converted to leftist politics. He became one of the foremost radicals of Indonesian nationalist history.[43] In his book he followed the familiar theme that Dutch colonialism rested on the impoverishment of Indonesia's people and the theft of its wealth. The nobility of pre-colonial rulers was, he claimed, demonstrated in the writings of (Javanese) *pujanggas* and *wayang* stories.

> The *wayang*, the *gamĕlan*, the books and the beautiful *candhis* [Hindu-Javanese temples] all are equally proof that before the time of the [Dutch East India] Company the land of Java had sufficient skills,

---

[38] *SH* 6 July 1920, in IPO no. 28/1920.
[39] McVey, *Rise of Indonesian Communism*, p. 36.
[40] *SR* 1 Sept. 1920, in IPO no. 36/1920.
[41] McVey, *Rise of Indonesian Communism*, pp. 113–4.
[42] *SH* 7–12 May 1924, in IPO no. 20/1924.
[43] He had born with the aristocratic title Sutan Ibrahim gelar Datuk Tan Malaka. For a biography, see Harry A. Poeze, *Tan Malaka: Strijder voor Indonesië's vrijheid; levensloop van 1897 tot 1945* (*VKI* vol. 78; 's-Gravenhage: Martinus Nijhoff, 1976).

wealth and civility, and had enough nobles to maintain that country and that civilisation…. Because of poverty, even the civility of earlier times has completely disappeared. For the *wayang* and *gamĕlan* nowadays are not as sublime as previously, but rather are just entertainments to satisfy the heart, as of a mere animal. *Dhalangs'* words nowadays are full of obscenities because social intercourse is full of obscenities.

Along with the influx of Dutch capitalists in general, the gramophone and cinema were also partly to blame for this decline of civilisation, wrote Tan Malaka.[44]

It is notable that the lost standards and values that Tan Malaka was bemoaning in this publication were those of the Javanese *priyayi* and *abangan*. The *putihan* had little sympathy for *candhis, gamĕlan* or *wayang*. PKI also sought to harness messianic prophecies attributed to the pre-Islamic king Jayabaya of Kĕdiri, saying that when the Just King (Ratu Adil) came it would not be as a person, but rather in the form of a peoples' government.[45] Again, such prophecies were an *abangan* set of ideas, anathema to many *putihan*. But by the time Tan Malaka's book and these Jayabaya references were published, the attempt at alliance with SI was collapsing, as will be seen below, so there would have been little point in PKI seeking the support of *putihan* anyway.

Idealisation of the *priyayi* or rulers of the past did not, however, prevent PKI from criticising contemporary *priyayi* and rulers, whom it saw as accomplices of the colonial government. The Communist newspaper *Sinar Hindia* published such denunciations on several occasions.[46] Not surprisingly, few of the Javanese bureaucratic elite were attracted to the PKI.

Until the late 1920 break with SI, PKI sought to avoid appearing anti-religious. In January 1920 *Sinar Hindia* reprinted an article from Tjokroaminoto's *Oetoesan Hindia* urging Muslims to maintain their religious duties.[47] It published advice to those making the pilgrimage to Mecca later that year.[48] Perhaps most remarkably, Semaun ended his

---

[44] Tan Malaka, *Toendoek kepada kekoeasaan, tetapi tidak toendoek kepada kebenaran* (Amsterdam: "De Strijd", [1922]), pp. 9–11.

[45] *SH* 13 Jan. 1921, in IPO no. 3/1921.

[46] E.g. *SH* 26 June 1920, 23 Feb. 1921, 15–21 May 1923, 22–28 May 1923, in IPO no. 26/1920, no. 9/1921, no. 21/1923, no. 23/1923.

[47] *SH* 24 Jan. 1920, in IPO no. 4/1920.

[48] *SH* 2 Oct. 1920, in IPO no. 40/1920.

1920 book on the "demands of the workers" with this thoroughly non-materialist admonition to trade-union leaders:

> Do not hope to receive praise in this world or other worldly things. A leader must hope for a gift from just one, that is, from Allah the Almighty. Do not hope for a gift from humankind, but instead employ the sayings,
> "With the Lord Allah for the Lord Allah (goodness)."
> "The heaven of a leader cannot be found in this world, while he lives here, rather it has to be sought in the Hereafter (in the future), after death. That is the legacy of the power to lead."[49]

The Party also sought neutrality in religious affairs — a position potentially antithetical to that of devout believers of a particular religion. In an article criticising "old-fashioned thoughts", adhering to the ideas of ancestors and setting one religion over another were both rejected.[50] In *Sinar Hindia* on Good Friday 1920, the great "revolutionary" Jesus Christ was praised and regret was expressed that his teachings were applauded but not followed.[51]

But this was not a time when ideological sophistication or purity was easy to maintain and PKI's increasingly numerous enemies were ready to find grounds to condemn its ideas. When, in May 1920, PKI's paper *Soeara ra'jat* criticised Sarekat Islam for not realising that religion was an "old model", incapable of bringing improvement, no major damage seems to have been done. But when the Comintern adopted Lenin's theses on the national and colonial questions in mid-1920, PKI's enemies were handed the weapon they needed. The increasingly shaky SI–PKI alliance collapsed and as it did so, the *putihan-abangan* divide which it had sought to bridge was reified in anti-colonial party politics and village-level conflict.

Lenin condemned Pan-Islam and, in doing so, also condemned the PKI–SI alliance to oblivion. His theses declared that it was

> necessary to struggle against Pan-Islamism and the Pan-Asian movement and similar currents of opinion which attempt to combine the struggle

---

[49] Semaoen, *Penoentoen kaoem boeroeh dari hal sarekat sekerdja* (Soerakarta: Pesindo, 1946) (first published in 1920), II, p. 27. The book was republished by Penerbit Jendela, Yogyakarta, in 2000, but the text was changed in places to make it conform with modern Indonesian usage, including the concluding section quoted here.

[50] *SR* 10 Mar. 1920, in IPO no. 11/1920.

[51] *SH* 3 Apr. 1920, in IPO no. 14/1920.

for liberation from European and American imperialism with a strengthening of Turkish and Japanese imperialism and of the nobility, the large landowners, etc.[52]

On 20 November 1920 the Dutch-language Communist paper in Indonesia *Het Vrije Woord* published Lenin's theses. Immediately there erupted a row over how to translate "Pan-Islam". SI translated it as *pergerakan persatuan Islam*, so that PKI was now painted as opposing "the movement for the unity of Islam". Among others, H. Fachrudin and H. Agus Salim — prominent Modernists and Pan-Islam supporters — could thereby denounce Communism for combating the ideas of the unity of Asia and the unity of Islam.[53] So did other writers from the *putihan* wing of the anti-colonial movement.[54] PKI insisted — valiantly if on utterly indefensible linguistic grounds — that "Pan-Islam" should be translated as *kemurkaan Islam* in Indonesian (the wrath or anger of Islam, or Islamic greed). Thus, it was claimed, Communism was only opposed to a perversion of Islam.[55] Darsono, along with others, thus rejected the claims of Fachrudin and Salim as lies and misrepresentations of PKI's positions.[56]

Conflict was now open, despite subsequent desultory efforts to bridge differences. Islamic Communism carried on in Java, mainly in Surakarta, attracting support from the anti-Modernist wing of the *putihan*, while Sarekat Islam came progressively more under the domination of the Modernist approach of Muhammadiyah. In 1924 Muhammadiyah declared Communism and Islam to be incompatible.[57] Meanwhile PKI's *Soeara ra'jat* declared that religion was unable to offer any betterment in this world; only Communism could do that.[58] The religious standing of Arabs was also criticised: "Goblog" ("stupid") wrote in *Sinar Hindia* that he found it strange that every year many natives made the pilgrimage to Mecca, while rich Arabs spent their money on property and automobiles, neglecting their religious duties.[59]

---

[52] Cited in McVey, *Rise of Indonesian Communism*, p. 61.
[53] *Islam bergerak* 10 Nov.–10 Dec. 1920, in IPO no. 51/1920.
[54] E.g. *Oetoesan Hindia* 9 Dec. 1920, in IPO no 50/1920.
[55] *Het Vrije Woord*, 5 Feb. 1921, p. 3.
[56] *SH* 14 Feb. 1921, in IPO no. 8/1921.
[57] McVey, *Rise of Indonesian Communism*, pp. 171–4.
[58] *SR* 31 Mar. 1921, in IPO no. 13/1921.
[59] *SH* 13 July 1921, in IPO no. 29/1921.

The conflict among the political elite was intensely personal. PKI figures accused Tjokroaminoto of being a whisky-drinker. Salim they denounced as "the Dutch *haji*". The SI leaders were accused of hypocrisy, indeed of being the cause of the decline of Islam in Indonesia, because they invoked God's name for their own interests.[60] Salim's God, said one article, was not the true God.[61] The Party's 1924 program called for the separation of religion and the state, "above all by withdrawing all state support which is given from the public purse to religious affairs".[62] While this would be seen as a threat by Christian schools and welfare institutions, it was even more politically significant as a direct threat to Muhammadiyah's activities. In return, Communists were accused of wanting to make women communal property and of being godless atheists. At an SI convention in Madiun in 1923, a leftist delegate who criticised the hypocrisy and avarice of pious Muslims had to flee the stage to avoid being thrashed.[63] Other political organisations found themselves pressured to take sides. Budi Utomo — the *priyayi* organisation *par excellence* — shared PKI's distaste for Islamic reform and, in 1924, even declared that if it were forced to choose between the approaches to religion of PKI and SI, it would choose the former.[64]

In the towns and villages of Java, local conflicts were triggered by these political disputes and, not surprisingly, at least to some extent these mirrored *putihan-abangan* differences. At the time there were no social surveys to assess *putihan* or *abangan* identities. Therefore, assuming that supporters of the PKI or "red SI" were *abangan* and those of "white SI" were *putihan* is largely a game of definitions, with "reds" by definition being *abangan* in Javanese and "whites" by definition being *putihan*. But we have seen sufficient other evidence of the emergence of this distinction in Javanese society since the mid-nineteenth century that it is reasonable to presume its salience in these conflicts. In 1924 the colonial government and its senior Javanese administrators encouraged the formation of gangs of thugs who attacked PKI and its peasant organisation Sarekat Rakyat (Peoples' union), disrupting meetings, destroying property and driving

---

[60] E.g. *SH* 17 Mar. 1923, 20–24 Mar. 1923, 3 Apr. 1924, in IPO no. 12/1923, no. 15/1924; *SR* 10 June 1924, in IPO no. 26/1924.

[61] *SH* 28 May 1924, in IPO no. 23/1924.

[62] Partai Kommunist Indonesia, Hoofdbestuur, *Partai-reglement dari PKI ... 1924* (Semarang: Drukkerij VSTP, 1924), p. 19.

[63] McVey, *Rise of Indonesian Communism*, pp. 144–5.

[64] Ibid., p. 171, citing articles in *Boedi Oetomo* of May 1924.

PKI supporters out of their villages. As violence spread, however, these groups became more difficult to direct and they also attacked SI followers.[65]

Sĕrat Dĕrmagandhul

In the midst of all this, *Sĕrat Dĕrmagandhul* — that anti-Islamic text of c. 1879 with its *Buda* and Christian sympathies that figured prominently in the previous chapter — arose as a heated public issue. We noted earlier in this present chapter the controversy that erupted in January 1918 when the Surakarta Javanese newspaper *Djawi Hisworo* published depictions from *Suluk Gatholoco* of the Prophet Muhammad as a gin-drinker and opium-smoker. This led Tjokroaminoto to found his "Army of the Lord Prophet Muhammad" (*Tĕntara Kangjĕng Nabi Muhammad*) to protest such slanders. *Djawi Hisworo* was widely condemned and there were protest meetings across Java. Now it was *Sĕrat Dĕrmagandhul's* turn to provoke controversy.

The Kĕdiri publishing house of Tan Khoen Swie (1882–1953) played a leading role in supporting Javanese literature. Tan Khoen Swie had a command of Javanese, as did many other Chinese in Java, and was a Javanese intellectual force of real significance. He patronised and published leading writers such as Raden Tanaya, Ki Mangunwijaya and Ki Padmasusastra. Their works were of a largely traditional style, uninfluenced by Islamic reform and of a kind that attracted readers inclined to the old mystic synthesis of Java. For example, among the many books brought out by Tan Khoen Swie was *Sĕrat Sastra Arjendra*, which purported to be a text gained from a Balinese *priyayi* setting out the nature of human kind and of being in general in discussions between Sang Hyang Guru and other Hindu gods, much of it explained with reference to the individual characters of Javanese script.[66] Another was *Sĕrat Pramanasiddhi*, by Mangunwijaya, describing how King Jayabaya of Kĕdiri — a real Hindu monarch of the twelfth century but a much-mythologised figure in more recent times — was taught the ultimate Islamic mystical sciences and prophesy by an Arab philosopher-king

---

[65] Ibid., pp. 295–6.

[66] *Sĕrat Sastra Arjendra anyariosakĕn pupuntoning kawruh kasampurnan Buddha, sarta cundhuk akaliyan pikajĕnganipun ngelmi makrifat* (5th printing; Kediri: Tan Khoen Swie, 1929).

Tan Khoen Swie (Courtesy of the
family of Tan Khoen Swie)

named Maolana Ngali Samsujen.[67] Tan Khoen Swie himself cut a
flamboyant figure. With long flowing bohemian hair and a splendid
moustache, he sometimes favoured a European suit and shirt with stiff
collar and tie, at other times a splendid white suit with high Javanese
collar. He was himself devoted to mystical practices and built a grotto
for meditation in his garden — now in a sadly neglected state.

In 1921 Tan Khoen Swie published *Sĕrat Dĕrmagandhul* for the first
time as a book.[68] It is not known how widely the work might have been
distributed previously in manuscript form, but now it was readily available
in print. Despite the blatantly and offensively anti-Islamic content of the
work, however, there seems to have been no reaction at first. The
Yogyakarta publishing firm of H. Buning then serialised *Dĕrmagandhul*
in its annual *Javaansche almanak* over 1922–24.

---

[67] [Mangoenwidjojo], *Sĕrat Pramansiddhi, inggih punika pengĕtan nalika Prabu Aji
Jayabaya ing Kadhiri puruita kawruh jangkaning jaman saha puruita ngelmi
kasampurnan saking agami Islam dhatĕng Sang Raja Pandhita Maolana Ngali Samsujen
saking ing tanah Ngarab* (2nd printing; Kediri: Boekhandel Tan Khoen Swie, 1935).
For an account of the actual time of Jayabhaya, see N.J. Krom, *Hindoe-Javaansche
geschiedenis* (2nd ed.; 's-Gravenhage: Martinus Nijhoff, 1931), pp. 293–6.
[68] This account of the *Dĕrmagandhul* controversy is based on Drewes, "Struggle",
pp. 310–3. Drewes was not, however, aware of the protest of 1923 described below;
he had the impression that all was quiet until 1925.

Tan Khoen Swie with Ki
Mangunwijaya (Courtesy
of the family of Tan
Khoen Swie)

Buning's *Javaansche almanak* and other publications precipitated complaints in 1923 from a writer identifying himself as "SI member from Blora". His views captured many of the issues then troubling *putihan*. This "SI member" opposed the spread of Christianity, against which Muslims should unite. *Buda* ideas[69] were also being used by the Dutch to attack Islam, he said. This was through the work of Dutch scholars and scholarly publications such as the Java Institute's journal *Djåwå*, in which Javanese art was associated with the age of *Buda*. All of this, he argued, had a political goal. So also did Buning's *Javaansche almanak*, which published *Buda* stories including *Dĕrmagandhul*, where the conversion of *Buda* people to Islam was depicted as a mistake. Buning's *Almanak* also published the *Pararaton* and other works which were full of *Buda* tales and put Islam in a bad light. *Pararaton* also

---

[69] The summary in IPO (see the following note) refers to "Buddhism" but I presume that the author would have used the usual term *Buda*, meaning the pre-Islamic age generally rather than specifically the doctrines of Buddhism. I have not been able to consult the original publication.

discredited the writings of Ronggawarsita and other writers who were respected by the Javanese. Indeed, this "SI member from Blora" admired Islamised Javanese culture more than many *putihan*. He (or she) complained that young people did not know the Javanese language, script or verse and could not play the *gamělan*, but were instead taking on Dutch manners. And there was much else done by the colonial regime in an attempt to split the Javanese people so that Christian missionaries could convert them.[70]

Further protest erupted when, in its 1925 *Javaansche almanak*, Buning published *Děrmagandhul's* final passages, denouncing the *walis* and Arabs, praising Christianity, comparing *santris* and *hajis* with stingy Chinese and generally ridiculing devout Javanese Muslims. At first it was Chinese who objected. Then the attention of the Muhammadiyah congress held in Yogyakarta in March 1925 was drawn to this publication. A mass meeting was held and sweeping demands were made of Buning. Tan Khoen Swie was also denounced. A committee was established called *Komite penyegah penghinaan* (Committee to prevent insults). But, as was the case with the "Army of the Lord Prophet Muhammad" of 1918, nothing more was heard of this organisation as the political conflicts of Java focused on other issues.

Failed Revolution

PKI was by now thoroughly exposed politically, targeted as an anti-religious party, frequently disrupted by anti-Communist vigilantes and the colonial police, penetrated by government agents, riding a wave of peasant activism which it could hardly manage and deeply divided at leadership level. Its leaders were frequently arrested or obliged to go into hiding or flee overseas to escape arrest. In this chaotic state, with Semaun and Darsono in exile in the Soviet Union, Tan Malaka in Manila and other top leaders out of action, PKI decided to launch a revolution. The revolutionary urge had been strongest in the branches along Java's *pasisir*, but the police arrested key figures there before they could act. When the revolutionary moment came on 12 November 1926, PKI rose only in West Java: in Batavia, Bantěn and Priangan. At the cost of one European killed, the rebellion was promptly crushed. It then broke out in West Sumatra and was put down there with somewhat greater difficulty by

---

[70] *SH* 8 Jan. 1923, in IPO no. 2/1923. There are further articles by "Lid SI Blora" in *SH* 9 Jan. 1923 and 9–16 Jan. 1923, in IPO no.2/1923 and no. 3/1923.

4 January 1927. Some 13,000 people were arrested. Some of these were shot, 4,500 were jailed and 1,308 were sent to a newly constructed prison camp in the malarial jungles of Papua, the infamous Boven Digoel camp. PKI was outlawed and disappeared, except for a small underground movement, until the Indonesian Revolution after World War II.

In the wake of PKI's disastrous failed rebellion of 1926–27, a thousand PKI prisoners (868 of them from Java) were analysed for their educational backgrounds. This revealed that 16 per cent had had some contact with western-style education although none had reached tertiary education. Only a quarter were illiterate — at a time when the adult illiteracy rate in Java and Madura was 94.5 per cent.[71] Five had titles of higher Javanese aristocracy (Raden Mas) and 52 of lower (Raden or Mas). There were 59 *hajis* amongst the group but no *kyais* were reported. Some were clerks and lower officials, thus lesser *priyayi*. So the educational and cultural mix was complex, reflecting both the Islamic Communist and the *abangan* versions of Communism that were found in the turbulent 1920s in Java.[72]

Abangan or *putihan* identities were not assessed by this analysis, but an interesting observation about the Communists was made by Sutan Sjahrir (1909–66). He was another of the national leaders to come from Minangkabau, one of Indonesia's foremost socialists, a man of European education, broad experience and integrity. Sjahrir also found himself imprisoned for over a year after his arrest in 1934 in Boven Digoel, before being moved to Banda in 1936. In Boven Digoel he met the imprisoned PKI people and found their Communism to be unlike the Marxism that he knew.

> For many it [their involvement in the rebellion] was perhaps nothing more than a crude mystical impulse, and for others it was perhaps a case of direct economic ambitions.... It is a strange sort of communism indeed, a mystical Hinduistic-Javanese, Islamic-Minangkabau, or Islamic-Banten sort of communism, with definite animistic tendencies. There are not many European communists who could recognise anything of their communism in this Indonesian variety![73]

---

[71] Departement van Landbouw ...& Departement van Econ. Zaken, *Volkstelling 1930*, vol. VIII, p. 110.

[72] W.M.F. Mansvelt, "Onderwijs en communisme", *Koloniale Studiën* 12, pt. 1 (1928): 205, 209–10, 212, 218–9.

[73] Soetan Sjahrir, *Out of exile* (transl. Charles Wolf Jr.) (New York: The John Day Company, 1949), pp. 73–4.

What Sjahrir was noting in the case of the Javanese was, of course, the *abangan* side of society.

Ongoing Conflicts

The crushing of the 1926–27 PKI uprising was not the end of conflict in Javanese society, although it was the beginning of serious government repression of anti-colonial movements, which would continue until the Japanese ousted the Dutch in 1942. Islamic puritans continued to provoke animosities. In 1927, for example, a fiery young Haji Saleh, who had been educated in Mecca, settled in the north coast village of Kajen, the site of the revered grave of the Kartasura-period figure Ky. H. Amad Mutamakin. In Kajen is also found an old mosque, which houses a *mimbar* (pulpit) said to have been made by Amad Mutamakin himself. The *mimbar* has carvings depicting two birds holding the ends of a crescent moon — evidently a visual chronogram which I have suggested elsewhere may mean AJ 1621 (AD 1697–98). There are also *naga* (serpent) heads carved on it.[74] H. Saleh insisted that the *mimbar* must be destroyed, for it offended the Islamic prohibition on depicting living beings. The old *kyais* of Kajen, who had at first welcomed Saleh, refused to destroy the *mimbar*. It was, they said, a legacy of the ancestors, who were better able to judge such things than they. No consensus was possible, so no action was taken. H. Saleh decamped to a nearby village, where his fiery sermons attracted many of the *putihan* of Kajen to join him.[75] The following year *kyais* in Cirěbon wanted to denounce the new and exclusivist Tijaniyya[76] Sufi *tarekat* as heretical. Tijaniyya had only just begun to attract followers in Cirěbon at that time. From there it would spread to other areas of Java. From 1928 until the early 1930s mutual denunciations and a war of pamphlets carried on. In 1931 the Nadhlatul Ulama — an organisation of traditionalist Shafi'i *kyais* founded in 1926 to defend their views against the Modernists — declared

---

[74] Ricklefs, *Seen and unseen worlds*, pp. 131–3; a photograph of the *mimbar* is found on p. 135.

[75] C.A.O. van der Plas, "Mededeelingen over de stroomingen in de Moslimsche gemeenschap in Nederlandsch-Indië en de Nederlandsch Islampolitiek", *Indisch Genootschap: Vergadering van 16 Februari 1934*, p. 256.

[76] Tijaniyya is an exclusive order that lacks a spiritual genealogy listing a chain of teachers going back to the Prophet, its eighteenth-century Algerian founder having been instructed in its teachings and practices directly by the Prophet's spirit. Nevertheless, it is now generally recognised as a legitimate (*muktabarah*) *tarekat*.

Tijaniyya to be legitimate, but it remains even today a controversial *tarekat*.[77]

Abangan, Putihan and *Priyayi*

Such conflicts amongst the *putihan*, however, had little significance for the majority *abangan* community or the *priyayi* elite. Among the latter, movements such as Theosophy and Freemasonry — anathema to the *putihan* leadership — remained popular, for they represented bridges between Javanese and Dutch, between "east" and "west". In a speech, Poerbo Hadiningrat, who had been *Bupati* of Sěmarang and Salatiga, praised Freemasonry for its lack of dogmatism. This was in contrast to Sarekat Islam, which was "in nature a religious body directed against propaganda for Christianity". Amongst the Javanese, he said dismissively, "the most extreme political ideas find a superficial but fanatical adherence, so long as they are given a religious tint by the *haji* and are aimed against the *kafir*".[78]

To many observers, that *putihan* were distinct from the majority of Javanese society, that they were somehow not really Javanese, was even more true in the 1930s than it had been when, in the previous century, Mangkunagara IV said in his *Wedhatama* that, "oddly enough they deny their Javaneseness". Writing in the late 1930s, Th.G.Th. Pigeaud commented,

> It is well known the Muslim "divines" in Java, above all nowadays, according to general opinion, must refrain from taking part in festivities where *gamělan* is played and Javanese dances and *wayang* are performed, that is, where one enjoys typically Javanese arts.[79]

Such restrictions were not new in the 1930s. In 1891, for example, it was forbidden in the religious district (*kauman*) of Surakarta to play

---

[77] Van der Plas, "Mededeelingen", p. 257; G.F. Pijper, *Fragmenta Islamica: Studiën over het Islamisme in Nederlandsch-Indië* (Leiden: E.J. Brill, 1934), pp. 97–121; Sri Mulyati *et al.*, *Mengenal dan memahami tarekat-tarekat muktabarah di Indonesia* (Jakarta: Kencana, 2004), pp. 219–52.

[78] Poerbo Hadiningrat, *Wat ik als Javaan voor geest en gemoed in de Vrijmetselarij heb gevonden* (Buitenzorg: Archipel Drukkerij, [1928]), pp. 29, 33. This published version of Poerbo Hadiningrat's speech had a foreword by prince Pakualam VII (1903–38) and was published by the Freemasons.

[79] Th. Pigeaud, *Javaanse volksvertoningen: Bijdrage tot de beschrijving van land en volk* (Batavia: Volkslectuur, 1938), p. 103.

the *gamĕlan*. On at least one occasion, *wayang* was nevertheless performed there but it was done without any music.[80] The *putihan* had
their own styles of performance, in which no bronze *gamĕlan* instruments
were played, but rather tambourines, drums and sometimes bamboo
instruments. In Banyumas was found a form of *topeng* (masked dance)
used to perform tales about Mecca and Medina, in the course of which
slawatan (religious songs) were sung. Such performances were also known
elsewhere. Pigeaud observed that "one can be confident that they almost
always are associated with the ... barely legalistic but very mystically
coloured old-fashioned Javanese Islam-current"[81] — what we have here
called the Javanese mystic synthesis.

The Mystic Synthesis, Just King and Newer Ideas

Readers should not imagine that the culture of hand-written manuscripts or devotees of the mystic synthesis style of religion had disappeared from Java. Among the *priyayi* there were still many followers of
the old-style religious life. In 1924, for example, as PKI and SI came to
blows in the pages of newspapers and conflict spread in villages, as the
colonial government acted to undermine the activist tendency in Javanese
society, in Yogyakarta R.Tg. Suryamurcita, a son of the former *Patih*
Danurĕja V (1879–99) and a senior official of the Sultanate, wrote out
a manuscript that he called *Piwulang monca warni-warni* (various
teachings). In this he conveyed multiple short texts of the mystic synthesis style, including the teachings of Pakubuwana II (1726–49: *Sĕrat
wulang Pakubuwana II*) that emphasised the need to command both
Arabic and Javanese to lead a full spiritual and temporal life.[82] The small
band of foreign aficionados of "traditional" Javanese literature and the
larger circle of Javanese who maintain an interest in such works know
of manuscripts of this kind being written well into the period of Indonesian independence.

Nor did more modern political organisations wipe out older forms
of association and action. In the midst of all the political agitation
depicted above, in 1918 an illiterate commoner in Wanagiri, south of

---

[80] *BM* 17 Feb. 1891.
[81] Ibid., pp. 103–4.
[82] SOAS 231965, pp. 213–6. The same text is to be found in Ricklefs, *Seen and
unseen worlds*, pp. 219–20. More details of the SOAS MS may be found in Ricklefs
& Voorhoeve, *Indonesian MSS*, p. 88.

Surakarta, received supernatural inspiration and became a religious teacher called Ky. Wirasanjaya. He taught his followers a secret *ngelmu* and invulnerability, and gathered a following said to amount to 10,000 people in the 1930s. His flock regarded him as the messianic Ratu Adil and built a hillside *kraton* for him modeled on that of the Susuhunan in Surakarta. When summoned to the *Bupati* of Wanagiri in 1935, Wirasanjaya went voluntarily but violence nearly broke out when he was told to close down his community. Shots fired in the air did nothing to calm the crowd, for they believed themselves invulnerable. So the *Bupati* drew his *kris* and identified it to the gathering as a powerful *pusaka* from the *kraton*: who would be the first to test its powers? None dared. Wirasanjaya was taken to jail, where he died in 1945.[83]

Similarly, and on a larger scale, a poorly educated prince of Yogyakarta named Png. Surjodiningrat established an "Association of the subjects of Yogyakarta" (*Pakĕmpalan Kawula Ngayogyakarta*) in 1930. Some of his followers, too, regarded him as the Ratu Adil. In 1931 the organisation claimed 100,000 members and by 1939 their numbers were said to be 260,000. The only other organisation with a following on such a scale in the entire Netherlands East Indies was Muhammadiyah. Despite government suspicion and police harassment, Surjodiningrat's association survived until World War II.[84]

These ongoing Javanese traditions, with roots deep in the past, were not immobile, of course. They, too, were open to new ideas and novel ways to encapsulate essential concepts and aspirations. A token of this is the work *Sĕrat Kĕmbar mayang* (the book of twin betel-blossoms).[85]

---

[83] Andrea Corsini Harjaka Hardjamardjaja, *Javanese popular belief in the coming of the Ratu-Adil, a righteous prince: An attempt at assessing its theological value and an inquiry into its adaptability to the incipient stages of evangelization in present-day Java* (Excerpta ex dissertatione ad lauream in facultate theologica Pontificiae Universitatis Gregorianae; Roma, 1962), pp. 31–5.

[84] William J. O'Malley, "The Pakempalan Kawulo Ngajogjakarta: An official report on the Jogjakarta People's Party of the 1930s", *Indonesia*, no. 26 (Oct. 1978): 111–58.

[85] Pujaarja, *Sĕrat Kĕmbar mayang*, SOAS 231970; see Ricklefs & Voorhoeve, *Indonesian MSS*, pp. 88–9. The work was published in Surakarta in 1927, but I have had access only to this MS copy. Another MS copy is held in the library of the Faculty of Letters of the University of Indonesia. See MS PW.29 in T.E. Behrend & Titik Pudjiastuti (eds.), *Katalog induk naskah-naskah Nusantara*, vols. 3-A, B: *Fakultas Sastra Universitas Indonesia* (2 vols.; Jakarta: Yayasan Obor Indonesia & École Française d'Extrême-Orient, 1997), vol. 3-B, pp. 688–9.

This was written by R. Pujaarja of Surakarta in 1927 as a guide to ulti-mate mystical insights. Pujaarja was a prolific if not a very well-known writer. He compiled a multivolume Javanese dictionary, published some 31 books over the period 1904–34, including edifying novels and other works of moral and religious instruction, and wrote still other manuscripts that remain unpublished. He also worked as an assistant to Th.G.Th. Pigeaud in compiling materials for a Javanese-Dutch dictionary.[86]

Sĕrat Kĕmbar mayang was presented in a format that might have seemed familiar in eighteenth-century Java except for the fact that it was written in prose rather than verse, yet it conveyed ideas that would have been revolutionary then. For some at least of its contents were consistent with — and probably influenced by — new free-thinking ideas from Europe, probably including existentialism:

> Almost everyone believes that Almighty God is located in heaven and that the place of this heaven is above. Where above is not made clear, for what is called "above" has many locations, and it is not only places alone. What is called "above" here is probably knowledge (*kawruh*) that is above or within. Whereas heaven is described as a place of pleasure and hell is a place that is not pleasurable, probably this just means that heaven is a very pleasant sensation and hell is a sensation that is very unpleasant. Thus, they are not places just like that, like a *kraton* or some such special place. So please don't go so far as to be deceived into thinking that the Lord God is located up in the air.
>
> And please remember that who is in charge of this world's affairs is humankind alone. Other than humankind there is none in charge of worldly affairs. The reason that humanity has charge of affairs is because of humanity's fervent desire. For humanity is inclined to set great store by our contentment, as if there were no disputes. Actually, there are few disputes and sometimes they just disappear altogether, leaving behind peace and tranquility.
>
> ... Clearly secret knowledge can be understood by humankind. Those who can grasp secret knowledge are those who practice good conduct, hold fast to standards and are modest in speech.[87]

We may be left wondering whether Pujaarja had read some Kierkegaard — or perhaps discussed such ideas with Theodore Pigeaud

---

[86] Behrend & Titik Pudjiastuti, *Katalog Fakultas Sastra Universitas Indonesia*, vol. 3-A, pp. 32–3.
[87] SOAS 231970, pp. 10–1.

— but the point is in any case demonstrated that even in metaphysical speculations, where we might imagine Javanese traditions to have been unchanging, there was evidence of openness to modernities.

Social Categories Multiple and Increasingly Fixed

By the 1930s the various categories in Javanese society were widely recognised, less bridgeable and more politicised than they had been at the start of the century. People in these contending categories had clashed at village and supra-village level. These groupings were reified in political organisations whose interest it was to maintain social distinctions in order to maintain their constituencies.

An illustration of these clearly recognised and socially accommodated distinctions may be found in a report from Bagĕlen in 1939. A *slamĕtan* was given by one of the local elite — the people generally called *priyayi* but in Bagĕlen given the title *kenthol* — and the open hall (*pĕndhapå*) in which it was given was divided into 3 areas. The left side was for the *wong abangan* who were not of the elite. The right was for the *putihan*, in Bagĕlen called *santri*. Between the two sat the elite *kenthols*.[88] In their three distinct seating areas, the Javanese of Bagĕlen exemplified the main categories of Javanese society of the time.

It is clear from the discussion in this and previous chapters, however, that Javanese were not just divided into *putihan*, *abangan* and *priyayi*. The *putihan* were divided into Modernists — represented in Java above all by Muhammadiyah — and traditionalists, who created their organisation Nahdlatul Ulama in 1926.[89] *Putihan* were also divided into Sufis and anti-Sufis, and the former were at times conflicted over the acceptability of Tijaniyya. Devout proponents of the old mystic synthesis were also to be found, but their views were under challenge from multiple directions. *Priyayi* were divided into those working for the colonial government and, in many cases, sharing the associationist aspirations of many Dutch "ethical" thinkers on the one hand, and those hoping to overthrow colonial rule on the other. *Abangan* were split among the followers of various political and other movements although many *abangan*, of course, chose to follow none.

---

[88] Soekardan Prånåhadikoesoemå, "De kénṭol der desa Kréndétan", *Djåwå* 19 (1939): 159.
[89] On the founding of NU, see van Bruinessen, "Muslims and the caliphate question", pp. 267–78; or Ricklefs, *History of modern Indonesia*, p. 223.

This chapter has not exhausted the new ideas and influences that poured into Java in the first three decades of the twentieth century from multiple sources. Print publications opened more doors than the many that have already been described. The government's Kantoor voor de Volkslectuur (Office for popular literature, in Javanese called Bale Pustaka, in Indonesian Balai Pustaka) played a major role in this regard. In Javanese it published much that we might call traditional: *wayang* stories, legendary tales, *babads* and such like. But Bale Pustaka also published children's reading books based both on local stories and imported ones, such as the fairy tales of the Grimm brothers. It brought out books that conveyed such matters as health and hygiene advice, how to run a cooperative and how to keep account-books. It also published translations of European novels — Jules Verne, H.C. Andersen and such like — in the hope of stimulating the writing of modern Javanese novels, some of which it then published.[90] Balai Pustaka also published widely in Indonesian, increasingly the second language (or the third, along with Dutch) of the modern leadership of Java, introducing new styles of literature and new ideas of social life.[91] Java was awash with new ideas in these decades.

We have tangentially noted another important development: in the context of the recently rounded-out conquests of the Netherlands East Indies, Java was now part of a larger state structure — what would shortly become the Republic of Indonesia. We have already seen above the role of Sumatran figures such as Agus Salim and Tan Malaka. From this time onwards, Javanese society was more open to influences from other Indonesian societies than it had ever been in the past. As it was also more and more exposed to new ideas coming from Europe and America.

By 1930 there had been dramatic changes in Java. A century before, Javanese society was, so far as can be known from the surviving evidence, generally united by a shared religious identity, here labeled the mystic synthesis. Now Javanese society was divided by contending identities:

---

[90] C. Hooykaas, "Javaansche uitgaven van Volkslectuur (Balé Poestaka)", *Djåwå* 12, nos. 2–3 (1932): 93–115. See also George Quinn, *The novel in Javanese: Aspects of its social and literary character*, VKI vol. 148 (Leiden: KITLV Press, 1992), particularly ch. 6, which objects to Hooykaas's contemporary criticisms of Javanese novels and the views of others (and includes a caricaturised version of my own observations).
[91] See Doris Jedamski, "Balai Pustaka: A colonial wolf in sheep's clothing", *Archipel*, no. 44 (1992): 23–46.

putihan, abangan, priyayi, Modernists, Traditionalists, Sufis, Christians, westernisers, Theosophists, Freemasons, anti-Islamic fans of pre-Islamic Javanese culture, perhaps even existentialists now contended for their own intellectual, social and political space. More tumult lay ahead. As we leave our discussion of Java c. 1930, its people stand on the verge of the Great Depression, World War II and the devastating Japanese occupation, the Indonesian Revolution and independence, all of which would have further impacts on the categories and conflicts we have considered here. Not just complexity, dynamism and change lay ahead, but also disputes and bloodshed. Javanese society was polarised in potentially dangerous ways.

Conclusions:

Religion, Politics and Conflicted Societies

In the preceding chapters, we have seen how a society that seems once to have been unified by a sense of religious identity came to be divided by conflicting senses of religious identity. As far as can be judged from the surviving evidence — which is voluminous but certainly less satisfactory with regard to religious matters than one would wish — from the beginnings of Islam in Java in the fourteenth century to the eighteenth century, the society went through several stages of conflict and reconciliation of religious identities. By the end of this period, the dominant mode of religious identity was what is here called mystic synthesis.

That mystic synthesis had three characteristic features, each of which came under challenge in the course of the nineteenth century. The first was a commitment to Islam as the religious element in being Javanese. With the exception of certain isolated pockets of population, to be Javanese was to be a Muslim. The second was a commitment to fulfilling the ritual obligations of Islam. So far as can be told from the evidence about elites and the much patchier information about other levels of society, fulfillment of the ritual five pillars of Islam — the confession of faith, ritual prayer, the giving of alms, fasting in the month of Ramadan and the pilgrimage to Mecca for those who were able to undertake it — was widely observed. Thirdly, this Javanese version of Islam nevertheless accepted the reality of many local spiritual forces, from village spirits, haunted sites and inanimate things "alive" with spirits to the immensely powerful Goddess of the Southern Ocean. All of this was within the capacious boundaries of Javanese Sufism. It seems

251

that there was consensus c. 1800–30 that these things defined what it meant to be a Javanese Muslim. Within a few decades each of these elements would be rejected by some part of Javanese society.

Java, 1830–1930

Dramatic change in Javanese society was triggered by three major developments after 1830. The first of these was the new context of Dutch colonial rule, at last firmly established after the devastation of the five-year Java War and over 150 years after the first Dutch military intrusion into the interior of Java. The Dutch-imposed *cultuurstelsel* brought significant social change to Java. Many of the *priyayi* elite and village landowners prospered. Officials received good salaries, percentages on crops compulsorily produced by the peasants under their authority, and greater certainty of tenure. Many peasants suffered, however, engaged in what Elson has called "coerced drudgery on a massive and relentless scale".[1] And in the interstices of the *cultuurstelsel*, and even more after its progressive dismantling from c. 1870, commercial middle classes began to grow. These middle classes were not one but several ethnically distinguishable groups. Chinese played a very important role. Indians did so, too, but on a lesser scale. So did Arabs, who also loomed large in the religious reform movements of the time. And there were also Javanese entrepreneurs, many of whom were leaders in the socio-religious changes of nineteenth-century Java. A concomitant of the growth of agricultural and other industry in Java in the nineteenth century was improved transportation and communication infrastructure, which facilitated the transport of products, the integration of Java's economy with that of the wider world, peasant mobility, private commerce and the spread of ideas.

A second driver of change in Java was population increase, although it must be said that it is difficult to assess its direct implications for the issues of concern in this book. Although there are no reliable base-line figures available for the beginning of the nineteenth century, it seems that the number of Javanese increased from five- to eightfold over that century, and continued to grow rapidly into the twentieth. Pressure on resources and social pressures of other kinds cannot have been avoided in the wake of such dramatic demographic change. In Chapter 2 above

---

[1] Elson, *Peasants*, p. 77.

we noted Poensen's comment from Kědiri in 1886 about "the alarming increase in population".[2]

A third major source of change was Islamic reform and revivalism. As noted in Chapter 3 above, in the course of the nineteenth century, and particularly from the 1850s, a life of Islamic piety began to mean different things to different people. The older mystic synthesis carried on, if under unprecedented challenge from reform movements. It was reflected in much of the Javanese literature emanating from the courts of Java. The most famous work was (and is) probably Mangkunagara IV's *Wedhatama*, with its admonition to the youth to follow the example of the founder of the Mataram dynasty Senapati Ingalaga, who met with the Goddess of the Southern Ocean and, should they turn to the model of the Prophet of Islam, to remember that, "seeing that you are Javanese, just a little is enough".[3]

Islamic reformist ideas evidently began to have an influence in Java from about the 1850s, almost half a century after they had begun to transform Minangkabau society in Sumatra. Arab communities of Java's *pasisir* towns seem to have played a leading role as transmitters of reform ideas. Many among the nascent Javanese middle class responded positively. The spread of printing played an important role, while the advent of steam shipping and the opening of the Suez Canal in 1869 greatly facilitated pilgrimage traffic. As the number of Javanese *hajis* grew, so reform ideas spread from their Middle Eastern heartland to the towns of Java. Increasing numbers of *pěsantrens* were vehicles for transmitting a purified Islam, although many of course still taught older ideas not in conflict with the mystic synthesis. Indeed, it seems that this was not simply a general wave of religious purification among pious Muslims, but rather something more complex. Not only were adherents of the mystic synthesis unmoved by it, but it seems that there was also a social distinction between the reformers and at least some — perhaps very many — of the existing Javanese religious teachers in the countryside, the *kyais*.

For adherents of the mystic synthesis, Sufism was a central element of the religious experience, but it, too, was subject to reform pressure in the nineteenth century. In particular, the Naqshabandiyya *tarekat* of

---

[2] C. Poensen, "Iets over het Javaansche gezin", Kědiri, Dec. 1886, in ARZ 161; also in *MNZG* 31 (1887): 225.

[3] Robson, *Wedhatama*, pp. 30–1, with a minor departure from Robson's translation.

the Khalidiyya branch and the hybrid Qadiriyya wa Naqshabandiyya evidently grew from the 1850s. They gave greater emphasis to observing Islam's five pillars than had the Shattariyya, previously the strongest *tarekat* in Java, and were less prepared to accept the compromises implicit in the mystic synthesis recognition of local spiritual forces. They thus formed an important part of the reforming spirit of the time, as well as playing a significant role in anti-colonial peasant movements.

In this environment, some of the purifiers, the pious Muslims who called themselves *putihan* — the white ones — looked down upon their fellow Javanese whom they thought ignorant, backward and impious. They derided them as *abangan* — the red or brown ones. The first evidence of this happening comes from the 1850s, a crucial decade in the developments studied in this book. The patchy evidence on this growing social distinction suggests that it spread across Java in the following years, evidently becoming a general and widely recognised phenomenon by the 1880s. The *abangan* themselves responded negatively to the pressures for a more purified form of religious life. If they had once generally been observers of Islam's five pillars, it seems that they began to attenuate their involvement in that ritual life. It is clear that these *abangan* were the majority of Javanese, while the *putihan* remained a small minority, strongest on the north coast and weakest in the interior. Poensen wrote from Kĕdiri in 1884 — after over twenty years of personal experience there — that Javanese were simply becoming "less religious and pious".[4] The minority of *putihan* families led more prosperous, disciplined, refined, pious lives, engaged in trade, lent money, rejected opium and did not gamble. The majority *abangan*, by contrast, neglected ritual prayer but observed some other Islamic social customs, provided no religious education to their children and enjoyed Javanese performances such as the *wayang* and lascivious dances. In Poensen's judgement, in *abangan* families there was "an absence of any profound, religious-moral tone in daily intercourse".[5]

While the *abangan* emerged as the majority social category and resisted what reformers now said was the proper understanding of Islam, a tiny minority of Javanese rejected Islam altogether and became Christians for the first time in Javanese history. Christianity began

---

[4] C. Poensen, "Iets over den Javaan als mensch", Kĕdiri, July 1884, in ARZ 261; also in *MNZG* 29 (1885): 118.
[5] C. Poensen, "Iets over het Javaansche gezin", Kĕdiri, Dec. 1886, in ARZ 161; also in *MNZG* 31 (1887): 259–60.

among Javanese at Ngara in the 1830s under the tutelage of the charismatic Russo-Javanese *kyai* C.L. Coolen. It grew in the East Java communities created and led by Paulus Tosari and the extraordinary Ky. Ibrahim Tunggul Wulung. It spread in Central Java through the work of Christina P. Stevens-Philips, her sister-in-law J.C. Philips-van Oostrom, E.J. de Wildt-le Jolle and above all Ky. Sadrach Surapranata, who converted thousands to Christianity before his death in 1924. The role of European missionaries in this conversion process was much less important than that of the Indo-European and indigenous Javanese proselytisers who successfully bridged the cultural gaps between Christianity and Javanese culture. Thus the early joke that Javanese Christians were "failed Dutchmen and half-baked Javanese" (*Landa wurung Jawa tanggung*) began to disappear: it became conceivable that one could be both Christian and Javanese. From around the turn of the century, the Jesuit order began converting Javanese to Catholicism, again embracing much of the Javanese culture that both Islamic reformers and European Protestant missionaries were more inclined to condemn.

The Dutch presence brought not only the Christianisation of a small minority of Javanese but also new ideas and intellectual horizons that transformed the life of the *priyayi*. The beginnings of modern education in Java, the appearance of *Bramartani* as the first indigenous-language newspaper in the Indies, the spread of printed books in Javanese, the general professionalisation of the Javanese bureaucratic elite and the rising wealth of that class all supported their positive, indeed often enthusiastic, embrace of the new information and ideas coming *via* their Dutch overlords. In towns across Java, and particularly in major places like Surakarta and Yogyakarta, a hybrid European-Javanese cosmopolitanism grew. It was not an intellectual and cultural style congenial to Islamic reform, but it evidently posed no problems for those whose religious life remained in the mystic synthesis mode. This new cosmopolitanism increased the social distance between the *priyayi* and commoners, whose practices and superstitions were frequently ridiculed in *Bramartani*. It went along with *priyayi* loyalty to the Dutch regime, distancing them still further from Islamic reformers who were often uncomfortable with and not infrequently hostile to the Christian Dutch.

It is particularly significant that among these modernising *priyayi* there grew also an interest in Java's pre-Islamic past, encouraged by the fruits of Dutch archaeological and philological research. This was being presented as a sort of "classical" age, on a par with the classical age of European history. It is not clear how much *priyayi* knew about ancient

The *Bupati* of Kudus, R. Panji Tg. Hadinoto, with his wife and children, 1924 (Photo Kreuger & Austermühle; Collection of KITLV, Leiden)

Greece and Rome. Certainly the more educated of their European contacts would have had ideas about Europe's classical past, and may have discussed them with *priyayi*. *Bramartani* published multiple accounts of European history. In 1876 C.F. Winter proposed to publish a Javanese translation of a Dutch-language history of the world which would include the history of Alexander the Great of Macedonia and the emperors of Rome, down its fall.[6] This was welcomed by a contributor to *Bramartani* for its usefulness in combating superstitions.[7] The history was subsequently serialised in *Bramartani* but was not completed, which another contributor lamented.[8] In 1886, one of *Bramartani*'s contributors who called himself (or herself) Lĕbdagama ("expert in religion") wrote of peoples who had once been clever but thereafter became ignorant, the two prime examples being the ancient Greeks and the ancient Egyptians.[9]

---

[6] *BM* 1 June 1876.
[7] *BM* 15 June 1876.
[8] *BM* 23 Nov. 1876.
[9] *BM* 4 Mar. 1886.

A parallel between pre-Islamic Java and classical Greece and Rome would, of course, implicitly position Islamic Java as the local equivalent to the "dark ages" of Europe. A parallel with ancient Egypt might be even more potent, for the view of "Lĕbdagama" that ancient Egypt went into civilisational decline — and no one would have needed reminding that this was coincident with its Islamisation — invited direct comparison with the history of Java.

While there is no evidence that many *priyayi* contemplated formally abandoning their Islamic identity, there is also none to suggest that they accepted the reformers' views of what constituted a proper Muslim life. Among other things, to embrace puritan piety would have so undermined their standing with the Dutch colonial regime that it would probably have brought an abrupt end to their bureaucratic advancement. Very few of the elite were attracted to Christianity. There were, however, some who were prepared to express open opposition to the influence of Islam within Javanese civilisation, not by embracing Christianity but by turning to Java's pre-Islamic past.

Anti-Islamic sentiments arose from this complex, polarising society by the 1870s. Proponents combined admiration for European learning with dislike of fervent Islamic purifiers and admiration for the glories of Java's older history, seeking to combine *budi* and *Buda*: modern learning and the pre-Islamic past of Java. In *Babad Kĕdhiri*, *Suluk Gatholoco* and *Sĕrat Dĕrmagandhul* these sentiments were expressed in ways deeply contemptuous of and insulting to Islam. The conversion of Javanese to Islam was depicted as the consequence of inexcusable treachery and treason by the evil Raden Patah, the first Sultan of Dĕmak. Islam was ridiculed extensively. In *Dĕrmagandhul* it was even predicted that Javanese would now convert to Christianity.

Thus, hardly more than a generation after 1830, cultural change led by two contending modernities in Java — that offered by Islamic reform and that offered by European learning — had contributed to social polarisation and conflicting religious identities.

In the early years of the twentieth century, in the midst of a tremendous fashion for creating modern organisations across the Netherlands East Indies, these various Javanese categories became reified in formal organisations and thus grew more rigid, more clearly defined and more conflictual. In 1908 those *priyayi* who found little or nothing of interest in Islamic reform set up Budi Utomo. Four years later Modernism — yet another element in the complex varieties of pious Islam in Java — was institutionalised in Muhammadiyah. In the same year, Sarekat Islam was set up as an expressly political movement, at first representing indigenous (but non-*priyayi*) Indonesians generally but progressively becoming the political vehicle of the Modernist *putihan*. SI members were involved in various forms of political violence. The *abangan* came to be represented more by the Communist Party (PKI), which at first worked within SI but was expelled beginning in 1920. Village-level conflicts followed. In 1926 non-Modernist Islam was reified in the establishment of Nahdlatul Ulama. Modern but non-Islamic educational ideas — to a considerable extent the product of the search for a union of *budi* and *Buda* — inspired the foundation of Taman Siswa in 1922.

We may say that this stage of social change, religious conflict and political organisation came to an end with the failed PKI uprising of 1926–27. As the colonial government clamped down thereafter, many of the developments of interest in this book were submerged under a government-imposed security regime. Both *abangan* and *putihan* were inclined to withdraw from the hazards of political activism, which had proved to be so fruitless, but where that was not so, they evidently continued to affiliate each to their particular organisations. The cultural gap between *abangan* and *putihan* persisted, indeed seems to have grown. There was a sense that, in some essential way, *putihan* were not fully or truly Javanese. As Ruslan Abdulgani (b. 1914) looked back upon his early years in Surabaya, he recalled that "We were not fully Javanese, for we were in the Islamic fold. Yet we were not fully Moslem in culture either."[10] Nor, given the divisions amongst *putihan* over such matters as Modernism and Sufism, were devout Muslims a single group. Nor, of course, were the *abangan* or the *priyayi*. As noted in the preceding chapter, Javanese were *putihan*, *abangan*, *priyayi*, Modernists, Traditionalists, Sufis, Christians, westernisers, Theosophists, Freemasons, anti-Islamic fans of pre-Islamic Javanese culture, perhaps even Existentialists. This was a polarised and conflicted society.

Parallels

The Javanese experience recounted in this book of course had many features unique to Java, to Islam and to the time period being discussed. The sequel to this period — to be adumbrated briefly below — similarly led to events that we may think of as characteristically Javanese and

---

[10] Ruslan Abdulgani, "My childhood world", p. 132.

Indonesian. But it is worth remembering that a pattern of reform and puritanism within a given religious tradition leading to social polarisation, political reification and violence is a wider, more common experience in human history. It is unique neither to Indonesia nor to Islam.

Probably the most extreme and bloody parallel is to be found in sixteenth- and seventeenth-century Europe. When Martin Luther pinned his 95 theses to the door of the church at Wittenberg in 1517, he cannot have guessed what bloodshed would follow. As the Protestant Reformation progressed, the religious environment polarised between loyal Catholics and Protestant schismatics, moderates lost their influence, and the religious divisions became reified in the loyalties of various principalities and kingdoms. Germany divided roughly between a Protestant north and a Catholic south, and the Lutheran church became the established church in Protestant states. A similar division was seen in the Calvinist Netherlands, as population shifts created a Protestant north and a Catholic south. Violence attended these changes and bred Europe's bloody and bitter wars of religion. While these wars were fought principally on German territory, they also included the Dutch, French, Danes and Swedes. What is commonly called in English the Thirty Years" War (1618–48), in the Netherlands known as the Eighty Years' War, began mainly as a conflict pitting Catholic and Protestant states against each other. The Peace of Westphalia in 1648 brought this particular phase to an end, but Catholic-Protestant bitterness abided in much of Europe down to recent times, was conveyed by migration across the Atlantic and into places like Australia, and persists dangerously in Ireland down to the present.

Intriguing parallels are also evident in what Kevin Phillips calls "the cousins' wars" of England and America: the English Civil War of the seventeenth century, the American Revolutionary War of the eighteenth and the American Civil War of the nineteenth. This involved English-speaking communities which, in the seventeenth century, were about the same size as was Java in the first part of the nineteenth century: around five million people. Just as, in Java, we have seen commercially oriented and mainly urbanite religious reformers at odds with *kyais* in the countryside, Javanese villagers and aristocratic *priyayi*, so Phillips writes of conflicts between "Low Church, Calvinistic Protestantism, commercially adept, militantly expansionist, and highly convinced ... that it represented a chosen people and a manifest destiny" on the one hand and "Cavaliers, aristocrats, and bishops" on the other. The emergence of the United States as a dominant power in the twentieth century, argues Phillips, represented the victory of "Puritans, Yankees, self-made entrepreneurs, Anglo-Saxon nationalists, and expansionists".[11] He does not argue that these three major conflicts were caused solely by puritan reform movements, but each was preceded and significantly shaped by Protestant religious revivals. Religion was a main cause only in the conflicts of the 1640s, but it remained a major element in those of the 1770s and 1860s.[12] In the words of the Battle Hymn of the Republic, their eyes had seen the glory of the coming of the Lord.

Phillips provides a description of the Protestant religious reformers that has obvious parallels with our picture of the pious, middle class, reforming *putihan* of Java.

> Puritanism, Presbyterianism, or Congregationalism in eighteenth- and nineteenth-century America, as in seventeenth-century England, resembled the continental Calvinism of the Reformation in providing quasi-economic belief systems for emerging capitalism. Theology and commerce ... became close allies in seeking to replace aristocratic and church hierarchies associated with old regimes; to clear away feudal, mercantilist, or guild-system rules that blocked entrepreneurialism; and to advance wage labour and enterprise rather than manorial relationships or slave labour. Puritanism was virtually an adjunct of economic development in encouraging temperance, neatness, education and hard work.[13]

We might recall Poensen's account, noted above, of *putihan* families leading their more prosperous, disciplined, refined and pious lives, while engaging in trade and lending money, turning their backs on opium and rejecting gambling.

But the conflicts in Java could not have the outcome that Phillips sees in his "cousins' wars": the triumph in America of the commercially oriented puritans. For Java was under the rule of another sort of puritans: the Dutch colonialists with their own background in the victory of Calvinism over Catholicism in the Netherlands. The circumstances of colonial rule prevented conflict in Java from escalating beyond the level of village squabbles and urban riots to real civil war. And it

---

[11] Kevin Phillips, *The cousins' wars: Religion, politics and the triumph of Anglo-America* (New York: Basic Books, 1999), p. xv. I am grateful to my colleague Dr Adam Fforde for bringing Phillips' book to my attention.
[12] Ibid., pp. 94, 159, 165.
[13] Ibid., p. 381.

guaranteed that the *priyayi* elite continued to play a key role, along with traditionalistic forms of Islam and the increasing *abangan* indifference towards Islam. Whatever the Dutch themselves might have thought in 1930, however, these circumstances were not to prevail for much longer.

The Sequel in Java

The Japanese occupation of Java from 1942 to 1945 and the subsequent Indonesian Revolutionary War of independence from 1945 to 1949 swept away colonial rule and the artificial constraints it had imposed on social and religious change and conflict. As political parties formed in revolutionary and newly independent Indonesia, Javanese society was mainly organised politically along *putihan-abangan* lines. This produced a communitarian rather than class-based political system based on what were called *aliran* (streams or channels). To a large extent, and not surprisingly given the colonial heritage of the political elite, this paralleled the political system of the Netherlands known as *verzuiling* (pillarisation), which had political parties, media channels, social organisations, sports groups and much else that reflected and channeled the main religious and social communities' allegiances.

Amongst the many conflicts of the Revolutionary period and the first years of Indonesian independence, some were along *putihan-abangan* lines. As in the Anglo-American cases discussed above, these violent clashes were not necessarily caused primarily by social or religious differences, but such differences nevertheless shaped allegiances and lines of conflict. The first major episode followed the attempt by the revived PKI in 1948 — in the Revolution's darkest hour — to take over the Republican government from the leadership of Sukarno and Hatta. This rebellion at Madiun was crushed by Republican forces, but it sparked killings along *putihan-abangan* lines.[14]

By the time that Clifford Geertz and his colleagues did their field work in the Kědiri area in the early 1950s, the division between *putihan* (for whom the term *santri* was used by the Geertz team) and *abangan* had come to be regarded as "a religious schism that cuts straight through the local society".[15] The classic case study of this phenomenon at this

---

[14] Ann Swift, *The road to Madiun: The Indonesian Communist uprising of 1948* (Ithaca: Cornell Modern Indonesia Project Monograph Series, 1989), pp. 42, 76n130.
[15] Robert R. Jay, *Javanese villagers: Social relations in rural Modjokuto* (Cambridge, Mass., & London: The MIT Press, 1969), pp. 4–5.

time remains Geertz's own *Religion of Java* — greatly influential, often criticised but still an important book, even if Javanese society has changed much since it was written. During campaigning for Indonesia's first general election of 1955, village-level conflicts between *putihan* and *abangan* frequently occurred. They were, indeed, intensified by the open political competition of the campaigning.[16] Throughout the rest of the 1950s and into the early 1960s, this *aliran* system was the principal way in which Javanese society was organised, understood and conflicted.[17]

Aliran political violence culminated in 1965–66, when an attempted coup in Jakarta precipitated widespread killings in the countryside, the worst being in Java and Bali. *Abangan* PKI supporters were the main targets of killing squads, amongst whom Islamic youth organisations took the lead.[18] Unknown numbers — probably several hundred thousand — were murdered. Thousands of others were imprisoned without trial for many years. The legacy of lost lives, shattered families, tormented memories, and of social and legal discrimination against ex-PKI and their descendants lingered long after. That legacy continues to cast its long shadow over the lives of many Javanese.

Yet, remarkably, this was the end of such violence on a major scale. *Putihan-abangan* conflict did not continue to escalate — as many Indonesians and foreign observers alike feared it might — into even more bloody social violence and, perhaps, outright civil war. Rather, it began to disappear from political calculations, from academic analyses, and indeed from social reality. The deep social chasm between *abangan* and *putihan* had seemed in the 1950s and 1960s to be "primordial" — "existing at or from the beginning, primeval; original, fundamental" as

---

[16] Herbert Feith, *The decline of constitutional democracy in Indonesia* (Ithaca: Cornell University Press, 1962), pp. 356–62; Clifford Geertz, *The interpretation of cultures: Selected essays* (New York: Basic Books, Inc., Publishers, 1973), pp. 150–2, 167.

[17] See Arbi Sanit, *Badai revolusi: Sketsa kekuatan politik PKI di Jawa Tengah dan Jawa Timur* (Yogyakarta: Pustaka Pelajar, 2000), pp. 198–222; Aminuddin Kasdi, *Kaum merah menjarah: Aksi sepihak PKI/BTI di Jawa Timur 1960–1965* (Yogyakarta: Jendela, 2001), pp. 341–4.

[18] There is substantial literature on these bloody events. For particularly useful analyses, see Robert Cribb (ed.), *The Indonesian killings of 1965–1966: Studies from Java and Bali* (Monash papers on Southeast Asia no. 21; Clayton: Monash University Centre of Southeast Asian Studies, 1990); Hermawan Sulistyo, *Palu arit di lading tebu: Sejarah pembantaian massal yang terlupakan (Jombang-Kediri 1965–1966)* (Jakarta: KPG [Kepustakaan Populer Gramedia], Yayasan Adikarya IKAPI, The Ford Foundation, 2000).

Oxford has it. But it was not that. It was not something that had existed from the beginnings of Islamisation in Java at all. It was, instead, a contingent circumstance arising from the specific historical experience of Javanese society over about a century, the period of interest in this book.

Explanations for the amelioration of *putihan-abangan* conflict since the 1960s are many and the matter still awaits further serious research. Obvious factors are the willingness and capacity of the Soeharto regime after 1965 to use unrestrained repression against any potential threats to social stability and economic development. Another is the regime's 1970s dismantling of the old party political structures that had reified *aliran* categories, thus depriving these categories of the organisational and identity structures that had reinforced them. Another is the success of the ongoing deepening of Islamisation within Javanese society. Nowadays, although opinions are divided, it is not difficult to find knowledgeable people who judge that the *abangan* have become the minority among Javanese.

Old animosities are not entirely dead. In a Javanese population of around 100 million, naturally one can find almost any imaginable opinion to be held by someone. For example, the 1870s *Babad Kĕdhiri*, *Sĕrat Dĕrmagandhul* and *Suluk Gatholoco* condemnation of Arabs and Islam was echoed in an anonymous internet appeal of April 2003. Arabs were denounced as being responsible for terrorism in Indonesia, culminating in the Bali bombings of October 2002. The email circular went on,

> Is it true that Arab descendants are *habibs* [descendants of the Prophet]? It's entirely possible that they are criminal fugitives from Arabia who settle in Indonesia and peddle Islam and claim themselves to be *habibs* so they can deceive our Muslims.... All this time we have been lied to by the Arabs! ... We no longer follow our own beliefs and convictions. We've been taken in by the Arabs with their products of loving war, sex and compulsion, that is, Islam. In fact, this Arab product is animism.... Islam teaches us to turn towards a black stone that lies in Mecca.... Reject contemptible Arab culture and language and clothes![19]

Such views are, however, now a great rarity in Indonesia, at least in public. But certainly there are still people who regard themselves as *abangan*, although in my experience they are more likely to prefer to call themselves *kĕjawen*, i.e. those who are (really) Javanese.

---

[19] Supplied by my colleague Prof. Martin van Bruinessen, 2 May 2003.

As we draw this book to a close, it is appropriate to suggest that the story of Islam in Java — of its successes and failures, its adherents and its opponents — has a wider significance in human history. Java is one of the rare cases where one can tell the story of how a society adopted and adapted a new religion over a period of more than 600 years. Despite all of the gaps in the evidence, we can see with some confidence how that new religion provoked both opposition and adherence from the beginning, and achieved reconciliation of Javaneseness and Islam by the later years of the eighteenth century. Those stages of the history are the subject of my book *Mystic synthesis in Java*, summarised in the first chapter of this book. For a period of something over a century, that reconciliation was then disrupted, challenged and in many ways overthrown by the tumultuous events described in preceding chapters of this book. It has been my purpose here to understand how that situation came to be, how a society once unified (so far as we can judge from the surviving evidence) by its religious identity came to be conflicted by contesting religious identities. A third book — for which the research is now under way — will be needed to understand how those social conflicts grew to produce the horrific bloodshed of the 1960s but then, against all expectations at the time, seemingly declined thereafter.

These matters are of more than abstract interest. Group conflict, especially when defined by religious differences, is a significant issue in human history. In our time, it is arguably among the most significant of human issues. How does such religiously defined conflict originate? How does it grow? How can it be brought to an end? In our attempt to answer such questions, the history of the Javanese people may have much to teach us.

Glossary

abangan	nominal or non-practising Muslims; literally "the red (*or* brown) ones"
babad	chronicle
bathik	wax-resist dyed cloth
bid'a	(unlawful) innovation, for which there was no precedent in the time of the Prophet
Buda	pre-Islamic; literally, Buddhist
budi	mind, intellect, reason, genius, wit, discretion, judgment, wisdom, aptitude, character, disposition, sense; desire, longing, etc.; a very positive concept associated with intellect, elevated character and striving
Bupati	Javanese regency head; the highest Javanese official in the colonial bureaucratic system
cultuurstelsel	cultivation system
dhalang	puppeteer in the Javanese *wayang*
dhikr	recitation of pious formulae as a mystic exercise
gamĕlan	Javanese orchestra, consisting mainly of percussion instruments

Garĕbĕg	Thrice-annual Javanese Islamic festivals, to celebrate the birth of the Prophet Muhammad (Garĕbĕg Mulud on 12 Mulud), to celebrate the end of the fasting month (Garĕbĕg Puasa on 1 Sawal) and to commemorate Abraham's willingness to sacrifice his son and the *hajj* (Garĕbĕg Bĕsar on 10 Bĕsar)
Haji	a person who has completed the *hajj* (pilgrimage) to Mecca
jakat	religious tax paid at the end of the fasting month to support the needy
jimat	amulet
kafir	infidel
kampung	hamlet
kaum	the pious, professional religious community
kawruh	knowledge, especially European learning
kitab	book, especially religious books
krama	high Javanese, used to address superiors
kraton	court of a Sultan or Susuhunan
kris	Javanese dagger, often thought to be "alive" with supernatural powers
kyai	term of veneration for Islamic teachers
macapat	Modern Javanese verse, written in one of around 20 standard metres, and traditionally sung aloud
ngelmu	mystical sciences
ngoko	low Javanese, used to address intimates or social inferiors

pangulu	chief religious officer, head of a mosque
pasisir	north coast of Java
Patih	Chief administrative officer of a Javanese court; also used for an official in the countryside
pěsantren	Islamic boarding school
priyayi	members of the Javanese administrative-aristocratic elite
pujangga	poet, literary master
pusaka	holy regalia, heirloom, usually believed to have supernatural powers
putihan	pious Muslim, professional religious; literally "the white ones"
regent	Dutch term for *bupati*
salat	ritual prayer
santri	student of religion
sěmbah	gesture of obeisance and respect made by placing the palms of the hands together before the nose
shari'a	Islamic religious law
sheikh	spiritual guide
slamětan	ritual communal meal to observe major occasions such as death, marriage, etc.
suluk	mystical poem in Javanese
sunan	Javanese title usually used for the first proselytisers of Islam in Java, the *walis*

tarekat	Sufi mystical order
tayuban	performance by Javanese dancing-girls, associated with prostitution
ulama	Islamic holy men, learned scholars
Vorstenlanden	Central Javanese principalities of the Susuhunan and Mangkunagara in Surakarta and the Sultan and Pakualam in Yogyakarta
wali	semi-legendary apostle of Islam in Java, of whom there are usually said to have been nine (the *wali sanga*)
wayang	Javanese shadow play; also used for other forms of theatrical performance such as *wayang wong* (dance drama) and *wayang topeng* (masked dance performance)

Bibliography

PRIMARY SOURCES

Javanese Manuscripts

Agami Jawi. Buku pĕpengĕtipun agami Jawi, ingkang mongka ancĕr-ancĕr ing agĕsang, badhe ngambah kalĕpasan. Copy of a MS owned by the *Bupati* of Purwarĕja (Kĕdu), dated AD 1907. 84 pp., 17.5 × 21.5 cm. LOr 6548.

Babad Mangkunagaran. Copy made for Th.G.Th. Pigeaud in 1937. 265 pp., 22 × 31 cm. LOr 6781. Notes on the text by Soegiarto in LOr 10,867–C no. 43.

Dialogues on *santri Dul* by Ky. Bĕstari, R. Atma and M. Danuwikrama. 19 pp., 20.5 × 32.5 cm. Poensen collection, LOr 5787.

Mangkunagara IV. *Sĕrat Pustakaraja.* Written at the wish of Pakubuawana VII, containing several texts:

    A: pp. [iii–iv], tables on divination etc.

    B: pp. 1–73, *Sĕrat Pustakaraja* covering the years *surya sangkala* 1 to 800/*candra sangkala* 1–824 and *Sĕrat Pustakaraja Puwara* for years 801–1400/825–1442; ending with the succession of Pakualam II, the exile of Pakubuwana VI and accession of Pakubuwana VII in *surya sangkala* 1705/*candra sangkala* 1757 [AJ 1757/AD 1829–30].

    C: pp. 74–585, *Pratelanipun urut-urut ing lalampahan ingkang sampun kasĕbut ing salĕbĕting Sĕrat Pustakaraja Purwa*, beginning with the *dewas* descending to Java, extending to Mĕdhang Kamulan, etc. At the end (p. [586]): *Tĕlas cariyos ing Sĕrat Maharata, anyandhak cariyos ing Sĕrat Mahatantra, taksih sami urut ing lalampahan ingkang kasĕbut ing salĕbĕt ing Sĕrat Pustakaraja Purwa.*

    D: p. [589], table of the names of 50 *taun Buda* with their meanings. MS is [iv] + [589] pp., 31.5 × 19.5 cm. KITLV Or. 661.

Notes on Javanese religion made for Carel Poensen by a Javanese Christian. Begins, *Punika buku cariosipun ing nagari Jawi, kang katingal dina niki.* 44 pp., 21.5 × 34.5 cm. LOr 5762.

Piwulang monca warni-warni. Owned (*kagunganira*) and presumably written by R. Tg. Suryamurcita, son of the late *Patih* Danurĕja V of Yogyakarta and a Knight of the Order of the Lion of the Netherlands. Dated Dal, *ponca Pandhawanipun astha Nata* [AJ 1855] and AD *catur mantri trus in bumi* [AD 1934, which is an error; the AD year should be 1924]. 351 pp., 33.5 × 21 cm. SOAS 231965.

Pralambange tanah Jawa. Predicting the coming of the Ratu Adil in AH 1299/ AD 1881. Copy of a MS (LOr 7175) originally owned by H. Abdullah b. H. Muhammad Salih of Sidayu which had been confiscated by Snouck Hurgronje. 191pp., 17 × 21 cm. LOr 6536.

Pujaarja. *Sĕrat Kĕmbar mayang, mratelakakĕn pratikĕlipun tiyang anggayuh kawruh yĕkti, inggih punika ngudi wosipun ingkang sinĕbut Pangeran, sarta mawi tondha saksi ingkang ringkĕs.* Dated Be, *rasa gati ngesthi wiji*, AJ 1856/ AD 1927 [*sic.* AJ 1856 was actually AD 1925–6]. 13 pp., 33.5 × 21.5 cm. SOAS 231970.

Ronggawarsita. *Sĕrat Maklumat Jati, tatĕdhakan sangking wuwulangipun Kyai Ronggawarsita pujongga ing Surakarta.* Copied in Ehe [AD] 1898. Dated at the end *sarira kalih nesthi tunggal*, AJ 1828/AD 1898. ff. 4r.–32r., 22 × 18.5 cm. SOAS 310763 (D).

Suluks. Dated Alip [AJ] 1803 [AD 1874–5]. 321 ff., 20 × 16 cm. SOAS 231925.

Published Primary Sources of Javanese Origin

Akkeren, Philippus van (ed. & transl.). *Een gedrocht en toch de volmaakte mens: De Javaanse Suluk Gaṭolotjo, uitgegeven, vertaald en toegelicht.* 's-Gravenhage: "Excelsior", 1951.

Anderson, Benedict (ed. & transl.). "The Suluk Gaṭoloco". *Indonesia*, no. 32 (Oct. 1981): 109–50; no. 33 (Apr. 1982): 31–88.

Bonneff, Marcel (ed. & transl.). *Pérégrinations javanaises: Les voyages de R.M.A. Purwa Lelana: Une vision de Java au XIXe siècle (c. 1860–1875).* Paris: Editions de la maison de sciences de l'homme, 1986.

Bramartani (in the period 1864–11 Aug. 1870 entitled *Jurumartani*), Surakarta, 1864–92.

Broek, P.W. van der (ed. & transl.). *De geschiedenis van het rijk Kĕdiri, opgeteekend in het jaar 1873 door Mas Soemã–Sĕntikã, gepensioneerd Wĕdãnã van het district Lèngkong.* Leiden: E.J. Brill, 1902.

Dewantara, Ki Hadjar. "Some aspects of national education and the Taman Siswa Institute at Jogjakarta". *Indonesia*, no. 4 (Oct. 1967): 150–68.

Djajadiningrat, Achmad. *Herinneringen.* Amsterdam & Batavia: G. Kolff & Col, [1936].

_____. "Het leven in een pasantren". *Tijdschrift voor het Binnenlandsch Bestuur* 34 (1908): 1–22.

Kartawidjaja. *Van Koran tot Bijbel, uit het Maleisch vertaald.* Rotterdam: Nederlandsche Zendingsvereeniging, n.d. [c. 1914].

Kartini. *Brieven aan Mevrouuw R.M. Abendanon-Mandri en haar echtgenoot met andere documenten.* Ed. F.G.P. Jaquet. Dordrecht & Providence: Foris Publications, 1987.

———. *Door duisternis tot licht: Gedachten over en voor het Javaanse volk.* Compiled by J.H. Abendanon. Revised ed. Ed. Elisabeth Allard. Amsterdam: Gé Nabrink & Zn, 1976.

———. "Educate the Javanese!" Ed. and transl. Jean Taylor. *Indonesia,* no. 17 (Apr. 1974): 83–98.

———. *Letters from Kartini, an Indonesian feminist, 1900–1904.* Transl. Joost Coté. Clayton: Monash Asia Institute in association with Hyland House, 1992.

———. *Letters of a Javanese princess.* Ed. Hildred Geertz. Transl. Agnes Louise Symmers. New York: W.W. Norton & Company, 1964.

Mangkunagara IV. *Sĕrat-sĕrat anggitanipun-dalĕm Kangjĕng Gusti Pangeran Adipati Arya Mangkunagara IV.* 4 vols. Jakarta: Kolĕp [Kolff], 1953.

[Mangoenwidjojo]. *Sĕrat Pramansiddhi, inggih punika pengĕtan nalika Prabu Aji Jayabaya ing Kadhiri puruita kawruh jangkaning jaman saha puruita ngelmi kasampurnan saking agami Islam dhatĕng Sang Raja Pandhita Maolana Ngali Samsujen saking ing tanah Ngarab.* 2nd printing; Kediri: Boekhandel Tan Khoen Swie, 1935.

Muchoyyar, M (ed. & transl.). "Tafsîr Faidl al-Raḥmân fî tarjamah tafsîr kalâm mâlik al-dayyân, karya K.H.M. Shaleh al-Samârani (suntingan teks, terjemahan dan analisis metodologi)". Doctoral thesis, IAIN Sunan Kalijaga, Yogyakarta, 2002.

Poerbo Hadiningrat. *Wat ik als Javaan voor geest en gemoed in de vrijmetselarij heb gevonden.* Buitenzorg: Archipel Drukkerij, [1928].

Purwalĕlana [pseud. for Condranĕgara V]. *Cariyos bab lampah-lampahipun Raden Mas Arya Purwalĕlana.* 2 vols. Batavia: Landsdrukkerij, 1865–66.

Radjiman. "De maatschappelijke loop van de Javaansche (Indonesische) bevolking". *Indisch Genootschap: Vergadering van 27 February 1920,* pp. 59–86.

———. "Het psychisch leven van het Javaansch volk". *Indisch Genootschap: Algemeene vergadering van 14 February 1911,* pp. 153–79.

Robson, Stuart (ed. & transl.). *The Wedhatama: An English translation.* KITLV working papers 4. Leiden: KITLV Press, 1990.

Ronggawarsita. *Sĕrat Paramayoga.* 3 vols. Djokja: Kolff-Buning, 1941.

———. *Sĕrat Pustakaraja Purwa.* 29 vols. Djokja: Kolff-Buning, 1938–39.

Ruslan Abdulgani. "My childhood world". Ed. & transl. William H. Frederick. *Indonesia* 17 (April 1974): 113–35.

Semaoen. *Penoentoen kaoem boeroeh dari hal sarekat sekerdja.* Soerakarta: Pesindo, 1946 [first published 1920].

Sĕrat Dĕrmagandhul, anyariosakĕn rĕringkĕsanipun babad bĕdah ing karaton Majapahit, sarta bantahipun Prabu Brawijaya kalayan Sabdapalon bab kawontĕnanipun agami Buda lan Eslam, sarta dunungipun carakan sastra Jawi. Kediri: Boekhandel Tan Khoen Swie, 1921.

Sĕrat Sastra Arjendra anyariosakĕn pupuntoning kawruh kasampurnan Buddha, sarta cundhuk akaliyan pikajĕnganipun ngelmi makrifat. 5th printing, Kediri: Tan Khoen Swie, 1929.

Simuh *et al.* (eds. & transls.). *Suluk: The mystical poetry of Javanese Muslims (41 suluks/LOR 7375).* Yogyakarta: IAIN Sunan Kalijaga, 1987.

Soetomo. *Toward a glorious Indonesia: Reminiscences and observations.* Ed. Paul W. van der Veur. Transl. Suharni Soemarmo & Paul van der Veur. Athens, Ohio: Ohio University Center for International Studies, Center for Southeast Asian Studies, Southeast Asia Monograph Series no. 81, 1987.

Tanaya. *Sang Pinudyasma R. Natarata iya R.Sasrawijaya sarta jasané kang arupa kasusastran 'ilmu luhung.* [Surakarta:] Para kadang mitra tresna budaya, 1977 (mimeo).

Yasadipura II. *Serat Sana Sunu.* Transl. Jumeiri Siti Rumidjah. Yogyakarta: Kepel Press, 2001.

Dutch Manuscripts

Archief Raad voor de Zending, held in the Utrecht city archives (het Utrechts Archief). The following boxes of missionaries' papers were consulted:

145	Boddé, A. Kruyt, H.C. Kruyt, Biegers
146	Gutzlaff
148	Poensen
206	Smeding
209	Douwes, Ganswijk
210	Hoezoo
261	Poensen
259	v.d. Valk, Harthoorn
378	Jellesma
447	Poensen
509	Hartig, Jellesma
511	Brückner
512	Gericke

National Archives, The Hague
Mailrapporten 1869–1917

Published Primary Sources of Dutch Origin

Algemeen vijfjarig verslag van het inlandsch onderwijs in Nederlandsch-Indië, loopende over de jaren 1878 t/m 1882. Batavia: Landsdrukkerij, 1885.

Algemeen vijfjarig verslag van het inlandsch onderwijs in Nederlandsch-Indië, loopende over de jaren 1883 t/m 1887. Batavia: Landsdrukkerij, 1890.

Algemeen vijfjarig verslag van het inlandsch onderwijs in Nederlandsch-Indië, loopende over de jaren 1888 t/m 1892. Batavia: Landsdrukkerij, 1894.

Algemeen vijfjarig verslag van het inlandsch onderwijs in Nederlandsch-Indië, loopende over de jaren 1893 t/m 1897. Batavia: Landsdrukkerij, 1901.

Anon. "Algemeen overzigt van den toestand van N.I. gedurende het jaar 1846". *TNI* 10, no. 1 (1848): 78–120, 200–25, 347–76.

Anon. "De Indische bedevaartgangers". *TNI* (n.s.) 3, no. 1 (1874): 55–67.

Anon. "De inlandsche school op Java". *MNZG* 11 (1867): 97–120.

Anon., "Oordeel van een Javaansch regent over het inlandsche onderwijs". *Koloniale jaarboeken* 4 (1864): 319–21.

Arsip Nasional Republik Indonesia. *Laporan-laporan tentang gerakan protes di Jawa pada abad-XX*. Jakarta: Arsip Nasional Republik Indonesia, 1981.

Arsip Nasional Republik Indonesia. *Memori serah jabatan 1921–30 (Jawa Tengah)*. Jakarta: Arsip Nasional Republik Indonesia, 1977.

—————. *Sarekat Islam lokal*. Jakarta: [Arsip Nasional RI], 1975.

B. "De godsdienstige beweging op Java". *Indische gids* 2 (1884): 739–44.

Berg, L.W.C. van den. "De Mohammedaansche geestelijkheid en de geestelijke goederen op Java en Madoera". *TBG* 27 (1882): 1–46.

—————. "Het Mohammedaansche godsdienstonderwijs op Java en Madoera en de daarbij gebruikte Arabische boeken." *TBG* 31 (1886): 518–55.

—————. "Over de devotie der Naqsjibendîjah in den Indischen archipel". *TBG* 28 (1883): 158–75.

Bleeker, P. "Hoodstuk II: Pasoeroeran". *TNI* 11, pt. 2 (1849): 17–55.

Cornets de Groot, A.D. "Bijdrage tot de kennis van de zeden en gewoonten der Javanen". *TNI* 14, pt. 2 (1852): 257–80, 346–67, 393–422.

Departement van Landbouw, Nijverheid en Handel & Departement van Economische Zaken, *Volkstelling 1930/Census of 1930 in Netherlands India*. 8 vols.; Batavia: Landsdrukkerij, 1933–36.

Deventer, C. Th. van. *Overzicht van den economischen toestand der inlandse bevolking van Java en Madoera*. Koloniaal-economische bijdragen I. 's-Gravenhage: Martinus Nijhoff, 1904.

Fokkens, F., jr. "De priesterschool te Tegalsari". *TBG* 24 (1877): 318–36.

Ganswijk, D.J. Ten Zeldam. "Iets over de Javanen, in betrekking tot de evangelieprediking in oostelijk Java". *MNZG* 1 (1857): 89–121.

Harthoorn, S.E. "Iets over den Javaanschen Mohammedaan en den Javaanschen Christen". *MNZG* 1 (1857): 183–212.

—————. *De toestand en de behoeften van het onderwijs bij de volken van Neêrlands Oost-Indie*. Haarlem: A.C. Kruseman, 1865.

—————. "De zending op Java en meer bepaald die van Malang". *MNZG* 4 (1860): 103–37, 212–52.

Hoezoo, W. "Verslag mijner werkzaamheden en bevindingen over het jaar 1861". *MNZG* 7 (1863): 163–99.

Jansz, Pieter. *"Tot heil van Java's arme bevolking": Een keuze uit het dagboek (1851–1860) van Pieter Jansz, doopsgezind zendeling in Jepara, Midden-Java*. Ed. A.G. Hoekema. Hilversum: Verloren, 1997.

J.L.V. "Bijdrage tot de kennis der residentie Madioen". *TNI* 17, pt. 2 (1855): 1–17.

Junghuhn, Fr. *Reizen door Java, voornamelijk door het oosterlijk gedeelte van dit eiland, opgenomen en beschreven in het jaar 1844.* 2 vols. Amsterdam: P.N. van Kampen, 1852.

[Keesteren, C.E. van]. v.K. "De Koran en de driekleur". *Stemmen uit Indie,* no. 1 (1870): 34–52.

Keijzer, S. *Onze tijd in Indië, beschreven in bundles.* 's-Gravenhage: H.C. Susan, C. Hzoon, 1860.

Mayer, L.Th. *Een blik in het Javaansche volksleven.* 2 vols. Leiden: E.J. Brill, 1897.

Overzigt van de Inlandsche en Maleisch-Chineesche Pers. Weltevreden: Kantoor voor de Volkslectuur, 1918–23.

Meulen, D. van der. "De Mekka-bedevaart en Nederlansch-Indië's belang darbij", *Indisch Genootschap: Verslag van de algemeene vergadering gehouden den 10 Nov. 1938,* pp. 17–34.

Plas, C.A.O. van der. "Mededeelingen over de stroomingen in de Moslimsche gemeenschap in Nederlandsch-Indië en de Nederlandsch Islampolitiek". *Indisch Genootschap: Vergadering van 16 Februari 1934,* pp. 255–72.

Poensen, C. "Bijdragen tot de kennis van den godsdienstigen en zedelijken toestand der Javanen: Eene beschouwing van den inhoud van eenige voorname geschriften der Javaaansche litteratuur". *MNZG* 13 (1869): 153–236, 313–56; 14 (1870): 259–90.

_____. *Brieven over den Islām uit de binnenlanden van Java.* Leiden: E.J. Brill, 1886.

_____. "Een en ander over den godsdienstigen toestand van den Javaan (uit een verslag over 1863, van C. Poensen, zendeling te Kediri)". *MNZG* 8 (1864): 214–63; 9 (1865): 161–202.

_____. "Gaṭo-lotjo (Een javaansch geschrift)". *MNZG* 17 (1873): 227–65.

_____. "Iets over den Javaan als mensch". *MNZG* 29 (1885): 26–74, 113–51.

_____. "Iets over het Javaansche gezin". *MNZG* 31 (1887): 113–50, 221–61.

_____. "Iets over Javaansche naamgeving en eigennamen". *MNZG* 14 (1870): 304–17.

_____. "De Javanen en het evangelie". *MNZG* 14 (1870): 123–216.

_____. "Een mohammadaansche traktaatje". *MNZG* 32 (1888): 1–23.

_____. "Naar en op de pasar". *MNZG* 26 (1882).

Schuurmans, N.D. "De tariqah Naqsjibendijjah op Java". *Nederlandsch Zendingstijdschrift* 2 (1890): 265–77.

Snouck Hurgronje, C. *Mecca in the latter part of the 19th century: Daily life, customs and learning; The Moslems of the East-Indian-archipelago.* Transl. J.H. Monahan. Leiden: E.J. Brill; London: Luzac & Co., 1931; reprinted Leiden: E.J. Brill, 1970.

Wal, S.L. van der (ed.). *Het onderwijsbeleid in Nederlands-Indië, 1900–1940: Een bronnenpublikatie.* Groningen: J.B. Wolters, 1963.
Winter, J.W. "Beknopte beschrijving van het hof Soerakarta in 1824". *BKI* 54 (1902): 15–172.

OTHER PRIMARY SOURCES

Bovene, G.A. van. *Mijn reis naar Mekka: Naar het dagboek van den Regent van Bandoeng Raden Adipati Aria Wiranatakoesoema.* Bandoeng: N.V. Mij. Vorkink, n.d. [c. 1925].
Crawfurd, John. *History of the Indian Archipelago, containing an account of the manners, arts, languages, religions, institutions, and commerce of its inhabitants.* 3 vols. Edinburgh: Archibald Constable and Co., 1820.
Kaptein, Nico (ed.). *The Muhimmât al-Nafâ'is: A bilingual Meccan fatwa collection for Indonesian Muslims from the end of the nineteenth century.* Seri INIS 32. Jakarta: INIS, 1997.
Partai Kommunist Indonesia, Hoofdbestuur. *Partai-reglement dari PKI ... 1924.* Semarang: Drukkerij VSTP, 1924.
Raffles, Thomas Stamford. *The history of Java.* 2 vols. 2nd ed. London: John Murray, 1830.
Sjahrir, Soetan. *Out of exile.* transl. Charles Wolf Jr. New York: The John Day Company, 1949.
Tan Malaka. *Toendoek kepada kekoeasaan, tetapi tidak toendoek kepada kebenaran.* Amsterdam: "De Strijd", [1922].
Vrije Woord, Het. Semarang, 1915–21.

Interview

Mohamad Roem, Jakarta, 3 August 1977.

SECONDARY SOURCES

Abdul Djamil. *Perlawanan Kiai desa: Pemikiran dan gerakan Islam KH. Ahmad Rifa'i Kalisalak.* Yogyakarta: LKiS, 2001.
Adaby Darban, Ahmad. *Rifa'iyah: Gerakan sosial keagamaan di pedesaan Jawa Tengah tahun 1850–1982.* Yogyakarta: Tarawang Press, 2004.
―――――. *Sejarah kauman: menguak identitas kampung Muhammadiyah.* Yogyakarta: Tarawang, 2000.
Adam, Ahmat B. *The vernacular press and the emergence of modern Indonesian consciousness (1855–1913).* Ithaca, NY: Cornell University Southeast Asia Program, 1995.
Adriaanse, L. *Sadrach's kring.* Leiden: D. Donner, 1899.

Akkeren, Philip van. *Sri and Christ: A study of the indigenous church in East Java.* London: Lutterworth Press, 1970.

Aminuddin Kasdi. *Kaum merah menjarah: Aksi sepihak PKI/BTI di Jawa Timur 1960–1965.* Yogyakarta: Jendela, 2001.

Anon. *The church of the Sacred Heart of Jesus at Ganjuran: Her concerns and hopes.* n.p., n.d., [c. 1999].

Anon. "Het onderwijs op Java, en de invloed daarvan op den toestand der bevolking". *TNI* (1849): 329–35.

Anon. "De regeering van Nederlandsch Indie tegenover den Islam". *TNI* (n.s.) 7 (1878): 205–21.

Arbi Sanit. *Badai revolusi: Sketsa kekuatan politik PKI di Jawa Tengah dan Jawa Timur.* Yogyakarta: Pustaka Pelajar, 2000.

Ardani, Moh. *Al Qur'an dan sufisme Mangkunagara IV: Studi serat-serat piwulang.* Yogyakarta: Penerbit Dana Bhakti Wakaf, 1995.

Azra, Azyumardi. "Hadhrâmî scholars in the Malay-Indonesian diaspora: A preliminary study of Sayyid 'Uthmân". *SI* 2, no. 2 (1995): 1–33.

Behrend, T.E. "Manuscript production in nineteenth-century Java: Codicology and the writing of Javanese literary history". *BKI* 149, no. 3 (1993): 407–37.

──────. "The writings of K.P.H. Suryanagara: Shifting paradigms in nineteenth-century Javanese thought and letters". *BKI* 155, no. 3 (1999): 390–415.

Boland, B.J. *The struggle of Islam in modern Indonesia.* VKI vol. 59. The Hague: Martinus Nijhoff, 1971.

Boomgaard, Peter. *Children of the colonial state: Population growth and economic development in Java, 1795–1880.* Amsterdam: Free University Press, 1989.

Brugmans, I.J. *Geschiedenis van het onderwijs in Nederlandsch-Indië.* Groningen & Batavia: J.B. Wolters' Uitgevers-Maatschappij, 1918.

Bruinessen, Martin van. "Muslims of the Dutch East Indies and the caliphate question", pp. 261–78 in *La question du califat.* Les Annales de l'autre Islam no. 2. Paris: Publication de l'ERISM, 1994.

──────. "The origins and development of the Naqshbandi order in Indonesia". *Der Islam* 67, pt. 1 (1990): 150–79.

──────. "*Pesantren* and *kitab kuning*: Continuity and change in a tradition of religious learning", pp. 121–45 in *Ethnologica Bernensia 4/1994: Texts from the islands.* Bern: Insitut für Ethnologie, 1994.

──────. *Tarekat Naqsyabandiyah di Indonesia: Survei historis, geografis dan sosiologis.* Bandung: Penerbit Mizan, 1992.

Burhani, Ahmad Najib. "The Muhammadiyah's attitude to Javanese culture in 1912–30: Appreciation and tension". MA thesis, Leiden University, 2004.

Chijs, J.A. van der. "Geschiedenis van het inlandsch onderwijs in Nederlandsch-Indië, aan officiëele bronnen ontleend". *TBG* 14, nos. 3–4 (1864): 212–323.

Coolsma, S. *De zendingseeuw voor Nederlandsch Oost-Indië.* Utrecht: C.H.E. Breijer, 1901.

Cribb, Robert (ed.), *The Indonesian killings of 1965–1966: Studies from Java and Bali*. Monash papers on Southeast Asia no. 21. Clayton: Monash University Centrer of Southeast Asian Studies, 1990.

Day, John Anthony. "Meanings of change in the poetry of nineteenth-century Java". PhD dissertation, Cornell University, 1981.

Dewantara, Ki Hadjar. *Beoefening van letteren en kunst in het Pakoe-Alamsche geslacht*. Djokjakarta: H. Buning, 1931.

Djoko Suryo. *Sejarah sosial pedesaan Karesidenan Semarang 1830–1900*. Yogyakarta: Pusat Antar Universitas Studi Sosial, Universitas Gadjah Mada, 1989.

Dobbin, Christine. *Islamic revivalism in a changing peasant economy: Central Sumatra, 1784–1847*. London & Malmö: Curzon Press, 1983.

Drewes, G.W.J. *Drie Javaansche goeroe's: Hun leven, onderricht en messiasprediking*. Leiden: Drukkerij A. Vros, 1925.

————. "The struggle between Javanism and Islam as illustrated by the Sĕrat Dĕrmaganḍul". *BKI* 122, no. 3 (1966): 309–65.

Eisenberger, Johan. "Indië en de bedevaart naar Mekka". Doctoral thesis, Leiden University. Leiden: Boekhandel M. Dubbeldeman, 1928.

Elson, R.E. *Javanese peasants and the colonial sugar industry: Impact and change in an East Java Residency, 1830–1940*. Singapore: Oxford University Press, 1984.

————. *Village Java under the cultivation system 1830–1870*. Sydney: Asian Studies Association of Australia in association with Allen & Unwin, 1994.

Farinia Fianto. "The Sarekat Islam Kudus: The rise, development and demise". MA thesis, Leiden University, 2002.

Fasseur, C. *Kultuurstelsel en koloniale baten: De Nederlandse exploitatie van Java 1840–1860*. Leiden: Universitaire Pers, 1975.

————. *The politics of colonial exploitation: Java, the Dutch and the cultivation system*. Transl. R.E. Elson & Ary Kraal. Ithaca: Cornell University Southeast Asia Program, 1992.

Feith, Herbert. *The decline of constitutional democracy in Indonesia*. Ithaca: Cornell University Press, 1962.

Florida, Nancy. "Reading the unread in traditional Javanese literature". *Indonesia*, no. 44 (Oct. 1987): 1–15.

————. *Writing the past, inscribing the future: History as prophecy in colonial Java*. Durham [N.C.] & London: Duke University Press, 1995.

Geertz, Clifford. *The interpretation of cultures: Selected essays*. New York: Basic Books, Inc., Publishers, 1973.

————. *The religion of Java*. Glencoe: The Free Press, 1964.

Groeneboer, Kees. *Weg tot het Westen: Het Nederlands voor Indië; een taalpolitieke geschiedenis*. VKI vol. 158. Leiden: KITLV Uitgeverij, 1993.

Guillot, C. *L'Affaire Sadrach: Un essai de Christianisation à Java au XIXe siècle*. Paris: Editions de la maison des sciences de l'homme, 1981.

Hadiwikarta, J. *Gua Maria Lourdes Puh Sarang, Kediri, Keuskupan Surabaya.* Kediri: Sekretariat Keuskupan Surabaya, 2001.

Hardjamardjaja, Andrea Corsini Harjaka. *Javanese popular belief in the coming of the Ratu-Adil, a righteous prince: An attempt at assessing its theological value and an inquiry into its adaptability to the incipient stages of evangelization in present-day Java.* Excerpta ex dissertatione ad lauream in facultate theologica Pontificiae Universitatis Gregorianae. Roma, 1962.

Haspel, C.Ch. van den. *Overwicht in overleg: Hervormingen van justitie, grondgebruiken en bestuur in de Vorstenlanden op Java 1880–1930. VKI* vol. 111. Dordrecht & Cinnaminson: Foris Publications, 1985.

Headley, Stephen C. *Durga's mosque: Cosmology, conversion and community in Central Javanese Islam.* Singapore: Institute of Southeast Asian Studies, 2004.

Herwanto, Lydia. *Pikiran dan aksi Kiai Sadrach: Gerakan jemaat Kristen Jawa Merdeka.* Jogjakarta: Matabangsa, 2002.

Hisyam, Muhamad. *Caught between three fires: The Javanese pangulu under the Dutch colonial administration 1882–1942.* Jakarta: INIS, 2001.

Hooykaas, C. "Javaansche uitgaven van Volkslectuur (Balé Poestaka)". *Djåwå* 12, nos. 2–3 (1932): 93–115.

Houben, Vincent J.H. *Kraton and Kumpeni: Surakarta and Yogyakarta 1830–1970. VKI* vol. 164. Leiden: KITLV Press, 1994.

Hourani, Albert. *Arabic thought in the liberal age, 1798–1939.* London: Oxford University Press, 1970.

Hugenholtz, W.R. "Taxes and society: Regional differences in Central Java around 1830", pp. 142–73 in *Papers of the fourth Indonesian-Dutch history conference, Yogyakarta, 24–29 July 1983,* vol I: *Agrarian history.* Ed. Sartono Kartodirdjo. Yogyakarta: Gadjah Mada University Press, 1986.

Hüsken, Frans. *Een dorp op Java: Sociale differentatie in een boerengemeenschap, 1850–1980.* Overveen: ACASEA, 1988.

Jaquet, F.G.P. "Mutiny en hadji-ordonnantie: Ervaringen met 19e eeuwse bronnen". *BKI* 136, nos. 2–3: 283–312.

Jay, Robert R. *Javanese villagers: Social relations in rural Modjokuto.* Cambridge, Mass., & London: The MIT Press, 1969.

Jedamski, Doris. "Balai Pustaka: A colonial wolf in sheep's clothing". *Archipel,* no. 44 (1992): 23–46.

Kahin, Audrey R. "The 1927 Communist uprising in Sumatra: A reappraisal". *Indonesia* no. 62 (Oct. 1996): 19–36.

Kartodirdjo, Sartono. *The peasants' revolt of Banten in 1888: Its conditions, course and sequel; a case study of social movements in Indonesia. VKI* vol. 50. 's-Gravenhage: Martinus Nijhoff, 1966.

————. *Protest movements in rural Java: A study of agrarian unrest in the nineteenth and early twentieth centuries.* Singapore: Oxford University Press, 1973.

Korver, A.P.E. *Sarekat Islam 1912–1916: Opkomst, bloei en structuur van Indonesië's eerste massabeweging*. Amsterdam: Historisch Seminarium van de Universiteit van Amsterdam, 1982.

Kraus, Werner. *Zwischen Reform und Rebellion: Über die Entwicklung des Islams in Minangkabau (Westsumatra) zwischen den beiden Reformbewegungen der Padri (1837) und der Modernisten (1908): Ein Beitrag zur Geschichte der Islamisierung Indonesiens*. Wiesbaden: Franz Steiner Verlag, 1984.

Krom, N.J. *Hindoe-Javaansche geschiedenis*. 2nd ed. 's-Gravenhage: Martinus Nijhoff, 1931.

Kuitenbrouwer, Maarten. *Tussen oriëntalisme en wetenschap: Het Koninklijk Instituut voor Taal,- Land en Volkenkunde in historisch verband, 1851–2001*. Leiden: KITLV Uitgeverij, 2001.

Kumar, Ann. *The diary of a Javanese Muslim: Religion, politics and the pesantren 1883–1886*. Canberra: Faculty of Asian Studies Monographs, new series no. 7, 1985.

————. *Java and modern Europe: Ambiguous encounters*. Richmond, Surrey: Curzon, 1997.

————. "The 'Suryengalagan affair' of 1883 and its successors: Born leaders in changed times". *BKI* 138, nos. 2–3 (1982): 251–84.

Kuntowijoyo. *Raja, priyayi dan kawula: Surakarta, 1900–1915*. Jogjakarta: Ombak, 2004.

Laffan, Michael F. "'A watchful eye': The Meccan plot of 1881 and changing Dutch perceptions of Islam in Indonesia". *Archipel*, no. 63 (2002): 79–108.

Linden, G.M. van der. "Wat zijn hadjie's en welke is hun invloed op het volksleven der Javanen". *Indisch Genootschap: Algemeene vergadering op 21 Maart 1859*, pp. 1–17.

McVey, Ruth T. *The Rise of Indonesian Communism*. Ithaca: Cornell University Press, 1965.

————. "Taman Siswa and the Indonesian national awakening". *Indonesia*, no. 4 (Oct. 1967): 128–49.

Mansvelt, W.M.F. "Onderwijs en communisme". *Koloniale Studiën* 12, pt. 1 (1928): 203–25.

Miert, Hans van. *Een koel hoofd en een warm hart: Nationalisme, Javanisme en jeugdbeweging in Nederlands-Indië, 1918–1930*. Amsterdam: De Bataafsche Leeuw, 1995.

Molen, Willem van der, and Bernard Arps (eds.). *Woord en schrift in de Oost: De betekenis van zending en missie voor de studie van taal and literatuur in Zuidost-Azië. Semaian* 19. Leiden: Opleiding Talen en Culturen van Zuidoost-Azië en Oceanië, Universiteit Leiden, 2000.

Nagazumi, Akira. *The Dawn of Indonesian nationalism: The early years of the Budi Utomo, 1908–1918*. Tokyo: Institute of Developing Economies, 1972.

Noer, Deliar. *The Modernist Muslim movement in Indonesia, 1900–1942*. Singapore: Oxford University Press, 1973.

Nugraha, Iskandar P. *Mengikis batas timur dan barat: Gerakan theosofi &*
nasionalisme Indonesia. Jakarta: Komunitas Bambu, 2001.

O'Malley, William J. "The Pakempalan Kawulo Ngajogjakarta: An official
report on the Jogjakarta People's Party of the 1930s". *Indonesia*, no. 26 (Oct.
1978): 111–58.

Onghokham. "The Residency of Madiun: Priyayi and peasant in the nineteenth
century". PhD dissertation, Yale University, 1975.

Peper, Bram. *Grootte en groei van Java's inheemse bevolking in de negentiende eeuw.*
[Amsterdam:] Afdeling zuid- en zuidoost-Asië, Antropologisch-sociologisch
centrum, Universiteit van Amsterdam, publicatie nr. 11, 1967.

Phillips, Kevin. *The cousins' wars: Religion, politics and the triumph of Anglo-*
America. New York: Basic Books, 1999.

Pigeaud, Th. *Javaanse volksvertoningen: Bijdrage tot de beschrijving van land en*
volk. Batavia: Volkslectuur, 1938.

Pijper, G.F. *Fragmenta Islamica: Studiën over het Islamisme in Nederlandsch-Indië.*
Leiden: E.J. Brill, 1934.

Poeze, Harry A. *Tan Malaka: Strijder voor Indonesië's vrijheid; levensloop van*
1897 tot 1945. VKI vol. 78; 's-Gravenhage: Martinus Nijhoff, 1976.

Pringgodigdo, A.K. *Geschiedenis der ondernemingen van het Mangkoenagorosche*
rijk. 's-Gravenhage: Martinus Nijhoff, 1950.

Pyenson, Lewis. *Empire of Reason: Exact sciences in Indonesia, 1840–1940.*
Leiden: E.J. Brill, 1989.

Quinn, George. *The novel in Javanese: Aspects of its social and literary character.*
VKI vol. 148. Leiden: KITLV Press, 1992.

Reid, Anthony. *The contest for North Sumatra: Atjeh, the Netherlands and Britain,*
1858–1898. London: Oxford University Press, 1969.

Ricklefs, M.C. "A consideration of three versions of the *Babad Tanah Djawi*,
with excerpts on the fall of Majapahit". *Bulletin of the School of Oriental and*
African Studies 35, pt. 2 (1972): 285–315.

————. *A History of modern Indonesia since c. 1200.* 3rd ed. Basingstoke:
Palgrave; Stanford: Stanford University Press, 2001.

————. *Jogjakarta under Sultan Mangkubumi 1749–1792: A History of the*
division of Java. London Oriental Series 10. London: Oxford University
Press, 1974.

————. *Mystic synthesis in Java: A history of Islamization from the fourteenth*
to the early nineteenth centuries. Norwalk: EastBridge, 2006.

————. *The Seen and unseen worlds in Java, 1726–1749: History, literature and*
Islam in the court of Pakubuwana II. St. Leonards, NSW & Honolulu: Asian
Studies Association of Australia in association with Allen & Unwin and
University of Hawai'i Press, 1998.

Ruiter, Tine. "The Tegal revolt in 1864", pp. 81–98 in *Conversion, competition*
and conflict: Essays on the role of religion in Asia, ed. Dick Kooiman *et al.*
Amsterdam: Free University Press, 1984.

Scherer, Savitri Prastiti. "Harmony and dissonance: Early nationalist thought in Java". MA thesis, Cornell University, 1975.

Schuurman, B.M. *Mystik und Glaube in Zusammenhang mit der Mission auf Java.* Haag: Martinus Nijhoff, 1933.

Schrieke, B.J.O. *Indonesian sociological studies: Selected writings of B. Schrieke.* 2 vols. The Hague & Bandung: W. van Hoeve Ltd., 1955–57.

Sears, Laurie J. *Shadows of empire: Colonial discourse and Javanese tales.* Durham [N.C.] & London: Duke University Press, 1996.

Shiraishi, Takashi. *An age in motion: Popular radicalism in Java, 1912–1926.* Ithaca & London: Cornell University Press, 1990.

Simuh. *Sufisme Jawa: Transformasi tasawuf Islam ke mistik Jawa.* Yogyakarta: Bentang, 1996.

Sitisoemandari Soeroto. *Kartini: Sebuah biografi.* Jakarta: Gunung Agung, 1986.

Soebardi. "Prince Mangku Nagara IV: A ruler and a poet of 19th century Java." *Journal of the Oriental Society of Australia* (Dec. 1971): 28–58.

Soekardan Prånåhadikoesoemå, "De kéntol der desa Kréndétan". *Djåwå* 19 (1939): 153–60.

Sri Mulyati *et al. Mengenal dan memahami tarekat-tarekat muktabarah di Indonesia.* Jakarta: Kencana, 2004.

Steenbrink, Karel. *Beberapa aspek tentang Islam di Indonesia abad ke-19.* Jakarta: Bulan Bintang, 1984.

————. *Catholics in Indonesia, 1801–1942: A documented history,* vol. I: *A modest recovery 1801–1903.* VKI vol. 196. Leiden: KITLV Press, 2003.

Stevens, Th. *Vrijmetselarij en samenleving in Nederlands-Indië en Indonesië 1764–1962.* Hilversum: Verloren, 1994.

Sudewa, Alex. "Sultan Hamengku Buwana V: Strategi sastra budaya menghadapi perubahan sosial". Unpublished paper presented to Seminar Sastra dan Budaya, Pusat Kajian Bahasa dan Kebudayaan Indonesia, Universitas Sanata Dharma Yogyakarta, 14 Juli 1997.

Suhartono. "The impact of the sugar industry on rural life, Klaten, 1850–1900", pp. 174–95 in *Papers of the fourth Indonesian-Dutch history conference, Yogyakarta, 24–29 July 1983,* vol I: *Agrarian history,* ed. Sartono Kartodirdjo. Yogyakarta: Gadjah Mada University Press, 1986.

Sulistyo, Hermawan. *Palu arit di ladang tebu: Sejarah pembantaian massal yang terlupakan (Jombang-Kediri 1965–1966).* Jakarta: KPG (Kepustakaan Populer Gramedia), Yayasan Adikarya IKAPI, The Ford Foundation, 2000.

Surjomihardjo, Abdurrahman. *Ki Hadjar Dewantara dan Taman Siswa dalam sejarah Indonesia modern.* Jakarta: Penerbit Sinar Harapan 1986.

Sutarman Soediman Partonadi. *Sadrach's community and its contextual roots: A nineteenth century Javanese expression of Christianity.* Amsterdam & Atlanta: Rodopi, 1990.

Sutherland, Heather. *The making of a bureaucratic elite: The colonial transformation of the Javanese priyayi.* Singapore: Heinemann Educational Books (Asia) Ltd, 1979.

Swellengrebel, J.L. *In Leijdekkers voetspoor: Anderhalve eeuw Bijbelvertaling en taalkunde in de Indonesische talen.* 2 vols. *VKI* vols. 68, 82. 's-Gravenhage: Martinus Nijhoff, 1974, 1978.

Swift, Ann. *The road to Madiun: The Indonesian Communist uprising of 1948.* Ithaca: Cornell Modern Indonesia Project Monograph Series, 1989.

Termorshuizen, Gerard, with the collaboration of Anneke Scholte. *Journalisten en heethoofden: Een geschiedenis van de Indisch-Nederlandse dagbladpers 1744–1905.* Amsterdam: Nijgh & van Ditmar; Leiden: KITLV Uitgeverij, 2001.

Tollenaere, H.A.O. de. *The politics of divine wisdom: Theosophy and labour, national and women's movements in Indonesia and South Asia, 1875–1947.* Nijmegen: Uitgeverij Katholieke Universiteit Nijmegen, 1996.

Van Niel, Robert. *The Emergence of the modern Indonesian elite.* The Hague & Bandung: W. van Hoeve, Ltd., 1960.

————. "Measurement of change under the cultivation system in Java, 1837–1851". *Indonesia*, no. 14 (Oct. 1972): 89–109.

Veth, P.J. *Java: Geographisch, ethnologisch, historisch.* 3 vols. Haarlem: Erven F. Bohn, 1875–82.

Vredenbregt, Jacob. "The haddj: Some of its features and functions in Indonesia". *BKI* 118, no. 1 (1964): 91–154.

Waal, E. de. *Onze Indische financien: Nieuwe reeks aanteekeningen.* 9 vols. 's-Gravenhage: M. Nijhoff, 1876–1907.

Wieringa, Edwin. "Het Christendom als het ware inzicht: Hendrik Kraemers uitgave van Paulus Tosari's *Rasa sejati*", pp. 56–88 in *Woord en schrift in de Oost: De betekenis van zending en missie voor de studie van taal and litteratuur in Zuidost-Azië. Semaian* 19, ed. Willem van der Molen and Bernard Arps. Leiden: Opleiding Talen en Culturen van Zuidoost-Azië en Oceanië, Universiteit Leiden, 2000.

————. "Ketzer oderer wahre Gläubige? Der Kampf zwischen Javanismus und Islam in *Suluk Lebé Lonthang*". *Der Islam* 78 (2001): 129–46.

Williams, Michael Charles. *Communism, religion and revolt in Banten.* Athens, Ohio: Ohio University Center for International Studies Monographs in International Studies, Southeast Asia Series number 86, 1990.

Zoetmulder, P.J. *Pantheism and monism in Javanese suluk literature: Islamic and Indian mysticism in an Indonesian setting.* Ed. & transl. M.C. Ricklefs. KITLV Translation Series 24. Leiden: KITLV Press, 1995.

————. *Pantheisme en monisme in de Javaansche soeloek-litteratuur.* Nijmegen: J.J. Berkhout, 1935.

Works of Reference

Behrend, T.E. and Titik Pudjiastuti (eds.). *Katalog induk naskah-naskah Nusantara,* vols. 3-A, B: *Fakultas Sastra Universitas Indonesia.* 2 vols. Jakarta: Yayasan Obor Indonesia, École Française d'Extrême-Orient, 1997.

Gericke, J.F.C. and T. Roorda. *Javaansch-Nederduitsch woordenboek*. Amsterdam: Johannes Müller, 1847.

————. *Javaansch-Nederlandsch handwoordenboek*. Revised ed. Ed. A.C. Vreede and J.G.H. Gunning. 2 vols. Amsterdam: Johannes Müller; Leiden: E.J. Brill, 1901.

Paulus, J., *et al.* (eds.). *Encyclopaedie van Nederlandsch-Indië*. 2nd ed. 8 vols. 's-Gravenhage: Martinus Nijhoff; Leiden: E.J. Brill, 1917–39.

Pigeaud, Theodore G. Th. *Literature of Java: Catalogue raisonné of Javanese manuscripts in the library of the University of Leiden and other public collections in the Netherlands*. 4 vols. The Hague: Martinus Nijhoff; Leiden: Bibliotheca Universitatis Lugduni Batavorum; Leiden: Leiden University Press, 1967–80.

Poersoewignja and Wirawangsa. *Javaansche bibliographie gegrond op de boekwerken in die taal, aanwezig in de boekerij van het Bataviaasch Genootschap van Kunsten en Wetenschappen/Pratélan kawontenaning boekoe-boekoe Basa Djawi (tjiṭakan) ingkang kasimpen wonten ing geḍong boekoe (Museum) ing pasimpenan (bibliothek) XXXIII*. Batavia: Bataviaasch Genootschap, 1920.

Ricklefs, M.C. and P. Voorhoeve. *Indonesian manuscripts in Great Britain: A catalogue of manuscripts in Indonesian languages in British public collections*. London Oriental Bibliographies, 5. Oxford: Oxford University Press, 1977.

Uhlenbeck, E.M. *A critical survey of studies on the languages of Java and Madura*. 's-Gravenhage: Martinus Nijhoff, 1964.

Wehr, Hans. *A dictionary of modern written Arabic*. Ed. Milton J. Cowan. Ithaca, NY: Cornell University Press, 1961.

Index

Waliyollah Imam Sampurna, Sunan, 136
Wanagiri, 245–6
Wanantara, 70
waringin, 128, 202
wayang, 8, 33–5, 37, 44, 62, 90, 102, 107–8, 110, 122, 127, 142, 148, 155, 173, 183, 184n21, 186n28, 221–2, 233–4, 244–5, 249, 254
Wedapaekarma, M.Ng., 141
Wederopbouw, 228
Wedhatama, Sĕrat, 38, 41–4, 74, 81, 106, 143, 164, 244, 253
Wellesley College, 158
Weltevreden, 156
Wĕwulang Kristen, 143
Widawati, 150–1
Wildt-le Jolle, E.J. de, 114, 255
Wilhelm, J., 117
Wilkens, J.A., 88, 132, 140
Willem I, 13
Willem III, 138, 156; Gymnasium Willem III, 88
Winter, C.F.: Sr., 88, 130, 140, 142; Jr., 143–4, 159, 256
Winter, F.L., 130, 136
Winter, F.W., 135, 144
Winter, J.W., 9–10
Wiranatakusuma, 219–20

Wirasanjaya, Ky., 246
Wirasari, 18, 169
Wose agama Kristen Katolik, 143
Wulang Brata, Sĕrat, 139
Wulang guru, Wulang murid, 143
Wulang Pakubuwana II, Serat, 208, 245
Wulangreh, Sĕrat, 6, 142
Wuruk Rĕspati, Sĕrat, 139

Xavier College, 121

Yasadipura I, 142
Yitnasastra, M., 146
Yogyakarta, 16, 48, 64, 66, 67–8, 71, 77, 104n39, 120–2, 126, 133, 137, 139, 142, 148, 160, 162, 168, 176, 208–9, 221–4, 230, 239, 241, 245, 255
Yudisthira, 8
Yusuf, Carita, 5

zakat, see alms
Zeehandelaar, S., 166–7
Zoetmulder, P.J., 32–5, 39, 121
Zuhdi, Sulaiman al-, 77